Picturing Genocide in the
Independent State of Croatia

War, Culture and Society

Series Editor: Stephen McVeigh, Associate Professor, Swansea University, UK

Editorial Board
Paul Preston *LSE, UK*
Joanna Bourke *Birkbeck, University of London, UK*
Debra Kelly *University of Westminster, UK*
Patricia Rae *Queen's University, Ontario, Canada*
James J. Weingartner *Southern Illinois University, USA (Emeritus)*
Kurt Piehler *Florida State University, USA*
Ian Scott *University of Manchester, UK*

War, Culture and Society is a multi- and interdisciplinary series which encourages the parallel and complementary military historical and sociocultural investigation of twentieth- and twenty-first-century war and conflict.

Published

Filming the End of the Holocaust: Allied Documentaries, Nuremberg and the Liberation of the Concentration Camps, John J. Michalczyk (2014)
South Africa's 'Border War': Contested Narratives and Conflicting Memories, Gary Baines (2014)
The Testimonies of Indian Soldiers and the Two World Wars: Between Self and Sepoy, Gajendra Singh (2014)
The British Imperial Army in the Middle East: Morale and Military Identity in the Sinai and Palestine Campaigns, 1916–1918, James E. Kitchen (2014)
The Japanese Comfort Women and Sexual Slavery during the China and Pacific Wars, Caroline Norma (2015)
Cultural Response to Occupation in Japan: The Performing Body During and After the Cold War, Adam Broinowski (2016)
Second World War British Military Camouflage: Designing Deception, Isla Forsyth (2017)
Jewish Volunteers, the International Brigades and the Spanish Civil War, Gerben Zaagsma (2017)
Women, Warfare and Representation: American Servicewomen in the Twentieth Century, Emerald M. Archer (2017)
Prisoners of the Sumatra Railway: Narratives of History and Memory, Lizzie Oliver (2017)
The Franco-Algerian War through a Twenty-First Century Lens: Film and History, Nicole Beth Wallenbrock (2020)

Forthcoming

The Lost Cause of the Confederacy and American Civil War Memory, David J. Anderson (2020)
The Irish Myth of the Second World War, Bernard Kelly (2020)

Picturing Genocide in the Independent State of Croatia

Atrocity Images and the Contested Memory of the Second World War in the Balkans

Jovan Byford

BLOOMSBURY ACADEMIC
LONDON • NEW YORK • OXFORD • NEW DELHI • SYDNEY

BLOOMSBURY ACADEMIC
Bloomsbury Publishing Plc
50 Bedford Square, London, WC1B 3DP, UK
1385 Broadway, New York, NY 10018, USA
29 Earlsfort Terrace, Dublin 2, Ireland

BLOOMSBURY, BLOOMSBURY ACADEMIC and the Diana logo are trademarks
of Bloomsbury Publishing Plc

First published in Great Britain 2020
This paperback edition first published in 2022

Copyright © Jovan Byford, 2020

Jovan Byford has asserted his right under the Copyright, Designs and
Patents Act, 1988, to be identified as Author of this work.

For legal purposes the Acknowledgements on p. viii constitute an extension of this copyright page.

Series design by Clare Turner

Cover image: Ustasa militia execute prisoners near the Jasenovac concentration camp.
(© United States Holocaust Memorial Museum, courtesy of Jewish Historical Museum, Belgrade)

All rights reserved. No part of this publication may be reproduced or transmitted in any form or by any means, electronic or mechanical, including photocopying, recording, or any information storage or retrieval system, without prior permission in writing from the publishers.

Bloomsbury Publishing Plc does not have any control over, or responsibility for, any third-party websites referred to or in this book. All internet addresses given in this book were correct at the time of going to press. The author and publisher regret any inconvenience caused if addresses have changed or sites have ceased to exist, but can accept no responsibility for any such changes.

Every effort has been made to trace copyright holders and to obtain their permissions for the use of copyright material. The publisher apologizes for any errors or omissions and would be grateful if notified of any corrections that should be incorporated in future reprints or editions of this book.

A catalogue record for this book is available from the British Library.

Library of Congress Cataloging-in-Publication Data
Names: Byford, Jovan, author.
Title: Picturing genocide in the independent state of Croatia: atrocity images and the contested memory of the Second World War in the Balkans / Jovan Byford.
Description: New York: Bloomsbury Academic, 2020. | Series: War, culture and society | Includes bibliographical references and index. | Identifiers: LCCN 2020009661 (print) | LCCN 2020009662 (ebook) | ISBN 9781350015968 (hardback) | ISBN 9781350015982 (ebook) | ISBN 9781350015975 (epub)
Subjects: LCSH: World War, 1939-1945–Atrocities–Croatia–Pictorial works–Historiography. | Croatia–History–1918-1945–Pictorial works–Historiography. | Ustaša, hrvatska revolucionarna organizacija–Historiography. | Collective memory–Former Yugoslav republics. | Collective memory–Balkan Peninsula.
Classification: LCC D804.C76 B94 2020 (print) | LCC D804.C76 (ebook) |
DDC 940.53/18094972–dc23
LC record available at https://lccn.loc.gov/2020009661
LC ebook record available at https://lccn.loc.gov/2020009662

ISBN: HB: 978-1-3500-1596-8
PB: 978-1-3501-9252-2
ePDF: 978-1-3500-1598-2
eBook: 978-1-3500-1597-5

Series: War, Culture and Society

Typeset by Deanta Global Publishing Services, Chennai, India

To find out more about our authors and books visit www.bloomsbury.com
and sign up for our newsletters.

Contents

List of illustrations		vi
Acknowledgements		viii
List of abbreviations		ix
Map		x
1	Introduction: Picturing genocide	1
2	Evidencing 'unprecedented acts of savagery': Atrocity photographs in occupied Yugoslavia	23
3	'Gather photographs!': The birth of the post-war visual memory of Ustasha violence	45
4	Why look at fascism? Visual propaganda and revolutionary justice in post-war Yugoslavia	63
5	Ustasha violence through the prism of 'brotherhood and unity': The dilemmas of visual memory in socialist Yugoslavia	81
6	'The dead open the eyes of the living': Atrocity images after Tito	101
7	Mobilizing images: Visual memory of the Ustasha genocide during and after the Yugoslav conflict of the 1990s	125
8	Conclusion: Atrocity photographs beyond idolatry and oblivion	151
Notes		157
Bibliography		193
Index		207

Illustrations

Figures

1.1 Visual symbols of perpetrators' triumph over the victim: Examples of trophy photographs taken by the Ustasha   13
1.2 'Turkish atrocities', *Ilustrovana ratna kronika*, 17 January 1913   15
1.3 Photograph evidencing Austrian atrocities in Serbia in 1914   17
1.4 Photographic postcard showing Serbs executed by hanging in Jagodina in 1916   18
2.1 German officers inspecting the bodies of Serbs killed by the Ustasha in the village of Gudovac   26
2.2 Ustasha atrocities through Italian eyes. Photographs of injuries sustained by two child survivors of the Ustasha massacre in Gračac in the summer of 1941   28
2.3 Photograph said to show the mutilated body of Miloš Teslić   32
2.4 Photograph of the body of Miloš Teslić, or Bishop Platon of Banja Luka?   34
2.5 Ustasha propaganda photograph of a victim of 'Chetnik-Communist' mutilation   38
2.6 Contrasting images of Partisan and Ustasha fighters in Ustasha propaganda   39
2.7 Ustasha propaganda photograph of 'abandoned' Serbian children   40
2.8 Ustasha propaganda photograph of troops 'horrifically mutilated and robbed' by rebels   41
2.9 Two of Edmund Stöger's propaganda photographs of Jasenovac, August 1942   42
3.1 Judges at the trial of the last chief of police of the Ustasha state Erih Lisak and his associates inspect atrocity images presented to the court by the prosecution   49
3.2 'Victims of German beasts': Appeal for information from the State Commission for the Investigation of the Crimes of the Occupiers and their Accomplices   50
3.3 Investigators from the Committee of Inquiry for Jasenovac in the company of journalists and photographers, during their visit to Jasenovac on 18 May 1945   54
3.4 Remains of the Jasenovac camp photographed during the investigation in May 1945   55
3.5 Images used in the Country Commission's report to illustrate the horror of Jasenovac killings: (a) 'Frontal bone shattered with a mallet' and (b) 'Victim with their belly slashed open'   56
3.6 Bodies on the riverbank in Sisak: Photographs used after the war to depict mass executions in Jasenovac   58

3.7	Endless line of death and suffering: Visualizing the scale of the killing at Jasenovac	59
4.1	Photograph published in the State Commission's report on crimes perpetrated by Austrian troops in Yugoslavia. It was accompanied by the caption 'German soldiers posing contentedly next to their victims'	65
4.2	Photograph used after the war as evidence of the collaboration between Italians and Chetniks, 'brothers in crime'	66
4.3	Article 'Death to German occupiers' published in *Borba*	73
4.4	Photograph featured in the article 'One photograph from a German soldier's album' published in *Borba*	74
4.5	Message to 'opportunists' and 'appeasers': The exhibition of atrocity photographs at the Ulrich Gallery in Zagreb, September 1945	77
4.6	Illustration of Chetnik-Ustasha collaboration: 'While Ustasha were killing Serbs, Chetniks of Draža Mihailović were drinking with them'	79
5.1	Stone Flower shortly after construction, Jasenovac Memorial Area	86
5.2	First permanent exhibition at the Jasenovac museum which opened in 1968	88
5.3	Souvenir postcard sold at the Jasenovac Memorial Museum in the 1970s	93
5.4	Photograph of corpses from Dachau occasionally attributed to Jasenovac	94
5.5	Exhibition 'Paths of Freedom', Museum of Bosanska Gradiška, 1973	96
5.6	Photographs of Chetnik and German atrocities featured in the 1966 documentary on Jasenovac	97
6.1	Touring exhibition 'Concentration camp Jasenovac 1941-1945', 1986	108
6.2	Photograph purporting to show the body of Petar Teslić	110
6.3	Photograph said to show 'Ustasha cutting off the head of Branko Jungić'	111
6.4	Atrocity photographs as 'proofs' of Andrija Artuković's crimes	115
6.5	Revised permanent exhibition at the Jasenovac Memorial Museum which opened in 1988	118
7.1	'History is repeating itself': extract from the catalogue of the 1992 exhibition 'Crimes of the State of Croatia '91'	128
7.2	Second World War-era Chetnik trophy photograph used in Croatian propaganda in the 1990s as an illustration of the history of 'mass atrocities' against Croats	139
7.3	Photograph of Roma in Jasenovac featured in the new permanent display at the Jasenovac Memorial Museum	143
7.4	Deportation to Ustasha camps of Serb population from Kozara	144
7.5	Landscapes as a proxy for atrocities: 'Poplar of Horror' in Donja Gradina and 'Grove of Sighs' in Jasenovac	147
7.6	Scenes from Stara Gradiška, April 1945: Bloodied staircase in the main building and a pile of inmates' possessions	147
7.7	Hitler giving his 'full support' to the genocide against Serbs, Jasenovac Memorial Museum	148

Map

1	The partition of Yugoslavia, 1941	x

Acknowledgements

My thanks are due first to the staff of the archives and museums where I conducted research for this book, above all the Archives of Yugoslavia and the Museum of Yugoslavia in Belgrade, the Archives of Vojvodina in Novi Sad, the Croatian State Archives and the Croatian History Museum in Zagreb, Archives of Bosnia - Herzegovina and the Historical Museum of Bosnia-Herzegovina in Sarajevo, Archives of Republika Srpska and the Museum of Republika Srpska in Banja Luka, and, last but not least, the Public Institution Jasenovac Memorial Area in Jasenovac. I am immensely grateful for all the assistance they provided me over the years, and for their hospitality, professionalism and kindness.

I gratefully received help and support also from staff at the National Library of Serbia and the University Library 'Svetozar Marković' in Belgrade, the Matica Srpska Library in Novi Sad, the library of the United States Holocaust Memorial Museum in Washington DC, and, of course, The Open University Library, whose interlibrary loan system I unashamedly exploited.

I should like to thank Hrvoje Gržina from the Croatian State Archives, Radovan Cukić from the Museum of Yugoslavia, Ivo Pejaković and Đorđe Mihovilović from the Jasenovac Memorial Area, Adam Sofronijević from the University Library in Belgrade, and Marko Radovanović and Đurđa Borovnjak from the Archives of Yugoslavia for their help with obtaining the photographs featured in the book. I am also grateful to the Jasenovac Memorial Area, the Military Museum in Belgrade, the Ministry of Defence of the Republic of Serbia and the Museum of Vojvodina in Novi Sad for granting me permission to reproduce images for which they own the copyright.

I am indebted to my employer, The Open University, for allowing me the freedom to pursue my intellectual interests without too much administrative interference and managerial scrutiny.

Part of Chapter 3 was published previously as 'Picturing Jasenovac: Atrocity photography between evidence and propaganda' in *Fotografien aus den Lagern des NS-Regimes: Beweissicherung und ästhetische Praxis*, eds Hildegard Frubis, Clara Oberle, and Agnieszka Pufelska (Vienna: Böhlau Verlag), pp. 227–248. I am grateful to the publishers of the volume for the permission to reproduce some of this material in the book.

Thanks are also due to the anonymous reviewers for their comments and suggestions, as well as to Beatriz Lopez, Laura Reeves and Rhodri Mogford of Bloomsbury Academic for their efficient handling of the publishing process, and for their patience and support.

Finally, I would like to thank my family, especially my partner Sabina Mihelj, and my two exceptionally clever and inquisitive daughters Clara and Emma for their love and encouragement, and for making me smile.

Abbreviations

ABiH.   Arhiv Bosne i Hercegovine / Archives of Bosnia - Herzegovina, Sarajevo
AJ.   Arhiv Jugoslavije / Archives of Yugoslavia, Belgrade, Serbia
ARS.   Arhiv Republike Srpske / Archives of Republika Srpska, Banja Luka, Bosnia-Herzegovina
AV.   Arhiv Vojvodine/ Archives of Vojvodina, Novi Sad, Serbia
HDA.   Hrvatski državni arhiv / Croatian State Archives, Zagreb, Croatia
HPM.   Hrvatski povjesni muzej / Croatian History Museum, Zagreb, Croatia
MIJ.   Muzej istorije Jugoslavije / Museum of Yugoslavia, Belgrade, Serbia
JUSPJ. Javna ustanova Spomen područje Jasenovac / Public Institution Jasenovac Memorial Area, Jasenovac, Croatia

Map

Map 1 The partition of Yugoslavia, 1941. From *War and Revolution in Yugoslavia 1941-1945: Occupation and Collaboration* by Jozo Tomasevich. Copyright © 2001 by the Board of Trustees of the Leland Stanford Jr. University. All rights reserved. Used by permission of the publisher, Stanford University Press, www.sup.org.

1

Introduction

Picturing genocide

On 21 November 1945, Robert H. Jackson, the US Chief of Counsel for the Prosecution at the International Military Tribunal in Nuremberg, delivered his historic opening statement. To the packed courtroom as well as to a global audience through journalists gathered in the nearby press room, Jackson introduced the 'twenty-odd broken men' in the dock as the 'living symbols of racial hatreds, of terrorism and violence, and of the arrogance and cruelty of power'. He accused them of 'abnormal and inhuman conduct', of leading 'their people on a mad gamble for domination' and of orchestrating a 'campaign of arrogance, brutality and annihilation as the world has not witnessed since the pre-Christian ages'.[1] For this, the men – all leading Nazi officials – stood charged with crimes against peace, the violation of the laws and customs of war and for the first time in history, crimes against humanity – the heinous acts of murder, enslavement, torture, imprisonment and deportation of millions of civilians throughout Nazi-occupied Europe.

In prosecuting the Nazi leadership, the International Military Tribunal was breaking new legal ground. Existing international legal theory and practice proved inadequate for bringing to book perpetrators of state-sponsored crimes of unprecedented scale and horror. New laws needed to be codified, and fresh procedures and rules of evidence devised. As Jackson admitted in his statement, the tribunal was 'novel and experimental', but at the same time vitally important: 'The wrongs which we seek to condemn and punish have been so calculated, so malignant and so devastating that civilisation cannot tolerate their being ignored, because it cannot survive their being repeated.'[2]

One of the novelties introduced at Nuremberg was that photographic and film evidence was accorded a prominent place in the proceedings. At key moments in the trial, the tribunal was shown graphic images and film footage of atrocities found among captured German records or taken by American, British and Soviet photographers and film-makers who accompanied the liberators of Nazi concentration camps. Importance attributed to visual material was reflected even in the spatial arrangement of the courtroom, organized around a large screen which hung on the wall facing the spectators, with the judges' bench on the right and the prisoners' dock on the left.

The reason for showing images that Robert H. Jackson warned would rob the viewer of their sleep and 'turn the stomach of the world' was that it was believed that to provide 'undeniable proofs of incredible events', Nazi crimes needed to be *seen* in all their horror.[3] Images were trusted to 'speak for themselves'; they offered, through their authenticity and vividness, direct access to and irrefutable evidence of the scale and horror of Nazism.[4] As the Soviet prosecutor Colonel Yuri Pokrovsky later told the tribunal chamber, visual images were the testimony of slain victims, of the dead who 'never lie'.[5] The verisimilitude conveyed by the images was thus meant to provide an antidote to suspicion and scepticism that had accompanied the tales of Nazi atrocities ever since the start of the war. Furthermore, because this very public trial was as much about history and memory as about law and justice, the dryness of the lengthy legal arguments and discussions of German documents – what Rebecca West described as the 'extreme tedium' of the courtroom – needed to be punctured by moments of spectacle.[6] The images, and the reactions to them in the courtroom, offered the 'dramatic contrast' needed to hold the attention of the media and maintain public interest in the trial.[7]

The use of photographs and film footage at Nuremberg marked a watershed moment in the history of visual culture of atrocity. As Susan Sontag argued, although 'photography has kept company with death' ever since the invention of the daguerreotype in mid-nineteenth century, it was only in 1945 – when the harrowing images from Majdanek, Buchenwald, Bergen-Belsen and Dachau entered popular consciousness – that the superior power of the visual image to 'define, not merely record, the most abominable realities' of war became fully recognized.[8] Images were validated as an 'unforgettable form of explanation' which could be legitimately and persuasively used, both in a court of law and outside it, to bear witness to and 'bring home' the horrors of Nazism.[9] Similarly, the reporting of Nazi atrocities in the press, and the numerous photographic exhibitions staged at the time, meant that the newly established, or emerging, categories of mass crimes, namely crimes against humanity, genocide and the Holocaust, became irrevocably visually defined in the public imagination. While the visibility of atrocity images ebbed and flowed over subsequent decades, there nevertheless remained the expectation that to attract the attention, and condemnation of the global public, contemporary mass atrocities needed to be evidenced, and rendered visible, with recognizably symbolic, dramatic and vivid images, evocative of the aesthetic and impact of those that shocked the world in 1945. According to Barbie Zelizer, Nazi-era photographs have become 'a frame for understanding contemporary instances of atrocity', 'a backdrop, or context against which to appropriate the more contemporaneous instances of barbarism'.[10]

The impact of the Second World War on the visual culture of atrocity was perhaps inevitable given the sheer number of images of death and suffering that it left in its wake. By the time the Nazi expansionist project began, photographic equipment was sufficiently small, light, affordable and easy to use, to become the ordinary soldier's faithful companion in war. Advances in photographic technology went hand in hand with, and were constitutive of, important cultural and creative developments.[11] These included the rising consumption of images through the illustrated press, photography's growing reputation as the medium that offers both an accurate record of reality and the means of constructing it and the realization that the camera, which was now a personal commodity as much as a professional tool, can be used to capture, narrate and share *individual* experience and perspective on the world. All this resulted in the Second World War being photographed not just by all sides in the conflict but also from a multitude of viewpoints – official and unofficial, professional and amateur. Among the resulting rich visual record was an unprecedented amount of incriminating evidence of crimes committed by the Nazis and their associates. Within just a few months of Germany's defeat, prosecutors at Nuremberg had amassed more than 25,000 still photographs, with tens of thousands more surfacing since.[12]

Over the years, the visual record of Nazi crimes has attracted considerable interest from scholars of different disciplines, including history, cultural and media studies and photography.[13] Their work has generated extensive debates about the historiographic, commemorative and educational value of violent images, about the precise source of their symbolic and evidential power, as well as about the ethics of their continuing dissemination and consumption. Given the unprecedented nature of the tragedy of European Jews under Nazism, and the central place it occupies in Western historical consciousness, imagery relating to the Holocaust has received most attention, as scholars sought to explore how the visual culture of atrocity reflected and, at the same time, helped to determine the course of post-war representation and understanding of the Holocaust.

In existing writing, much of which comes from and is focused on the West, there is a tendency to presume that engagement with atrocity images typical of Western societies and cultures (especially the United States) is universally relevant. This is manifested in the adherence, in the literature, to a Western-centric narrative of the Second World War and Nazi atrocities (including the focus on the liberation of concentration camps), in the choice of photographs and assumptions about what they signify or what makes them 'iconic', but also in considerations of the ethics of looking, namely, the question about when and how it might be appropriate (if at all) for 'us' to gaze at images of past suffering. Relatively little attention has been paid to the social and cultural contingency of, and variability in, visual representations of atrocities, or to the question of how the rest of the world visualizes and remembers Nazi-era crimes.

The importance of this blind spot becomes clear when one turns to Eastern Europe, a region where the memory of Nazi occupation has always had a very different flavour, and social and political function, compared to the West. For one thing, throughout Eastern Europe the Holocaust – while unparalleled in terms of overall scale and intended totality – often took place alongside, and in conjunction with, other instances of racial, ethnic and political persecution or the implementation of brutal counterinsurgency or punitive measures against non-Jewish civilians. This means that Nazi-era atrocities, incorporated into *national* memories of the war, have had a different meaning for, and a more direct emotional and political impact on, local societies and majority populations compared to, for instance, in Britain or the United States, where Nazi crimes were, for the most part, experienced from a distance and where they are today remembered mainly through the prism of the Holocaust. Also, under communism, the selective and carefully managed memory of the Second World War was much more directly political.[14] Motifs of resistance and suffering were an intrinsic part of state and nation building projects. They were used not only to legitimize communist rule and foster social and political unity but often also to divert attention from the delicate issues of local collaboration with Nazi Germany and the uniqueness of the Holocaust. Yet the role of visual culture in this politics of memory, and how ideological and political concerns affected the visibility, choice and interpretation of images of Nazi crimes, has not been adequately explored. The evolution of visual memory over time, including after the fall of communism, has also received little attention, despite the abundance of literature on the wave of historical revisionism that swept the region after 1989.[15]

This book begins to address some of these gaps in research, by looking at visual culture of atrocity in the former Yugoslavia. The book's specific focus is the history and politics of visual representation of the bloodiest, but also the most controversial and politically divisive episode of the Nazi occupation of Yugoslavia, namely genocidal violence against Serbs, Jews and Roma perpetrated by the pro-Nazi, collaborationist, Ustasha regime in the Independent State of Croatia. It explores how Ustasha atrocities have been represented in public exhibitions, documentaries, books and the press from 1945 to the present. The book is especially concerned with the politics of atrocity images and how they were selectively mobilized at different times, and by different memory communities and stakeholders, to *do* different things: to justify retribution against collaborators and their sympathizers in the immediate aftermath of the war, sustain the discourses of national unity on which socialist Yugoslavia was founded, or in the post-communist era, prop up different nationalist agendas, and in many ways 'frame' the Yugoslav wars of the 1990s.

Why examine the visual record of Ustasha violence?

The Ustasha genocide took place on the periphery of the European theatre of war, and, in the context of the overall devastation that Nazi Germany and its allies brought upon the continent, was an event primarily of regional relevance. Nevertheless, there are several reasons why the genocide – especially that against the Serbian population of the Independent State of Croatia – constitutes a particularly apposite case study for examining the power of visual images to shape collective memory of mass violence.

First, the genocide against Serbs – who were the main target of Ustasha persecution – occurred in the context of a bloody and traumatic civil war of unprecedented complexity. The warring factions included the mostly Croatian Ustasha units and the regular army of the Independent State of Croatia (the Home Guard or *Domobrani*), bands of Serbian Chetniks (who opposed the Ustasha while collaborating to varying degrees with Germans and Italians in the fight against communist Partisans), Muslim militias (who were loyal to the Independent State of Croatia and the Germans and fought against Chetniks and Partisans) and the multi-ethnic, communist Partisan army, which fought not just against the Germans and the Italians, but also against collaborators of all backgrounds and persuasions. The prolonged and fluid conflict between the different sides, in which hundreds of thousands of civilians – Serbs, Muslims and Croats – perished, left a deep and enduring scar on community relations in post-war Yugoslavia. This presented a unique political challenge for the authorities.

Fratricidal violence, collaboration with the occupiers, countless atrocities and so on all needed to be explained and committed to memory in a way that did not jeopardize Yugoslavia's identity as a multi-ethnic state or undermine the doctrine of 'brotherhood and unity' on which communist authorities staked their legitimacy. The main legacy of the Ustasha genocide – the damaged relationship between the country's largest constituent nations, Serbs and Croats – was, obviously, the most sensitive issue. As we shall see, atrocity images were mobilized from the outset to render visible the horrors of fascist violence and delegitimize collaborationist forces, but also to promote national reconciliation and build a future-oriented socialist state. How this was achieved is one of the main themes of this book.

Also, the specific circumstances of Yugoslavia's post-communist transition – its violent dissolution in the 1990s and the rekindling of hostilities that had been dormant since 1945 – offer a new way of looking at how the visual record of a past conflict shapes the presentation and perception of a more recent one. Existing literature on this topic mainly focuses on the role that visual analogies (especially those relating to the Holocaust) have played in shaping public opinion in Western societies, about conflicts taking place far away: in Cambodia, Bosnia, Rwanda, Kosovo and so on.[16] This Western-centric focus on the visualization of *remote* suffering inevitably assumes a geographical distance between locations of past and present instances of mass violence, and the social and political context in which the analogy between them is made. By contrast, Yugoslavia – the only European country to have experienced large-scale military conflict on its territory since 1945 – provides a unique opportunity for examining the dynamics, and politics, of analogy-driven visual memory in a context where no such geographical distance exists.

In fact, Yugoslavia's bloody demise provides a compelling example of how in times of social and political upheaval, iconography of violence and polemics over the relevance of images as a mode of historical representation become a medium through which identities are constructed and challenged, and political projects forged and contested. In the late 1980s and early 1990s, at a time of rising nationalism and worsening political crisis in Yugoslavia, graphic atrocity images from the Second World War became a core component of Serbian nationalist discourse and propaganda. They were used to promote the message that the present-day plight of Serbian communities in Croatia and Bosnia-Herzegovina was a continuation of the genocide endured in the Independent State of Croatia, and, by extension, that armed uprising and secession were the only ways to prevent renewed suffering. Among Croatian nationalists, by contrast, the emphasis was on challenging the authenticity and relevance of both the images and the events they represent. The exclusion of atrocity photographs from public gaze was an important part of the broader drive, apparent in Croatia in the 1990s, to whitewash the lamentable historical record of the Independent State of Croatia.

Arguments over the relevance, and use, of atrocity images persist to the present day. In Serbia and in the Bosnian Serb entity of Republika Srpska, even the most graphic atrocity photographs still feature regularly in the mainstream press, in news reports, documentaries and exhibitions devoted to the suffering of Serbs. One can even speak of a distinct atrocity-focused aesthetic of memory, captured in recurring, graphic images of mock or actual executions, decomposing bodies, decapitated or disembowelled victims, corpses of children and the like, which frame public understanding of war and genocide.¹⁷ Exposure to the spectacle of suffering is accepted within these societies as both normal and necessary, even if often disturbing. As the website of the Military Museum in Belgrade explains, scenes of mutilated and dismembered bodies found in its collection of Second World War-era photographs

> leave a heavy and painful impression on all those who look at them, even fleetingly. Yet these photographs are exceptionally important, because they represent almost the only way for the viewer today to appreciate the real horrors of war, short of experiencing them firsthand.¹⁸

Thus, gruesome photographs are treated as both historical evidence and a source of unique vicarious experience, a means of transmitting traumatic memory across generations.

Meanwhile, in Croatia, the same photographs are seldom seen in public. The argument there is that explicit images of brutality are incompatible with a more ethically informed, victim-focused memory of the genocide, one that respects the dignity of the dead and moves away from the aesthetic of shock.¹⁹ Also, it is argued that the legacy of propagandistic misuse by Serbian nationalists has compromised the status of violent images as a vehicle for public remembering. Regrettably, the taboo surrounding atrocity images helps to sustain the almost complete suppression of the genocide against Serbs as a topic of public memory. In Croatian bookshops today, one is more likely to encounter glossy books with photographs glamorizing the Ustasha army than any trace of the visual record of their crimes.²⁰ In fact, photographs of Ustasha brutality have something of a subversive character in Croatia. Their presence tends to be limited to social media, blogs or internet portals, where they are used sparingly and strategically, to puncture the prevailing political taboos and expose, and counter, the failure of mainstream institutions and the media to confront the country's violent past.²¹

A major aim of this book is to deconstruct the two dramatically different approaches to images of Ustasha violence and analyse their origins, evolution and interdependence. Placing the two cultures of visual memory in the appropriate historical context is especially important. Up until the early 1990s, societies that today treat atrocity images so differently were part of the same country and shared a distinctly 'Yugoslav' memory of the Second World War. Yet if one was to believe the today dominant interpretations of the former Yugoslav regime's approach to Ustasha genocide, one would struggle to find evidence of a shared past. In Serbia, there is a widely held view that the martyrdom of Serbs at the hands of the Ustasha was a suppressed topic under communism, part of history swept under the carpet by Yugoslavia's leader Josip Broz Tito and his clique. Hence, the proliferation of atrocity images in Serbia in the late 1980s was part of a broader pushback against the perceived injustices of a state-controlled history and the 'oblivion and taboo' that had supposedly surrounded the genocide against Serbs.²² Meanwhile, in Croatia, the memory of the socialist period is based on the opposite premise, namely that Yugoslav authorities had deliberately created, sustained and promoted the various 'myths' about the Ustasha and exaggerated their iniquity. As Franjo Tuđman – the first president of the Republic of Croatia – argued in his 1989 book *Horrors of War*, these myths were a 'black legend of the historical guilt of the entire Croatian nation, a guilt which should be expiated', and a political instrument utilized to 'keep Croatianness in shackles' and instil a sense of national shame.[23] In Croatian nationalist discourse ever since, atrocity images and their uses and alleged abuses, have been considered an important symbol of this long-standing political, 'anti-Croat' manipulation of history.[24] As we shall see, both positions harbour an element of truth, but they also simplify and misrepresent socialist Yugoslavia's complex and inherently ambivalent attitude towards the Second World War-era ethnic violence and its memorialization. What is more, both sides will be shown to draw on representational strategies that originate from the very same Yugoslav culture of memory that they today so vociferously condemn.

Photographs of Jasenovac and the question of authenticity

In considering visual representations of the Ustasha genocide, forthcoming chapters will use the memory of the Ustasha-run Jasenovac concentration camp as the main case study. Established in August 1941 on the marshes at the confluence of the rivers Una and Sava, around 100 km southeast of Zagreb, Jasenovac was the largest concentration camp in occupied Yugoslavia and, in terms of the number of deaths, among the ten largest camps in Nazi-occupied Europe. According to current estimates, around 83,000 inmates were killed there, of whom 47,000 Serbs, 16,000 Roma, 13,000 Jews, 4,000 Croats and 2,000 victims of other nationalities.[25] Also, Jasenovac was the only camp of its size in the Second World War operated entirely by a collaborationist administration, without the involvement of, or much encouragement from, Nazi Germany.

Throughout the post-war period Jasenovac occupied a central place in both official and vernacular memory of Ustasha crimes. Even today, the word 'Jasenovac' serves as a metonymy for the entirety of the genocide perpetrated in the Independent State of Croatia. Jasenovac owes its metonymic status partly to the fact that in socialist Yugoslavia the number of victims was grossly exaggerated, with the official estimate standing at 700,000 dead. This figure, which was routinely used but never officially debated or justified, implied that as many as 40 per cent of Yugoslavia's assumed 1.7 million wartime casualties perished in Jasenovac.[26] As a result, remembrance of Ustasha crimes inevitably gravitated towards this camp, which eventually became the site of a national memorial. Because of its symbolic importance and political sensitivity, Jasenovac has been the subject of constant instrumentalization and politicization, first by Yugoslav communist authorities, and later also by Serbian and Croatian nationalists. Endless debates between the latter over the number of victims and the nature and purpose of the camp, which date back to the 1980s and refuse to go away, have been explored and written about in considerable detail.[27] Much less scholarly attention has been devoted to the deep divisions regarding the photographic record of Jasenovac and the role of atrocity images in representing the horrors of this camp. This is a surprising omission, given that the question about how Jasenovac should be represented visually, and specifically what should and should not be seen in the Jasenovac Memorial Museum, remains a significant barrier to regional reconciliation, comparable in importance to the polemics over casualty figures. To begin to address the ongoing controversies over the museum in Jasenovac, this book offers the first detailed, comparative examination of the use of visual images in the three permanent displays, from 1968, 1988 and 2006.

The single most contentious aspect of the photographic record of Jasenovac is the questionable 'authenticity' of many of the images that have been used over the years to depict the killings at the camp. As Nataša Mataušić has shown in her book on photographic sources relevant to Jasenovac, images that demonstrably have little to do with this camp have frequently been attributed to it.[28] Photographs depicting Ustasha killings perpetrated at other, usually indeterminable locations, crimes committed by German, Italian or Hungarian troops, even photographs purporting to show Partisan atrocities which appeared in Ustasha propaganda literature during the war, have all been used in publications and exhibitions about Jasenovac. Through erroneous, or in some instances deliberately misleading captions, descriptions and attributions, these photographs, Mataušić argues, have become an 'instrument of untruth'.[29]

The misattribution of images to which Mataušić and others have drawn attention is not unique either to Jasenovac or to the Yugoslav context. The Second World War produced an imperfect photographic record. Photographs uncovered by victorious armies after the war – especially the harrowing images of Nazi atrocities taken by perpetrators or bystanders – often lacked reliable information about their provenance, authorship, subject matter or the circumstances in which they were taken. Many of them ended up being used to illustrate multiple, unrelated locations and events.[30] And yet, very little has been written to date on *how* and *why* these misattributions happen. In the case of photographs of Ustasha crimes, causes are usually sought either in 'human error' or, more commonly, in propagandistic motives.[31] While the latter assumption is not unreasonable, explanations that over-rely on intentionality seldom tell the complete story when it comes to the dynamics of collective remembering. To explain the various misattributions and understand their complex and multifaceted causes, it is necessary to delve deeper into the history of the images and the processes of their collection, curation and dissemination, and scrutinize the complex web of institutional and social practices by which photographs are constituted as authentic, credible and appropriate (although often contested) representations of the past. At the same time, it is just as important to critically examine the rhetoric of doubt and suspicion about the credibility and relevance of images, and consider how it is being used, often just as selectively and tendentiously, to render some photographs, and aspects of the past, invisible.

Genocide in the Independent State of Croatia: The historical context

The Independent State of Croatia, on whose murderous legacy the book focuses, was established by Nazi Germany and Fascist Italy in April 1941, in the aftermath of the Axis invasion and dismemberment of the Kingdom of Yugoslavia. It encompassed the territory of today's Republic of Croatia (without a large part of the Adriatic coast and the Baranja region which were ceded to Italy and Hungary, respectively), the whole of Bosnia-Herzegovina and the Srem region of what is today the northern Serbian province of Vojvodina. The country was placed under the control of the Ustasha, a brutal Croatian fascist terrorist organization that before the war had mostly operated from military training camps in Italy and Hungary.[32] Although the Ustasha, led by the *poglavnik* ('leader') Ante Pavelić and his government, were formally in power, for most of its existence the Independent State of Croatia was an 'Italian-German quasi-protectorate': it was split into a German and an Italian 'sphere of interest', with their respective security forces and military-diplomatic representatives often influencing key decisions.[33] Amid the inevitable power struggle and rivalry among the Ustasha, the Italians and the Germans, the Ustasha embarked on a ruthless campaign of terror against Serbs and the much smaller Jewish and Roma communities, with the aim of creating an ethnically homogenous and 'pure' Croatian state.[34]

For the Ustasha, the 1.9 million Serbs living in the Independent State of Croatia – almost a third of the country's population – represented the main obstacle to the fulfilment of their nationalist dream. Drawing on popular resentment over what was perceived by many Croats as the oppression of their nation by the Serb-dominated, centralized, pre-war Yugoslav state, the Ustasha portrayed Serbs as the arch-enemy, an alien, disloyal, culturally and morally inferior group that poses a threat to the stability, if not existence, of the newly founded independent Croatia. For the ideologues of the Ustasha movement, the 'Serbian question' had always been something of an obsession. Even before the war, Ustasha publications called for a violent reckoning with the Serbs and wished for the day when 'razor-sharp daggers of the Croatian Ustasha will cut out all the rotten flesh from the body of the Croatian nation'.[35] Thus, when the Ustasha, radicalized by years in exile, returned to their homeland in 1941, they saw the Nazi-sponsored Independent State of Croatia as providing both the rationale and an opportunity for the fulfilment of their violent ambitions. Other 'undesirable elements' in the new state – Jews, Roma and communists – were also targeted. Defined in racial terms, Jews and Roma were subjected to Nuremberg-style racial laws and faced mass arrests, internment and, ultimately, mass murder in concentration camps.

Between 1941 and 1945, as many as 330,000 Serbs, 30,000 Jews and 20,000 Roma perished in the Independent State of Croatia.[36] With regard to Serbian victims in particular, the multidirectional nature of the violence and the absence of reliable wartime or post-war records make it virtually impossible to partial out military from civilian losses or determine with any precision what proportion of victims were killed in the genocide, as opposed to other war activities.[37] The fact that the genocide has always been a politically sensitive issue has not helped. Tomislav Dulić estimates the number of Serbian victims of Ustasha genocide to be around 245,000, although other researchers have put forward a higher figure.[38]

While Serbs, Jews and Roma were all victims of horrific and sustained violence at the hands of the Ustasha, there are significant differences between the fate of Serbs, on the one hand, and that of Jews and Roma on the other. Marko Attila Hoare even writes about 'two overlapping but distinct genocides with very different causes and serving different purposes'.[39] The first and main difference is that the destruction of Jews and Roma was part of the Nazi project of extermination that was taking place throughout occupied Europe. Although the Ustasha were both racist and antisemitic, for them the complete annihilation of Jewish and Roma communities was, ideologically speaking (and because of their relatively small size), of secondary importance. Diligence shown in the implementation of the Holocaust was mainly a way of demonstrating adherence to the Nazi principles of racial purity.[40] By contrast, the intolerance of and violence against Serbs reflected a strong, 'home-grown' form of hatred. The persecution of Serbs was pursued even though it eroded popular support for the regime, fuelled Serbian rebellion and jeopardized the security situation in the country.[41]

The second difference is that the persecution of Jews and Roma was more systematic. Most Jews (those who did not go into hiding, join the Partisans or flee to the relative safety of the Italian zone of occupation) were rounded up by the Ustasha, deported to concentration camps and killed.[42] The same happened to the arrested Roma, most of whom were murdered in Jasenovac in the summer of 1942.[43] The organized nature of the persecution accounts for the devastating losses among the two communities: the Ustasha killed around 76 per cent of Croatian and Bosnian Jews and almost all the interned Roma.[44] The fate of the Serbs was different. Because they were more numerous, and largely inhabited rural areas, Serbs could not be easily rounded up, deported to camps and killed. Only around 90,000 Serbian victims of Ustasha genocide were murdered in concentration camps. The rest perished in what is commonly referred to as 'direct terror': punitive expeditions against Serbian settlements (usually accompanied by theft, looting and repossession of land) which often resulted in whole villages being raised to the ground and residents killed, or in numerous pogroms, massacres and sporadic executions perpetrated mostly in 1941 and 1942.[45] Also, because Serbs, unlike Jews and Roma, were defined in ethno-religious rather than racial terms, the Ustasha state subjected them to forced assimilation, mainly through religious conversion to Catholicism, or deportation. Hundreds of thousands were banished to Serbia or fled across the border to escape persecution, while thousands of others were deported to German-run labour camps throughout Europe.[46]

The somewhat chaotic nature of the 'direct terror' means that there was much greater geographical and temporal variation in the persecution of Serbs, compared to Jews and Roma. The scale and ferocity of the violence was often determined more by local social and intercommunal relations, and the proclivities of local warlords, than by any well thought-through, regime-driven policy.[47] Also, the killings were often part of the complex cycle of multidirectional violence and retribution, or were perpetrated under the guise of counterinsurgency operations. And yet, there is no doubt that the campaign of terror was inspired and enabled by the Ustasha regime's broader policy towards Serbs, which included systematic discrimination, open threats of annihilation and concerted efforts to eradicate any trace of Serbian cultural life in the country.

One of the distinguishing features of Ustasha violence, whether directed at Serbs, Jews, Roma or political enemies, was its excessive, sadistic ferocity, which spread fear among the population and sometimes alarmed Italian and German troops. Victims were often, although by no means always, bludgeoned with a mallet or axe, stabbed to death, pushed off a cliff or thrown down a ravine, or had their throats slit with a knife. The partiality for 'cold weapons' was partly due to the shortage of firearms and ammunition, especially in the early stages of the war.[48] But it also reflected an adherence to the culture of violence that glorified the knife as a 'cult object' and regarded intimate forms of killing as a sign of commitment to the Ustasha cause.[49] After the war, the image of the bloodthirsty, knife-wielding Ustasha became the dominant motif of the memory of genocide in the Independent State of Croatia, culminating in the today common, albeit somewhat misguided inference that the sadism of the Ustasha made them 'worse' than their Nazi counterparts.[50]

The fact that the violence against Serbs was not as methodical as that against Jews and Roma, that it occurred alongside the policies of expulsion and assimilation and that it was often exacerbated by the Serb-dominated uprising has led to polemics about whether the fate of Serbs amounted to genocide.[51] While this may sound like a matter of semantics, in a region where 'genocide' is a politically highly charged term (both in relation to the Second World War and the wars of the 1990s), terminology is important. On the one hand, those who argue against the use of the term 'genocide' (at least those who are well intentioned and who question the categorization of the crime rather than its scale) are correct to point out that the often-used phrase 'genocide against Serbs, Jews and Roma' obscures the important differences between the fate of these communities in terms of intent, systematicity and magnitude of the violence. They are also right that the failure to acknowledge those differences fuels the rhetoric of competitive martyrdom and the appropriation of the Holocaust that has been a notable feature of Serbian nationalism since the 1980s.[52] But claiming that the persecution of Serbs was *not* genocide, and focusing on the differences between their fate and that of Jews and Roma, also stimulates nationalist myths: it legitimizes (even if unintentionally) attempts by some in Croatia to minimize, trivialize or deny the scale of Serbian suffering. More importantly, while it may be true that the Ustasha did not have a premeditated plan to kill *all* Serbs, and that losses among the Serbian community were proportionally lower than among Jews and Roma, it is undeniable that the dynamic of destruction bore the hallmarks of genocide. The aim of the Ustasha was, from the outset, to 'destroy the Serbs in Croatia and Bosnia as a distinct national community capable of independent life'.[53]

Importantly, by this definition, the brutal campaign of murder and expulsion that Serbian Chetnik militias waged against Muslim civilians in eastern Bosnia in 1942 and 1943 – which left tens of thousands of civilians dead – was also genocide. This crime may have been more localized and smaller in scale compared to Ustasha violence against Serbs, but its aims, calculated cruelty and devastating impact on the victim community were comparable.[54] While recognizing that Muslims in eastern Bosnia were also victims of genocide, this book will not focus on their fate or its visual representation. This is partly because within the bloody vortex of fratricidal violence among Serbs, Croats and Muslims during the Second World War, the Ustasha genocide against Serbs stands out. For one thing, Serbs, unlike Bosnian Muslims, had the infrastructure, bureaucracy and security apparatus of a state, albeit an imperfect and dysfunctional one, intent on their destruction. The state-sponsored nature of the violence is, in part, why Serbs from Croatia and Bosnia suffered among the highest death tolls in Europe during the Second World War and why they account for as many as two-thirds of all civilian casualties in the Independent State of Croatia.[55] Also, the Ustasha persecution of Serbs, on which much of this book focuses, played a more prominent role in the post-war politics of memory, and, as an object of remembrance, was more strongly visually defined. And yet, Chetnik violence will not be completely overlooked. As we shall see, throughout the socialist era the juxtaposition of Ustasha and Chetnik crimes was a prominent motif in the state-sponsored, 'Yugoslav' memory of the war which had ethnic balance in villainy and suffering as one of its basic principles.

The politics of atrocities and atrocity images

In the book *Explaining Yugoslavia*, John Allcock described collective violence in the Balkans as an area of inquiry 'where angels fear to tread' and warned researchers that 'serious dangers await the fool who enters there'.[56] The main source of danger is that, when it comes to accounts of Yugoslavia's violent past, 'disentanglement of myth from reality' is a delicate affair. Past suffering is often remembered through elaborate stories of atrocities, which, although based on real events, have acquired, through repeated transmission and embellishment, the attributes of myth. The past has been reduced to 'powerful symbolic compilations, whose importance has long since ceased to depend in any way upon their veracity'. As a result, 'the truth is hard to establish, and to separate from various forms of deliberate or incidental fiction'.[57]

Representations of Ustasha atrocities are a prime example of this mingling of fact and fiction. Although the bloodthirstiness of the Ustasha and their penchant for 'intimate' killing methods are well documented, the genocide against Serbs is often remembered through striking and exaggerated atrocity stories which, while built on kernels of truth, belong firmly in the realm of myth.[58] These include tales of children being thrown in the air and impaled on bayonets, foetuses being ripped out from the bellies of pregnant women, victims having their genitalia or breasts mutilated, hearts extracted or noses and ears cut off and kept as trophies, or indeed tales of prominent Ustasha slitting the throats of thousands of Serbs in a single killing spree, sometimes even tasting the blood of their victims. Referring to these stories as 'myths' is not to say that perpetrators never mutilated the corpses of victims, collected body parts as trophies or engaged in mass murder or macabre killing rituals. The Ustasha committed unimaginable atrocities, and they may even have occasionally acted out the various gory rumours that followed them, to shock victims and bystanders, and augment the unsavoury reputation in which many of them revelled. After all, certain forms of violence – throat-slitting, decapitation, genital mutilation, sexual violence and so on – are inherently symbolic and operate within a culturally embedded framework of meaning, a 'rhetoric of atrocity', that is often shared by perpetrators and victims.[59] When carried out, boasted about or documented in a 'trophy photograph', demonstrative violence is a form of communication (e.g. Figure 1.1). It reaffirms the perpetrator group's cult of militarism and masculinity, and conveys to fellow soldiers, victims and bystanders, but also to the outside world, the scale of the triumph over the vanquished enemy. Throat-slitting, for instance, is a method traditionally used to slaughter animals. When used against a human being in war, as the Ustasha frequently did, it becomes an act of almost ritualistic dehumanization.[60] Decapitation and the removal of body parts (usually ones linked to a person's identity such as parts of the

Figure 1.1 Visual symbols of perpetrators' triumph over the victim: Examples of trophy photographs taken by the Ustasha (AJ-337-110-II-156 and HR-HDA-1422, Z-362).

face or genitalia) are similarly symbolic. Transforming parts of the human anatomy into objects to be held, possessed or discarded is a 'ruthless expression of [a soldier's] supremacy', but also an affront to the sanctity of the human body.[61] Violation of women and children outrages because it breaches patriarchal norms about the inviolability of the family and the female body. Yet amid the horrific reality of Ustasha violence, it is also undeniable that the various grisly motifs and recycled tropes that stretch the limits of plausibility and often verge on the pornographic occur with far too great a regularity to be plausibly true in every case.

Atrocity myths about the Ustasha have always had a strong *visual* component. Photographs depicting the cruelty of perpetrators reflect the same 'semiotics of the representation of atrocities' as verbal accounts and descriptions.[62] As we shall see throughout this book, the two modalities have always been locked in a relationship of mutual reinforcement, each deriving meaning and authority from the association with the other.

Importantly, motifs permeating the accounts of Ustasha violence are not unique. Comparable tales of sadistic murder and mutilation have featured (albeit less commonly) in descriptions of actions of other protagonists of the war in occupied Yugoslavia, including Germans, Hungarians, Chetniks and even Partisans. What is more, as Marc Bloch noted shortly after the end of the First World War, the grisly tropes of atrocity propaganda – virtually identical to those commonly associated with Ustasha violence – have been 'ceaselessly recycled since the dawn of time' and have accompanied most wars throughout history.[63] Their stubborn persistence and uniformity is commonly understood in psychological terms: tales of atrocity are part of a coping mechanism, which by fusing reality, folklore and unconscious fantasy allows people caught up in war – civilians and soldiers alike – to give meaning to the world around them; to articulate the fear of, and legitimize their hatred for, the enemy. And yet, the continuity that runs through atrocity accounts and the fact that they span different cultures, political contexts and historical periods cannot be explained solely by reference to the human mind's inherent, and seemingly universal, susceptibility to 'mythification'. Vernacular responses to the horrors of war have strong sociopolitical as well as psychological dimensions; they are mediated by 'top-down' processes and influences. Especially as for the past century and a half, the term 'atrocity' has been a *political* category, associated with a distinct style of rhetoric and manner of reporting and representation.

The concept of atrocity, as understood today, entered political discourse only in the mid-nineteenth century, when it became the favoured term for describing organized and deliberate acts of mass violence against civilians in the context of war, insurgency or revolution. An atrocity typically referred to violence motivated by political or religious reasons and accompanied by mutilation, rape, looting, arson and the destruction of cultural heritage.[64] Importantly, 'atrocity' was seldom a purely descriptive term: to call an act of violence an atrocity was to mark it as a particularly egregious 'violation of a fundamental cultural value' and a source of moral outrage.[65] Accounts of atrocities (whether true or false) pointed the finger at the alleged perpetrators as the embodiment of inhumanity. They also constructed a moral basis for some form of social action. The label 'atrocity' served to provoke righteous indignation and mobilize the intended audience for, and often against, something or someone.

The roots of the political and moral connotation of atrocities are to be found in the internationalization of conflicts on the outer borders of Europe in the second half of the nineteenth century, and in the emergence of advocacy groups in European capitals which campaigned for the rights of oppressed nations overseas. Drawing on the tradition of the anti-slavery movement, these groups advocated intervention by the great powers to protect the lives of endangered civilians beyond national borders. Many of the early campaigns were linked to events in the Middle East and, significantly, the Balkans, where Ottoman Turkish authorities carried out frequent punitive, counterinsurgency measures which resulted in brutal massacres of Christian populations. Eventually, saving the lives of civilian victims of 'massacres' and 'atrocities' in faraway lands became an important political and diplomatic issue for governments of European powers, and a source of political and moral capital, both at home and internationally.[66]

This development had profound implications for the framing and representation of military conflict. The prospect of international patronage for victims of massacres and persecution meant that protagonists of local wars (especially smaller, emerging nations seeking international recognition and support) often-used claims and counterclaims, accusations and denials about atrocities to convince foreign governments, as much as the public at home, about the legitimacy of their cause.[67] By the early twentieth century, and especially by the time of the First and Second Balkan Wars (1912–13), courting the world's public opinion and bidding for neutral support by assuming the role of victim of an atrocity became an inevitable part of waging war.[68]

Atrocities were typically documented in a specific genre of pamphlet, or report, supposedly based on eyewitness testimonies, journalistic reports or correspondence of locally based diplomats and envoys. These reports were full of lurid details of the primitive and brutal methods of killing that violated moral norms and social taboos. At the time when 'the gloomy festival of punishment' was dying out in Europe, the spectacle of tortured, dismembered or maimed bodies became associated with the conduct of intrinsically violent, less enlightened peoples, stuck in the pre-modern, medieval era.[69] Tales of brutality were often gendered, featuring rape, the mutilation of female breasts or infants killed in their mothers' arms.[70]

Visual images from the outset were an important feature of atrocity reporting. In late nineteenth and early twentieth centuries, mainly due to limitations of photographic technology, photographs of atrocities were rare. When present, they tended to show healed wounds of survivors, photographed well after the atrocity had taken place.[71] Killings were usually depicted through elaborate drawings or lithographs (supposedly based on eyewitness reports), which contained both symbolic representations and vivid details of the violence.[72] These were published in books and the illustrated press which promised to convey the horrors 'so effectively that [readers] could imagine being there'.[73] The artwork relied on not only the iconography of martyrdom found in Christian religious art but also the visual rhetoric that emerged in the sixteenth and seventeenth centuries, and was manifested, for instance, in depictions of massacres committed during the French Wars of Religion (1562–98) and the Irish Confederate Wars (1641–53).[74]

Consider, for instance, Figure 1.2, a depiction of 'Turkish atrocities' published in 1913 in *Ilustrovana ratna kronika*, an illustrated magazine printed during the First Balkan War. The magazine was edited and distributed in the city of Novi Sad by the well-known Serbian journalist and publicist Kamenko Subotić. Given that Novi Sad was in the Austro-Hungarian Empire, the aim of *Ilustrovana ratna kronika* was to

Турска зверства: Турци у бегству, видећи да се никад више неће вратити у Стару Србију, касапе Србе

Figure 1.2 Illustration of 'Turkish atrocities', *Ilustrovana ratna kronika*, 17 January 1913, 100 (courtesy of the University Library 'Svetozar Marković', Belgrade).

publicize, among local Serbs, the heroism and suffering of their brethren across the border, who were engaged in the 'war for freedom and civilization' against Ottoman Turkey.⁷⁵ Subotić's patriotic publishing venture was building on a longer tradition: a publication of the same name, and similar visual style and content, was printed in the city in 1877–8, during the Second Serbian–Ottoman War.⁷⁶

The caption accompanying the illustration suggests that it shows retreating Ottoman troops 'butchering' Serbian civilians. It is uncertain whether the illustration was produced specifically for this publication: similar images featured in the magazine were sometimes reprinted from other sources, including old issues of the French magazine *L'illustration* which had a tradition of publicizing depictions of political violence and atrocities.⁷⁷ The drawing contains many clichés of atrocity propaganda of that era. It shows excessive violence: grim-faced Turkish soldiers decapitating victims, gouging their eyes, severing a woman's breast and so on. All those being killed are women, children or elderly, which identifies the crime as a violation of the rules of war; the victims' white attire is a further symbol of their innocence. The most gruesome acts of violence, including a dead girl resting her head on the body of her decapitated mother, feature prominently in the foreground. In the background is another familiar theme: flames engulfing houses, but also a church tower. In atrocity drawings, burning temples were a common way of representing the ethno-religious nature of the violence and the threat to a whole culture and way of life, in the same way that dishevelled clothing, or exposed breasts of female victims, signified sexual violation.⁷⁸

Similar illustrations were to be found also in the Western press throughout the First World War, where, in the absence of material evidence of widely reported German atrocities, editors resorted to emotive drawings, sketches and cartoons.⁷⁹ However, during the First World War, figurative illustrations began to give way to forensic photographs of crime scenes, which provided graphic depictions of the dead and injured, and gave visual representations of atrocities an aura of authenticity and referentiality. By the 1920s, the close-up of a dead or mutilated body became the typical atrocity photograph.⁸⁰

One of the earliest examples of the shift towards a forensic visual register was a series of reports on atrocities perpetrated by the Austro-Hungarian army in Serbia during the First World War. In 1914, the Serbian government commissioned Rodolphe Archibald Reiss – 'a distinguished man of science (who furthermore is a neutral)' – to investigate, document and publicize myriad crimes committed against Serbs during the Austro-Hungarian occupation of the country.⁸¹ Reiss, a Swiss national, was a pioneer of modern forensic science and the founder of one of the world's first police laboratories in Geneva. Given that Reiss's background was in photography (he authored one of the first manuals of forensic photography published in 1903), it should come as no surprise that images taken by Serbian military photographers occupied a central place in the reports.⁸² For Reiss, the camera was an essential tool in any criminal inquiry, and photography served as 'humanity's artificial memory and the automatic, impartial recorder of events'.⁸³ Thus, his reports from Serbia featured not only detailed statistics about the number of victims who suffered different types of mutilation and verbal descriptions of these acts ('disembowelment', 'arms cut off or broken', 'noses cut off', 'eyes gouged out', 'breasts cut off' and so on) but also 'ocular proof': numerous graphic photographs of maimed and murdered victims in situ as well as close-ups of wounds inflicted by explosive 'dum-dum' bullets allegedly used by the Austrians.[84]

Reiss's reports, although partisan and prone to exaggeration, were ground-breaking in the way they brought the forensic lens to atrocity reporting. The scientific rhetoric accompanied by explicit photographs, including those documenting sexual mutilation and rape, was both shocking and convincing, especially to audiences in the West, where reports of German atrocities were still based mainly on sensationalist and usually uncorroborated witness accounts, and somewhat old-fashioned cartoons and sketches. Reiss's use of images also provides an early example of the atrocity photograph's reliance on descriptive captions which guide the viewer's interpretation of the depicted event as an atrocity. For instance, in one report, the caption accompanying Figure 1.3 described the victims as 'young persons from 15 to 17 years of age massacred at the village of Grushitch' and invited the reader to 'notice the wounds at the apex of the skull and the eyes gouged out'.[85] The age of the victims marked the killing as a violation of the rules of war, but it was the alleged sadistic manner of the execution and the mutilation of the bodies that framed it as an 'atrocity'.

There is, however, a further aspect of Reiss's work that warrants attention. As well as publishing photographs taken by the Serbian army, Reiss drew attention to a relatively novel type of visual evidence, which was to gain prominence after the Second World War: the trophy photograph. In a series of reports, published as articles in the European press in 1916 and 1917, Reiss revealed the existence of photographic images, printed as souvenir postcards, which showed the execution by hanging of Serbian civilians by Austro-Hungarian troops. These were said to have been found in

Figure 1.3 Photograph evidencing Austrian atrocities in Serbia in 1914. From Rodolphe A. Reiss's, *Report upon the Atrocities Committed by the Austro-Hungarian Army during the First Invasion of Serbia* (London: Simpkin, Marshall, Hamilton, Kent & Co, 1917, 97).

Figure 1.4 Photographic postcard showing Serbs executed by hanging in Jagodina in 1916 (courtesy of Library of Congress, https://www.loc.gov/item/2014646262/).

the possession of dead or captured Austrian soldiers. A postcard that Reiss described in detail in one of his reports showed the execution of hostages in the Serbian town of Jagodina in 1916 (Figure 1.4). The photograph featured 'youthful Austrian soldiers [...] standing "in a photographic pose"', with officers and civilians assembled nearby 'contemplating the scene' and 'taking a lovely interest in the disgusting spectacle'.[86] The contrast between the 'morbid scenes' depicted in the photographs and the medium of the picture postcard – 'a record of happy incidents and so true a picture of happy places!'– offered a 'damning indictment' of the collective Austrian 'mentality' and proof of the perpetrators' depravity. For Reiss, the most incriminating was the facial expression of the executioners and bystanders, the smiles on their faces revealing 'all the savage glee afforded [to them] by this despicable act'.[87] At the same time, as an investigator working on behalf of the Serbian government, Reiss welcomed the existence of these 'ribald postcards'. Because 'photography never lies', they constituted the 'most formidable indictment' against the Austro-Hungarians, a source of 'documentary evidence, proving in incontestable fashion' their brutal crimes against Serbs.[88]

As this book will show, visual memory of Ustasha crimes, while borne out of the post-Second World War endeavours to evidence the crimes of the Nazis and their associates, is also rooted in this longer tradition of representing and reporting atrocities. The latter's conventions and practices (including the importance attributed to trophy photographs) influenced the choice of images for public consumption as well as their dissemination and interpretation. However, the brief history of the concept of 'atrocity' provided here is important for two further reasons, which help set the scene for the forthcoming chapters.

First, it clarifies what is meant by the term 'atrocity photograph'. In everyday language, there is a tendency to define atrocity photographs purely by their often-gruesome subject matter and to treat any graphic depiction of violent death or injury as an 'atrocity photograph'. And yet, it could be argued that for this label to apply, a further condition needs to be met. A photograph needs to be suffused with appropriate political symbolism and set within a context of meaning that establishes the depicted death as a crime worthy of universal moral condemnation. In other words, atrocity images are defined not by visual or aesthetic properties but by their framing and performative function, by the reaction they provoke and by the things they *do*.

The reaction that atrocity images provoke, or seek to provoke, is one of shock, anger and indignation. As such they are very different from, for example, humanitarian or anti-war images, which they might resemble visually, and which also aim to incite strong, affective responses. An atrocity image does not convey the universal message of revulsion for the brutalities of war, nor is its primary aim to provoke in the viewer compassion for the victims. Its rhetorical connotations and political objectives are quite different. An atrocity photograph directs the gaze of the viewer at the act of violence and brings into focus the perpetrators' irredeemable depravity. This emotional dimension of the atrocity image is an important source of its rhetorical and political power.

Second, because of the evolved political connotations and function of the concept of 'atrocity', atrocity photographs are always set in an emotionally charged argumentative context, where their authenticity and relevance is contested. This is perhaps unsurprising given that photography's long-standing claim to mechanical objectivity and referentiality (on which the authority of atrocity images rests) has always gone hand in hand with scepticism about its ability to fulfil its evidentiary promise.[89] After all, despite the commonplace assertion that 'camera never lies', everyone knows that photographs can be, and often are staged, edited, cropped, or doctored in some other way, either for artistic purposes or to mislead the viewer. In fact, it is precisely the assumed persuasiveness of the visual image that drives the temptation to fake it or makes people look for evidence of fakery. Similarly, photographs do not 'speak for themselves'. One can never be certain, just by looking at a photograph, that it shows what is being claimed. Photographs 'wait to be explained or falsified by their captions', with their capacity to display the truth always contingent upon the knowledge that the viewer brings to them.[90]

Things are complicated further by the fact that photography's (contested) evidentiary and documentary potential has always been only one part of its appeal as a mode of representation. Photographs, especially those representing violent death, derive power also from their assumed ability to steer the audience towards appropriate feelings and action. They do so not necessarily by way of unquestionable provenance and authenticity, but through the intricate web of signs and codes that the audience recognizes in, or reads into, an image. Through aesthetic appeal, familiarity and symbolism, striking, evocative photographs – just like the hand-drawn illustrations that adorned atrocity reports in the nineteenth century – trigger associations and emotions and capture some *broader truth* about the world. As Zelizer put it, bearing witness to past horrors sometimes involves wresting images 'free of detail so that they can be effectively utilised to tell a story larger than that of the scenes they depict'.[91] This is photography's crucial symbolic, *illustrative* role. As we shall see throughout this book, the atrocity photograph's contested epistemological status and its tendency to 'hover uncomfortably between illustration and proof' are issues that haunt the history of visual representations of Ustasha violence.[92] They also pervade the ongoing debates about the legitimacy and relevance of violent photographs as 'vessels of memory' and proofs of a historical grievance.[93]

Outline of the book

In tracing the trajectory of visual memory of Ustasha genocide, the book adopts a chronological approach. Chapter 2 focuses on images of Ustasha atrocities collected and circulated at the height of the genocidal campaign in 1941 and 1942. It explores why German and Italian armies were the first to document, and photograph, the excesses of Ustasha violence, and what role atrocity images, alongside witness testimonies about the suffering of Serbs, played in the political life of neighbouring Nazi-occupied Serbia. Also, the chapter analyses the atrocity-focused (counter-) propaganda that the government of the Independent State of Croatia produced in 1942 to defend its reputation against accusations of brutality and to justify the violent campaign against Serbs. Through the analysis of this material the chapter explores the link between visual images, political propaganda and wartime rumour and considers how the relationship between them shapes the engagement with atrocity photographs more generally.

Chapters 3 and 4 explore the activities of the Yugoslav State Commission for the Investigation of the Crimes of the Occupiers and their Accomplices. Between 1944 and 1948, the State Commission, established by Yugoslavia's communist government, collected thousands of images pertaining to war crimes perpetrated in Yugoslavia, including those depicting Ustasha violence. Chapter 3 examines the commission's approach to evidence gathering and the importance it attributed to photographs as a source of proof of fascist criminality. Also, using as an example the commission's early report on the killings in Jasenovac, it shows how the tension between the evidential/documentary and illustrative/symbolic role of atrocity photographs manifested itself in practice and how this paved the way for many of the controversies that have plagued the visual memory of Jasenovac ever since.

Chapter 4 moves on to examine how photographs collected by the State Commission were mobilized in the service of propaganda, both at home and internationally. Abroad, including at Nuremberg, the Yugoslav government deployed the motif of victimhood in the pursuit of its foreign policy agenda and to enhance its international reputation. On the home front, photographic exhibitions, film documentaries, illustrated press reports and so on were used to incite hatred of collaborators and justify retribution, but also to promote the idea of Yugoslav unity based on shared suffering. With regard to the latter, the chapter looks at how photographs taken by perpetrators – especially 'trophy photographs' – were used to formulate a generic theory of 'fascist mentality', one that obviated the need to delve into the complex and politically delicate questions about the causes of the fratricidal violence among Yugoslav nations.

Chapter 5 looks at the memory of Ustasha crimes in socialist Yugoslavia. The period between the 1950s and the 1980s was marked by a general decline in public interest in atrocities perpetrated during the Second World War, as attention was firmly focused on the heroism of the Partisans as the main object of public memory and source of national pride. However, by examining the content of the first permanent exhibition at the Jasenovac Memorial Museum which opened in 1968, as well as a number of publications and film documentaries from that era, the chapter shows that Ustasha brutality was nevertheless a visible component of the story of the Second World War, albeit one that, for political reasons, needed to be managed carefully.

Chapter 6 examines the period of the 1980s which was marked by a proliferation of images of Ustasha atrocities and a resurgence in public interest in the theme of genocide in the Independent State of Croatia. The chapter argues against the conventional view that these developments were the outcome of the rise of Serbian nationalism after the death of Josip Broz Tito. It shows that, on the contrary, for much of the decade, the greater visibility of atrocity images was sanctioned by the authorities as a way of buttressing the dominant, 'Yugoslav' narrative of the war and promoting, especially within Croatia, an anti-fascist and anti-nationalist message. However, the chapter also shows that the greater emphasis on Ustasha brutality and the genocidal nature of their project exposed the limitations of the Yugoslav culture of remembrance and its cautious approach to the history of ethnic violence. This eventually allowed the motif of Serbian suffering, and the relevant atrocity photographs, to be appropriated by Serbian nationalists and instrumentalized by the Milošević regime in Belgrade.

Chapter 7 looks at the impact that the violent breakup of Yugoslavia had on the visual memory of Ustasha genocide in Serbia and Croatia. First, it looks at the role that atrocity images, historical and contemporary, played in the wartime propaganda in the 1990s, and specifically how the events of the 1940s were used, in both Serbia and Croatia, to 'frame' the war of the 1990s. Then, by deconstructing the radically different approaches to atrocity photographs in present-day Serbia and Croatia, the chapter considers the continuing influence of the events and political agendas of the 1990s on the interpretation and visualization of Ustasha genocide.

The concluding chapter, Chapter 8, revisits the key themes of the book and addresses two broader questions about atrocity photographs, namely what they are for and what role they *should* play in the remembrance of the genocide in the Independent State of Croatia. It also ponders the possibility of a new, critically informed approach to visual memory, one that would allow contentious photographs of Ustasha atrocities to be incorporated into public memory in a more productive and conciliatory way.

Finally, a brief note on the photographs featured in the book and on the captions that accompany them. The book contains around sixty images, some of which are graphic and potentially upsetting depictions of atrocities. In selecting this material, I have taken care to include only photographs which I consider integral to the analysis or which illustrate important aspects of visual rhetoric discussed in the text. Hopefully, the reader will be satisfied that I have not used the images gratuitously or with the intention to shock, inflame passions or cause distress.

The atrocity photographs were obtained from archives and museums in Serbia and Croatia, and the source and the unique reference number are indicated in the captions.

Importantly, however, the *descriptions* in the captions are my own. This is because, in most instances, the description found in the records of the source institution was either demonstrably incorrect or was just one of myriad conflicting interpretations of that image. Thus, to avoid reproducing and perpetuating past inaccuracies or misattributions – which are themselves a subject of critical scrutiny in the book – I included new captions. These are grounded in the analysis and allude to the specific issue or point in the book to which the photograph pertains or which it is meant to illustrate. In other words, the captions are not necessarily about what is *in* the photographs; they are part of the broader story about what individuals and institutions *made of* the photographs, over the years, as they sought to make sense of and remember the horrors of Ustasha genocide.

2

Evidencing 'unprecedented acts of savagery'
Atrocity photographs in occupied Yugoslavia

The publication of photographs of liberated concentration camps in 1945 is often regarded as the moment when the world finally confronted the reality of Nazi crimes. One reason for this is that the images were explicitly framed as such, especially in North American and British media. Photographs and film footage of Allied soldiers gazing at corpses of victims, or of German civilians being compelled to do so by the victorious armies, made the photographic record of the liberated camps as much about the first visual encounter with the 'horrors of German brutality', as about atrocities themselves. The Western public's vicarious participation in this act of witness, discovery and confrontation was inevitably absorbed in the way atrocities were subsequently represented and remembered.

And yet, photographic evidence of Nazi atrocities had been in the public domain since the start of the war. As early as in 1940, members of the Polish underground movement began smuggling atrocity photographs out of occupied Europe.[1] These were published in reports and pamphlets prepared by the London-based Polish Ministry of Information or by various Jewish organizations in the United States.[2] The Soviet propaganda machine in London also issued dozens of communiqués on mass crimes perpetrated on Soviet territory, mainly through the *Soviet War News Weekly*, an English-language newspaper launched in January 1942. Several richly illustrated compendia of these reports were also printed.[3] Graphic, violent images included in these publications, which were often of poor quality and uncertain provenance and credibility, were greeted with a mixture of suspicion and indifference by a substantial proportion of the British and American public. Nevertheless, they received favourable coverage in the press, and were shown in officially sanctioned and well-attended photographic exhibitions organized on both sides of the Atlantic.[4]

The importance that the Soviet Union and the Polish government in exile placed on publicizing Nazi crimes illustrates well the political, and propaganda, function of atrocity accounts and images. By 1940, claims of atrocities had been widely recognized as a vital instrument of international public diplomacy. The problem, however, was that this instrument was available to all parties in the conflict and was often misused. In the fog of war, it was not always possible to determine who is telling the truth and who is merely spreading 'atrocity propaganda'. For instance, in 1940, the German Foreign

Office published the pamphlet *The Polish Atrocities Against the German Minority in Poland* which falsely alleged that, in the weeks leading up to the German invasion of Poland in September 1939, as many as 58,000 men, women and children of the German minority had been murdered and mutilated by 'the Polish armed forces and by Polish civilians'.[5] Then, in April 1943, using a very similar mixture of witness testimonies, records of medico-legal examinations and graphic images of human remains, the Nazi propaganda ministry exposed another massacre: the execution, in 1940, of thousands of Polish civilians by Soviet forces in the Katyn forest in western Russia. Unlike the alleged massacres of ethnic Germans, this was a very real atrocity whose uncovering, the Nazi leadership had hoped, would drive a wedge between Western Allies and the Soviet Union. A year later, following German withdrawal from western Russia, Soviet investigators re-examined the mass graves at Katyn and, unsurprisingly, confirmed their government's previous disingenuous denials of culpability. The 'Truth about Katyn' report, circulated widely among Western Allies, blamed the killings on the Germans and dismissed the previous attempt at implicating 'the Soviet Power' as a 'German provocation' and 'agitation'.[6] Key to pulling off the Katyn deception was the involvement in the Soviet investigation of the government-sponsored Extraordinary State Commission, an institution which between 1942 and 1948 investigated and reported on thousands of genuine Nazi crimes in the Soviet Union.[7] Meanwhile, the Polish government in exile, which had brought news of Nazi crimes against Jews and Poles to British and American audiences, found itself, in 1943, defending the finding of the German-sponsored Katyn investigation. In doing so, it left itself exposed to accusations that it was colluding with Nazi Germany in the propaganda war against the Soviets.[8] All this confusion and uncertainty over what is real and what is not, and what, and who, should and should not be believed is another reason why scenes from liberated Nazi concentration camps, seen through the eyes of trustworthy Allied soldiers and photojournalists, were perceived as clearing the air and providing a different order of proof of atrocities in Europe.

The role that atrocities stories and images played in international diplomacy during the Second World War has been extensively researched and is relatively well understood. The same cannot be said about the dissemination and consumption of images in occupied Europe itself. This is important because atrocity claims, while addressing a global audience, are the product of local social, cultural and political circumstances, and often perform important local functions before entering the international stage. Ustasha genocide against Serbs offers a useful example of this. The first reports of Ustasha atrocities reached Britain and the United States in the autumn of 1941, via the London-based Yugoslav government in exile. Konstantin Fotić, the government's representative in the United States, publicized the content of these reports through diplomatic channels, and passed them on, unofficially, to the Chicago-based Serbian newspaper *Amerikanski Srbobran* which began printing them in November 1941. Ustasha atrocities later received coverage also in the mainstream press in Britain and the United States.[9] In 1943, the North American diocese of the Serbian Orthodox Church published an illustrated, 300-page book in English about Ustasha atrocities, entitled *Martyrdom of the Serbs*.[10] And yet, the diplomatic agenda pursued through these reports and images, the division they caused among the Yugoslav diaspora and the government in exile, or the reaction to them in the corridors of power in Washington and London, are only part of the story. As important is the dynamic by which this material came into existence in the first place, and the role that it played in the political power-play, and everyday life, in Nazi-occupied Yugoslavia.[11] These issues, which left an enduring mark on representations of Ustasha violence, are the topic of this chapter.

Monitoring the undependable ally: German and Italian investigations into Ustasha crimes

On 14 April 1941, only four days after the Independent State of Croatia was established, the Ustasha publication *Hrvatski narod* announced that the 'resurrection' of the Croatian state cannot fully take place without a 'bloody confrontation with our eternal enemies, our native Serbs'.[12] In the days and weeks that followed, the Pavelić regime initiated such a 'confrontation' through virulent anti-Serbian propaganda, accompanied by a wave of arrests, kidnappings, looting and sporadic killing of Serbs. These largely uncoordinated acts of violence and intimidation soon escalated into mass murder and a programme of physical annihilation.[13] The first mass killing of Serbs took place on 28 April 1941, in the village of Gudovac, near the Croatian city of Bjelovar. That day, a local Ustasha commander ordered the rounding up of around 200 Serbs from the village and the surrounding hamlets. At dusk, the men were escorted to the field that normally hosted the village farmers' market and were executed by firing squad.[14] Those who survived the initial salvo of bullets were finished off with knives and bayonets. Later that night, a group of residents were issued shovels and lanterns and ordered to dig shallow graves where the bodies were hastily covered with quicklime and buried.[15]

The Gudovac execution took place a day after two members of a local armed posse, the 'peasant guard', were killed in armed skirmishes, probably with members of the defeated Yugoslav army who refused to surrender their weapons and were hiding in the woods.[16] Even before the precise circumstances of the guardsmen's death could be ascertained, Ustasha officials pinned the blame on an 'organized attack by Chetniks from Gudovac', and used this as a pretext for the mass arrest, and killing, of Serbs. Upon hearing the news that Serbs were being rounded up in large numbers in a village near Bjelovar, Eugen Dido Kvaternik, a senior Ustasha official from Zagreb who would become one of the masterminds of the genocide against Serbs, immediately set off for the area, to personally coordinate the action.[17]

The shooting in Gudovac is an event of considerable historical, and symbolic, importance. As the first mass execution in the Independent State of Croatia, it set in motion the initial wave of Ustasha genocide against Serbs. In the weeks and months that followed, similar killings were carried out in countless towns and villages throughout Croatia and Bosnia: Blagaj, Velun, Banski Grabovac, Glina, Gacko, Stolac, Čapljina, Knin, Gračac, Slunj, Sanski Most, Prijedor and others.[18] But the Gudovac massacre is important also because it yielded the earliest photographic evidence of an

Ustasha crime. Because perpetrators made little attempt to conceal the nature, or the scale, of the shooting, news of the event soon reached the city of Bjelovar, including the commanders of a German garrison stationed there. German officers, who had not been given notice of the action, swiftly assembled a 'commission' which visited the execution site and carried out an investigation. Accompanied by a local translator and a doctor, investigators interviewed witnesses, and carried out a partial exhumation of the bodies, which were examined and photographed.[19] Among the photographs – of which around twenty have been preserved – there are several showing corpses laid out on the ground, awaiting inspection (Figure 2.1).

Why did the German military formally investigate an execution carried out by its ally, of whose bigotry and murderous proclivities it was undoubtedly aware? German officers stationed in Bjelovar were clearly dismayed by the unprovoked killing of Serbian civilians. The day after the shooting, they even ordered the arrest of around forty of the perpetrators. At the same time, it is unlikely that in the relative confusion of the first month of the occupation, bringing to book those responsible for the shooting would have been a priority for the Germans or that this was the main reason for embarking on an official, quasi-legal evidence-gathering exercise. A more likely explanation is that the act of investigation, just like the arrest of suspects, was a demonstration of German authority, a way of appeasing the local population, restoring order and sending a message to the Ustasha that they could not operate with impunity. As such, the response to the Gudovac shooting was an early manifestation of the tension that permeated German-Ustasha relations for much of the war. Most Wehrmacht officers in Croatia deemed mass violence against civilians justified when carried out as part of counterinsurgency measures, or when a territory, and its inhabitants, needed to be 'pacified'. During the four years of occupation, the German army carried out numerous ruthless, punitive military operations in Croatia and Bosnia (often with the assistance of local Ustasha and Domobrani forces) in which tens of thousands of civilians were

Figure 2.1 German officers inspecting the bodies of Serbs killed by the Ustasha in the village of Gudovac (HR-HDA-1422, Z-793).

killed or deported to concentration camps. But Germans perceived their 'space-centred' approach to violence as very different from the 'people-centred' approach of the Ustasha, whose aim was to rid the Independent State of Croatia of the Serbs.[20] What is more, they saw the two approaches as having conflicting objectives: Ustasha brutality was blamed for fuelling the armed rebellion that the German army sought to quash. As the German artillery general Paul Bader observed in the spring of 1942, German troops should be ordered to shoot at Ustasha committing atrocities 'not out of consideration for the Serbs, but to restore order'.[21] Arguably, therefore, officers who ordered the investigation of the shooting in Gudovac were not collecting evidence of a specific crime but were documenting the *nature* of Ustasha violence. They were laying the foundation for the 'discursive divisions in Wehrmacht perceptions of violence', between the 'chaotic, unmeasured, and fundamentally irrational' terror of the Ustasha and the supposedly goal-oriented, rational and justified anti-insurgency efforts of the Wehrmacht.[22]

The distinction between the two forms of violence informed also the Ustasha response to German criticism over the treatment of Serbs. The Gudovac massacre was forgotten within a few days, and the arrested perpetrators were released after the German ambassador to Zagreb, Siegfried Kasche, chose to accept the falsehood that this was a retaliatory execution in response to the killing of eleven Ustasha soldiers in the area.[23] Ustasha later used the same excuse to justify other atrocities. Nevertheless, complaints over the mindlessness of Ustasha terror – supported with atrocity stories – persisted as a prominent feature of the German military's rhetoric, mainly because it provided a convenient explanation, and excuse, for the failure of the Wehrmacht to subdue Partisan resistance.[24]

Gudovac was not the only Ustasha crime investigated, and photographed, by the Germans. In early September 1941, Ustasha units went on a violent rampage through villages near Sarajevo, in which around 300 Serbian civilians were killed, some by being locked up in buildings which were then set ablaze. Shortly after, representatives of the German army visited one location at Alipašin Most where they photographed around sixty burned bodies which the Ustasha left unburied.[25] Another crime near Sarajevo perpetrated in April 1942 was also photographed, and a report was filed with the local office of the German Security Police and Security Service.[26] However, much more diligent in documenting and reporting Ustasha crimes were the Italians, in whose 'sphere of interest' the violent and often out-of-control irregular, 'wild Ustasha' units were particularly active. The Italian army reported on and photographed the aftermath of numerous Ustasha atrocities, including those in Trojvrh, Smiljane, Gračac, Čapljina and Knin.[27] In September 1941, they also investigated the abandoned sites of the Ustasha concentration camps at Jadovno near Gospić and Slano on the island of Pag.[28] Visits to these sites were triggered by reports of hundreds of dead bodies which had been thrown down pits and ravines and which the Italians feared could lead to water contamination and the spread of infectious diseases.[29]

Although many in the Italian military were genuinely concerned about the indiscriminate and barbaric nature of Ustasha violence – one report described it as echoing the 'darkest times of the Middle Ages' – the motive for documenting atrocities was not purely humanitarian.[30] Accounts and images of Ustasha, but also Chetnik and Partisan violence, helped sustain the prevailing stereotype of Balkan nations as treacherous 'savages', 'barbarians' and 'blood thirsty beasts' to whom the usual customs of 'moral, juridical and military law' do not apply.[31] These were then used to legitimize a range of repressive measures which the Italians deployed to control and dominate occupied territories. Fascist Italy had used the same strategy six years earlier, during its military campaign in Ethiopia.[32] On the whole, however, the Italians, just like the Germans, turned a blind eye to Ustasha (and Chetnik) violence when it suited their political and military interests, but then criticized it, or acted to curb it, when there was some practical benefit to doing so. In August 1941, for example, the Italian army used Ustasha atrocities, and the threat to security that they posed, as the pretext for taking full military control over large parts of the Independent State of Croatia.[33] Some of the photographs of Ustasha brutality taken over the preceding months, many of which deployed familiar, gendered visual clichés of atrocity propaganda, were put to practical use (e.g. Figure 2.2). They were shown to Serbs in reoccupied areas, as a way of enhancing the image of the Italian army as a benevolent force and protector of Serbs.[34] Unsurprisingly, Ustasha officials were furious at the Italians' curiosity about the locations of execution sites, and they opposed 'arbitrary and illegal' investigations into the killings of Serbs. The tendency of the Italians to 'publicly grieve over rebel casualties and photograph their remains' was dismissed as little more than 'political preparation' for the complete takeover of the country.[35]

Germans and Italians did not photograph Ustasha crimes solely in the context of formal investigations. Soldiers who owned a camera and used it to document wartime experience – their own, or that of their military unit – also took images of atrocities they encountered. Some did so because they were shocked by the brutality of their cobelligerents, others as part of the more routine practice of creating 'a memento from a life being lived' and detailing the realities, and horrors, of war in the Balkans.[36] These photographs were occasionally handed over to superiors or the security services

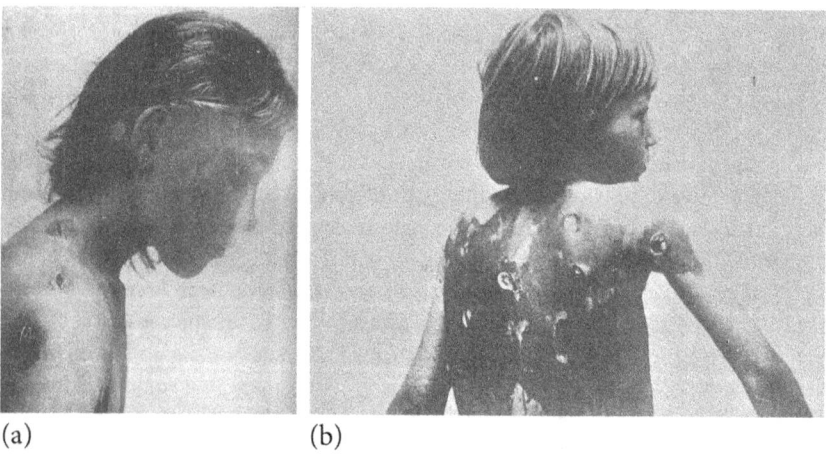

(a)   (b)

Figure 2.2 Ustasha atrocities through Italian eyes. Photographs of injuries sustained by two child survivors of the Ustasha massacre in Gračac in the summer of 1941 (from *Note Relative All'occupazione Italiana in Jugoslavia*, date and publisher unknown, 75).

and became part of the formal record, what was referred to in German documents as *Ustascha Gräuel* – Ustasha atrocities.³⁷ Others remained in personal collections. Either way, after the capitulation of Italy in the autumn of 1943 and the defeat of Germany eighteen months later, many of these photographs found their way into the hands of Yugoslav authorities and became an important source of visual proof of Ustasha genocide.

The politics of atrocity images in occupied Serbia

The mass killings of Serbs in the late spring and early summer of 1941 led to the exodus of thousands of civilians across the border into Serbia. By July, Serbian authorities had between 130,000 and 200,000 refugees on their hands, with the number rising further over subsequent months.³⁸ Refugees brought with them harrowing stories of Ustasha persecution which caught the attention of the authorities. Two institutions were set up in the summer of 1941 to systematically document refugees' testimonies. First was the collaborationist administration's Commissariat for Refugees, whose officials interviewed many of the arrivals about events leading up to their escape or deportation from Croatia and Bosnia.³⁹ Around 3,000 testimonies collected in this way were transcribed, collated and bound, forming what one contemporary called the Commissariat's unique 'library of horror'.⁴⁰ The second institution was the Serbian Orthodox Church. Among the refugees from the Independent State of Croatia were around 500 priests and their families, who turned to the Patriarchate in Belgrade for assistance.⁴¹ Upon hearing about the arrests and murder of Orthodox clergy, the secretariat of the Synod established a commission tasked with collecting evidence of these crimes. The commission comprised around a dozen representatives of the clergy, tutors from the local seminary, and clerical staff, many of whom were themselves refugees.⁴²

The primary audience for reports compiled by the two institutions were German officials in Belgrade. Already in June 1941, representatives of the collaborationist administration began to send 'memoranda' detailing Ustasha atrocities to the head of the German administrative apparatus in Serbia, Harald Turner, and the top military commander, General Ludwig von Schröder, calling upon them to intervene on behalf of the Serbs.⁴³ In subsequent months, the Serbian Orthodox Church issued its own appeals to Schröder and later also to his successor, General Heinrich Danckelmann.⁴⁴ It is the copies of these memoranda that were later sent to the London-based Yugoslav government in exile, with the view of raising awareness among the Allies about the plight of Serbs.⁴⁵ In late 1941 and 1942, Milan Nedić, who formed a permanent collaborationist government in August 1941, continued to send letters to Turner with details of Ustasha atrocities.⁴⁶

Memoranda sent to German officials were sometimes accompanied by atrocity images.⁴⁷ The photographs of the Gudovac massacre were appended to one of the first appeals that the collaborationist administration sent to Harald Turner. On 25 June 1941, in response to what he referred to as a 'confidential report' from the Serbs, Turner wrote a letter to the German embassy in Zagreb in which he listed twenty instances of murder, torture and mutilation perpetrated by the Ustasha. In the letter, Turner 'once again' appealed to the ambassador to 'urgently file a complaint with the government of Croatia' and urge them to stop what he referred to as 'acts of terrorism'.[48] Notably, the motive for writing the letter was not the concern over the well-being of Serbs but the fact that rumours of atrocities represented a security risk. 'Because of the fate of their compatriots in the Independent State of Croatia', Turner wrote, 'the Serbian population on the Territory of the Military Commander [in Serbia] has been overcome by a state of quiet desperation, which I regard as a significant threat'. As 'evidence' of the veracity of the atrocity claims, Turner submitted fourteen photographs 'of the way in which the Ustasha killed Serbs in the village of Gudovac near Bjelovar'.[49] Surprisingly, the photographs which, as we have seen, were taken by *German* investigators were said to have originated from 'the Serbian Ministry of Interior'. This was probably a reference to the fact that Milan Aćimović, the head of the temporary collaborationist administration who also led the Ministry of the Interior, was involved in the preparation of the memorandum, and is likely to have sent it, if not delivered it personally, to Turner.[50] Turner did not elaborate on *how* collaborators might have gotten hold of the photographs. Stanislav Krakov – who edited several Belgrade newspapers during the Nazi occupation and who was closely associated with the collaborationist administration – wrote after the war that the Gudovac images were brought to Serbia by regular German soldiers, who then shared them with the landlord of the flat in Belgrade where they resided.[51] A much more plausible explanation is that someone within the German security apparatus in Belgrade received the photographs from colleagues in Zagreb, and then, unbeknownst to Turner, passed them onto the collaborationist authorities. After all, offices of the German Security Police and Security Service (SiPo and SD) in Zagreb, Sarajevo and Belgrade regularly exchanged reports on security-related matters (sometimes accompanied by photographs), including on Ustasha atrocities.[52] The same 'photographs of the gruesome scenes' in Gudovac were later mentioned in other reports, including the memorandum which the Serbian Orthodox Church sent to General Dankelmann in August 1941.[53]

Memoranda to German authorities were never made public in occupied Serbia, at least not officially. The church and the collaborationist administration did not print pamphlets or books, and details of Ustasha violence were conspicuously absent from the collaborationist press, even as thousands of refugees were crossing the border into Serbia.[54] The main reason was that the Independent State of Croatia was Germany's ally, so open and public criticism of its criminal regime would not have been tolerated by the occupying army and its sensors.

And yet, collaborators had a vested interest in disseminating atrocity stories about Ustasha treatment of Serbs. In a country where there was little public support for cooperation with Nazi Germany, the easiest way to justify collaboration was to present it as a necessity, a sacrifice for a higher, national cause. Claims that collaborators were saving Serbia from destruction and ensuring the biological survival of the nation were staple ingredients of this rhetoric of self-legitimization.[55] Atrocity propaganda about events in the Independent State of Croatia was a way of persuading Serbs that only through collaboration can their country remain an 'oasis of Serbdom', a sanctuary for the wretched fugitives from Croatia and Bosnia.[56]

The principal means by which atrocity stories spread among the population was rumour. The Independent State of Croatia's chief diplomatic representative in Belgrade, Consul General Ante Nikšić, complained to his superiors in Zagreb that the Serbian capital was buzzing with 'deliberate rumours' about Ustasha bestialities, which the consulate collected from informants frequenting the city's bars, cafés and brothels. The Consul General conceded that refugees were probably the main source of the rumours. However, he reported also the existence of 'proofs of these so-called bestialities and atrocities' which circulated in the form of 'photographs and detailed descriptions of the so-called victims'.[57] The latter included clandestinely produced and distributed pamphlets, which were passed from hand to hand or sold under the counter in the city's bookshops.[58] A particularly notable example was the copy of a letter which the Belgrade-based politician of Croatian descent Dr Prvislav Grisogono purportedly sent to the Catholic archbishop of Zagreb Alojzije Stepinac in February 1942. Forged while Grisogono was imprisoned by the Gestapo as a suspected British agent, the letter accused the Catholic Church of complicity in Ustasha crimes and brought together many of the atrocity tropes that circulated in Belgrade at the time. Supposedly penned by a known public figure, and more importantly a Croat and a Catholic, the letter was intended to lend credence to rumours of torture and mutilation, including children being roasted or boiled alive, foetuses being extracted from belies of pregnant women, victims being made to drink blood of slain compatriots and so on.[59] That this letter and similar material were widely available and talked about in Belgrade points to the likely involvement in their distribution (if not creation) of the collaborationist security apparatus and its network of agents and informants.[60]

Collaborators also used rumours of Ustasha atrocities to stoke the fear among the population that, unless Serbia collaborates, it too might be engulfed in the tragedy unfolding across the border. In memoirs published after the war, individuals close to the Nedić government consistently justified their wartime actions by citing a threat supposedly made by German officials in Belgrade (Turner, Dankelmann or someone else, depending on the version of the story) that Nedić's failure to extinguish Partisan resistance would have lead Hitler to withdraw German troops from Serbia and hand control over large parts of the country to the Independent State of Croatia and Bulgaria.[61] The idea of the 'secret German plan' that would bring Ustasha rule to Serbia, although implausible, was effective in transforming the harrowing reports of Ustasha atrocities into a dystopian vision of Serbia's future that only collaboration could prevent from coming to pass.

Photographs were instrumental in driving this politics of fear. One image in particular became an icon of Ustasha atrocities in the summer of 1941. It showed a group of men, some in uniform, others in civilian attire, standing above a mutilated body, laid out on what looks like a workbench (Figure 2.3). Some of the men in the photograph appear to be smiling, and one of the soldiers (third on the left) is holding an implement or a tool, probably a bow saw.

This image was said to depict the killing of Miloš Teslić, a prominent Serbian businessman from the Croatian city of Sisak, who was arrested by the Ustasha at the end of April 1941 and killed shortly after.[62] The motive behind Teslić's arrest and murder was, likely, financial as much as ideological. Around that time, Ustasha

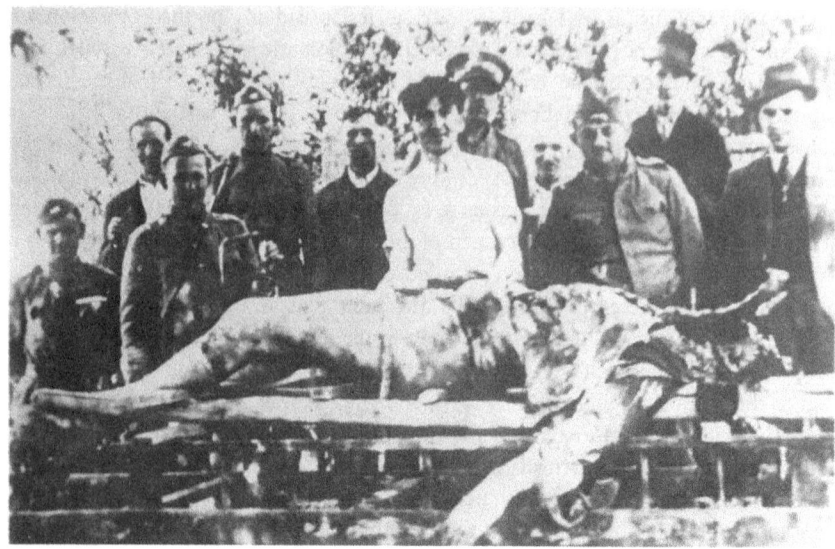

Figure 2.3 Photograph said to show the mutilated body of Miloš Teslić (AJ-337-110-II-361).

deliberately targeted wealthy Serbs so that they could appropriate their assets, money and possessions.[63] In memoranda and reports compiled in occupied Serbia, however, the central aspect of the murder was the perpetrators' sadism and the gruesome details of the execution. Teslić was said to have been killed 'in the most bestial manner' and was 'literally cut to pieces' by the executioners.[64] The fact that Teslić's business empire included a furniture factory and a sawmill led to speculation that the horrific injuries were inflicted with a rotary saw.[65] Also crucial to the photo's persuasive power was the fact that it featured Ustasha soldiers 'gloating over the body'. This not only authenticated the photograph but also confirmed the rumours that perpetrators took perverse pleasure in the suffering of victims.

The precise circumstances of Teslić's death have never been established, so it is impossible to say which of the various versions of the execution, if any, is accurate.[66] It is noteworthy, however, that different accounts of the 'bestial manner' in which Teslić was killed are all based on what can be seen in (or read into) the photograph, which remains the only 'evidence' of the brutal nature of the murder. Yet because the provenance of the image is unknown (most sources simply suggest that it was 'brought to Serbia by refugees') there is no proof that it indeed shows the body of Miloš Teslić. It is possible, and even likely, that the unidentified and unattributed (although probably genuine) photograph arrived in Serbia around the same time as the news of Teslić's death and that the two became fused into, and disseminated as, a single, powerful symbolic marker of Ustasha depravity.

The photograph of Miloš Teslić circulated widely in occupied Belgrade. Aleksandar Ajzenberg, a Holocaust survivor who was in the city in the summer of 1941, recalls that as an eleven-year-old boy he 'saw several photographs of a group of Ustasha soldiers gathered around a table on which lay the spread-out body of the owner of the vinegar factory in Sisak. Visibly cheerful, they had a photo taken, with knives and daggers in their hands'.[67] Also, the same photograph was carried around by Milan Aćimović as he agitated for the collaborationist cause. In June 1941, Aćimović visited the head of the Serbian Orthodox Church, Patriarch Gavrilo Dožić, who was under house arrest at the Rakovica monastery near Belgrade. The purpose of the visit was to obtain the Patriarch's support and blessing for collaboration. Dožić's posthumously published diaries contain a detailed description of Aćimović's visit and his lengthy exposé on the situation in the war-torn country. This included a description of the worst of Ustasha atrocities, including the following 'unprecedented act of savagery' in Sisak:

> The Ustasha arrived at [Teslić's] store in their trucks and took away everything. Materials, money, everything. When they finished, they dragged him in front of the building and nailed him, alive, to a large table. Then they carved up his body, piece by piece, and skinned him. This poor fellow died under this horrific torture, and when they saw that he was no longer giving any sign of life, they ripped his heart out of his chest. After they did all this, they took a photo of him, all mutilated. They made thousands of copies and distributed them in the surrounding areas, and in Serbian villages, to show Serbs what awaits them unless they adopt the Catholic faith.

According to Dožić, Aćimović then reached into his bag and pulled out a copy of the photograph in question, 'which Serbian refugees preserved and brought with them to Belgrade'.[68]

The fact that Aćimović took the photograph to the meeting with Dožić, and chose to produce it in a dramatic fashion, testifies to his belief in the persuasive power, and revelatory promise, of the atrocity image. Also interesting is that Aćimović explicitly alluded to the propaganda potential of the photograph, when he claimed that Ustasha 'made thousands of copies' and distributed them to sow fear among the Serbian population. There is no evidence that the Ustasha – or indeed any other party in the war in Yugoslavia – ever used photographs of their own crimes in this way, at least not in as organized and systematic way as Aćimović alleged. Almost by definition, atrocity photographs only ever show crimes perpetrated by others. If anyone, it was the collaborationist authorities in Nazi-occupied Serbia who mobilized this photograph in the pursuit of their political goals, just as Aćimović had done during the visit to the Rakovica monastery.

Figure 2.3 is not the only photograph linked to the tragedy of the Teslić family. In 1943, the North American diocese of the Serbian Orthodox Church published the book *Martyrdom of the Serbs* comprising English translations of several of the memoranda and atrocity reports compiled by the church in previous years. The book included numerous photographs of Ustasha atrocities, among them that of 'Croat Ustashi gathered around the corpse of the Serbian martyr, Teslich'.[69] Yet earlier in the book, a very different photograph was used to depict 'the well-known Serb, Teslich, whose heart the Croat Ustashi extracted through the hole in his chest'.[70] This was an outdoor shot of the head and torso of a male victim laid out on the ground, whose clothing had been partially removed to expose large penetrating wounds and lacerations to the

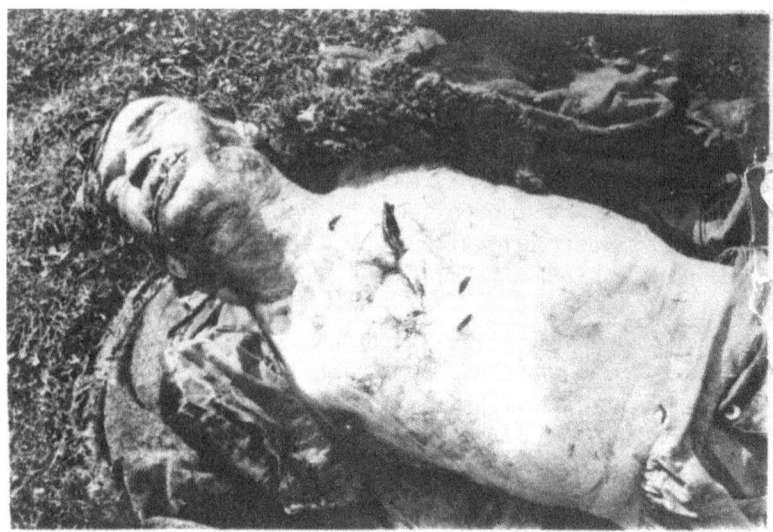

Figure 2.4 Photograph of the body of Miloš Teslić, or Bishop Platon of Banja Luka? (AJ-337-110-II-423).

chest (Figure 2.4). Given that one of the reports in the book alleged that 'the River Sava threw up his corpse with gouged eyes, a horribly mutilated face and his body and chest cut wide open', it is likely that this photograph was meant to illustrate the state of the body at the point of discovery.[71] Also, as a close-up of the body, it offered visual proof of the alleged mutilation, including the extraction of the heart.

Martyrdom of the Serbs is the sole source where Figure 2.4 appears in relation to the murder of Miloš Teslić.[72] After 1945, and almost certainly also during the war, this photograph was used to depict another well-known Ustasha crime: the murder of the Serbian Orthodox bishop of Banja Luka, Platon Jovanović.[73] Bishop Platon, a prominent figure within the Serbian church, was arrested on 5 May 1941 on the orders of the notorious Ustaša commissioner for Banja Luka, Viktor Gutić. Together with another priest, he was driven to a secluded spot outside the city and killed, and their bodies were thrown in the River Vrbas. The bishop's remains were found washed up on the bank of the river a few weeks later and were taken to the local hospital morgue. Once his death was confirmed, rumours began to spread among the local population, as well as within the church hierarchy, about his body being massacred beyond recognition, about his beard being torn out, nose cut off, salt poured in his wounds, his heart extracted and so on.[74] These tales of 'horrific torture' and death persisted in subsequent decades and became an inherent part of the overall discourse of the Christ-like suffering of the Serbian Orthodox Church in the Independent State of Croatia.[75]

The photograph in Figure 2.4 is, however, *not* of Bishop Platon's body. In October 1941, three months after he was deported to Serbia, Dušan Mačkić, a priest from Banja Luka, wrote a detailed report on events surrounding the bishop's death. The report stated that after the discovery of the body, Ljubo Jovanović, a local undertaker who knew the bishop well, was sent to the hospital to perform formal identification and make funeral arrangements. Jovanović reported back to Mačkić that he examined the bishop's body thoroughly and discovered three bullet wounds, two to the head and one in the back. He made no reference to signs of torture and mutilation. The undertaker also reported that the bishop was found wearing just his underpants, with a leather belt around his waist and distinctive elasticated shoes on his feet, and that 'half of his beard [or jaw] had been eaten away by fish, while the other half was still visible'.[76] This description of the injuries and the state of the by-then probably badly decomposed body does not correspond to what can be seen in the photograph. Evidently, just like in Teslić's case, the photograph was used to illustrate and validate the rumours about the brutal nature of the Bishop's execution. The fact that the corpse in the photo obviously looked nothing like the bearded figure of Bishop Platon only served as definitive proof that he had been tortured and disfigured beyond recognition.[77]

More importantly, there is now conclusive evidence as to when and where this photograph was taken. The body shows one of the victims of the massacre in Gudovac. Archives of Vojvodina in Novi Sad recently uncovered a cache of documents and photographs relating to Ustasha atrocities, which the office of the German Security Police and Security Service in Belgrade compiled in 1941–2. Among them is a set of fourteen photographs labelled as showing the execution in Gudovac. These are probably the same fourteen photographs that Harald Turner appended to his letter to the German embassy in Zagreb in June 1941. Besides the wide-angle shots of the exhumed bodies (including Figure 2.1), there are also close-ups of injuries sustained by the victims.[78] Among them is Figure 2.4, labelled as 'Murdered Serb from the district of Bjelovar'.[79]

The fate of Figure 2.4, and the way it has been associated with different crimes, points to a broader tendency in the use of atrocity photographs, which, as we shall see, persisted after the war. Institutions in Nazi-occupied Serbia were receiving reports of an unprecedented number of Ustasha crimes. Casualty estimates went as high as hundreds of thousands of dead. Yet photographic evidence to support the atrocity stories was scarce. What is more, most of the available images depicted a single event, the killing in Gudovac. Eventually, this set of photographs was broken up, either intentionally or inadvertently, and images ended up being used either as generic illustrations of Ustasha crimes or as representations of disparate events, usually the murder of prominent Serbs whose fate had captured the public's imagination. In *Martyrdom of the Serbs*, for example, images from Gudovac were used to represent multiple themes: 'A Serbian victim of Croatian Ustasha whose brain was extracted', the body of 'martyr Teslić' or 'German soldiers and Croatian Ustashi shooting enmasse [sic] Serbian war victims'.[80] Only one of the photographs was explicitly linked to Gudovac.[81] Labelled and presented in this way, photographs of a single atrocity became the means of conveying the overall horror, scale and pervasiveness of the 'martyrdom of the Serbs'.

The dissemination and consumption of atrocity photographs in Nazi-occupied Serbia reveals also how words and images work together to make sense of atrocities. Photographs depicting Ustasha crimes, far from speaking for themselves, were viewed, and read, through the prism of the prevailing tropes and clichés, which were incorporated into captions and descriptions. Photographs acquired relevance and meaning from their correspondence with atrocity rumours, while, at the same time, they helped reinforce and authenticate those same rumours. They offered demonstrative evidence that horrendous stories of Ustasha bestiality were not a figment of the collective imagination or simply 'atrocity propaganda'.

Furthermore, the rhetoric of atrocity influenced not just the choice and interpretation of the images but also how they were remembered. Because people glance at photographs of atrocities only fleetingly, they tend to remember the gist of the photograph and its connotation rather than details. Human memory, after all, is anything but 'photographic', even in the best of circumstances. So, at the point of recall, or more accurately, reconstruction, gaps in memory are embellished with details which reinforce aspect of a photograph that made it an object of interest in the first place. In the case of Ustasha violence, this tends to be the horror of the killings and mutilations, and the perpetrators' depravity. Thus, when Stanislav Krakov recalled the Gudovac photographs in his memoirs written after the war, he described them as showing 'hundreds, maybe a thousand bodies' arranged in 'tens of rows'. He wrote that visible among the dead were 'men, women, and male and female children', and that close-ups revealed that victims' eyes had been gouged out and bellies ripped open. Similarly, Aleksandar Ajzenberg's memory of the photograph of Miloš Teslić's body was embroidered with the prevailing stereotype about the Ustasha: he misremembered the perpetrators standing above Teslić's body holding 'daggers and knives in their hands'. These examples highlight a broader truth about atrocity photographs that is worth bearing in mind: their symbolic power lies not just in what is captured in the image but also in what viewers take away with them, after they stop looking.

Atrocity propaganda in the Ustasha state

The political reverberations of atrocity rumours and propaganda circulating in Nazi-occupied Serbia were felt across the border in Croatia. In early June 1942, Croatia's Consul General in Belgrade noted (somewhat belatedly) that Serbian authorities were passing the information about 'supposed Ustasha atrocities' to the Germans and were using them to tarnish the reputation of the Pavelić regime. He recommended a swift response in kind, namely, 'that we immediately begin with publicizing the countless atrocities by Communist-Chetnik gangs, because it is obvious that the enemies of our state are intent on attributing their atrocities and bestialities to the actions of our army and state security units'. He noted that this 'requires urgent action, otherwise our enemies will always be one step ahead of us with their machinations'.[82]

As Nikšić was making these observations, a response was already under way in Zagreb. That same month, the Croatian Ministry of Foreign Affairs published, in Croatian and German, a 150-page book entitled *Rebel Atrocities and Devastation in the Independent State of Croatia in the First Months of Existence of the Croatian National State*.[83] The purpose of the book, prepared by the regime's leading propagandist, Matija Kovačić, was to stem the tide of 'Judeo-masonic, Bolshevik-Anglo-Saxon, and Greater Serbian propaganda' and debunk the damaging allegations against 'the Croatian people and their state'.⁸⁴ According to Kovačić, the Independent State of Croatia deserved international recognition and gratitude for its sacrifices in the defence of 'European civilization and culture' and for the way it stood up to the 'bloodthirsty rebels of a different nationality' intent on halting the 'victorious march of the great European project'.⁸⁵ Another publication containing similar material, penned by the journalist Franjo Rubina, was published later that summer under two different titles: *Bloody Secrets of Mount Kozara* and *Kozara: the Partisan Graveyard*.⁸⁶ Rubina was the war correspondent of *Nova Hrvatska*, the second most prominent daily newspaper in the Independent State of Croatia.⁸⁷ He was well known for reports extolling the virtues of 'heroic' Ustasha soldiers, and inflammatory articles which described in lurid detail atrocities perpetrated by Serbs and Partisans.⁸⁸ *Bloody Secrets of Mount Kozara* was published by the education section of the Ustasha army, and was distributed to soldiers, while *Kozara: the Partisan Graveyard*, which was more richly illustrated, was probably intended for general distribution.⁸⁹ Rubina's pamphlets focused on alleged Partisan atrocities perpetrated near Mount Kozara in western Bosnia, where a large-scale joint German-Ustasha offensive against the Partisans was carried out in July 1942. The book was clearly intended to legitimize, and celebrate, this brutal 'cleansing' operation, in which thousands of Serbian civilians were killed, and tens of thousands more deported to concentration camps from which very few returned.

In painting the picture of the 'disturbed and sick state of the Serbian soul', Ustasha propaganda mirrored the rhetoric of atrocity found in rumours circulating in Serbia at the time.⁹⁰ It was the Chetniks or Bolshevik Serbs, not the Ustasha, who were 'killing for the sake of killing' who were 'severing or smashing heads, slashing throats, gouging eyes, cutting off noses, hands and feet, flaying the skin off the head and body, chopping off genitalia, or the breasts of girls and mothers, or in acts of unprecedented sadism, leaving infants to suckle on the severed breast'.⁹¹ Printed material comprised detailed and repetitive descriptions of such acts, which, in the case of *Rebel Atrocities*, were interspersed with statements from witnesses and official reports of medico-legal investigations of mass graves.

Photographs used to support claims of Chetnik and Partisan atrocities included close-ups of bodies, with suggestive captions emphasizing the brutality of torture and execution which was not always evident in the photos themselves. Just like in the examples circulating in Nazi-occupied Serbia, the more-or-less visible signs of injury or tissue damage were automatically read as evidence of deliberate mutilation and torture. Other possible explanations – the effects of natural decomposition, the impact of explosions or large-calibre bullets and the scavenging action of rodents or wild animals – were typically ignored.⁹² Figure 2.5, for instance, was described as the body of the child of a 'Muslim Croat from the village of Košutica, whom Chetnik-Communists mutilated'. The visible chest wound (probably caused by a bullet) was presented as evidence of the 'incomprehensible sadism' of the rebels who 'extracted the child's heart'.⁹³ The extraction of the heart was the authors' favourite motif, mirroring its presence in the Serbian material. It featured in captions accompanying three other images and was mentioned countless times in the text.⁹⁴ Photographs were also used to substantiate claims that victims were 'impaled on a stake and roasted', 'skinned alive', 'emasculated', had symbols carved into their skin, or were maimed in some other, equally horrific way.⁹⁵

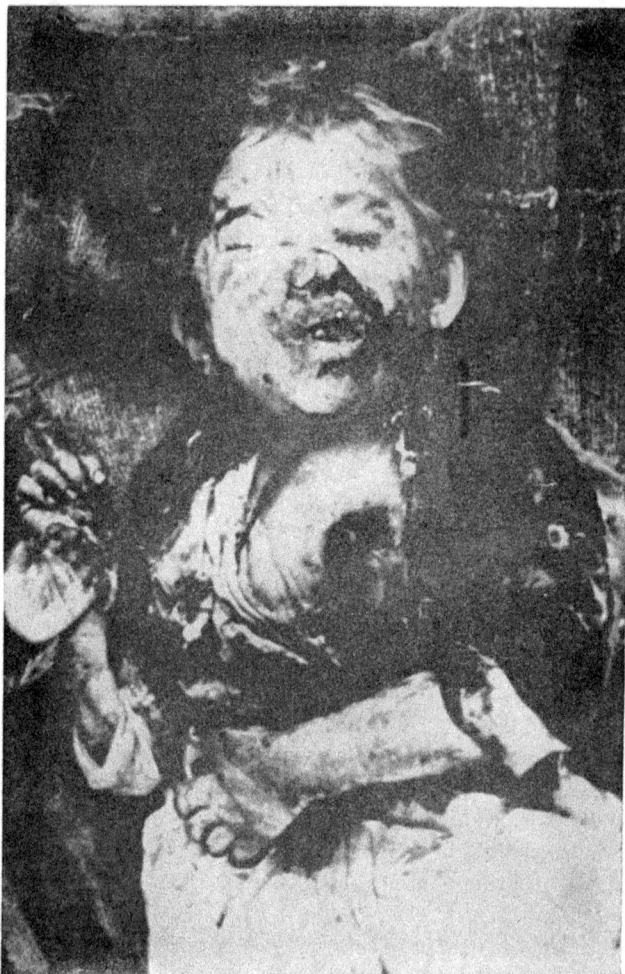

Dicte jednog Hrvata muslimana iz sela Košutica, koje su četnici-komunisti strašno iznakazili. U svom nepojmljivom sadizmu izvadili su djetetu srdce.

Figure 2.5 Ustasha propaganda photograph of a victim of 'Chetnik-Communist' mutilation (from *Odmjetnička zvjerstva i pustošenja u Nezavisnoj Državi Hrvatskoj*, 1942, photoplates, p. ix).

The focus on barbaric means of execution reflected, and reinforced, the racist ideology of the Ustasha. Serbs were portrayed as inherently primitive, backward and menacing. This was conveyed through 'ethnographic-racist' photographs of Serbian civilians and mugshots of captured rebel combatants, which were carefully selected to emphasize their supposed cultural and racial inferiority.[96] Partisan men were depicted unshaven and dishevelled, their 'dark exterior' a marker of 'spiritual dimness', the 'perfidious stare' hinting at an 'evil character' (e.g. Figure 2.6a).[97] By contrast, the 'noble and determined' Ustasha soldier was visualized through a publicity image of

Figure 2.6 Contrasting images of Partisan and Ustasha fighters in Ustasha propaganda: (a) 'Types of Partisan heroes captured in Kozara' and (b) 'noble and determined expression of the Ustasha fighter' (from Rubina, *Kozara: groblje partizana*, 65, 79).

a tidy, clean-shaven and distinctively 'Aryan'-looking man in uniform (Figure 2.6b). Also, Serbian civilians caught up in the fighting in Kozara were said to be 'wretched' and naïve, susceptible to Partisan propaganda and manipulation. They were generally photographed in passive and compliant poses, squatting or sitting down in groups, or walking along obediently under Ustasha escort. Crucially, photographs depicting columns of such misguided Serbian civilians who were being 'allowed to return home' looked identical to those showing 'captured Partisan gangs' being escorted to concentration camps. This visual similarity clearly conveyed the message that when it comes to Serbs, the boundary between civilians and combatants, between the 'wretched' and the 'perfidious', was inherently blurred.

Representations of perpetrators of alleged atrocities, just like those of victims, had a gender dimension. Serbian women were portrayed as the antithesis of the idealized, patriarchal notions of femininity, chastity and traditional morality which were core to Ustasha ideology.[98] Women fighters were said to be particularly 'fanatical and bloodthirsty' and inventive when it came to methods of torture.[99] Serbian women were also presented as neglectful mothers, prone to child abandonment, which in the context of the cult of motherhood that the Ustasha promoted was especially damning. This stereotype served to legitimize the Ustasha policy of separating Serbian children from their mothers and interning them in cruel, disease-ridden concentration camps

(a) (b)

Figure 2.7 Ustasha propaganda photograph of 'abandoned' Serbian children before (a) and after (b) they were taken into 'care' by the Ustasha state (from Rubina, *Kozara: groblje partizana*, 1942, p. 22 and 85).

masquerading as orphanages. During the Kozara offensive, thousands of Serbian children suffered this fate, as their mothers were deported to concentration and labour camps. Figure 2.7 offers two examples of images of Serbian children published in Ustasha propaganda literature. Figure 2.7a is one of several images used to illustrate 'innocent peasant children' that Ustasha soldiers supposedly found abandoned and saved them from 'hunger and disease'. Figure 2.7b illustrates the civilizing influence of the Ustasha-run state. It shows 'abandoned' Serbian children 'fully recovered and healed' in an idealized, well-ordered domestic setting of one of the 'special children's homes'.[100] As we shall see in Chapter 5, other photographs of Serbian children in 'care' emerged after the war, which exposed the brutal reality of these Ustasha-run 'children's homes'.[101]

Also featured in Ustasha propaganda literature were images of enemy combatants killed in action as well as those of dead Ustasha and Domobrani soldiers. Ustasha units often photographed the enemy dead for reasons of identification, and, in the case of better-known outlaws, also for purposes of propaganda.[102] What is more, local Ustasha commanders were keen to obtain visual proof of military engagement with, and successes against, the enemy to demonstrate to superiors the effectiveness of their troops.[103] As for bodies of dead Ustasha and Domobrani fighters, *Rebel Atrocities* featured four images showing 'mutilated bodies of Croats', namely, thirteen Ustasha killed by Partisans near the town of Lipik in May 1941 (Figure 2.8). The bodies were photographed laid out on a bed of straw, probably in a barn, with their shirts unbuttoned and wounds exposed.

Despite the reference to 'horrific mutilations', there are no visible signs of torture, and the photographs are not nearly as gruesome as those of dead civilians featured in the book. The inclusion of these images is noteworthy however, because the publication of photographs of one's own dead is generally frowned upon by any military and is often regulated by strict censorship rules. And yet, the propaganda potential of these images is clear. As we have seen earlier in this chapter, in their communication with German

Figure 2.8 Ustasha propaganda photograph of troops 'horrifically mutilated and robbed' by rebels (from *Odmjetnička zvjerstva i pustošenja u Nezavisnoj Državi Hrvatskoj*, 1942, photoplates, p. xi).

representatives in Zagreb, the Ustasha justified many of their actions against Serbs as retaliation for attacks on their forces. Images of dead soldiers in a book intended for the eyes of German officials helped to reinforce this narrative. On the domestic front, these photographs illustrated the sacrifices made in the war against a ferocious, uncivilized enemy. However, there may have been another reason for allowing them to be published. We know, for example, that the German army in Serbia did little to dispel rumours circulating among their troops that Partisans were torturing prisoners of war and killing them in horrific ways. In October 1941, after a group of German soldiers were killed in an ambush near the Serbian town of Topola, it was reported that their bodies had been 'partly mutilated, skulls shattered, legs cut up, faces disfigured'.[104] Although subsequent medical examination found no evidence of mutilation – according to survivor reports the soldiers had been cut down by machine gun fire which caused extensive injuries – military authorities suppressed this disconfirming information and allowed rumours to persist. They even dispatched a photographer from the propaganda section to document the autopsy. They did this, first and foremost, because they knew that stories about Partisan savagery, although potentially damaging to troop morale, discouraged German soldiers from surrendering.[105] They also lessened the sympathy for the enemy, encouraged revenge and rationalized acts of reprisal and brutal conduct towards civilians during counterinsurgency operations. There is even some evidence that Wehrmacht soldiers in Serbia were shown photographs of slain comrades as part of psychological preparation for retaliatory executions of civilians.[106] The Ustasha propaganda machine probably hoped that images, and rumours, of mutilation suffered by comrades would instil a similar mind-frame in their troops.

Figure 2.9 Two of Edmund Stöger's propaganda photographs of Jasenovac, August 1942: (a) inmates repairing a steam-powered machine in one of the camp factories and (b) building a perimeter wall around the camp (courtesy of the Jasenovac Memorial Museum).

The books published in Zagreb in the spring and summer of 1942 were part of a wider, orchestrated effort to misrepresent the realities of Ustasha rule. In August that year, Edmund Stöger, a photographer affiliated with the government propaganda office, visited the Jasenovac concentration camp, where he took staged photographs of inmates building flood defences or working in various workshops and factories within the camp complex (Figure 2.9). Around the same time, a similarly deceptive and misleading film footage of camp conditions was recorded.[107]

It is not difficult to see where Stöger found inspiration for his work: photographs of Jasenovac were virtually identical, in terms of composition, choice of motifs and aesthetic to those of Dachau published in the Nazi propaganda newspaper *Illustrierter Beobachter* in 1936.[108] Stöger's work was put on display in Zagreb in September 1942, at a public exhibition marking the first anniversary of the camp's existence. The exhibition was staged in a purpose-built replica wooden barracks from Jasenovac. At the end of what would prove to be the bloodiest summer at the camp, the photographs were meant to create the illusion that the Jasenovac slaughterhouse was 'neither a sanatorium nor a torture chamber', but a well-ordered labour camp and a refined correctional facility for Croatia's enemies.[109] As a report on the exhibition published in *Hrvatski narod* explained, 'Those who once hoarded money and profiteered from the bloody calluses of Croatian workers are working today, working steadily to repay their debt to the Croatian people, whom they had exploited for years.'[110]

As we shall see in later chapters, after 1945, Stöger's photographs and the propaganda film footage were absorbed into the official memory of Jasenovac, often in a way that did not adequately acknowledge their provenance and connotations. Meanwhile, the exculpatory interpretation of the Ustasha regime that these and other propaganda images sought to substantiate retreated to the margins, and, for much of the post-war period remained confined to pro-Ustasha organizations in the diaspora. It made a return to public discourse in Croatia only in the 1990s, when Croatian nationalists fully embraced the idea that Yugoslavia's communist rulers had misrepresented the bloody legacy of the Independent State of Croatia and that Serbs and communists were the real villains of the war, while Croats were the main victims. Some even regarded the fifty-year-old Ustasha stereotypes and propaganda myths about Serbs as the appropriate prism through which to view the worsening crisis in Yugoslavia: the violence that erupted following Croatia's declaration of independence in the summer of 1991 inspired the publication of a reprint of *Rebel Atrocities*. Importantly, the situation was similar in Serbia, where the opposition to Croatia's independence and the threat of war also involved the resurrection of occupation-era atrocity myths. It should therefore come as no surprise that, ever since, the 'memory wars' between Serbian and Croatian nationalists have been fought on similar lines, and using similar arguments and iconography, as the propaganda battles in the early 1940s.

Partisan photography and enemy atrocities

In the early stages of the violence in the Independent State of Croatia, the side that was least actively involved in the collection and dissemination of visual evidence of enemy atrocities were the Partisans. This may seem surprising given that the Ustasha campaign of terror was the driving force behind the Partisan insurgency in Croatia and Bosnia. What is more, the motif of atrocities was frequently mobilized in Partisan propaganda to explain why 'avenging the rivers of blood of our people' was the appropriate emotional and behavioural response to persecution, and why the Partisans were the natural home for those dispossessed and uprooted by ethnic violence.[111]

For the Partisans the focus on atrocities was a twin-edged sword, however. The movement's communist leaders knew that their success depended on their ability to appeal to different ethnic groups and be recognized as a credible alternative, rather than a party to the vicious cycle of ethnic violence and bloodletting that was tearing the country apart. To achieve this, Partisan rhetoric emphasized the 'joint struggle of Serbs, Croats and Muslims for the cleansing of [Yugoslavia] of the common enemy' and adopted a more balanced framing of ethnically motivated mass killing.[112] Even when descriptions of mass violence drifted into gruesome atrocity myths, great care was taken to maintain a symmetry in villainy between the different 'domestic traitors and hirelings' (primarily the Ustasha and the Chetniks) and to include multiple ethnic groups (and, of course, Partisan sympathizers and communists) among the victims. As we shall see in Chapters 4 and 5, this became a vital and an enduring feature of the 'Yugoslav' memory of the war.

Ambivalence towards atrocities was reflected in the approach to visual propaganda. When Partisans deployed images to promote resistance and drive recruitment, they did not resort to potentially inflammatory and divisive photographs of Ustasha, or Chetnik, violence. On one occasion, Partisan propaganda explicitly condemned the dissemination of gruesome photographs of Ustasha violence by collaborators in Serbia as part of the 'wicked plans of the blood-soaked enemy' to sow discord between Serbs and Croats.[113] Instead they used affirmative images showing military successes and the movement's multi-ethnic composition. These were smuggled into Zagreb, Sarajevo and other cities, as a way of debunking Ustasha stereotypes about the Partisans as disorganized, ineffectual and murderous bands of 'Chetnik-Bolsheviks'.[114] Žorž

Skrigin, one of the best-known Partisan photographers and the author of many of the early propaganda images, explained after the war that photographs 'spoke persuasively that we had a regular and disciplined army, equipped with artillery, even anti-aircraft guns'.[115] This propaganda activity eventually acquired an international dimension, as the Partisan movement sought recognition, and military assistance, from the Allies.[116]

For much of the war, Partisan photography remained skewed towards documenting the life of resistance fighters and capturing their heroism and sacrifice.[117] However, in late 1942 there was a notable shift in the perceived importance of evidencing fascist atrocities. In late October that year, Moša Pijade, one of Tito's closest associates, issued a series of orders instructing military units in Croatia, Slovenia and western Bosnia to begin collecting evidence of atrocities perpetrated by 'the occupiers, Ustasha and Chetniks'.[118] An article in *Borba* published shortly after, stated that collecting this material was nothing less than the 'sacred duty of all patriots' and a central task for both military and civilian authorities.[119] Pijade's orders referred to the need to photograph traces of fascist crimes in liberated territories, but also to surrender to the Supreme Command 'all seized enemy photographs (especially photographs of fascist bestialities)'. Thus, images hitherto collected as curiosities and war souvenirs were now to be treated as compelling evidence which, after the war, would help convict 'fascist bandits who happen to still be alive'.[120]

The newly discovered interest in evidencing atrocities was a reaction to events overseas. A week before Pijade issued his orders, the Soviet government published a note on 'the responsibility of Hitlerite invaders and their accomplices for crimes perpetrated in occupied Europe'. The note expressed solidarity with occupied nations and called for international cooperation in the gathering of evidence needed to bring to justice the 'Hitlerite clique'.[121] By responding to the note and committing to cooperation with the Allies, the Partisan leadership sought to enhance its international profile, and to try to wrest, from the London-based royalist government in exile, the role of the voice of the Yugoslav people in global affairs. Moreover, the Soviet note was interpreted as signalling that atrocities were acquiring 'political value', which presented new opportunities for 'agitation and propaganda'. Pijade's orders specifically highlighted the importance of harnessing the evidence of atrocities to 'inform the domestic and foreign public' about the suffering of the Yugoslav people and seize the 'avenues which are opening for our propaganda in Soviet and international press'.[122]

It took another eighteen months before the collection of evidence of fascist atrocities in Yugoslavia became a systematic and organized endeavour. Instrumental in this development was the creation, in late 1943, of the State Commission for the Investigation of the Crimes of the Occupiers and their Accomplices. The State Commission's activity and vital role in shaping the visual culture of atrocity in postwar Yugoslavia is the focus of the next two chapters.

3

'Gather photographs!'

The birth of the post-war visual memory of Ustasha violence

In the final days of November 1943, the small Bosnian town of Jajce hosted the second session of the Antifascist Council of National Liberation of Yugoslavia. The Antifascist Council, better known by the acronym AVNOJ, was founded a year earlier as the representative body of the Partisan movement. It comprised delegates from different parts of Yugoslavia and functioned as a quasi-government tasked with overseeing the administration of liberated territories and facilitating the continuing armed struggle for the liberation of the country.[1]

The second session of AVNOJ was held after an eventful six months, marked by important military victories for both the Partisans and the Allies. Sensing that the tide of war was turning in their favour and that they were finally receiving the international support and recognition they deserved, the leadership of the Partisan movement embarked on a sustained project of state and nation building. The second session of AVNOJ was a landmark event in this process, in that it was in Jajce that the post-war communist-led Yugoslav state began to take shape.

On the night of 29 November (sessions were held at night for fear of German bombardment), amid rapturous applause and periodic outbursts of cheering and slogan shouting, AVNOJ delegates passed a series of motions that heralded the new constitutional order in Yugoslavia. The royalist government in exile was divested of its powers, and a National Committee was inaugurated as a provisional government, with AVNOJ as the supreme legislative body and 'bearer of national and state sovereignty'.[2] The king was prohibited from returning to the country, while the title of 'marshal' was bestowed on the Partisan movement's charismatic leader Josip Broz Tito. This affirmed Tito's status as the supreme authority, even if not yet the head of state. The federal organization of the country was also agreed, and territorial claim was laid to parts of the Adriatic coast annexed by Italy after the First World War. Even a new national coat of arms was showcased at the event, symbolizing the birth of the new Yugoslavia.

Among decisions taken at the second session of AVNOJ was the creation of the State Commission for the Investigation of the Crimes of the Occupiers and their Accomplices. Although not as far-reaching as some others, this decision was intrinsic to the project of state building. A month before the meeting in Jajce, leaders of the

United States, Great Britain and the Soviet Union signed the Moscow Declaration on Atrocities, in which they asserted their commitment to the post-war prosecution of the Nazi leadership. The Declaration pledged that perpetrators of 'atrocities, massacres and cold-blooded mass executions' would be 'sent back to the countries in which their abominable deeds were done, in order that they may be judged and punished according to the laws of those liberated countries and of the free governments which will be erected therein'.[3] Yugoslavia was listed in the Declaration as one of the occupied countries where 'abominable deeds' had taken place, and which would, therefore, play a role in the post-war quest for justice. Around the same time, the newly formed United Nations War Crimes Commission called for the establishment of national bodies that would take on the task of gathering evidence of Nazi crimes.[4] The creation of the State Commission – just like Moša Pijade's orders examined in the previous chapter – was a direct response to these international developments. It helped to situate the new Yugoslavia within the emerging transnational legal order and affirm AVNOJ as a shining example of a 'free government' rising from the blood-soaked soil of occupied Europe.

The structure and remit of the State Commission

The State Commission, which formally began to operate on 8 May 1944, was constituted as a complex, hierarchically structured and highly bureaucratic institution. At the top of the pyramid was the federal State Commission, which, as a coordinating body, oversaw the undertakings of seven subsidiary commissions: a 'country' or 'land' commission (*zemaljska komisija*, sometimes abbreviated to *zemkom*) for each of the six newly formed Yugoslav republics and one 'provincial' commission (*pokrajinska komisija*) for Vojvodina, which, within the emerging federal organization of the country, had the status of an autonomous province within Serbia.[5] These commissions coordinated their own network of regional branches, which, in turn, had their own subsidiaries. The pyramid-like structure of the institution, although not uniform throughout the country, usually cascaded down to the level of boroughs and municipalities.[6] The obvious similarities in name as well as in structure and modus operandi between the Yugoslav State Commission and its Soviet counterpart, the Extraordinary State Commission for the Establishment and Investigation of Atrocities Committed by the German-Fascist Invaders and their Accomplices, provides a strong indication as to where Yugoslav leadership drew inspiration when drawing up the institutional framework for evidencing war crimes.[7]

The State Commission's main responsibility was to document crimes committed on Yugoslav territory and gather statistical data on human losses and material damage. Much of its daily activity consisted of taking down statements from witnesses and survivors. By the time the Commission was disbanded in 1948, a staggering figure of 1,487,730 'voluntarily submitted claims and witness statements' had been collected, mostly in 1945 and 1946.[8] In addition, teams of investigators inspected enemy archives seized in liberated territories and conducted field investigations at major killing sites.[9] The Commission also compiled a register of 66,420 suspected war criminals, liaised with the United Nations War Crimes Commission and Allied governments over extradition requests and coordinated Yugoslavia's involvement in the prosecution of Nazi war criminals at the International Military Tribunal at Nuremberg.[10]

The State Commission's remit included the collection of photographs of fascist atrocities. Article 4 of the State Commission's statute mandated the preservation of 'photographic images which show either a criminal act, the site or traces of a crime, weapons used in the perpetration of a crime, or the perpetrators'.[11] Protocols and instructions which the Country Commissions issued to local branches were replete with reminders that photographs are essential to proving fascist crimes.[12] In a public appeal entitled 'Gather photographs!' issued by the Country Commission for Bosnia, individuals, military units and local authorities were urged to hand over atrocity images, and in doing so help document 'the crimes, murder, slaughter, shootings, gassing, arson, looting and other horrors which the war brought upon us, and everything the blood-soaked occupier, the Schwab and the Italian, and their helpers the Chetniks and the Ustasha did to our innocent nations'. Any attempt to hang onto images of atrocities 'as precious souvenirs' was deemed unpatriotic, amounting to complicity in the crimes.[13]

Most photographs collected by the State Commission originated from what was referred to as 'enemy sources', that is they were found among the property left behind by retreating armies or defeated collaborationist regimes. Others were received from official photographers affiliated with agitation and propaganda sections (Agitprop) within larger Partisan military units, or amateur photographers from both within and outside the Partisan movement. Also, agents of OZNA, the Partisan secret police, confiscated photo archives of newspapers and news agencies in liberated cities and raided photographic studios whose owners often documented local events, and where enemy soldiers had their portraits taken or films developed. Some of this material was later forwarded to the State Commission and used to identify prominent local collaborators and officers of the occupying armies.[14] In addition, the commission's staff sometimes photographed investigations at major killing sites.[15] Because of a general shortage of equipment, materials and expertise within the commission, such investigations were seldom detailed or well documented. The most thorough ones were carried out by specialist Committees of Inquiry (*anketne komisije*) appointed to investigate major concentration camps and killing sites, such as Jasenovac, Stara Gradiška and Lepoglava in Croatia, Banjica, Sajmište and Jajinci in Serbia, or execution sites around Sarajevo in Bosnia. Elsewhere, whether or not a detailed investigation or exhumation was carried out depended entirely on the availability of qualified staff, diligence of local investigators or how vocal relatives of the victims or local communities were in their demands to have bodies exhumed and, where possible, returned to the families. By extension, whether and how these exhumations were photographed depended on the presence of photojournalists or the availability of local photographers who could be co-opted to record the investigation. Only three Country Commissions (for Croatia, Slovenia and Bosnia) and the Provincial Commission for Vojvodina had specialist 'photo sections' with staff dedicated to photographing field investigations, preparing images for publications and making duplicate prints for the central photo archive in Belgrade.[16] Yet even these comparatively well-resourced teams frequently had to improvise and outsource work to professional or amateur photographers.

By the end of 1947, there were 5,816 photographs in the commission's central photo archive in Belgrade.[17] However, not all photographs collected by the commission's subsidiaries and local offices reached the central archive. Local branches suffered from a chronic lack of resources and qualified personnel. In parts of the country, investigations were sometimes brought to a complete standstill by the shortage of the most basic equipment, such as pens and paper. In rural areas, regional branches struggled to recruit enough literate personnel, so many local offices consisted of a single 'rapporteur'.[18] Given these dire circumstances, expectations regarding the collection of photographs (for instance, that local branches should submit three copies of each photograph in their possession to their designated Country Commission) were impossible to meet.[19] Thus, most local and even some regional branches only forwarded images deemed to be particularly poignant, relevant or illustrative, and instead of making copies, they parted with the originals.[20] This means that the total number of photographs collected across Yugoslavia is likely to have been higher than 5,816, but probably lower than the upper estimate of 10,000 mentioned in some State Commission's documents.[21] What proportion of this number related to crimes perpetrated by the Ustasha is impossible to determine, given that neither the complete collections nor any of the original catalogues and inventory books have been preserved. One thing that *is* certain, however, is that most atrocity images that later formed the core of the visual memory of Ustasha genocide, and which are the focus of this book, originated from and came into the public domain via the State Commission's photographic collection.

Atrocity photographs as legal proof

The importance which the State Commission attributed to the collection of visual evidence reflected the belief in the direct, persuasive power of photographs. Photographs were thought to strengthen the credibility of documents and testimonies. A memo issued by the State Commission in January 1945, which criticized some Country Commissions for neither collecting nor forwarding enough photographs asked: 'Does the importance of this kind of evidence, and the credibility which photographs lend to text, really need emphasising?'[22]

The State Commission also regarded photographs as a potential source of legal proof. Photographs that could be matched to a specific crime or suspected war criminal were included in the relevant casefile, alongside documentary evidence and witness statements.[23] Some of these were later taken up by public prosecutors and entered in evidence in domestic war crimes trials. In the trials of leading Ustasha and Chetnik officials, most commonly used photographs were of defendants (or their associates) in the company of German or Italian officers or dignitaries, as these were considered incontrovertible proof of collaboration and treason. However, atrocity photographs were also shown, to corroborate and illustrate the harrowing testimonies of survivors and witnesses (see Figure 3.1).

Figure 3.1 Judges at the trial of the last chief of police of the Ustasha state Erih Lisak and his associates inspect photographs presented to the court by the prosecution (HR-HDA-1422, Z-1319).

The evidentiary value of photographs was acknowledged in the guidance pertaining to their collection. Instructions issued to investigators implicitly recognized that to qualify as legally admissible evidence of a crime, a photograph must be accompanied by at least basic information about its subject, provenance and authenticity. Regional branches were instructed that 'all photographs must, if such information exists, be well explained' and that they should accurately record 'the name of the crime [sic], the name of the victim, the date when it took place, the place where it was committed and how' and 'state who they received the evidence from, and how that person came in possession of the said evidence'.[24] The State Commission was eager to be seen to be adhering to these principles. The commission's report to the International Military Tribunal at Nuremberg stated, somewhat over-confidently, that 'the majority' of the ninety photographs submitted in evidence had been 'identified' (presumably a reference to the location where they were taken and the crimes which they depict) and that in many cases 'even the persons in the photographs have been identified'.[25] Dušan Nedeljković, the president of the State Commission, later signed a formal guarantee to the Nuremberg Tribunal that the Commission identified and established the authenticity of not the majority but *all* the images 'based on documents and witness statements'.[26]

In the effort to identify and authenticate photographs, the State Commission occasionally sought assistance from the public. This was done either at public exhibitions of atrocity photographs or through the press. A report on an exhibition which toured Bosnia in 1945 mentions 'distressing scenes' as some visitors 'recognised crimes in which they lost members of their families, friends, or acquaintances' and lists examples of successful identifications.²⁷ A similar exhibition in Vojvodina was organized with the specific purpose of gathering intelligence about crimes depicted in the photographs.²⁸ In late 1944 and early 1945, the daily *Borba*, published in liberated Belgrade, printed several 'appeals from the State Commission for the Investigation of the Crimes of the Occupiers and their Accomplices' in which readers were invited to help identify persons or events depicted in photographs. The first such appeal featured a photograph of two bloodied corpses of 'victims of German beasts', supposedly found among the possessions of a German soldier captured in Serbia (Figure 3.2).²⁹ The next appeal, published ten days later (this time featuring photographs of Chetniks executing civilians) revealed that it had taken just two days for the slain 'Orthodox priest and a woman' to be successfully identified by a reader.³⁰

The preoccupation with authenticating and verifying photographs, and the commission's apparent confidence in its ability to link photographs to crimes, concealed a much less rigorous approach to the collection, to archiving and to the use of visual images. Although many photographs in the State Commission's possession could be matched to specific events, this was by no means the norm. The commission obtained photographs from a variety of sources – Partisan units, security services, members of the public and so on – who generally did not record, or possess, the relevant information. Moreover, most photographs changed hands numerous times before they reached one of the commission's local branches, and then again as they were passed

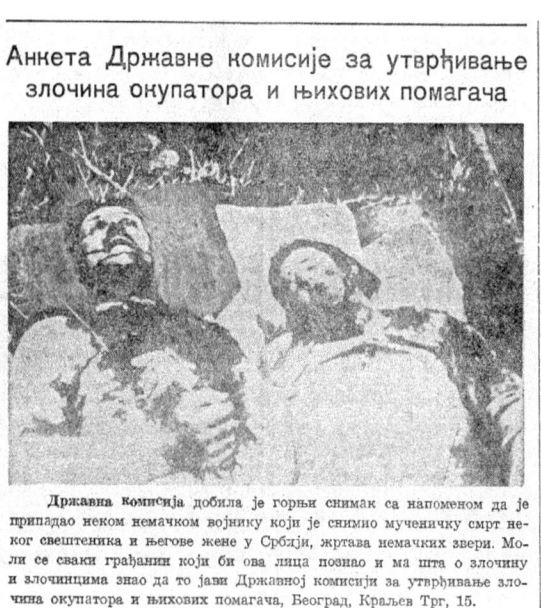

Figure 3.2 'Victims of German beasts': Appeal for information from the State Commission for the Investigation of the Crimes of the Occupiers and their Accomplices (*Borba*, 30 November 1944, 5).

up the hierarchy. The brief and often generic descriptions with which most images reached their destination – usually in the form of hand-written scribbles on the back or in the margin of the photograph – could have been added, amended or embellished at any point in this often-broken chain of custody and probably by individuals who had little direct knowledge of the photograph's origins.

The paucity of reliable information about photographs influenced also the management of photographic collections. Because the identification of every image was an unattainable goal, the commission's local branches were instructed to adopt a pragmatic approach and arrange images in boxes or thematic photo albums, simply 'according to the nationality of the perpetrators, then territorially, by the location where the war crime was committed'. The classification 'by perpetrator' was deemed especially important and applied to other types of evidence, while the reference to 'location' mostly meant stating in which republic (e.g. Bosnia, Croatia) or region (Kozara, Banija, eastern Bosnia and so on) the crime had been committed.[31] Much of this work was based on conjecture underpinned by the assumption that all photographs of atrocities inevitably represent crimes committed by the fascists. This is how some of the photographs published in Ustasha propaganda as illustrations of Partisan atrocities ended up classified as crimes of the occupiers or their accomplices.

The unfastidious approach to collecting and managing photographs was not unique to Yugoslavia. Efforts by British and American prosecution teams preparing for the Nuremberg Trials exhibited similar shortcomings: their management of photographic collections was, in the words of Robert Wolfe, 'highly unsystematic', and geared towards finding poignant examples of atrocities to be presented in court, rather than 'collecting source documents for any logical historical purpose'.[32] Nevertheless, the State Commission's handling of photographic evidence reflects a broader truth about its investigative methods. This was an under-resourced institution committed to gathering as much evidence as possible, as quickly as possible, without taking much notice of the quality of the material or trustworthiness of the sources. The speed with which it conducted inquiries and interviewed witnesses and survivors, and the difficult conditions in which it did so, led to many factual errors and inconsistencies in the findings.[33] It should therefore come as no surprise that, despite all the claims about the importance of verification, or perhaps because of them, in the commission's photographic collection, and even in its publications, one finds glaring mistakes, including copies of the same image with two different captions or photographs of the same event linked to two different crimes. This was the case even with some of the photographs submitted to the Nuremberg Tribunal, where the state formally guaranteed their authenticity and the accuracy of the captions.[34]

The State Commission's 'political remit'

Errors and omissions in the identification of photographs, even if they did not pass unnoticed, did not seem to matter at the time. This was largely because gathering legally admissible evidence and 'helping to bring perpetrators to justice' was not the State Commission's only purpose. The commission also had an explicitly 'political' remit, namely, to 'inform the domestic and foreign public' about enemy atrocities and publicize the suffering of the Yugoslav people.[35] The public relations or, more accurately, propaganda aspect of the commission's work was arguably the more important one. For one thing, the State Commission operated outside Yugoslavia's criminal justice system and its work was not treated seriously by the courts, the prosecutor's office or the secret police. None of the commission's decisions and pronouncements – not even those which resulted in individuals being placed on the register of war criminals – were legally binding.[36] They had a 'declarative character', and were meant to initiate and guide more formal legal proceedings.[37] This was a deliberate decision by the commission's creators, who wanted to separate its work from that of the nascent civilian and military courts or the security services.[38] Also indicative of the State Commission's priorities is that at its helm was Dušan Nedeljković, a Marxist philosopher and university professor, who had no legal training or experience in overseeing or conducting criminal investigations. What qualified him for the role, apart from his political steadfastness and academic credentials (Nedeljković was a vocal critic of fascism in the 1930s), was that, having joined the Partisan uprising in the summer of 1941, he became actively involved in setting up and editing the main voice of Partisan propaganda, the newspaper *Borba*.[39]

The State Commission pursued its 'political' objective mainly through links with the media.[40] Its press releases and communiqués on major crimes committed in Yugoslavia, ninety-three of which were issued between 1944 and 1946, were publicized in the main daily newspapers such as *Politika*, *Vjesnik*, *Narodni List*, *Oslobođenje* and *Borba*. A further 160 reports were produced on specific crimes or aspects of the occupation, some of which were later published as books and pamphlets and distributed at home and abroad.[41] The State Commission also produced a weekly twenty-minute programme broadcast on Radio Belgrade and Radio Ljubljana and organized public lectures and photographic exhibitions.

Atrocity photographs were essential to this broader propaganda effort. In his final report, Dušan Nedeljković listed among the commission's achievements the fact that it responded to over 7,000 requests for photographs of 'war criminals and war crimes' from the media.[42] While this figure is probably an exaggeration, it reveals that photographs were vital to promoting the commission's political message. Photographic exhibitions modelled on those organized around liberated Europe at the time, were another means by which the authorities ensured that the motif of atrocity was seared into the memories of the citizens of post-war Yugoslavia. The State Commission's central exhibition, which opened at the 'Cvijeta Zuzorić' art pavilion in Belgrade on 15 March 1946 included over a thousand exhibits, including more than 800 photographs. According to official records, as many as 53,963 residents of the capital visited the exhibition over the five-and-a-half weeks that it remained open. The exhibition later toured other major Yugoslav cities, including Zagreb, Ljubljana, Sarajevo and Cetinje, where it was seen by further 50,000 visitors.[43] Other, smaller touring exhibitions were organized by the Country Commissions. Between 1945 and 1947, these were displayed in more than fifty towns and cities across Yugoslavia.[44]

In Chapter 4, we will examine in more detail *how* atrocity images were mobilized in the pursuit of communist government's political and ideological agenda. However, before we do so, it is important to consider in more detail an important conundrum that the State Commission faced when investigating and publicizing enemy atrocities, one that drove many of the early misattributions or misinterpretations of photographs in its collection. If visual images were vitally important for evidencing and representing fascist crimes – that is, if the legacy of fascism truly needed to be seen to be believed – how does one convey the horror of atrocities of which there is not an adequate photographic record, especially when traces of the most dreadful crimes were often rendered invisible by deliberate actions of the perpetrators? This was a challenge that the commission faced when dealing with the scene of the largest concentration camp in Yugoslavia, Jasenovac.

Smashed skulls and dead bodies washed up on the river bank: Visualizing the horrors of Ustasha 'hell'

By the time the State Commission was founded, Jasenovac was already widely regarded as the epitome of suffering of Yugoslavs under fascist yoke. In April 1942, the Moscow-based radio station Free Yugoslavia mentioned the 'bestiality of the Ustasha mob in the concentration camp near Jasenovac' as a prime example of the 'bloody fascist terror in Yugoslavia'.[45] Seven months later, Moša Pijade's order concerning the collection of evidence of 'crimes against the people of Yugoslavia perpetrated by fascist butchers' was publicized in the Partisan newspaper *Borba* in the context of an article on Jasenovac.[46] Shortly after, the Council for National Liberation of Croatia printed the booklet *Jasenovac camp: testimonies of inmates who escaped from the camp*, the first publication of its kind in occupied Yugoslavia.[47] What made Jasenovac stand out in the eyes of the Partisan leadership was not just the scale and viciousness of the killings, but also the fact that it was a concentration camp – a place of large-scale, industrial killing that, as the war progressed, was becoming recognized as emblematic of fascist criminality. In the summer and autumn of 1944, when images from Majdanek – the first concentration camp liberated by Soviet troops on 24 July that year – started to receive international attention, the belief in the symbolic importance of concentration camps increased further.[48] It is not a coincidence that it was around that time, in October 1944 – more than six months before Partisan units entered Jasenovac – that regional branches of the Country Commission for Croatia were instructed to get ready for an investigation, which was to include 'photographing all building, camps, and means of torture [...] immediately, as soon as these sites are liberated'.[49] Yugoslavia, just like Poland and the Soviet Union, needed powerful visual icons of atrocity that would tell the story about the scale and horror of suffering, and tie the fate of Yugoslavs to that of other martyred nations in Europe.

The Croatian Country Commission's investigators arrived in Jasenovac on 18 May 1945, a couple of weeks after Partisan units first entered the camp and almost a month after it was abandoned by Ustasha guards.[50] Among the investigators were photojournalists, invited to document the inquiry and create a photographic record of this iconic place of fascist brutality (Figure 3.3).[51] However, upon arrival in Jasenovac, the investigators encountered the camp and the adjacent village deserted and practically

Figure 3.3 Investigators from the Committee of Inquiry for Jasenovac in the company of journalists and photographers, during their visit to Jasenovac on 18 May 1945 (HR-HDA-1422, Z-49).

razed to the ground. The camp buildings had been blown up by the Ustasha prior to their retreat, leaving little for the investigators to examine and record. Among the eerie ruins, there were no masses of emaciated bodies or piles of skeletal human corpses, no crowded barracks, gas chambers or crematoria, or piles of personal possessions. There were, therefore, no opportunities to create striking and harrowing images that would match the liberation photographs from Majdanek, Auschwitz, Dachau or Buchenwald which adorned the front pages of the international press. Investigators discovered some badly decomposed bodies floating in the shallow, murky waters of the Sava, and many more skeletal remains set into the muddy clay on the riverbank (Figure 3.4). But there was little that differentiated these scenes from those encountered at other locations that did not have the resonance of Jasenovac as the place of unimaginable suffering and unprecedented cruelty. The situation was similar in Stara Gradiška, a subsidiary of Jasenovac located some 30 kilometres from the main camp. In late April 1945, a Partisan unit entered the buildings of the abandoned camp and encountered the horrific aftermath of its 'liquidation' a few days earlier, during which around 300 remaining inmates were slaughtered. The scenes, which were later described in forensic detail by investigators from the local branch of the Country Commission, were documented in around twenty photographs which Mato Tašković, a fighter with the 28th Slavonian Brigade, took that day.[52] But these too were photographs of individual corpses left to rot in burned-out prison cells or in the nearby river. None of them could capture the horror of the mass killing at Jasenovac, or its sheer scale, which at that time was estimated at around 500,000–700,000 victims.

Figure 3.4 Remains of the Jasenovac camp photographed during the investigation in May 1945 (HR-HDA-1422, clockwise from top left Z-32, Z-63, Z-83, Z-95).

The shortage of suitably poignant visual material presented a problem. No other visual record of Jasenovac existed at the time, except for Stöger's propaganda photographs and film footage examined in Chapter 2, which showed everything that the camp was *not*.[53] In the absence of powerful imagery, how does one portray and bring home that which in the commission's own words would seem 'unbelievable, impossible' to 'any normal human being who did not witness or experience these atrocities'?[54] How does one reconcile what *happened* at Jasenovac with what could be *seen* in the somewhat ineffective photographs taken at the scene after liberation?

The solution was to turn other available images of Ustasha brutality into visual symbols for Jasenovac. The earliest official post-war account of crimes perpetrated at the camp – the Country Commission for Croatia's eighty-five-page booklet on Jasenovac, published in 1946 – offers a relevant example. *Crimes in the Jasenovac Camp* contains fourteen photographs, including those showing the ruins of the camp and skeletal remains found at the site after the war, as well as portraits of the 'main Ustasha criminals – throat-cutters'. Of interest, however, are images which appear in the section on the treatment of inmates by the Ustasha.[55] This section comprises selected extracts from witness testimonies, with vivid descriptions of the worst excesses of Ustasha brutality. These are accounts of arbitrary punishments and killings, sadistic methods of torture, blood drinking, sexual mutilation, decapitation and dismemberment, children being impaled on bayonets and descriptions of the most common methods of killing – throat cutting and a blow to the head with a mallet or hammer. Quotations from witness statements pertaining to the latter are accompanied in the report by a photograph of 'a wooden mallet that Ustasha used to kill their victims'.[56] This was one of several makeshift murder weapons discovered and photographed by war crimes investigators during their visit to Jasenovac. On the next page, there is a head shot of a recently deceased male victim, laid on a wooden surface (Figure 3.5a). Clearly visible is a large laceration and skull fracture on the right side of the forehead, exposing what appears like an empty cranial cavity. The caption reads 'frontal bone shattered with a mallet'. A few pages later, shortly before the description of Ustasha cutting open a pregnant woman's abdomen and extracting the unborn child, there is photograph of a fresh, partially clothed male corpse, with intestines visibly protruding through a gash across the lower abdomen. The caption reads 'victim with their belly slashed open' (Figure 3.5b).

It is obvious just from reading the text of the report that neither of the two images could have been taken in Jasenovac. The pathologist who examined the bodies during the commission's second visit to the site in June 1945, and whose words are quoted in the report, noted that corpses at Jasenovac were 'two to three months old, in some cases even older' and all badly decomposed.[57] Three photographs of skeletal remains featured in the penultimate section of the report clearly show this. In fact, one of these images is remarkably similar, in terms of composition, subject matter and caption, to that used to illustrate the execution with a mallet, except that it shows skeletal remains

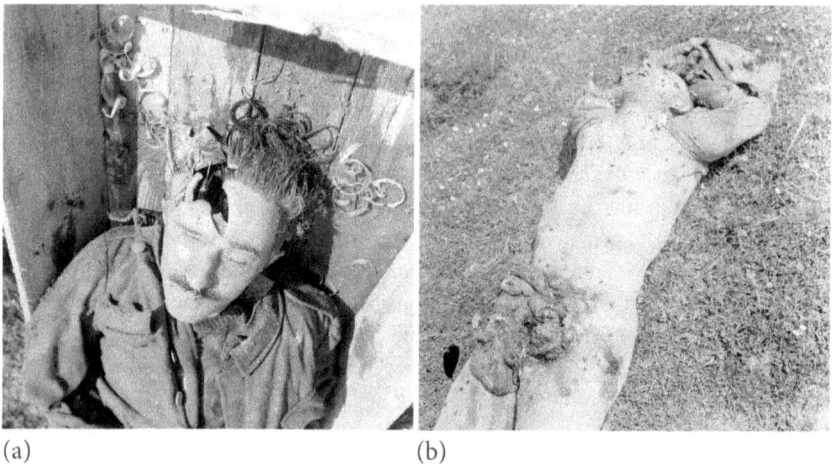

(a) (b)

Figure 3.5 Images used in the Country Commission's report to illustrate the horror of Jasenovac killings: (a) 'Frontal bone shattered with a mallet' and (b) 'Victim with their belly slashed open' (HR-HDA-1422, Z-234 and Z-220).

rather than a fresh body. It is a photograph of a smashed human skull, accompanied by the caption 'A blow to the frontal bone with a mallet'. We can only speculate why this image was not used in the earlier section instead of that showing the fresh corpse. One possibility is that the purpose of the image was not to present the anatomical consequences of the blow to the head – the photograph of the skull would have been adequate for that – but to convey the actual horror and goriness of the execution. The skull was what the investigators found in 1945; the much more graphic image represented what the survivors, whose words the photograph illustrated, witnessed and described in their testimony.

The origin of the photographs in Figure 3.5 has not been difficult to trace. They belong to a large collection of photographs, around 160 in total, which document the retrieval and burial of victims from the town of Sisak, executed by the Ustasha and thrown in the river Sava shortly before their retreat from the city in early May 1945.[58] When the press first reported on the Sisak executions several weeks later, it mentioned 'between 350 and 400' dead, although this number should be treated with caution given the more general tendency, at the time, to inflate the number of victims.[59] An official memorandum, which Branko Drezga, the public prosecutor for the region of Banija, sent to his superiors in Zagreb on 15 May 1945 cited a more probable, albeit approximate figure of 150 victims.[60]

The Sisak collection includes mainly forensic photographs of the corpses in situ, on the banks of the river or in the shallow water, or of victims after they were recovered and lined up for inspection and identification, either in simple wooden coffins or on the ground.[61] Many photographs of individual victims show them with clothes partially removed, so that their wounds could be examined, and the cause of death confirmed. Among them are two different versions of the photographs in Figure 3.5, taken from slightly different angles.[62] There are also images of the recovery process – the retrieval of the victims from the river, the removal of mud from their faces – and of civilians, including women wearing mourning attire, who had gathered in the hope of finding and identifying their loved ones. The mixture of different photographic genres within the collection – the aesthetically unpretentious forensic photographs alongside the artistically much more accomplished images of grieving wives and mothers or the wide angled shot of the row of bodies and coffins – suggests that they were probably taken by a professional photographer or a photojournalist.[63]

The challenge of representing Jasenovac revealed in the Country Commission's report was apparent also in the fifteen-minute documentary film *Jasenovac*, released in August 1945. This work, produced by the official state-owned film studio, was shown in cinemas in major cities, often alongside other short propaganda films and newsreels. In the part of the documentary which describes conditions in the camp, the authors Gustav Gavrin and Kosta Hlavaty utilized Ustasha propaganda footage taken at the camp in the summer of 1942. A review of the film published in *Borba* praised the authors for using this footage and for 'skilfully weaving together extracts from the Ustasha film, and testimonies from survivors' which were spoken in the film by a narrator.[64] Yet the use of propaganda footage created an obvious incongruity between the relatively benign working conditions shown on film and the voiceover which describes summary executions and exhausted inmates coiling under 'Ustasha whips and riffle buts'. Likewise, there was a discrepancy between descriptions of malnourishment and deprivation and footage of prisoners being handed bread and soup, footage which, incidentally, was created by the Ustasha precisely to counter the reports of starvation at Jasenovac. Atrocity photographs, including many of the forensic close-up shots of the victims from Sisak showing slit throats, split skulls or slashed abdomens, provided the necessary corrective. They feature in the film, individually or as a sequence, to demonstrate the 'horrific and indescribable' torture of prisoners and the 'sadistic and pathological urges' of the perpetrators.[65] Decomposed corpses discovered in Jasenovac are also shown, but mainly at the end of the film. They are offered as a demonstration of the failure of the 'crazed Ustasha executioners' to destroy all traces of their crime and as evidence of what the camp looked like in 1945. Just like in the Country Commission's report on Jasenovac, decaying bodies and skeletons in the mud offered incontrovertible proof that the crimes had taken place, while other, more graphic and shocking photographs were needed to capture the brutality, the 'blood and guts' of Jasenovac executions.[66] The fact that many of the images were not taken in Jasenovac was of course concealed. The public was meant to believe – as did the author of the review of the film published in *Narodni List* – that harrowing photographs of 'smashed skulls and slashed bellies' were authentic images of victims slain in the 'Jasenovac swamps'.[67]

The Ustasha 'perspective of death': Visualizing the scale of atrocities

The relevance of the Sisak photographs for representing Jasenovac extended beyond the fact that they contained forensic close-ups of victims. They provided also a way of visualizing the scale of the killings. Three images from the collection have been used regularly to that effect, including in the 1945 documentary *Jasenovac*.[68] Two show tangled corpses on the steep slope of the riverbank (Figure 3.6), while the third is of a

(a) (b)

Figure 3.6 (a) and (b). Bodies on the riverbank in Sisak: Photographs used after the war to depict mass executions in Jasenovac (HR-HDA-1422, Z-177 and Z-176).

Figure 3.7 Endless line of death and suffering: Visualizing the scale of the killing at Jasenovac (HR-HDA-1422, Z-193).

row of bodies laid out on the muddy ground, with people gathering around to inspect and identify them (Figure 3.7).

It is easy to see why these images presented suitable illustrations of Jasenovac. Sisak and Jasenovac are on the same river, 60 kilometres apart. There is a remarkable similarity between the terrain of the riverbank in Jasenovac visible in some of the images taken during the Country Commission's investigation and the scenes in Figure 3.6, taken in Sisak. There is one difference, though: the riverbank in Sisak was 'populated' with bodies. In the light of the emphasis, in representations of Jasenovac, on *mass* executions on the infamous Granik loading dock – the execution site where victims were slain and thrown into the river – this was a crucial difference. After the war, Figure 3.6b was often cropped to reduce the empty spaces and make the riverbank seem even more crowded with dead bodies.

Figure 3.7, showing a different scene, is visually the most striking of the three photographs. The row of neatly arranged bodies recovered from the river stretches from the foreground to the background of the photograph, giving the impression of an endless line of death and suffering. Egon Berger, a Jasenovac survivor, would later call this the Ustasha 'perspective of death'.[69] The fact that visible in the photograph are survivors searching for dead relatives makes this also a poignant symbol of grief, loss and witnessing. There are several similarly composed iconic images from the concentration camp in Nordhausen, in Germany, taken around the same time, which also offer a long view of bodies lined up in the camp courtyard or a nearby burial site.

As Barbie Zelizer points out, such scenes of mass, 'outdoor horror' were common, because they were highly effective in representing visually the *scale* of the murder in concentration camps.[70] This was precisely the aspect of Jasenovac that images *from* Jasenovac could not adequately capture, but those from Sisak could. This image was also often cropped and presented in vertical orientation, which further accentuated the 'perspective of death'.

The use of the photographs from Sisak as illustrations of Jasenovac, or indeed other Ustasha concentration camps, began on the very same day that the news of the mass execution in Sisak was first reported in the Zagreb daily *Vjesnik* on 19 May 1945. In the same issue of the paper, only a couple of pages after the article on Sisak, a photograph from the exhumation appeared in an unrelated piece on the killings in the Stara Gradiška camp.[71] On the following day, another accompanied an article on atrocities in Jasenovac.[72] Later that month, in *Narodni List*, a photograph of a disembowelled victim from Sisak featured in the text of the Country Commission for Croatia's communiqué on the Ustasha camp in Lepoglava.[73] On these occasions, the captions correctly identified the photographs as showing victims recovered from the Sava in Sisak. Nevertheless, they were used as generic 'visual appendages' to stories about Ustasha brutality at other sites.[74] By 31 May, the photographs were being published with much more generic captions 'Ustasha crimes over our innocent people' or 'A document of Ustasha terror'.[75] On the other hand, images of dead bodies from Sisak were so ubiquitous in the Croatian press in May and June 1945 that editors assumed that *any* photograph of dead bodies laid on muddy ground must be from Sisak. On one occasion, *Narodni List* printed such a photograph showing the corpses of a man and a woman, with the caption 'Another document of Ustasha crimes committed in the vicinity of Sisak'.[76] The photograph had nothing to do with Sisak; it was the one featured in Figure 3.2 that had appeared in *Borba* six months earlier as the body of the 'Orthodox priest and a woman' killed by German soldiers in Serbia.

The recurrent use of the photographs from Sisak in *Vjesnik* and *Narodni List* was undoubtedly driven by their visual properties as well as by the fact that editors had them at hand. However, the linking of these photographs to Jasenovac was facilitated also by the fact that, from the outset, crimes at Jasenovac and Sisak were seen as connected. When *Vjesnik* and *Borba* reported the recovery and burial of the bodies in Sisak, they mentioned that the majority of those killed had been arrested by the Ustasha in April 1945 and were destined for Jasenovac. But, as Jasenovac was being 'liquidated' at the time, prisoners were locked up in a local factory, from where they were taken to the execution site by the river and killed just before the Ustasha fled town.[77] In addition, *Vjesnik* claimed that among those killed were members of a unit of the regular Croatian army, the Domobrani, who had previously been stationed in Jasenovac and who were executed as potential eyewitnesses to the horrors at the camp. This implied that some of the perpetrators of the killing in Sisak were in fact Ustasha retreating from Jasenovac, who were trying to destroy evidence of their crimes. The accuracy of this version of events, based mostly on testimonies of local residents, is impossible to verify. A point made in *Vjesnik*'s report, which was perhaps why the Sisak killings received widespread coverage in the Croatian press, was that most of those executed were Croats. Presenting Sisak's Croat population, and even the regular army of the Independent State of Croatia, as victims of the Ustasha and tying their fate to the horrors of Jasenovac may have been a way for the authorities to counter widespread perceptions in liberated Croatian towns and villages that Partisans were waging a vengeful, pro-Serbian war.[78] What is important, however, is that uncertainty about the nature of the link between events in Sisak and Jasenovac created opportunities for errors and misunderstandings. When the prosecutor Branko Drezga reported on the situation in Sisak to his superiors on 15 May 1945, he described the victims not as inmates *destined* for Jasenovac but as 'inmates from Jasenovac'.[79] A similar 'slippage' in meaning was apparent in the reading of photographs. By the time a selection of images from Sisak reached the State Commission's central photo archive in Belgrade, some were correctly identified, others were said to show Jasenovac victims killed in Sisak, while the image shown in Figure 3.6b was accompanied by the following description: 'During their retreat, the Ustasha in Jasenovac killed all the inmates and threw the bodies in the river.'[80]

Atrocity photographs between evidence and illustration

Confusion over what the photographs from Sisak show persisted in subsequent decades. The image of the victim with the shattered skull in Figure 3.5a, remained so firmly associated with Jasenovac that it has never been published as showing anything other than the body of a camp inmate slain with a mallet. Others, such as photographs in Figures 3.6 and 3.7, have been used to represent the killing in Sisak or, more commonly, Jasenovac, and occasionally both locations simultaneously, in line with the assumption that the two are somehow inherently connected.

As we have seen, in the months after the end of the war the misattribution of the Sisak images was mainly driven by the genuine desire to render visible and drive home the message about the very *real* horrors of Jasenovac. In the State Commission's publications, in the 1945 documentary, just like in the press, images from Sisak were used to show what photographs of the slaughter in Jasenovac *would have looked like* had someone been there to take them. This practice of using visual images of one event or place as an illustration for a story about another was widespread at the time. In the press throughout Europe and North America it was common for photographs of one concentration camp to be used in reports about another, or for a smaller number of images to be repeatedly used as generic illustrations for the broader theme of 'Nazi atrocities'.[81]

And yet, the State Commission's approach to representing Jasenovac is important because it exposes the problem that arises when boundaries become blurred between the evidentiary and illustrative function of the atrocity photograph. As a quasi-legal institution, the State Commission was dedicated to collecting photographs *as evidence*, and this involved a commitment to 'authenticating' and 'verifying' photographs, and assembling information about their provenance, authorship and the circumstances in which they were taken. Yet when it came to the commission's 'political' role, authenticity and provenance were much less important than whether a photograph's composition or subject matter captured the meaning and symbolism of an event or place, or whether it had the potential to arouse the appropriate sentiment in the audience. In the work of the State Commission, these two concerns were deeply intertwined. The institution's capacity to execute its political, or propaganda, role depended on the aura of credibility and authority derived from the assumption that it followed proper rules of evidence. At the same time, collection, interpretation and presentation of the evidence (especially when it was inconclusive and there were gaps to be filled) were driven by its political function. The outcome was that images selected as an *illustration* of an event could be, and often were, transformed into visual *proof* of that event, simply by being treated as such by the State Commission. This is what happened with the images from Sisak examined in this chapter.

As we shall see later in the book, this tension between the illustrative and documentary power of visual images persisted long after the State Commission ceased to exist. Visual memory of Ustasha genocide continued to be marked by an unwavering belief in the indexicality of the image and its status as the 'vessel of accuracy, authenticity, verisimilitude and truth'.[82] Yet this belief went hand in hand with a somewhat cavalier approach to photographs as historical artefacts, marked by a blatant disregard for the limits of their evidentiary and illustrative potential. In other words, atrocity photographs continued to be *revered* as compelling form of proof, but *utilized* primarily as 'visual soundbites', to illustrate and corroborate harrowing accounts of Ustasha depravity and, more importantly, provoke the sense of horror and outrage.[83]

4

Why look at fascism?

Visual propaganda and revolutionary justice in post-war Yugoslavia

In this chapter we turn our attention to *how* Yugoslavia's nascent communist regime, working through the State Commission for the Investigation of the Crimes of the Occupiers and their Accomplices, used photographs of fascist atrocities as a propaganda tool. As we shall see, much of the propaganda activity was directed at the public at home and was aimed at legitimizing the post-war social and political order. This involved justifying retribution against 'domestic traitors' and promoting a narrative of the Second World War that would bring closure to a country torn apart by four years of fratricidal violence. However, atrocity-focused propaganda was also aimed at the international audience. After the signing of the Moscow Declaration on Atrocities in October 1943, it had become apparent to Tito and his associates that in the post-war world, national suffering would be recognized as a source of moral authority and that nations perceived to have endured injustice under Nazism would be endowed with visibility and influence. Thus, in 1945, as it negotiated a place for Yugoslavia in the post-war international order, the communist-led government frequently alluded to the country's tragic wartime history. As a country that suffered, resisted and ultimately won the war, Yugoslavia was to be listened to and taken seriously.[1]

Photographs played an important role in this international propaganda effort. The leaflet 'Gather photographs!', which was mentioned in the previous chapter, stated explicitly that atrocity images, which 'speak even without words', would 'recount to the whole freedom-loving humanity the horrors of the occupation'. They would do so by cutting through the complexity of other forms of evidence and by directly communicating to the world the essence of suffering and fascist depravity. 'It is on photographs that one most clearly sees all the horrors of the bloody terror against our innocent people,' the leaflet stated, so 'it will be enough for our allies to look at the photographs. There will be too many documents for them to look at every page. But these photographs will tell a story. A story of terror and devastation.'[2]

Atrocity propaganda and international diplomacy

One way in which Yugoslav authorities conveyed to the world the 'terror and devastation' endured under Nazi occupation was through photographic exhibitions, of the kind that were common in Europe and North America after the war. In 1945, the State Commission contributed material to two international exhibitions on Nazi crimes held in Paris and London.[3] The Yugoslav Ministry of Foreign Affairs organized a further exhibition on the occupation of Yugoslavia which was staged in Geneva, for the benefit of the diplomatic corps and staff at the UN Office in the city. Although material exhibited overseas focused primarily on the crimes of the occupiers, especially the Germans and the Italians, photographs of Chetnik and Ustasha crimes were also displayed. The inclusion of the latter was considered by some to be a risky strategy, for reputational reasons. On seeing photographs of Ustasha and Chetnik atrocities at the exhibition in Geneva, the famous Croatian sculptor and architect Ivan Meštrović warned the organizers that 'foreigners won't be able to tell apart Chetniks from the Ustasha from the Partisans', so the horrific, violent images of bloodletting among Yugoslavs will only serve to 'reinforce the view that we are all barbarians'.[4] And yet, as we shall see shortly, there was an important political reason why it was deemed pertinent to remind Western governments and international institutions of the crimes of collaborators.

In the immediate aftermath of the war, the motif of enemy atrocities was especially important in the context of Yugoslavia's bitter diplomatic disputes with her neighbours, Italy and Austria. These were mainly territorial disputes, over Trieste and the Adriatic coast with Italy, and southern Carinthia and parts of Styria with Austria. There was also the issue of Yugoslavia's claims for war reparations against the two states, and the latter's reluctance to collaborate with Yugoslav authorities on bringing to justice suspected Austrian and Italian war criminals or collaborators who found shelter in these countries. The Yugoslav side was especially troubled by the fact that both Italy and Austria were wholeheartedly whitewashing their wartime record and were cynically playing down their role in the bloody occupation of Yugoslavia. In 1946 and 1947, the State Commission prepared two extensive, richly illustrated reports on the crimes committed by the Italian army and Austrian officers and military units in Yugoslavia. The 150-page *Report on the Crimes of Austria and the Austrians against Yugoslavia and Her Peoples* included numerous photographs of Nazi atrocities, including several of Wehrmacht soldiers 'posing contently next to their victims' (e.g. Figure 4.1).[5] Given that the report alluded to the Austrians' long-standing hostility towards the people of Yugoslavia, and the fact that they had twice in the twentieth century been the 'main perpetrators of war crimes against Yugoslavs', it is impossible not to see, in the choice of illustrations, a nod to Rodolphe Archibald Reiss's reports on Austrian crimes during the First World War, which used similar trophy photographs to illustrate the pathological nature of Austrian 'mentality'.[6]

Atrocity propaganda was even more prominent in the dispute with Italy. A disproportionate number of the State Commission's early communiqués, published in 1944 and 1945, were devoted to crimes perpetrated by the Italian army in Yugoslavia.

Why Look at Fascism? 65

Figure 4.1 Photograph published in the State Commission's report on crimes perpetrated by Austrian troops in Yugoslavia. It was accompanied by the caption 'German soldiers posing contentedly next to their victims' (MIJ, III-11002).

The focus on Italian atrocities was necessitated by 'external political factors', namely, the need to strengthen Yugoslavia's position in the dispute over the Dalmatian coast, and counter Italian 'profascist', revisionist propaganda.[7] The latter referred to the fact that, in downplaying its role in the crimes committed in Yugoslavia, the Italian government resorted to atrocity propaganda of its own. It publicized photographs of Ustasha, Chetnik and Partisan atrocities collected by the Italian military and used them to portray the Balkans as a cesspit of violence, murder and 'indescribable barbarism'. Italian occupying army was thus cast in the role of bystander, caught up and forced to mediate in a brutal, internecine conflict.[8]

Responding to this self-exculpatory narrative, the Yugoslav side promoted the alternative view, namely that 'Italian occupiers were as brutal as the Germans and, in some cases, were even more perfidious'.[9] This was evidenced with photographs of notorious 'round-ups' (*rastrellamenti*) and other counterinsurgency and retaliatory operations carried out by the Italian army and security forces. Also, various communiqués on Italian atrocities, and the 200-page *Report on Italian Crimes against Yugoslavia and Its People* (published in time for the Paris Peace Conference in the summer and autumn of 1946), attributed very different meaning to photographs of Ustasha and Chetnik atrocities that the Italians had used to present themselves as mere onlookers.[10] The Yugoslav authorities argued that the fact that Italian officers 'used cameras to take photographs of mutilated bodies and horrific scenes of mass slaughter' proves that they were *present* when their protégés, the Chetniks and the Ustasha, did their killing and that they 'actively participated' in the crimes.[11] What is more, because the Italians funded and armed the Ustasha and the Chetniks, and 'kindled the criminal fury' of the murderous 'hordes' among the collaborators, they were said to bear the greatest responsibility for the atrocities in parts of Yugoslavia formally under Italian control.[12]

Figure 4.2 Photograph used after the war as evidence of the collaboration between Italians and Chetniks, 'brothers in crime' (from *Državna komisija za utvrđivanje zločina okupatora i njihovih pomagača, Saopštenja br. 7-33*, Belgrade, 1945, 177).

Photographs such as Figure 4.2, which show Italian soldiers and Chetniks posing *together* next to victims, were especially common in the State Commission's publications and the press, as they offered seemingly incontrovertible proof of Italian complicity in, and responsibility for, the ethnic violence in the Independent State of Croatia.[13]

'Photographs of Hitlerite crimes in Yugoslavia' at Nuremberg

The most high-profile opportunity for the Yugoslav government to showcase to the international audience the crimes endured under Nazi occupation was at the International Military Tribunal at Nuremberg. The Nuremberg Tribunal was established in 1945 by the four victorious Allied powers: the Unites States, the Soviet Union, the United Kingdom and France. It was the governments of these four nations that agreed on the constitution, jurisdiction and functions of the tribunal, appointed judges and prosecution teams, and oversaw its functioning. However, a number of other European countries that had been occupied by the Nazis, including Poland, Czechoslovakia and Yugoslavia, were also involved in the proceedings and submitted evidence relevant to crimes committed on their territory. As of January 1946, Yugoslavia had a small permanent delegation at Nuremberg, which liaised with the four main prosecution teams and prepared evidence for presentation to the tribunal by Soviet prosecutors. On 26 December 1945, the Yugoslav government submitted to the tribunal an eighty-six-page overview of Nazi atrocities in Yugoslavia, alongside twenty-six original documents and ninety 'photographs of Hitlerite crimes in Yugoslavia'.[14] The latter were described as a small sample of 'more than ten thousand photographs confiscated by the Yugoslav Army from captured enemy soldiers'.[15]

At the time of the trial, the Yugoslav press eagerly reported that material submitted by the State Commission was judged by observes and the international media to be 'among the richest and technically most accomplished'.[16] This assessment reflected the widespread and, as it turned out, misplaced belief in the Commission's competence and international standing. Upon arrival at Nuremberg, the Yugoslav delegation was taken aback by the tribunal's prioritization of documentary evidence over witness statements. Because prosecutors focused their attention on proving the 'organized' nature of the criminal conspiracy, aggression and violations of international law, precedence was accorded to Nazi documents.[17] Witness statements and survivor testimonies detailing specific crimes or acts of depravity – the collection of which had been the Yugoslav State Commission's central focus – were viewed as undermining the expediency of the proceedings and were confined to a small number of 'representative examples'.[18] What is more, the Yugoslav delegation had always counted on the fact that, formally, the tribunal was not bound by the usual 'technical rules of evidence' and was supposed to take 'judicial notice of official government documents and reports'.[19] In other words, it was meant to treat the State Commission's findings as established facts. In practice, however, the Western judges, keen to avoid the tribunal turning into a Soviet-style show trial, applied stricter rules of procedural fairness. Thus, the fact that witnesses who testified before the Yugoslav State Commission had not been formally sworn in, or that the precise provenance of the submitted documents could not always be established, weakened the perceived validity and relevance of the Yugoslav material. Correspondence from early January 1946 between the State Commission's president, Dušan Nedeljković, and the de facto head of the Yugoslav delegation at Nuremberg, Albert Vajs, suggests that both were aware that this may lead to the commission's evidence being sidelined. Subsequent efforts to persuade the chief Soviet prosecutor Roman Rudenko to relax these 'procedural formalities' when considering material collected by the fledgling Yugoslav government operating in extremely difficult circumstances were unsuccessful.[20] To address what Nedeljković later called the 'excessive pedantry' of the international legal system, the Yugoslav delegation decided to foreground 'only the strongest material', namely documents (more of which were sent to Nuremberg) and photographs.[21]

In early February 1946, just two weeks before Yugoslav evidence was scheduled to be presented in the tribunal chamber, copies of the ninety photographs included in the State Commission's report were sent to London, where they were made into a film. This was effectively a slide show, with a voiceover reading the captions and descriptions in Russian.[22] The film, or 'photo-document', as one of the Soviet prosecutors, Counsellor Lev Smirnov, introduced it during the court proceedings, was entered as Exhibit Number USSR-442. An extract deemed relevant to the charges of crimes against humanity (on which the Soviet prosecution team took the lead) was shown in the tribunal chamber on 26 February, around the same time as the films on Nazi crimes prepared by the Soviet government.[23]

The last-minute decision to create the 'photo-document' was a response to the fact that the 'the filmic witness' was a novel feature of the Nuremberg trial.[24] The Yugoslav delegation clearly wanted a share of the courtroom spectacle. Also, the 'photo-document' provided a way of maximizing the impact of the photographs and diverting attention from the perceived shortcomings of the other material. In other words, foreign prosecutors and judges may have chosen to disbelieve the witness statements and question the State Commission's evidence-gathering methods, but they would not be able to help being moved by the powerful images depicting the suffering of Yugoslav nations at the hands of the Nazis. Indeed, as the daily *Politika* later reported, photographs from Yugoslavia shown in the tribunal chamber were 'the most eloquent indictment of the fascist war criminals' which left the 'the strongest impression' on the judges and journalists.[25]

Alongside the version in Russian which was shown at Nuremberg, a copy of the film was made with the voiceover and captions in Serbo-Croatian for screening in major Yugoslav cities. There was also some interest from the US military for producing an English version, for use in their educational programme on Nazi war crimes.[26] In the end, only one Russian and one Serbian copy were made, neither of which appears to have been preserved. On 16 March 1946, a plane transporting evidence back from Nuremberg crashed during take-off in Budapest, where it stopped for refuelling.[27] The cargo, including the Russian version of the film, was destroyed in the fire that ensued.[28] The fate of the Serbo-Croatian version, which in the end was screened only in Zagreb and Belgrade, is unknown. It does not appear to be in possession of any of the relevant institutions in the former Yugoslavia, but one should not discount the possibility that it languishes, unmarked, in some long-forgotten depot or attic.

Atrocity photographs as a source of 'sadistic gratification'

The ninety photographs which the State Commission submitted to Nuremberg on behalf of the Yugoslav government, and which were included in the 'photo-document', were divided into nine uneven sections, containing between one and thirty-five images.[29] Despite the specific remit of the Nuremberg Tribunal, and the focus on the conduct of the Nazi leadership, the State Commission took the unusual step of devoting the first section (comprising eighteen photographs) to the 'manifold fifth column', including members of the Royal Family and the pre-war Yugoslav government (who were said to have colluded with Nazi Germany before 1941), the Chetniks, the Ustasha and the pro-Nazi elements among Yugoslavia's Volksdeutche community, who 'faithfully implemented the criminal fascist plans aimed at the extermination of our people'.[30] The next thirty-seven photographs, divided into seven smaller sections, covered the theme of war crimes. These sections were carefully designed and labelled to cover the different categories of war crimes listed in Count Two of the Nuremberg indictment: wanton destruction of cities, murder of civilians, deportation to slave labour and concentration camps, plunder of property and so on. The final and largest section contained thirty-five photographs of 'unimaginable bestialities that German soldiers perpetrated in Yugoslavia'.[31]

The foregrounding of 'domestic traitors' in the Nuremberg photographs is indicative of the extent to which the Yugoslav government saw the tribunal as a platform for international agitation. On 29 November 1945, just as finishing touches were being put on the Nuremberg report, a general election, mandated by a negotiated settlement between Tito and the British government, was held throughout Yugoslavia. This was effectively a plebiscite on whether Yugoslavia was to revert to a monarchy with a multiparty parliamentary system or become a one-party, Soviet-style, socialist republic led by Tito and the Communist Party of Yugoslavia. The election, marked by numerous irregularities about which Western governments were understandably concerned, handed the communist-led Popular Front a resounding victory and soon after, the monarchy was abolished. Photographs alluding to the treachery of the Karađorđević royal family and its pre-war political protégés were a way of restating, for the benefit of the international audience, the central anti-monarchist argument and legitimizing the outcome of the election. Also, Yugoslav newspapers at the time were highly critical of Western Allies for their reluctance to extradite collaborators who found themselves under British and American jurisdiction, mainly in Italy and Austria. These criticisms went as far as to describe the Allies as 'the international reaction, which offers assistance and refuge to war criminals'.[32] The inclusion in the Nuremberg material, but also in the photographic exhibition shown in Geneva, of images depicting Chetnik and Ustasha collaboration and criminality hinted at the duplicity of the Allies, who were prosecuting the Nazis while allowing their faithful servants to elude justice. What is more, the British and American policy on extradition, of which the Yugoslav government was so critical, was informed, in part, by the disapproval of Yugoslav regime's violent retribution against the defeated parties in the war, including the expulsion of ethnic Germans from the country in 1945. The inclusion of the Volksdeutche among the 'manifold fifth column' could therefore be read as an attempt to explain, and justify, Yugoslav government's policy of ethnic cleansing of the German minority.

It was however the final section, the one depicting fascist bestialities, that was deemed especially 'striking' and was screened at Nuremberg.[33] It included multiple photographs of not only death marches, hangings, shootings and beatings but also victims who were said to have been burnt alive by German soldiers, fed to animals, mauled by Nazi guard dogs or had a red star cut into their faces. There were also photographs of a female victim with a severed breast, a decapitated child, and a series of four images depicting the beheading with an axe of two captured Partisan fighters. Further five images were of smiling German soldiers posing next to victims who had been hanged or shot.[34] This section supported the count of the indictment concerning crimes against humanity, whose defining feature was not just the scale of the killing but its barbaric, savage, 'medieval' quality.[35]

The State Commission regarded these photographs as especially incriminating not just because of their graphic and violent content, but also because many were taken by perpetrators. By that time, it had been widely accepted that German soldiers were keen photographers and that, despite official prohibition, they frequently documented the humiliation, maltreatment and execution of victims. Other examples of such 'souvenir' photographs were shown by prosecutors at Nuremberg and were even mentioned in Robert H. Jackson's opening address. As a manifestation of the 'Teutonic devotion to detail' and the 'vanity' of German officers, the perpetrator-generated images fitted well with the rationale underpinning the trial, namely, that for justice to be seen to be done, Nazi leaders had to be convicted not 'on the testimony of their foes', but on their own, in this case visual, record.[36] The Yugoslav State Commission, however, took this argument a step further. In addition to providing unequivocal proof of a criminal act, the gruesome trophy photographs were said to offer a glimpse into the perpetrators' depraved minds, the pathological, murderous mentality which turned death into a spectacle, and found in suffering a source of pleasure, humour and titillation.

The State Commission's documents made frequent reference to perverse pleasure that fascists purportedly derived from inflicting pain and suffering and from observing, recording and sharing images depicting their crimes. Captions accompanying the photographs in the Nuremberg report emphasized that German soldiers were 'smiling' or 'joking around' and that both the creation and consumption of the images were a source of 'sadistic gratification'.[37] The State Commission's president, Dušan Nedeljković, made this point in a letter to Soviet prosecutors, when he explained that the images prove that Nazi criminals 'enjoyed recording their horrific offenses on these pictures, often photographing themselves in a proud or cynical pose, next to the victims, carrying these pictures like war trophies'.[38]

The focus on pleasure derived from the creation and consumption of violent images reflected the quasi-psychological interpretation of fascist criminality that permeated the State Commission's publications.[39] This interpretation was most clearly articulated in Nedeljković's short essay entitled 'Contribution of the crimes of the fascists and the fifth column to the history of criminality'.[40] Given that Nedeljković's background was in Marxist philosophy and ethnopsychology, it is perhaps unsurprising that, having witnessed the horrors of the war, he became interested in the fascist mind and the causes of what Marxist thinkers had identified as early as in the 1930s as the distinct 'barbarity and bestiality' of Nazism.[41] Unlike many of his contemporaries, however, Nedeljković did not view the iniquity of the Nazis as unique to the German national character. After all, the work of the State Commission demonstrated clearly that Italians, Hungarians, Bulgarians and, perhaps most importantly, some Yugoslavs were capable of similar, if not greater savagery.

In the essay, Nedeljković argued that what makes fascism unique are not just its aggressive, imperialist pretentions or the planned annihilation of whole peoples and nations. Fascism was characterized also by 'unprecedented mass sadism' of its exponents. Hitler's 'infernal propaganda' managed to 'draw a whole people, the whole [German] nation, into a murderous psychosis'. It turned not only German soldiers but also armies of their partners and the myriad 'fifth column' in occupied lands into furious 'cannibals', 'rabid dogs who sowed death around them'.[42] Individuals contaminated by fascist 'psychosis' – including the Ustasha and the Chetniks – derived almost sensual pleasure from frenzied killing orgies, the murder of women and children, mutilation of victims' bodies, rape and other unimaginable crimes.[43]

This account of fascism, which mirrored the rhetoric of Soviet propaganda, was politically advantageous for several reasons. First, it portrayed the 'modern-day cannibals' who succumbed to fascist psychosis as brainwashed, degraded and violent creatures, deprived of human characteristics. Nedeljković, for instance, recalled an encounter with captured German soldiers in Užice in Serbia in 1941 and the inability of the Partisans to 'awaken the humans in them'. Out of touch with reality and lacking elementary human compassion, fascists were considered beyond redemption and therefore as deserving of the ultimate punishment. Their physical destruction was deemed justified, even necessary to prevent any future 'rising from the dead of the fascist plague'.[44]

Second, attributing the recently ended 'reciprocal slaughter' among Yugoslav nations to an ideologically mediated, 'murderous' mental affliction and 'psychosis' obviated the need for the deeper causes of the ethnic conflict in Yugoslavia to be given serious consideration. As Nedeljković explained, fascism created the 'fifth column', and it so happened that 'the most odious specimens' of this treacherous class were to be found in Yugoslavia.[45] All 'servants of the occupiers' – but especially the Ustasha and the Chetniks – were given the same diagnosis and were therefore to be regarded as equals in terms of iniquity. Also, the ultimate responsibility for atrocities committed in Yugoslavia was laid at the door of the foreign occupiers who brought the fascist 'psychosis' to the country.

This was the prism through which the State Commission viewed atrocity photographs and their evidentiary and symbolic importance. Photographs of mutilated bodies of victims validated the claim about 'mass sadism' and inhumanity of the fascists. The grinning faces on the perpetrator-generated trophy photographs were treated as both proof and *symptom* of the fascist 'psychosis': only the deranged mind of 'modern-day cannibals' would have had the inclination to document, share, view and take pleasure in photographs of bestialities. But equally importantly, atrocity photographs were believed to be one of the methods by which the fascist 'psychosis' was transmitted. In the State Commission's submission to Nuremberg, Nedeljković explained that 'Hitlerites' documented their atrocities not just for their own personal 'enjoyment' but because these images could be used to 'infect others with the desire for bestial gratification' and make them derive pleasure 'from the torture and murder of victims'.[46] Photographs were believed to have been intentionally created and disseminated with the aim of 'cultivating sadistic tendencies' among fascist troops.[47]

Importantly, the assumption that perpetrator-generated photographs were central to turning ordinary people into frenzied, murderous hordes did not result in them being quarantined or destroyed like some perilous, infectious virus. On the contrary, Yugoslav authorities actively encouraged the public to view them. They reclaimed the images and harnessed their persuasive power to engender a different kind of 'desire' in the audience: a desire for revenge against fascists and other 'enemies of the people'.

Atrocity photographs and revenge

Throughout the Second World War, hatred and revenge were important motifs in Partisan propaganda.[48] Although Partisan proclamations and communiqués occasionally drew the distinction between 'revenge' and 'punishment', the Manicheanism of the Partisan world view meant that, for the most part, the two terms were interchangeable.[49] Revenge, provided it was measured and driven by the correct motives (hatred of fascism rather than ethnic intolerance), was encouraged and seen as a marker of 'heroism and patriotism'.⁵⁰ One of the best-known wartime expositions of the idea of revenge was the text 'Noble hatred' by Milovan Đilas, published in *Borba* in October 1942.⁵¹ Đilas, who was one of Tito's closest associates and member of the politburo of the Communist Party of Yugoslavia, argued that 'noble' and merciless hatred for fascists and their ultimate physical destruction are a central military and political goal for the Partisans. 'The depth of hatred felt towards the enemy', Đilas wrote, was the only relevant measure of patriotism: 'To hate the occupier and their servants, that monstrous tumour on the beautiful body of the nation, to hate them from the depth of one's soul, with every thought and every drop of one's blood – is to be infused with the noble feeling of the people's avenger, to be faithful to one's people, its history and future'. He also warned against any 'sentimentality' or 'vacillation'. In the war against fascists – 'truly beasts in human form' – mercy is a sign of weakness, a form of treason.⁵² In his war memoirs published in 1977, Đilas, who was by that time Yugoslavia's best-known dissident, admitted with a hint of embarrassment that the rhetorical flourishes in 'Noble hatred' were 'inspired by the writing of Ilya Ehrenburg', the Soviet writer and journalist whose propaganda pieces published in the Red Army newspaper *Krasnaya Zvezda* frequently called for hatred and merciless vengeance against German occupiers.⁵³ Nevertheless, the central message of Đilas's article captured well the spirit of revenge that permeated Partisan politics.

This spirit infused the language of the State Commission. Moša Pijade's order in October 1942 regarding the collection of evidence of atrocities referred to the Partisan army as the instrument of 'people's vengeance against the bloody villains', which was already 'punishing by death organizers and perpetrators' as well as 'traitors who assist the occupiers'. It also cited the 'approaching hour of retribution' as 'one, perhaps the most important reason for gathering evidence pertaining to war crimes'.⁵⁴ A memo to local officials which the Country Commission for Bosnia issued in September 1944 also stated as one of the main aims of the evidence-gathering process to 'reinforce the hatred that people feel towards the occupiers and their mercenaries' and legitimize retribution that will bring 'moral and material satisfaction' to victims.⁵⁵ Broadsides displayed in public spaces and proclamations issued by Country Commissions routinely called for the destruction of the enemy 'without compassion, without clemency' and declared: 'No mercy for the murderers of our children!'.⁵⁶

Photographs helped sustain this spirit of revenge. In November 1944, *Borba* (which resumed publication as a daily newspaper in Belgrade after the liberation of the city in October that year) printed three graphic photographs showing the decapitation of two captured Partisans by a German military unit in Slovenia (Figure 4.3). Two showed the act of decapitation (with perpetrators 'sadistically grinning' in the background), while the third was of the severed heads laid on a table, one of which 'had a cigarette shoved in its mouth'.⁵⁷ The photographs – described as 'horrific records of the cannibalism of Hitler's hordes' – dominated the page of the newspaper and were published under the title, 'Death to the German occupiers: Let us avenge the blood and suffering of our brothers from the Slovenian littoral'. The article condemned the deeds of the 'savages from Germania … freaks in human form' and concluded with the following rallying cry: 'Patriots of Belgrade, remember that thousands of our people are suffering under Hitler's yoke. Let's avenge our brothers from the Slovenian littoral, let's avenge our

Figure 4.3 Article 'Death to German occupiers' (*Borba*, 29 November 1944, 4).

mothers and sisters from all over our yet to be liberated Yugoslavia. Blood for blood, death for death.'[58]

An even more poignant photograph was published in a similar context several months later under the title 'One photograph from a German soldier's album'.[59] The photograph, which was printed prominently at the top of the page, across three columns, is one of the most graphic and disturbing images from the State Commission's photo archive. It shows a decapitated boy, around ten or eleven years old, whose naked body is laid in the prone position on a table or a bed, with the severed head resting alongside it, facing the camera at a slight angle (Figure 4.4). The photograph appears to have been taken in a domestic setting, in that the body was placed on a striped blanket or tablecloth, with a white, metal washbasin and chair visible in the background. What makes this image particularly striking is not just its graphic nature or that the victim is a child, but the fact that the macabre scene appears to have been arranged for the purpose of the photograph. The severed head was neatly positioned next to the body, with bloody fingerprints visible on the forehead hinting at how it was held as the

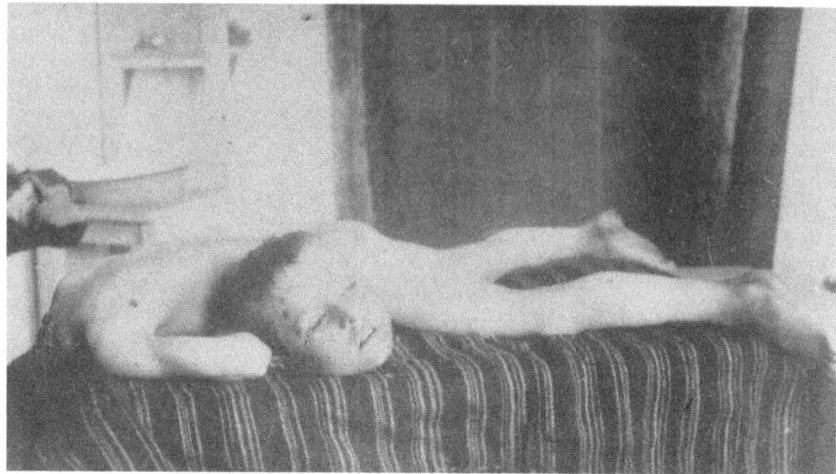

Figure 4.4 Photograph featured in the article 'One photograph from a German soldier's album' published in *Borba* (AJ, 337-110-II-1238).

scene was prepared. What is more, the lighting and composition give the photograph a curiously aesthetic quality, reminiscent of Theodore Jericault's or Antoine Wiertz's nineteenth-century paintings of severed heads. The photograph of the decapitated boy was included in the Nuremberg report, although it also featured in a collection of the State Commission's communiqués as an illustration of crimes committed by Hungarian troops in Vojvodina.[60]

According to the article in *Borba,* the photograph was discovered in the town of Pančevo near Belgrade by the State Commission's investigators who were sifting through abandoned German records. One of a 'huge number' of similar 'souvenir' snapshots recovered from German sources, it was said to capture 'the inhumane vileness, the moral decline of today's German man, who takes pride in such sadistic murders and photographs the mutilated body of his victim in order to preserve, for the post-war years, a memento of his atrocious crimes'.[61] The author of the article then explains:

> Today, as they look at the photograph which we bring, some people will ask how is it possible that anyone calling themselves human can commit such a deed? Well it is possible. The human capable of committing such a deed exists in this world, and his name is the German. The German, who with two bullets murders the boy, then carries the body into his room, undresses him, severs the dead boy's head, bathes him to remove traces of blood and ensure that the skin is pure and white, and then positions the severed head. He does all this, like a proper German, calmly, pedantically, so that he would have as 'interesting' a shot as possible, for his album 'souvenirs from Yugoslavia'.

There is something profoundly unsettling about this account. As if showing the image was not enough, the author invites the reader to vicariously partake in the imagined ghoulish, necrophilic ceremony which culminates in the act of taking the picture. The nakedness of the body and the reference to 'undressing' and 'washing' subtly hints also at a ritualistic, sexual, paedophiliac dimension of the crime. While 'trophy' photographs often draw the viewer into unwittingly identifying with the killer by adopting their gaze, in this instance the accompanying text extends the identification to the sequence of macabre, deviant actions leading up to the pressing of the shutter. Also, the description is exclusively about the killer, their actions, motives and disposition. Like a true atrocity photograph, the image signifies an abomination and, in seeking to stir the feelings of shock, anger and outrage at the heinousness of the perpetrator, leaves little space for mourning the victim.

Aware that some readers might recoil at the horror of the image and avert their gaze, the article in *Borba* instructs them to 'scrutinize it carefully'. Readers were clearly expected to own, and savour their discomfort, and channel it in the appropriate way. 'Our fighters', in particular, 'should preserve photographs' such as this,

> and then, as they go into battle against the Germans, they should look at them not once, but a hundred times. These photographs in the hands of our fighters will become a tremendous weapon against the Germans. The photographs will help each of our fighters realise how great and noble is the struggle against the German plague. When charging at the enemy trench, or bunker, one should be aware that sitting in that bunker is not just the enemy who, like in so many previous wars, finds himself fighting against our peoples. One should know that in the trenches is the fascist criminal, who killed for entertainment, who severed the heads and arms of dead boys, just so that his camera would not have to photograph 'dull motifs'.[62]

Therefore, this and other perverse 'mementos of atrocious crimes', which were said to have served as the source of sadistic gratification for the perpetrators, were still to be gazed at, shared and relished, now as revenge souvenirs – talismans against mercy, compassion and hesitation in the final reckoning with fascists.[63]

Both examples from *Borba* called for revenge against *German* perpetrators, rather than fascists generally. This was in part because the paper was published in Serbia, where most crimes had been committed by the occupying forces, so there was already widespread animosity specifically towards Germans. Also, after the liberation of Serbia in the autumn of 1944, as the final push against the retreating German army was under way, there was a flurry of articles in the press which sought to remind the relieved residents of Serbia that the struggle for national liberation was not yet over and to mobilize them for war. To achieve this, the articles, including the two discussed above, emulated Soviet propaganda and drew, often explicitly, on the tradition of Ehrenburg's inflammatory rhetoric of hate and dehumanization of Germans.[64]

Meanwhile, in Croatia and Bosnia, there was greater focus on the crimes of the Ustasha. There too, photographs were used to legitimize the campaign of retribution.[65] The documentary film *Jasenovac*, considered in the previous chapter, is a case in point. In the film, over a mixture of footage of the banks of the river in Jasenovac and still shots of atrocities from other locations, the narrator explicitly called for revenge: 'Disembowelled corpses, mutilated bodies and skeletons, victims from earlier in the war and the last days of the camp, are all crying out for revenge, in their own name and in the name of their fallen comrades'.[66] The film ends with the footage of an anti-fascist march in Zagreb, featuring people carrying banners with slogans 'victims of Jasenovac are crying out for vengeance' and 'death to those who spilled the blood of innocent people!'. A similar message was imparted through photographic exhibitions organized by the State Commission and its subsidiaries. An internal report on the exhibition organized by the Country Commission for Bosnia proudly stated that 'many visitors left the venue with the feeling of bitter contempt, and called for vengeance', particularly against the 'traitors of our people, the Ustasha and the Chetniks, the photographs of whom attracted most attention'.[67] A report on a similar exhibition which opened at the Ulrich art gallery in Zagreb in August 1945 mentioned, as a key lesson of the event, that the 'the deceased' – namely victims featured in the atrocity photographs – 'demand justice, they demand that the fascist criminals – domestic and foreign – are given the punishment they deserve'. Or as the authors of the report put it bluntly, the photographs demonstrated why the slogan of Yugoslav Partisans 'death to fascism – freedom to the people' needed to be taken '*literally*'.[68]

Who was the intended audience for the gruesome photographs and footage of Ustasha atrocities, and associated calls for revenge? The propaganda drive appears to have been aimed at those who, in the opinion of the authorities, had not yet embraced the regime's uncompromising stance towards the enemy. Following the liberation of Zagreb in May 1945, security services expressed concern that many Ustasha had gone into hiding and that arrests and reprisals were not progressing with the required urgency.[69] Part of the problem were 'opportunists' and 'appeasers' who opposed the implementation of revolutionary justice and refused to cooperate with the secret police. In the weeks and months that followed, 'spontaneous' public protests were organized, and a media offensive launched, warning the 'vacillators' and 'doubters' of the danger posed by the presence of 'unpunished criminals' in their midst.[70] The photographic exhibition in Zagreb and the Jasenovac documentary were part of this propaganda effort.[71] Reporting on the Zagreb exhibition, the press pointed out that images of crimes committed by 'Ustasha beasts' contained a message above all for those who 'still do not appreciate the need for the merciless punishment of perpetrators'.[72] Or as the organizers of the exhibition called them, 'hypocrites who are disturbed by the just punishment of fascist criminals'.[73] The message was the same in Belgrade. The article 'One photograph from a German soldier's album' explained that, alongside Partisan fighters, it was the 'ditherers' who should 'take a particularly good look at the boy with the severed head'. This will help them to confront the reality of the fascist menace and accept that 'all-out, merciless revenge' is both legitimate and necessary.[74]

It is, of course, questionable whether the authorities in Yugoslavia ever truly believed that the ideologically suspect waverers, appeasers and doubters would be persuaded by, or even engage with, atrocity images published in the state-controlled press, displayed in officially sanctioned exhibitions or shown in documentaries with an overtly propagandistic tone. Especially as some internal reports on the photographic exhibitions acknowledged that they often failed to reach the section of the population for whom they were intended and that most who attended did so as part of planned and often compulsory group visits.[75] One could argue, therefore, that

Figure 4.5 Message to 'opportunists' and 'appeasers': The exhibition of atrocity photographs at the Ulrich Gallery in Zagreb, September 1945 (from *Ilustrirani Vjesnik*, no 5, 15 September 1945, 12).

the primary objective of the atrocity-focused visual propaganda was not to *persuade* the 'vacillators' and dissenters or convert them to the government's cause through a ritual of confrontation. The objective was simply to call them out. By publishing or displaying atrocity photographs, by explaining their meaning and setting out what was considered to be the normative emotional and behavioural reaction to them, the authorities were fashioning, in a rhetorically effective way, the new post-war moral and political order, one that extolled revenge and equated indecisiveness and compassion with 'treason'. The real message (and threat) communicated through the hard-hitting, emotive atrocity photographs and their discursive framing was, first, that the depravity of the enemy makes 'all-out, merciless revenge' morally justified and, second, that in the black-and-white universe of revolutionary justice, anyone who did not fully, and demonstrably, embrace (or at least accept) the spirit of retribution would be treated as an 'advocate of the fascists and their assistants' and an accessory to the gruesome crimes portrayed in the photographs.[76]

Managing Ustasha exceptionalism: Regular 'domestic traitors' or uniquely violent 'cannibalistic beasts'?

In the examples examined so far, there was little evidence of a qualitative distinction being made between the Ustasha and other fascists in terms of depravity. On the contrary, in line with the understanding of fascism expounded in Dušan Nedeljković's essay, authorities often went out of their way to present different perpetrator groups as equally depraved and sadistic. In the State Commission's visual propaganda, this was achieved by ensuring that comparable atrocity photographs were present in representations of all perpetrators. The largest photographic exhibition, which opened in Belgrade in March 1946 and later toured the capitals of Yugoslav republics, offers a relevant example. There, German, Italian, Ustasha and Chetnik atrocities were all represented through familiar clichés of atrocity reporting, and included trophy photographs, as well as images of decapitations and mutilations, of victims having symbols carved into their skin and so on. A report on the exhibition published in the Zagreb daily *Naprijed* picked up on the intended ideological message behind the choice and juxtaposition of images when it noted that the exhibits demonstrated clearly that 'German, Italian, Ustasha and Chetnik butchers' *all* had photographs taken 'standing next to slaughtered women, massacred children or beheaded fighters for freedom'.[77]

The parity between the Ustasha and the Chetniks, mandated by the principle of symmetry in heroism, victimization and villainy between Serbs and Croats, was especially important. In the exhibition, the 800 or so photographs on display were divided into 26 thematic sections or 'wall panels', each containing between 20 and 30 captioned images. Of the twenty-six panels, ten were devoted to crimes perpetrated by German forces. Three were on Italian, two on Hungarian and one on Bulgarian crimes. This allocation of space pointed to a hierarchy of culpability among foreign occupiers. Yet no comparable hierarchy existed in representations of Ustasha and Chetnik atrocities. The panels on 'Hitler's multiple Fifth Column' and 'Domestic traitors', shown at the start of the exhibition, presented the Chetniks and the Ustasha (alongside other collaborators) as a single, homogenous, traitorous category. The exhibition also featured the same number of additional panels – four each – specifically about Chetnik and Ustasha crimes. Within the captions accompanying the photographs, a parallel was consistently drawn between the two, especially in terms of bloodthirstiness and sadistic killing methods. Above one of the wall panels stood the large banner stating, 'Both Chetniks and Ustasha killed and slit throats'.[78] Also common were photographs showing Chetnik and Ustasha officials together, in the company of German or Italian officers. One such photograph, similar to Figure 4.6, if not the same one, was accompanied by the caption 'While Ustasha were killing Serbs, Chetniks of Draža Mihailović were drinking with them'.[79] Such photographs signified the similarity in treachery between the collaborators, but also helped to undermine their nationalist credentials: the supposedly rival extreme nationalist groups were exposed as having colluded not just with the occupiers but also with each other, against the interests of the Yugoslav people.[80]

The assumption of equivalence between the Ustasha and the Chetniks and the tendency to subsume both under the all-encompassing category of 'collaborators of the occupiers' or 'domestic traitors' persisted in public discourse until the 1980s. This was part of the ideological common sense that underpinned the doctrine of 'brotherhood and unity' on which the Yugoslav federation was founded and which helped keep it together for more than four decades.

And yet, things were not that simple. No matter how hard the authorities tried to present all collaborators as equal, there was no escaping the fact that, by 1945, the Ustasha had deservedly acquired notoriety, both among the population and the ruling elite, for bloodthirstiness and unprecedented brutality. This reputation was not only

Why Look at Fascism? 79

Figure 4.6 Illustration of Chetnik-Ustasha collaboration: 'While Ustasha were killing Serbs, Chetniks of Draža Mihailović were drinking with them' (MIJ, III-8151).

impossible to avoid or supress but, at times, the authorities consciously harnessed it, especially when denouncing 'domestic traitors' in Croatia. For example, an appeal for information issued by the Country Commission for Croatia and published on the first page of the daily *Vjesnik* in May 1945, referred to the enemy in general terms, as 'rabid fascist beasts who spattered every part of our country with blood'. But it then proceeded to emphasize the distinctiveness of 'Ustasha killers, cannibalistic beasts', who executed people

> in the most brutal ways, with axes, mallets, iron bars, by suffocation, they threw people into rivers and down ravines, they burned people alive, raped women and girls, they tortured in thousands of different ways, including by cutting flesh, breaking bones, inserting wire into the nose and ears, and hammering nails into the skull, they starved inmates in prisons and camps, they forced them to work, they ordered deportations, looting, and the destruction of property.[81]

The voiceover in the 1945 Jasenovac documentary also highlighted the 'sadistic and pathological urges' of the Ustasha and even suggested that 'there are no other examples in history remotely like the Ustasha crimes in Jasenovac'.[82] In the aforementioned photographic exhibition in Zagreb, which was officially devoted to the crimes committed by occupiers and collaborators generally, the brutality of the Ustasha was the main theme, with 'numerous photographs of mangled human corpses', of 'smashed skulls' and bodies 'floating down the River Sava' or 'piled upon its riverbanks' dominating the display.[83]

This motif of Ustasha exceptionalism, which lurked in the shadow of the broader denunciation of fascism, is important to bear in mind. As we shall see in the next chapter, for much of the post-war period it persisted on the visible margins of the collective memory of the crimes of the Ustasha. In fact, it was its stubborn persistence, especially in vernacular memory, that necessitated the constant affirmation of the principle of symmetry in brutality between the Ustasha and the Chetniks, and drove the tendency to blame the Germans, or fascists generally, for the genocide. On the other hand, an important and enduring legacy of the State Commission's propaganda work in the mid-1940s was that it exposed the effectiveness of atrocity photographs, and the motif of Ustasha brutality more generally, as a way of highlighting, and denouncing, the excesses of Croatian nationalism. This means that, in the decades that followed, photographs of Ustasha atrocities were never just a means of evidencing or illustrating crimes of the Independent State of Croatia. They were also a weapon that, while requiring careful handling, could be relied upon whenever the scourge of nationalism and chauvinism showed signs of 'rising from the dead'.

5

Ustasha violence through the prism of 'brotherhood and unity'

The dilemmas of visual memory in socialist Yugoslavia

In the winter of 1947–8, the work of the State Commission for the Investigation of the Crimes of the Occupiers and their Accomplices was drawing to a close. At the headquarters in Belgrade, Dušan Nedeljković was compiling the final report for the Yugoslav government, while the remaining office staff prepared the Commission's records for handover to state institutions that would continue its work in the years that followed.

On 10 December 1947, the State Commission's secretary, Ivan Grgić, sent a letter, marked 'confidential', to the federal Ministry of the Interior informing it of the existence of a substantial collection of large-format photographic prints of war crimes and war criminals that had been used in public exhibitions. Grgić proposed that, because war crimes are 'a specific category of criminality' and the focus of 'significant international attention', this valuable material, which presently 'lies unused, in crates', should be displayed in the Museum of Criminology, which the Ministry of the Interior was planning to open.[1] Ten days later, the ministry responded favourably to Grgić's proposal, agreeing to take possession of the photographs. Once relevant permissions had been obtained, the State Commission dispatched three crates of photographs containing 1,289 items, followed by a second, smaller consignment of 114 photographs and 2 artefacts – iron shackles brought to Belgrade from Jasenovac.[2]

The ministry never opened the Museum of Criminology, and the material from the State Commission's exhibitions was never put on display again. Crates containing the prints languished for almost forty years in the attic of a police training college in Zemun, near Belgrade. They were discovered there during a clear-out in the mid-1980s, and what could be salvaged was donated to the Historical Archives of Belgrade and the Museum of the Revolution in the city.

The fate of the exhibits is in many ways symbolic of the general decline in the interest in, and public visibility of, atrocity images in Yugoslav society after the State Commission ceased to operate in 1948. By the late 1940s, the topic of 'fascist bestialities' had lost much of its political currency. Albert Vajs, who headed the Yugoslav delegation at Nuremberg, anticipated this development in 1946, when he recommended ordering multiple copies of the 'photo-document' submitted to the tribunal, for screening in Yugoslav cities. Correspondence relating to this matter hints at a sense of urgency: Vajs considered it important for the public in Yugoslavia to see the film before it was 'too late', that is, while the issue of war crimes was still 'current'.[3] He later observed that the speed with which the commission as a whole gathered and publicized evidence of war crimes was driven in part by the realization among its staff that 'political and legal interest' in this matter would not last, either at home or internationally.[4]

The change in official attitudes towards atrocity images was not a uniquely Yugoslav phenomenon. In the West, the onset of the Cold War altered the stance towards German society and its past. For the governments of the United States and Britain, the reconstruction and renewal of Germany became more important than the pursuit of retributive justice, so Nazi crimes slipped down the political agenda. In 1955, a US-sponsored photographic exhibition at Dachau – of the kind that ten years earlier was deemed essential to the process of denazification– was 'closed until further notice' because atrocity photographs were now deemed 'offensive to good taste' and 'damaging to international relations'.[5] The changing international political landscape and new alliances had less of an impact on the treatment of Nazi crimes in the Soviet Union, although the veneration of war heroes and the focus on labour feats and industrial progress inevitably resulted in the marginalization of the motif of civilian suffering that during the war served to inspire hatred of Germans.[6]

In Yugoslavia, the declining interest in fascist atrocities and associated imagery reflected some of these broader developments but was also driven by local factors. First, by 1947 the leadership of Yugoslavia's Communist Party had consolidated its grip on power and defeated its 'internal enemies' of various ideological persuasions. In Croatia, this meant a final reckoning with the Ustasha and their followers, the eradication of all forms of political opposition from the country's body politic and the marginalization of the Catholic Church as a source of nationalist and anti-Communist agitation.[7] There was, therefore, no longer the strong need to stir up the feelings of hatred and revenge towards 'traitors' and collaborators. Also, the authorities understood quite early on that dwelling on the past, including the horrors of war and occupation, distracted from practical problems of renovation and reconstruction. Public discourse became more future-oriented, and focused on measures portrayed as necessary for the creation of a successful and prosperous socialist society: centralization of the economy, agricultural reform, industrialization, the construction of railway networks and motorways, and so on.[8] This message was not hard to sell to the Yugoslav public, which was genuinely tired of violence and keen to escape the dark shadow of a very bloody and divisive war.

Second, the Tito-Stalin split in the spring and summer of 1948 brought about a comprehensive and far-reaching reinterpretation of the history of the Second World War. This involved downplaying the contribution of the Red Army to the liberation of parts of Serbia in the autumn of 1944 and eradicating from the history of the Communist Party of Yugoslavia any reference to the long-standing and decisive political and ideological influence of the Soviet Union and its Communist Party. Intrinsic to this new 'de-Sovietized' history of the Second World War in Yugoslavia was the glorification of the Partisan movement and the portrayal of the 'struggle for national liberation' as a unique accomplishment of the Yugoslav people and, crucially, Yugoslav communists. The principal exponents of this view of the past were veterans of the Partisan movement, whose organization – the Union of Fighters of the People's Liberation War – acquired a virtual monopoly over history writing and memory making relevant to the period of 1941–5. Veterans oversaw the construction of monuments, commissioned and edited books and other publications, organized commemorative ceremonies and so on, all with the aim of safeguarding the 'revolutionary traditions' forged during four years of armed struggle against fascism.

The inevitable consequence of the glorification of Partisan resistance was that 'victims of fascism' became sidelined as an object of memory. In the 1950s, for instance, commemoration of civilian victims was actively discouraged, in favour of memorials honouring heroes and landmark events of the Partisan war.[9] Also, many execution sites and mass graves of civilian victims were assimilated into the pervasive narrative of resistance and commemorated as graves of 'Partisan fighters', 'heroes' or 'patriots'.[10] The suffering of civilians was, of course, never denied, and its commemoration was never completely suppressed, but within the dominant discourse of remembrance, a special place was reserved for executed Partisans or communist sympathizers.

There was also a third, more practical reason why images of fascist atrocities became less visible after 1948. When the State Commission was officially abolished in April that year, jurisdiction over the investigation of war crimes and the extradition of war criminals was transferred to the Federal Office of Public Prosecutor and the Ministry of the Interior. The commission's records, including its photo archive, were divided between these institutions, but also the Ministry of Foreign Affairs, the Yugoslav Army's Historical Institute, the Historical Section of the Central Committee of the Communist Party and so on. Records of the six Country Commissions (which were abolished at the end of 1947) were taken over by equivalent institutions operating at the level of republics. The largest collection of photographs of fascist atrocities was thus not only broken up but also placed beyond the reach of the public. There were not many atrocity photographs left in the public domain, except what remained in the archives of daily newspapers or collections of state-owned photo-agencies, such as the Photographic Documentation Agency in Zagreb. Only in the late 1960s and early 1970s did government bodies begin to release the photographs from the State Commission's collection – partially, gradually and unsystematically – to archives and museums.

This chapter examines the impact of these developments on visual representations of Ustasha violence in socialist Yugoslavia. The focus will once again be on the visual memory of the Jasenovac concentration camp, which in the mid-1960s became the site of the only national memorial in Yugoslavia devoted specifically to victims of fascist terror and the bloody legacy of the Independent State of Croatia. Crucially, the things that made Jasenovac the focus of public memory – the scale and brutality of the killings – were also a source of political controversy and sensitivity. Fragile inter-ethnic relations in Yugoslavia and the dominant doctrine of 'brotherhood and unity' meant that the history of ethnic violence and bloodletting during the Second World War, of which Jasenovac was an important symbol, needed to be managed carefully.[11] By exploring the creation and the content of the first permanent display at the Jasenovac Memorial

Museum, the chapter considers the challenges, both political and practical, that official memory makers faced when forging the memory of Jasenovac and determining what it is about Ustasha atrocities that the Yugoslav public should see.

The challenges of Jasenovac memorialization in post-war Yugoslavia

Like most Nazi-era concentration camps both in Yugoslavia and elsewhere, Jasenovac did not become the object of organized or public remembering until the 1960s. A large memorial monument was unveiled at the site in the summer of 1966, followed by the opening of a museum two years later. These developments were the culmination of a gradual, intricate and politically delicate process of memory making, which began more than ten years earlier.

In the early 1950s, as part of national commemorations of the tenth anniversary of the beginning of the Partisan uprising, local authorities throughout Yugoslavia started building memorials commemorating their community's 'revolutionary history' and contribution to the 'struggle for national liberation'.[12] In the case of the village of Jasenovac, which was rebuilt after the war, this contribution lay in the fact that on its outskirts was the site of 'one of the most notorious concentration camps in the world' where 'hundreds of thousands of citizens of this country laid their lives for the liberation of our people'.[13] Thus, in 1952, the local Communist Party organization proposed the construction of 'a monumental sculpture surrounded by an international park'. The memorial would include a new primary school for the village and a museum dedicated to 'victims of fascism'.[14] Backing for this initiative was sought from the relevant authorities in Zagreb and Belgrade, who, although broadly supportive, considered Jasenovac to be far too important, and politically sensitive, to be left in the hands of the local party organization. Before the end of the year, the federal leadership of the Union of Fighters declared Jasenovac a site of 'pan-Yugoslav significance', effectively taking control over its memorialization. An important factor that led the Union of Fighters to act was the emergence of informal, unsanctioned forms of commemoration that threatened the veteran organization's monopoly over the memorialization of the war. The local diocese of the Serbian Orthodox Church, for instance, had begun collecting donations for a memorial church in Jasenovac, while survivors and relatives of victims (mainly Serbs from western Bosnia) started to hold candle-lit vigils and wreath-laying rituals at the site of the camp. Although commemorative visits were not yet organized or well attended, they nevertheless exposed the mismatch between the official silence surrounding Jasenovac and the prominent place it occupied in vernacular memory of the Second World War.

Little progress was made on the construction of the memorial until the early 1960s, unless one counts the informal signposting, by survivors and victims' families, of key landmarks at the site, or the creation in 1954 of an improvised and unsanctioned 'museum': a wooden shed housing a few artefacts, including implements used in the executions of inmates, chains and several human skulls.[15] The delay was caused by limited financial resources and the more general prioritization of places of Partisan heroism and sacrifice. But it was also because Jasenovac was a political 'hot potato'. In 1959, Aleksandar Ranković, one of Yugoslavia's top-ranking communist officials, who, as president of the Union of Fighters of the People's Liberation War, chaired the committee that oversaw the construction of memorials at sites linked to the Second World War, noted that creating a large memorial at Jasenovac 'could be costly, for political reasons': a monument or a museum would need to specify who perished there, and at whose hands, and this could upset the balance of brotherhood and unity.[16] Another challenge surrounding Jasenovac was that the official estimate of the number of victims – which stood at between 500,000 and 700,000 dead – was clearly an exaggeration, arrived at in the immediate aftermath of the war, and allowed to stand. By the mid-1950s, the figure became so widespread and entrenched in public memory that it was impossible for the authorities to revise it down to a more plausible level, without inviting allegations of appeasement, and provoking the wrath of the victims' families.[17] For these reasons, Ranković and a number of other leading figures within the communist establishment advocated a modest memorial museum, aimed primarily at accommodating the needs of survivors and families of victims who visited the site every year.[18] Others, such as the defence minister, general Ivan Gošnjak, held the opposite view and backed the creation of a more representative, national memorial. This was also the position of Jasenovac survivors and descendants of victims, growing numbers of whom participated in the annual pilgrimage to Jasenovac. Attendance at the event rose from 700 in 1956 to 10,000 in 1962, leading the authorities to label the gathering a 'public demonstration', a form of popular protest that could no longer be ignored.[19]

A further problem with the memorialization of Jasenovac was the question of *how* it was to be represented. Bogdan Bogdanović, the author of the monument that was erected at the site in 1966, remarked that even ten or fifteen years after the end of the war, remembrance of victims of fascism was still 'unbearably preoccupied with representing the act of violent death, and with naturalistic, almost sadistic representations of the victim'.[20] This was a feature of both the dominant 'social-realist funereal art' and vernacular memory focused on graphic, and, in Bogdanović's words, 'necrophilic' portrayals of suffering. As we have seen in the previous chapter, this was a rhetoric, and iconography, of violence which the authorities encouraged in the immediate aftermath of the war. However, they were now just as keen to tone it down, because feelings of hatred and revenge were no longer politically expedient. Several proposals for the memorial in Jasenovac were rejected because, as one official put it, they took 'the full naturalism' to an extreme and 'made the hairs on one's neck stand on end'.[21] The authorities favoured a different solution, one that would allow Jasenovac to be remembered (thus placating public opinion), but in a way that also made it possible for important, but politically sensitive or divisive aspects of its history to be sidelined.

Disagreements over the memorial in Jasenovac eventually led Josip Broz Tito – the supreme authority in Yugoslavia at the time – to take personal responsibility for this issue. At a meeting in Belgrade in February 1963, Tito approved the basic design of the Stone Flower, a large 25 metre tall concrete monument by Bogdan Bogdanović,

Figure 5.1 Stone Flower shortly after construction, Jasenovac Memorial Area (courtesy of the Jasenovac Memorial Museum).

one of Yugoslavia's best-known designers of memorial architecture (Figure 5.1). The appeal of the monument lay, as Bogdanović put it at the time, in the fact that 'it does not evoke images of horror and disgust' but affirms 'one universal human truth – that life is indestructible'.[22] As such, the Stone Flower had a 'calming effect' on the memory of the war and served as a 'a talisman which would help all of us Yugoslavs to dispel the demons of hatred and ghosts of the past, and grab hold of the thread of the harmonious and peaceful common existence'.[23]

The Stone Flower monument, formally unveiled on 4 July 1966, infused Jasenovac with new meaning, but also offered a new visual marker for this place of suffering. Over the decades that followed, the image of the monument standing in an empty field devoid of all traces of the camp that once stood there featured prominently in the press, in books and publicity material, on memorabilia: pins, keyrings, postcards and so on. Thus, the Stone Flower did not symbolize 'triumph over suffering and mindless violence' in a purely abstract sense; it provided a way of visualizing Jasenovac that did not immediately conjure up horror and death.[24] On the other hand, violence was an indelible part of Jasenovac memory that could not be circumvented completely. Even Bogdanović's monument had built into its core a crypt, a solemn memorial space, where verses from Ivan Goran Kovačić's harrowing wartime poem 'The Pit' – which describes an Ustasha massacre from the perspective of the victim – reminded visitors that the flower, with all its life-affirming symbolism, is nevertheless rooted in darkness, suffering and death. Striking a balance between the affirmation of life and the remembrance of the horrors of Jasenovac would become a key challenge for the memorial museum, which opened at the site two years later.

The first exhibition at the Jasenovac Memorial Museum (1968)

The Jasenovac Memorial Museum, a modest single-storey building on the periphery of what used to be the main camp complex, opened to the public on 4 July 1968. The exhibition space within the museum building comprised a single hall, with the floor area of just 171 m². Adjacent to it was another, smaller room, used mainly for screening documentary films. The museum building also housed a small shop which sold souvenirs and books, as well as the offices of the Jasenovac Memorial Area, the public body charged with coordinating commemorative activities and maintaining the site.

The Jasenovac Memorial Area entrusted the design of the museum exhibition to curators from the Museum of the Revolution of the People of Croatia, based in Zagreb. At the time, the Museum of the Revolution was the main institution in Croatia charged with preserving the memory of the Second World War. Its involvement in the design of the Jasenovac Memorial Museum reflected the perceived importance, and politically sensitive nature of the project, but also the need for the memory of Jasenovac to be assimilated into Yugoslavia's foundation myth, namely the story of the struggle for national liberation and the socialist revolution. As Radovan Trivunčić, the first director of the Jasenovac Memorial Area put it, the aim of the museum was not just to honour victims but also to 'show that the people who died were not devoid of consciousness or ideas. Their vast sacrifices are inseparable from our Revolution'.[25]

Very little information about the first exhibition at the Jasenovac Memorial Museum has been preserved. In the museum's publicity material from the 1970s there are several photographs showing the layout of the exhibition and the content of some of the display cases. Also, outtakes from Lordan Zafranović's 1983 documentary *Blood and Ashes of Jasenovac* include footage of some of the exhibits.[26] Among the documents preserved in the Jasenovac Memorial Area's institutional archive, of relevance are an early conceptual plan of the exhibition and a provisional list of exhibits, both drafted by Ksenija Dešković, the curator from the Museum of the Revolution who led the project. Although limited, this material sheds important light on the content of the exhibition, the sourcing of exhibits (including photographs), and the process by which a politically opportune interpretation of Jasenovac was created in 1960s Yugoslavia.

Figure 5.2, taken in the early 1970s, reveals the simple spatial organization and minimalistic design of the exhibition. Exhibits were presented in long rows of wall-mounted and tabletop glass display cases, which were arranged along the side walls. There were four additional free-standing, tabletop display cases on the right-hand side of the central area and a further three placed against the wall opposite the entrance. Hanging on the wall was the centrepiece of the exhibition, a large sculpture by the artist Dušan Džamonja, in the shape of a stylized gate, made of metal chains and wood carved to resemble human bones. A large drawing of the layout of the camp was suspended from the ceiling, near the entrance to the hall. Exhibits in the display cases comprised original artefacts (such as objects manufactured in the camp's workshops and inmates' personal possessions), photographs and copies of documents, public notices, newspaper articles and so on. Also present were original shackles and remains

Figure 5.2 First permanent exhibition at the museum in Jasenovac which opened in 1968 (courtesy of the Jasenovac Memorial Museum).

of murder weapons – hammer, wooden mallet, axe and several daggers – some of which were displayed suspended on a mock prison fence.

The content of the exhibition can be partially reconstructed from the draft list of exhibits. Hand-written comments and amendments of unknown provenance, which are visible on the undated document, suggest that this was a provisional list, one that is likely to have undergone modifications before the project was finalized in the summer of 1968. However, changes are likely to have been at the level of individual exhibits or captions, not the overall framing of Jasenovac, or the structure and layout of the exhibition.

Of the 226 items listed in the document, 84 are photographs, 54 copies of archival documents and 50 original artefacts. The rest are interpretive legends, maps, panels with quotations from speeches and documents and so on. The exhibits were arranged into fifteen thematic sections of unequal size. The first four set the scene for the story of Jasenovac by explaining the fascist nature of the Ustasha regime and its reign of terror. Here, 'patriots, communists, Serbs and Jews' were identified as targets of Ustasha violence, with 'antifascist, democratic and progressive forces, especially their vanguard, the Communist Party' clearly positioned as the primary victim group. Prominent party members and communist activists were also the only victims mentioned by name. On the other hand, the exhibition did include a separate, lengthy section specifically devoted to the 'implementation of policies of discrimination and extermination of Serbs and Jews'.

The overlapping categories of victim groups and their ordering warrant attention: the prioritization of 'antifascists', 'patriots' and 'communists' reflected the dominant, and by that time well-established, 'inclusive' construction of the Second World War as a common struggle of Yugoslav nations, who suffered and died together, first and foremost for their patriotism and anti-fascism. As Tito put it in a speech delivered in Glina in 1952, Ustasha killed 'both Serbs and Croats', but their violence was directed above all at 'progressive forward-thinking people, communists, who strived for something better than what they had'.[27] And yet, the emphasis on progressive Yugoslav nations united in suffering did not prevent Serbs, Jews and less commonly Roma from being specifically identified as targets of Ustasha violence. As Emil Kerenji has shown, attaching ethnic labels to victim groups was permissible in socialist Yugoslavia, as long as 'one simultaneously downplayed the genocidal nature of these crimes and connected them to all other crimes that had been committed in Yugoslavia during the war'.[28] This is why in commemorative speeches, reports in the press and so on, Jasenovac was often described in generic terms, as a place of 'fascist' rather than specifically Ustasha bestiality. This broad interpretative pattern was central to the Jasenovac exhibition: according to the conceptual plan, the museum's main aim was to commemorate the victims of 'monstrous fascist ideology', of which the Ustasha were mere 'representatives'.[29] It is also revealing that the section of the exhibition on Ustasha 'discrimination and extermination' of Serbs did not reflect on the *cause* of the violence. Nor was the official, inflated figure of 700,000 victims broken down by ethnicity, so there was no reference to how many Serbs were killed. Also, most of the exhibits dealt with confiscation of property and forced religious conversion of Serbs (an unavoidable gibe at the Catholic Church) rather than mass killings. There was no mention of the scale and the scope of the 'direct terror' against the Serbian population, or its genocidal nature.

The largest part of the exhibition was devoted to Jasenovac itself, and included sections on deportations, different workshops and factories that existed at the camp, the appalling living conditions, the 'pathological types' among camp commanders and perpetrators and so on. Life at the camp was presented through Ustasha propaganda photographs, without flagging their origin. The horror and brutality of the violence was conveyed through sections on 'methods and means of killing people in the camp', 'mass liquidations' and 'individual executions', which comprised original murder weapons and photographs of execution sites. The final part of the exhibition covered the theme of resistance. It described the activity of Communist Party members among the inmates, who were credited with raising morale, and organizing various successful escapes, including the final breakout on 22 April 1945. The exhibition concluded with images of camp ruins taken by the Country Commission's investigators in 1945 and a photograph of the fighters of the 21st Serbian Partisan Brigade who liberated the village of Jasenovac. Even though the Partisans entered Jasenovac ten days after the Ustasha abandoned the camp, the exhibition's final section tied the camp's closure to the glorious victory of the liberating Partisan army. This was in line with the museum's objective to commemorate 'the struggle and ultimate victory of antifascist forces gathered in the Struggle for National Liberation, whose organiser and leader was the Communist Party of Yugoslavia, the bearer of humane, Marxist ideology'.[30] The final panel bore a brief message condemning fascism generally and warning younger generations that crimes of Jasenovac must not be allowed to be repeated.

One of the main challenges that the authors of the exhibition faced was that they had little material on Jasenovac to draw on. A seven-page overview of the history of the camp, which constituted the starting point for the conceptual plan, was based on twelve published sources, of which only four were directly related to Jasenovac: three were memoirs of survivors published in the 1940s, the fourth was the Country Commission report on Jasenovac from 1946.[31] The absence from the bibliography of Egon Berger's memoir *44 Months in Jasenovac* and Mirko Peršen's book *Ustasha Camps* – both of which were first published in 1966 – suggests that work on the conceptual plan began sometime in 1965 or earlier.[32] More importantly, the bibliography clearly shows that in the first twenty years after the end of the Second World War, not a single scholarly piece of work on Jasenovac had been written. Survivor testimonies and the report of the Country Commission were still the only available sources.

A related challenge was the lack of photographs. By the mid-1960s, the Museum of the Revolution in Zagreb had amassed a sizeable collection of photographs related to the Second World War, through donations, acquisitions of personal collections or institutional exchanges. Although some of this material was relevant to Ustasha crimes, there was not enough on Jasenovac to meet the needs of a museum exhibition. Concentration camps, unlike the struggle for national liberation and the socialist revolution, were never part of the museum's remit.[33] Only in the late 1960s, in part because of its involvement in the creation of the Jasenovac exhibition, did the Museum of the Revolution start to collect, in a more systematic way, photographs related to the suffering of 'victims of fascism' in Croatia.[34]

To address the paucity of relevant photographs, curators of the exhibition turned to published works: the publications that informed the conceptual plan and the books by Peršen and Berger published in 1966. In fact, if one cross-references the description of the eighty-four photographs from the draft list of exhibits with photographs published in these books, one finds a match in more than 80 per cent of cases.[35] Captions for the photographs were also reproduced from the published sources either verbatim or in a slightly modified form. By far the most common source was Nikola Nikolić's memoir *The Jasenovac Camp* published in 1948.[36]

The correspondence between the list of exhibits and the published images does not imply that photographs for the exhibition had to be *literally* reproduced from the books. This would have been unnecessary because in May 1967, just a few months before he laid the foundation stone for the Jasenovac Memorial Museum, Egon Berger donated to the Museum of the Revolution around 180 photographs which he had copied sometime earlier from the Photographic Documentation Agency in Zagreb, probably for the purposes of his 1966 memoir.[37] A year later, the museum also made copies of photographs from Nikola Nikolić's personal collection. Around the same time, the Croatian Secretariat of the Interior released to the Museum of the Revolution in Zagreb the first tranche of photographs that had once belonged to the photo archive of the Croatian Country Commission.[38] Most photographs mentioned in the provisional list of exhibits would have been among at least one of the three acquisitions. Nevertheless, the curators' initial reliance of what was, literally, an 'off the shelf' solution illustrates the lack of availability of atrocity images at the time. Unlike in the mid-1940s, when designers of exhibitions or publishers could simply turn to the State Commission or one of its subsidiaries and request suitable photographs of fascist atrocities, in the 1960s, even an important state institution like the Museum of the Revolution had to work hard to find suitable photographs of an iconic place of suffering.

Forging 'humanist broadmindedness' in a place of fascist terror

The conceptual plan for the exhibition, just like the choice of images, was based mainly on Nikola Nikolić's 450-page memoir *The Jasenovac Camp*. This is unsurprising given that this was not only the most detailed work on Jasenovac available at the time but also one whose interpretation of the occupation, collaboration and killing at the camp was perfectly aligned with that which the Jasenovac Memorial Museum sought to project. Nikolić placed Jasenovac in the roll call of *Nazi* camps, he equated Ustasha with other collaborators, such as the 'Chetnik-royalist-Nedić clique' in Serbia, and emphasized the heroism of communists. He stressed the ethnic and social diversity of the inmate population: Jasenovac was the 'horrific slaughterhouse of our people' bound by anti-fascist convictions and dedication to 'brotherhood and unity'.[39]

Also, unlike most memoirs of Jasenovac survivors published immediately after the war, Nikolić's book included close to a hundred illustrations. Among them were photographs of Ustasha killings, propaganda images taken in Jasenovac in 1942, photographs taken during post-war investigations, various drawings and sketches, photographs from his personal collection and so on. Gathering visual material was an important aspect of Nikolić's broader endeavour to document the horrors of Jasenovac, to which he was committed throughout his life. Already during the war, Nikolić was known among his contemporaries as a devoted communist with 'a primordial, irrepressible hatred of violence, of Ustasha ideology'.[40] Nikolić channelled this hatred into an obsession with, as he put it, honouring 'victims of the Jasenovac camp, my wretched comrades, who lie brutally slain in the clay of those six giant necropolises of Jasenovac'.[41] Soon after his release from the camp as part of a prisoner exchange in September 1942, Nikolić – a trained doctor – joined the Partisan medical corps and almost immediately began collecting material on Jasenovac. This included seeking out other survivors and noting down their stories, collecting photographic evidence and even planning a permanent memorial at Jasenovac.[42] In 1943, during a stay in the Bosnian town of Jajce, Nikolić had a chance encounter with relatives of one of the most notorious killers at Jasenovac, the former Catholic priest Miroslav Filipović-Majstorović. From them he obtained a rare photograph of Filipović leading his first mass.[43] After the war, Nikolić visited Jasenovac with his teenage son Sergej, who photographed the remains of the camp specifically for the purposes of Nikolić's memoir. The precise source of the rest of the images included in the book is unknown, but it is likely that Nikolić obtained them either during the war (from the photo archive of the Supreme Staff to which he was affiliated as a doctor in late 1943 and early 1944) or immediately after liberation, when he had privileged access to the State Commission's material. In 1945, Nikolić was a member of Yugoslavia's military-diplomatic mission in Switzerland and was the main organizer of the exhibition of atrocity photographs in Geneva mentioned in the previous chapter.

In selecting photographs for his 1948 book, Nikolić did not opt for the most gruesome or explicit images, even though he undoubtedly had access to them. Included were photographs of Ustasha soldiers posing above pits and mass graves, but none showing the effects of decapitations and disembowelments, or close-ups of slashed necks. This is even though the book contains detailed medical observations and forensic analysis of Ustasha killing methods. For instance, there is a lengthy section of almost a hundred pages devoted specifically to categorizing and describing the 'mechanisms of the mobile human slaughterhouse', with detailed accounts of different firearms and cold weapons used by the Ustasha and of executions by hanging, immolation, starvation, exhaustion, gassing, deliberate spreading of infectious diseases and so on. Notably, communists were the only category of inmates whom Nikolić describes as having been *shot* rather than slaughtered with knives or killed in some other gruesome way. This was clearly a nod to partisan martyrology, which viewed execution by firing squad or hanging (preceded by acts of defiance by the condemned men and women) as a more heroic and noble way of dying. Correspondingly, a photograph showing the 'liquidaton of communists' was the only one in the book depicting execution with firearms. Mass killing was represented also through shots of specific locations within the camp complex which Nikolić and his son visited after the war, with only the captions revealing their role in the site's tragic past. The likely explanation for the choice of images, which, of course, may have reflected the editors' rather than Nikolić preference, is the broader shift, in the late 1940s, away from overwhelming the audience with explicit visual images of atrocity.

Curators of the Jasenovac Memorial Museum adopted a similar strategy. Although *some* graphic images were exhibited, including those of Ustasha killers standing on a pile of dead bodies in a mass grave, or the tangled, muddied corpses on the riverbanks of the Sava in Sisak, they were peripheral to the museum's overall message, and tended to be presented alongside various weapons and implements used by the murderers. The scarcity of graphic images was perhaps unsurprising given the political considerations, but also the fact that within a memory culture that privileged heroic resistance, death of civilians was often regarded as 'a necessary sacrifice that must be made for one's community' rather than an object of memory in its own right.[44] Thus, in terms of the number of photographs on display, as well as their size, content and prominence, the exhibition was visually very different from those organized by the State Commission after the war. As Đuka Kaurić, the architect who designed the interior of the museum explained, Jasenovac was never meant to be 'a museum of horror and terror, of the urge for vengeance and bloodletting'. Its aim was to forge 'the new man, marked by humanist broadmindedness', something that called for a different representational strategy and aesthetic.[45]

Atrocity photographs were even less visible in the publications of the Jasenovac Memorial Area. Over thirty books published by the institution between 1971 and the mid-1980s contained mainly images of the camp ruins taken after the war or photographs of the Stone Flower and other scenery from around the memorial area. The souvenir postcard sold in the museum shop, shown in Figure 5.3, is illustrative

Figure 5.3 Souvenir postcard sold at the Jasenovac Memorial Area in the 1970s (Photographic Documentation Agency, Zagreb).

of this approach. Also present in the publications were artist's impressions of various aspects of life in the camp, images of chains or shackles, or photographs that had little to do with Jasenovac, but which were used as generic (and not particularly graphic) illustrations of specific motifs, such as the suffering of children at the camp.

The memorial area's bulletin *Poruke*, which mainly contained reports of the institution's activities and extracts from survivor testimonies, also rarely featured graphic images. Death was occasionally represented in the publication through photographs of skeletal remains uncovered at the site.[46] These were clearly deemed less distressing and more acceptable for public consumption than archival photographs of fresh and decomposing bodies, especially as human bones served as both visual markers for the killings at the camp and evidence of the continuing effort to document the site's tragic history. And yet, their use, and the fact that local schoolchildren were involved in the excavations, suggests that Jasenovac was sometimes treated more like an ancient archaeological site than the hallowed place of (relatively recent) national suffering.[47]

The general absence of graphic imagery in publications of the Jasenovac Memorial Area was not the result of formal state censorship or strict rules about what could or could not be published. It was an editorial choice informed by broader ideological currents, and one that was not consistently applied. For example, the first edition of Egon Berger's memoir *44 Months in Jasenovac*, published in Zagreb in 1966, included thirty photographs, many of which were graphic images of dead bodies.[48] These were not photographs of Jasenovac, and the captions were erroneous and misleading. One showed a group of men dressed in white coats and wearing gloves, leaning over a dead body in a forest. These were undoubtedly pathologists photographed during one of the exhumations carried out after the war. In Berger's book, however, the image was said to show 'Ustaša hyenas [...] exhuming slaughtered victims so that they can extract their gold teeth'.[49] It is unclear whether this was Berger's interpretation of the photograph or whether it was captioned as such in the photo archive of the institution where he obtained it.[50] Either way, it made it into the memoir as a fitting illustration of the extreme violence and trauma recounted therein.

Berger's book was well received and the choice of illustrations, which must have been approved by the book's editors and publisher, did not cause controversy. Nevertheless, twelve years later, when the Jasenovac Memorial Area published the second edition of *44 Months in Jasenovac*, all atrocity images were removed, leaving only photographs of buildings and deportations.[51] This is even though, around the same time, the Jasenovac Memorial Area co-published another illustrated book about Jasenovac, by Nikola Nikolić. This book included a smaller number of photographs compared to Nikolić's 1948 memoir, but among them were some very graphic ones.[52] They were certainly as graphic as the ones removed from Berger's book, and with similarly inaccurate descriptions. For instance, alongside photographs with captions such as 'After raping her, the Ustasha extracted the woman's heart', or 'Ustasha beasts about to drink the murdered victim's blood', there were two photographs of piles of corpses from Dachau, which were used to illustrate the scale of the killing in Jasenovac (e.g. Figure 5.4).[53] While it is possible that the Jasenovac Memorial Area, as the junior partner in this publishing venture, did not have a say in the choice of illustrations, there is no indication that they objected to the inclusion of graphic and quite obviously

Figure 5.4 Photograph of corpses from Dachau occasionally attributed to Jasenovac (HR-HDA-1422, Z-1108).

erroneously attributed photographs. On the contrary, they later hailed the book as a 'publishing feat' not only on account of its scope but also for the superior 'technical-graphic solutions' which referred to the high-quality tipped-in plates with over fifty black-and-white photographs.[54]

Importantly, in using images from Dachau in a book about Jasenovac, Nikolić was perpetuating existing misattributions rather than creating new ones. By the mid-1970s, several institutions in Bosnia – including what was then the Museum of the Revolution in Sarajevo, from where Nikolić sourced some of the images for his book – had these photographs in their collections labelled as showing Jasenovac.[55] Figure 5.4 had already been published as such in 1969, in a large edited volume of testimonies of Yugoslav concentration camp survivors entitled *Resistance among the Wires*.[56] Clearly, because of its growing symbolic importance, Jasenovac was attracting and arrogating atrocity images, just as it had done in the immediate aftermath of the war with the images of the mass execution in Sisak. As we shall see in the forthcoming chapters, this trend continued in the decades that followed, as more and more graphic images, especially those representing mass violence and sanguinary death, came to be associated with this camp, reinforcing its status as a metonymy of Ustasha genocide.

The variability in the presence of atrocity images in printed material relevant to Jasenovac is important because it shows that in socialist Yugoslavia there was no single, consistent way of representing Ustasha violence. There were some basic obligations, for instance to place Partisan resistance at the core of the story of the Second World War, observe the principles of 'brotherhood and unity', or downplay the inter-ethnic dimension of the violence. But within these parameters, there was a scope for creativity and different aesthetic approaches and representational strategies. This was the case with museum exhibitions too. In the 1970s, several exhibitions relevant to the Second World War were put up in museums across Bosanska Krajina, the western part of Bosnia-Herzegovina where the Serbian population suffered devastating losses during the Second World War, and from where tens of thousands of Serbs were deported to Jasenovac. Among the exhibitions was the permanent display entitled 'Paths to Freedom', which opened in 1973 in the local museum in the town of Bosanska Gradiška (Figure 5.5).

The difference between this exhibition and the one in the Jasenovac Memorial Museum is obvious. Here, distressing photographs of emaciated or dead children interned in Ustasha-run children's camps and orphanages dominated the display. These photographs throw in sharp relief the perfidy of Ustasha propaganda about these facilities discussed in Chapter 2. By contrast, the Jasenovac Memorial Museum included only a single photograph on this theme. Photographs on display in Bosanska Gradiška were also larger in size, they covered the walls from floor to ceiling, and were clearly the dominant medium. But the ideological message was the same in the two museums. In Bosanska Gradiška, the top row of photographs, which ran along the whole exhibition, contained portraits of Partisan heroes, which ensured that the motif of heroism and resistance was present throughout. Also included was the ubiquitous photograph of Ustasha and German officers sitting together at a table. This provided a subtle reminder that Nazi occupiers bore the ultimate responsibility for the atrocities. In several books on the suffering of the children from Kozara, which the curator of this

(a) (b)

Figure 5.5 Exhibition 'Paths of Freedom', Museum of Bosanska Gradiška, 1973 (AJ, Archival records of the TANJUG news agency, AJ 122-25251-7 and AJ 122-25251-8).

exhibition, Dragoje Lukić, published in the 1970s, captions accompanying many of the photographs seen on Figure 5.5 did not identify the young victims as Serbs. Nor did Lukić challenge in any way the official interpretation of Ustasha violence or the primacy of Partisan resistance as an object of memory.[57] There is no reason to doubt that this was the case also with legends accompanying the exhibits in Bosanska Gradiška. Thus, despite the greater visibility of atrocity images, this and similar exhibitions remained faithful to the canon of the 'Yugoslav' memory of the Second World War.

Jasenovac documentary films and the 'nationalist euphoria' of the late 1960s and early 1970s

The museum in Jasenovac comprised more than just the display in the main exhibition hall. Curators and guides were at hand to talk the visitors through the camp's history, and documentaries were shown in the museum's designated auditorium. During busy times of the year, films were sometimes screened up to twenty times a day. Although a copy of the 1945 Jasenovac documentary was donated to the museum shortly after it opened, there is only anecdotal evidence that it was shown to the public. Featured instead were newer films, which had a more contemporary, politically appropriate message and visual style.

The first of these films, by the Croatian filmmaker Bogdan Žižić, was made in 1966, around the time of the unveiling of the Stone Flower. This film comprised footage from the unveiling ceremony, combined with archival material, namely the 1942 Ustasha propaganda footage from Jasenovac and that recorded at the site in 1945 for the purposes of Gustav Gavrin and Kosta Hlavaty's documentary. Unnamed survivors, who are shown in the film talking to each other in front of the monument or visiting the site of one of the mass graves, are the dominant voice in the film. Extracts from their testimonies are played over the film footage, and are the only words spoken in the film.

Survivors' recollections include references to beatings, maltreatment and killing, but detailed accounts of slaughter are conspicuously absent. The motif of loss and mourning is signified through the figure of a woman dressed in black, who is shown weeping, as well as by the (female) scream of 'Nooo!', which occasionally pierces the eerie silence.

The motif of slaughter in Jasenovac is introduced on two occasions in the film. Half way through, there is a minute-long segment which features scenes from Jasenovac recorded in 1945. Footage of decomposed bodies floating in the River Sava or resting on its muddy embankment is accompanied by mournful, rhythmic sounds of a slow rendition of the second movement of Beethoven's 7th Symphony. The contrast with the 1945 documentary, where the same footage is accompanied by the narrator angrily warning that victims of 'crazed Ustasha killers' will not find peace until they have been avenged, is stark. Then, at end of the film, ten photographs (displayed for about four seconds each) are shown in two brief segments, without captions or descriptions. The first set of six photographs shows acts of execution, the second – featuring four close-ups of smashed skulls and dead bodies – the aftermath. The images were almost certainly sourced from the Photographic Documentary Agency in Zagreb, whose album on 'war crimes' includes all ten photographs.

The choice of photographs representing executions is especially interesting. First four show Ustasha killing victims above a mass grave. These are followed by a photograph of a Chetnik holding a knife to a victim's neck (Figure 5.6a) and one of the photographs of German soldiers decapitating a Partisan fighter in Slovenia, which were mentioned in Chapter 4 (Figure 5.6b). In the Photographic Documentation Agency's album of photographs, these two images appear side by side, so they were probably picked as a pair.⁵⁸ Why these photographs, clearly identified in the agency's inventory books as images of 'slaughter' by Chetnik and German forces, respectively,

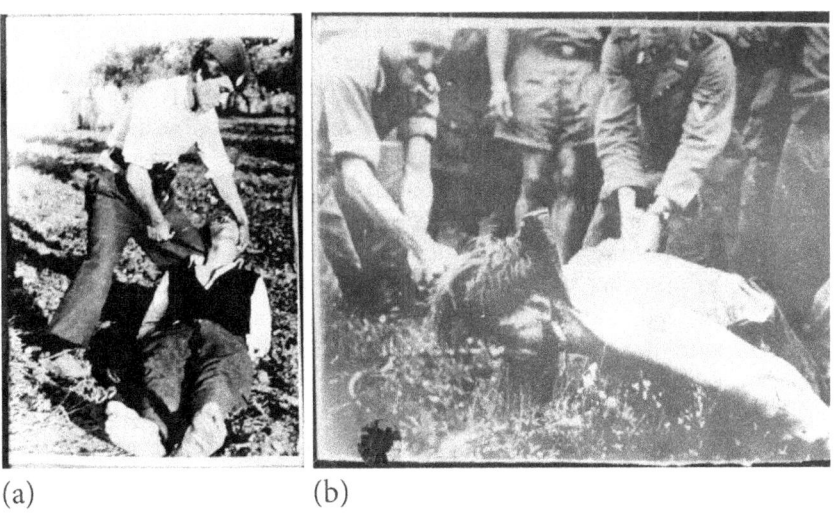

(a) (b)

Figure 5.6 Photographs of (a) Chetnik and (b) German atrocities featured in the 1966 documentary on Jasenovac (HR-HDA-1422, Z-525 and Z-527).

were included in a documentary about Jasenovac is unclear. They may have been selected in error or as a part of the emerging tendency to treat any image of brutal, sadistic, intimate form of violence, as an illustration of atrocities in Jasenovac. There is, however, another, arguably more plausible explanation. Their inclusion may have been a clumsy attempt to convey a very different and for that era ideologically much more appropriate message, namely, that other exponents of fascism, the German Nazis and the Chetniks, were as sadistic and bloodthirsty as the Ustasha. However, in the absence of any commentary or contextual information, the meaning of these photographs (which were not particularly well known at the time) was ambiguous and invited misinterpretation. As we shall see in the next chapter, by the mid-1980s, the photograph of the decapitation would become ubiquitous in representations of *Ustasha* depravity.[59] It is therefore possible that Žižić's documentary, in trying to *undermine* the premise of Ustasha exceptionalism, inadvertently helped to create what would become one of its most recognizable and enduring icons.

In the early 1970s, the Jasenovac Memorial Area funded the production of a second film, the documentary *The Gospel of Evil* by the Montenegrin filmmaker Gojko Kastratović. Initially, the Jasenovac Memorial Area approached Veljko Bulajić, the director of numerous epic Yugoslav war films, including the 1969 Oscar-nominated classic *Battle of Neretva*. However, Bulajić was busy with other projects, so he recommended Kastratović who was assistant director on *Battle of Nertva*.[60]

Kastratović's sixteen-minute film begins with a two-minute segment featuring contemporary film footage from Chile, Germany and other unspecified countries, showing neo-Nazi marches and desecrated Jewish cemeteries. Weaved into the footage are shots of headlines from the Yugoslav press stating that 'Black shirts are on the march again' and that fascism is on the rise around the world. This is followed by five minutes of archival footage of the Nuremberg rally, of Hitler, Mussolini, and fascist politicians from across Europe (including Yugoslavia), of Nazi atrocities (among them were photographs of the beheading in Slovenia) and scenes encountered by allies after the liberation of concentration camps. There is no narration in the first half of the film, only ominous drumbeat and harrowing music.

In the second half, attention turns to Jasenovac. Over familiar archival footage and photographs of slain victims, the narrator tells the story of Jasenovac through extracts from genuine and fictitious inmates' letters, Ustasha documents, confessions of perpetrators and transcripts of interrogations. This kind of blending of fact and fiction was not unusual for the period; it was used in recitals performed at commemorative ceremonies to convey, in a dramatic and poignant fashion, historical 'truths' and memorial tropes.[61] Importantly, the script highlighted the brutality and sadism of Ustasha killers much more directly than either Žižić's film or the museum exhibition. Although the overall number of atrocity images was not much higher than in the 1966 film (fourteen compared to ten), they were more graphic, and were on the screen more frequently, and for longer.[62] Despite assurances that the aim of the film was not to 'provoke fear' in the audience, *The Gospel of Evil* had a deliberately harrowing tone and feel.[63]

The reasons for this shift in tone should be sought in the political context out of which the film arose. The juxtaposition of images of fascism past and present and fascists domestic and foreign was doing more than to draw the audience's attention to the *general* resurgence of 'anti-human and antidemocratic tendencies' in the world.[64] Kastratović's 'artistically and ideologically mature work' was indirectly commenting on events closer to home, namely the resurgence of nationalism in Croatia in the late 1960s and early 1970s, during the so-called Croatian Spring.[65]

In the late 1960s, a movement developed in Croatia which began to question the constitutional arrangements in Yugoslavia and Croatia's position within the federation.[66] The issues at stake were mainly political, economic and cultural, and amounted to a call for greater liberalization of Yugoslav society, and increased autonomy for the republics. However, the movement quickly acquired strong nationalist overtones, which cast a dark shadow over its supposedly progressive agenda. For instance, in the name of greater pluralism and freedom of expression, and as a test of newly found national assertiveness, the movement's exponents began to probe politically 'sensitive' topics. One of these was Jasenovac. In 1969, an article in *Hrvatski književni list* publicly questioned the official number of victims, and put the real figure at 60,000.[67] Later, the Croatian writer Vjekoslav Kaleb claimed that 'most of those killed [in Jasenovac] were Croats' and that official figures had been inflated to conceal that fact and keep the Croatian nation down.[68] These and similar supposedly taboo-breaking discoveries – another was that that Jasenovac was just a 'labour camp' rather than a place of mass slaughter – were, of course, not underpinned by a genuine, or well-intentioned, desire to discover the truth about the country's past. Rather, they served to prop up what would become one of the main pillars of Croatian nationalism, namely, the idea that Yugoslavia was founded on the 'demonization of everything that bore a Croatian name' and that federal authorities were manipulating the Ustasha wartime record so as to silence, threaten and undermine the Croatian nation.[69]

By the end of 1971, Tito crushed the Croatian Spring and purged its political and intellectual leadership. Nevertheless, the turmoil left an indelible mark on the Jasenovac Memorial Area. In 1971 the situation in Croatia was so volatile that the annual wreath-laying ceremony at the Stone Flower was cancelled. In January 1972, the institution's governing council took the unprecedented step of issuing a statement criticizing the 'traders in dead souls' who sought to revise the official casualty figures, and deny the suffering of Serbs, Jews and Roma.[70] More importantly, the staff at Jasenovac saw the 'nationalist euphoria' as a wake-up call, a confirmation of the importance of their social mission.[71] The institution's programme for 1971 pledged a 'more intensive and modern educational-propaganda activity' that would include the 'use of suitable visual and other means of communication'.[72] Shortly after, the Jasenovac Memorial Area launched its publishing venture, applied for permission to build an extension to the museum building, and initiated an annual summer youth work action in Jasenovac that would serve as a 'school of brotherhood and unity'.[73] This new agenda mandated also greater 'visual and auditory' engagement with the past, to impart on visitors the message: 'So that we don't forget! ... So that it is never repeated!'.[74] *The Gospel of Evil* was the product of these developments, its emphasis on the horrors of the killings a filmic riposte to what the Memorial Area dismissed as the 'minimization of the suffering of the inmates' by Croatian nationalists and malicious references to Jasenovac as a 'labour camp'.[75]

The film's increased focus on violence signalled the Jasenovac Memorial Area's readiness, in times of political crisis, to turn to a visual rhetoric that would shock, horrify and mobilize the public. In other words, events of the Croatian Spring revealed that, in addition to affirming the values of 'humanist broadmindedness', the Jasenovac Memorial Museum had another, equally important function. It was there to instil a hatred of fascism and train the collective 'iron fist' so that, when such need arises, it can 'crush evil in its infancy'.[76] The idea that graphic images of atrocities were the appropriate tool for this task was, just like in the 1940s, regarded as entirely self-evident.

Less than a decade after the end of the Croatian Spring, official curators of the past in Yugoslavia found themselves once again compelled to reach for atrocity images in the fight against resurgent nationalism. This, however, was just one of several developments in the aftermath of Tito's death in 1980 that contributed to the unprecedented rise in the interest in and the visibility of photographs of Ustasha crimes. In the next chapter, we examine these developments and assess the role which the growing preoccupation with Ustasha genocide in the 1980s played in Yugoslavia's steady demise.

6

'The dead open the eyes of the living'

Atrocity images after Tito

In the afternoon of 4 May 1980, television broadcasts across Yugoslavia were interrupted to announce that Josip Broz Tito, or 'Comrade Tito' as he was known to his many devoted followers in Yugoslavia, had died. The news plunged the country into a state of collective grief, which culminated in the spectacle of the state funeral. The event was attended by 700,000 mourners, among them close to a hundred heads of state and dignitaries from around the world. Tito was buried in Belgrade, in the House of Flowers, a winter garden turned mausoleum on the grounds of his official residence. The final resting place was his choice; the man who held Yugoslavia together for more than three decades wanted his tomb on a hill above the capital to become a place of pilgrimage, a symbol of enduring 'Yugoslav unity'.[1]

Tito's passing left Yugoslavia leaderless and rudderless. The country quickly descended into a state of perpetual economic and political crisis from which it never recovered. In the absence of a unifying figure and political authority, the long-standing divisions between constituent republics that ran along political, cultural and economic lines steadily deepened. Inevitably, ethnic tensions started to simmer. One of the first casualties of these developments, especially of the rising nationalism in Serbia and Croatia, was the country's past, which became a key symbolic battleground in the bitter disputes between the emerging nationalist elites and the old communist establishment, but also between nationalists on different sides.

As Jasna Dragović-Soso has shown, the initial wave of revisionism was most visible in Serbia, whose intellectual elite and well-developed public sphere took full advantage of the political liberalization of Yugoslav society that followed Tito's death.[2] 'Taboos' being confronted at the time included the personality cult surrounding Tito, post-war communist repression, the wartime record of the Chetnik movement and, perhaps inevitably, the history of the suffering of Serbs in the Independent State of Croatia.[3] Key to the thematization of Serbian victimhood during the Second World War was the formation, in 1983, of the Committee for the Collection of Material on the Genocide against the Serbian People and Other Nations on the Territory of Yugoslavia in the First and the Second World War, which operated within the Serbian Academy of Arts and Sciences (SANU).[4] The creation of the committee (colloquially known as the Committee for Genocide) signalled not only a shift in the focus of public memory from Partisan resistance to civilian suffering but also the emergence of a new institutional base for national history writing and memory making. Around that time, the Serbian Orthodox Church emerged as another important player in this regard. In 1984, amid considerable publicity and in the presence of 20,000 faithful, Patriarch German consecrated the Orthodox temple in Jasenovac.[5] This event formally instituted the religious cult of the Serbian victims of the camp, the New Martyrs of Jasenovac. Ever since, the Church has seen itself as the main guardian of the memory of Jasenovac and Serbian suffering more generally.[6] By the end of the decade both the SANU and the Serbian Orthodox Church would take over from the likes of the Union of Fighters of the People's Liberation War as the foremost interpreters of the events of the Second World War in Serbia.

Debates in the early 1980s about the genocide in the Independent State of Croatia inevitably touched on the contentious topic of the number of victims of Jasenovac. In the summer of 1983, the historian Velimir Terzić called for the opening of controversial historical questions and for exposing 'historical facts, regardless of whom they might offend, now and in the future'. In this context, he mentioned Jasenovac as a place where at least 'one million Serbs' were killed 'not counting the victims of other nationalities'.[7] Despite its implausibility, the hyperbolic figure quickly gained ground among some Serbian nationalists, as a potent symbol of the magnitude of Serbian suffering.

Meanwhile, in Croatia, revisionist tendencies and the 'questioning' of official history progressed along the path set a decade earlier, during the Croatian Spring. This included challenges to the official estimates of the number of victims of Jasenovac and an emphasis on unacknowledged suffering of Croats. These came from the usual suspects: the Catholic Church and 'veterans' of the events of the early 1970s.[8] Croatian revisionists were dismissed by the authorities as 'sowers of nationalist hatred', 'forces of darkness' and enemies of 'brotherhood and unity', but this only enhanced their popular appeal given that, just like in Serbia, misguided nationalist myths had the attraction of dissident and subversive ideas.[9] On the other hand, it has to be acknowledged that both Serbian and Croatian nationalists exploited very real shortcomings of the Yugoslav memory culture: the figure of 700,000 victims of Jasenovac *was* an exaggeration, and Yugoslav authorities never adequately acknowledged the scale, scope or specificity of Serbian suffering in the Independent State of Croatia.

As nationalists on both sides chipped away at Yugoslavia's ideological foundations, state institutions persevered in their defence of the established historical narrative. After Tito's death, Yugoslavia witnessed a surge in commemorations linked to the Second World War. The communist establishment naively believed that 'renewed revolutionary engagement' through the memorialization of Partisan struggle and the socialist revolution offers the best antidote to the myriad 'negative tendencies' and 'weaknesses' in Yugoslav society, including the return of 'the greatest enemy of socialist development in Yugoslavia' – nationalism.[10]

This was the context in which the Jasenovac Memorial Area operated in the early 1980s. Its work was dedicated to fighting the 'darkest forces ... eager to take the country back to the times of fratricidal destruction, disunity and fascism'.[11] Initially, this referred mainly to Croatian revisionists (probably due to sensitivities dating back to the Croatian Spring), but criticism was soon extended to 'chauvinist and criminal extremists' on all sides, including those who 'do not accept anything less than a million victims, all of them Serbs'.[12] Nationalism in general, rather than specifically *Croatian* nationalism, was identified as 'the greatest evil' and the force behind the dark legacy of Jasenovac.[13]

To meet the political challenges of the post-Tito era, 'defeat the falsifiers' and put an end to nationalist instrumentalization of the past, the Jasenovac Memorial Area expanded its activities.[14] Just like after the Croatian Spring, new annual events were initiated, aimed mainly at the country's youth.[15] Several sites outside Jasenovac relevant to its history – most notably the building that once housed the camp at Stara Gradiška – were brought under the jurisdiction of the Jasenovac Memorial Area, with the aim of turning them into permanent memorials. The decision was taken to revise and update the more-than-a-decade-old exhibition at the Jasenovac Memorial Museum. Also, polemics surrounding the number of victims tilted the institution's activity in the direction of 'establishing' the truth about the camp, rather than simply conveying it.[16] Annual scholarly round-table discussions were held at Jasenovac, and links and collaborations were established with archives, museums and historical institutes in Croatia, Bosnia-Herzegovina and Serbia. As part of this endeavour, the museum in Jasenovac began to expand and systematize its archive, including the collection of photographs. [17]

The effort to protect the memory of Jasenovac from the 'assault by various quasi-historians, clerical nationalists, Greater Serbian hegemonists and exponents of ideologies defeated during the Second World War' also led to greater focus on taking the message of Jasenovac beyond the gates of the memorial.[18] As Ana Požar, who led the Jasenovac Memorial Area for much of the 1980s, put it, to end the 'profanation of victims' it is necessary to 'take the evidence about the camp out of museum depots and archive attics, and turn them into an intimate message, and a warning to all generations'.[19] The best known and most controversial of these outreach activities, which we will examine shortly, was a photographic exhibition which toured Yugoslavia between 1986 and 1989. However, five years before this exhibition opened, the Jasenovac Memorial Area became involved in another project with a similar purpose, one that, in terms of *how* the 'warning to all generations' was to be articulated, set the scene for the rest of the decade. The project in question was the documentary film *Blood and Ashes of Jasenovac* by Lordan Zafranović.

Searing Ustasha violence into the brain of the Yugoslav public: *Blood and Ashes of Jasenovac*

In the late 1970s, Lordan Zafranović was one of Yugoslavia's most highly regarded film-makers. In 1978 his best-known work, the feature film *Occupation in 26 Scenes*, was released to critical acclaim.[20] Set during the Second World War, the film examined the phenomenon of fascism and its causes and consequences, through the lives of three friends, an Italian, a Croat and a Jew living in occupied Dubrovnik, in Zafranović's native Dalmatia. The film was considered provocative, even controversial at the time, because of the inclusion of a particularly violent portrayal of Ustasha slaughter. About two-thirds into the film, there is a scene where a group of prisoners – Serbs, Jews and Croats – are transported, under Ustasha escort, out of the city. During the journey in an ordinary passenger bus, the guards start killing the prisoners. What ensues is a violent killing orgy lasting about four minutes, which features naturalistic and overstated depictions of the extreme methods of killing and mutilation typically associated with the Ustasha. One victim's skull is smashed with a mallet, a large nail is hammered into another's head, a third is stabbed and thrown down a ravine. There is an explicit portrayal of decapitation with an axe, of a tongue being cut, eyes being gouged. A woman among the prisoners is raped, before her breast is slashed with a knife. In a recent interview Zafranović explained that he included this shocking scene, whose violence was incongruous with the rest of the film, because he wanted the horror to be 'seared in the brain of every viewer' and to 'inspire in people a kind of respect for evil, and respect for peace'. The film, and this scene in particular, was a 'cry against aggressive nationalism and hate' and a 'warning' about where they can lead.[21]

In the aftermath of the film's success, Zafranović decided to make a documentary about Jasenovac that he hoped would convey a similar message.[22] In 1981, he teamed up with the Jasenovac Memorial Area, and Duško Lončar – a local poet who was member of the memorial's governing council – was nominated to help write the script. Two years later, the film *Blood and Ashes of Jasenovac* was complete.[23]

Zafranović's film is very different to Žižić's and Kastratović's documentaries on Jasenovac examined in the previous chapter. It is considerably longer – around fifty minutes – and much closer in style and rhetoric to an expository documentary. The dominant voice in the film is that of the narrator, who explains to the viewer, often using poetic language, the history and the horror of Jasenovac. Also, the authors gave the film a more conventional narrative structure that closely resembled that of the 1968 permanent exhibition in the Jasenovac Memorial Museum: themes covered in the film broadly corresponded to the different sections of the exhibition and were presented in similar order.[24] This was probably deliberate: *Blood and Ashes of Jasenovac* was meant to take the museum's message on the road, so it needed to replicate, rather than complement, the content of the exhibition. The film's ideological message was also very similar to that of the museum display. Victims of Ustasha persecution were said to have included 'political enemies, Serbs, Jews and Roma', in that order. Racially motivated violence is mentioned, but anti-communism is singled out as a particularly prominent aspect of Ustasha ideology. Included also were the mandatory themes of resistance under the leadership of the Communist Party and the liberation of Jasenovac by the Partisans. The film concludes with the recording of the speech that Tito delivered in the town of Glina in 1952, in which he condemned all collaborators, and called for brotherhood and unity among Yugoslav nations, especially Serbs and Croats.

Where the film differed substantially from the museum exhibition was in the approach to violence. Zafranović's belief in the didactic potential of naturalistic portrayals of savagery, apparent in *Occupation in 26 Scenes*, was even more prominent in *Blood and Ashes of Jasenovac*. For instance, the segment in the film that deals with life in the camp is composed almost entirely of short vignettes in which survivors recount, on and off camera, episodes from their camp experience. In sharp contrast to Žižić's

1966 film *Jasenovac*, which also gave a voice to survivors, extracts from testimonies in Zafranović's work mainly contain lurid descriptions of torture and killing, including macabre practices such as Ustasha drinking the blood of victims. Topics such as cannibalism among inmates, which were frowned upon in the 1960s and 1970s and occasionally censored in survivor memoirs, are discussed openly in the film.[25]

Also, the film is saturated with atrocity photographs. References in the script to killing or torture, or allusions to Ustasha depravity, are accompanied by black-and-white images of rotting dead bodies and mutilated corpses. Close-ups of slain victims are used to represent the brutal methods of killing, while wide-angle shots are used to convey the scale of the violence. The camera often zooms in and out of the photographs, drawing the viewer's attention to the horrors of the injuries, especially those to the head, neck and face. Just like in *Occupation in 26 Scenes*, graphic violence is deliberate, aimed to shock, haunt and provoke, to jolt the audience into appreciating the consequences of fascism.

In terms of the selection of images, Zafranović treated photographs purely as illustrations. There appears to have been hardly any consideration for the origins of the photographs or their authenticity. For instance, when the voiceover mentions the use of a crematorium in Jasenovac, images of crematoria from Nazi concentration camps are presented on screen; a reference to Ustasha using the axe as a killing weapon is illustrated with images of the decapitation of Partisans by German soldiers in Slovenia; mass executions at the Granik loading dock in Jasenovac are illustrated with the familiar images from Sisak, and so on. Correspondence to words spoken by the narrator or the survivors and the capacity to shock were, it appears, the only criteria for inclusion.

Zafranović's film was met with approval from his peers and received several professional awards. However, Zafranović would later claim that the authorities disapproved of the film and tried to sabotage it by, for instance, broadcasting it on television at a time when most of the viewing public was watching a popular music show on the main channel. Or, on another occasion, by moving it to a late night slot, supposedly to avoid a clash with an important basketball match. In this Zafranović saw a cover-up and a symptom of the general lack of readiness, especially among the Croatian political and media establishment, to confront the horrors of Jasenovac.[26] While it is possible that television executives in Croatia had some reservations about *Blood and Ashes of Jasenovac* and its potential impact on the public, the Jasenovac Memorial Area enthusiastically embraced the film. It considered its provocative style a valuable contribution to the ongoing battle against rising revisionism, and a good example of how the emotional power of violent images can be harnessed to raise awareness of the perils of nationalism and chauvinism.[27] According to Zafranović, the only objection the Jasenovac Memorial Area raised about the film was the absence of any reference to the number of victims. Although the film alludes to the scale of the killing – it mentions, somewhat hyperbolically, hundreds of inmates being transported daily across the river to be slaughtered and buried in mass graves in Donja Gradina – Zafranović refused to include the official figure of 700,000 dead. This was on the grounds that his team of researchers failed to find credible evidence of its veracity.[28] The fact that Zafranović did not apply the same judicious approach to evidence when selecting photographs is indicative of the extent to which he, and the Jasenovac

Memorial Area for that matter, viewed visual material purely as a device for driving home the horror of Ustasha violence and provoking a reaction in the audience. In the years that followed, this approach to atrocity images gradually infiltrated other areas of the Jasenovac Memorial Area's activity, including the museum's permanent display.

The 1986 touring exhibition 'Concentration camp Jasenovac, 1941-1945'

Shortly after the release of *Blood and Ashes of Jasenovac*, the Jasenovac Memorial Museum became involved in the organization of touring exhibitions. The first such event was a small and largely unknown exposition entitled 'The dead open the eyes to the living' which toured four towns in western Serbia in 1984.[29] This was a locally organized event, initiated by a group of Jasenovac survivors from Belgrade, in whose set-up the museum played an advisory role. A year later work began on a much more ambitious and consequential exhibition, which toured over thirty towns and cities between 1986 and 1989 and, according to reports at the time, was seen by as many as 400,000 visitors.[30]

The 1986 touring exhibition is today often incorrectly referred to as also having borne the title 'The dead open the eyes to the living'.[31] Its title was, in fact, much more prosaic: 'Concentration camp Jasenovac, 1941-1945'. The phrase 'The dead open the eyes to the living' – inscribed on a monument in Jasenovac village centre – was frequently used in the 1980s as the title for Jasenovac Memorial Area's educational ventures and outreach activities.[32] The phrase may have been used in publicity material related to the 1986 exhibition, but only as a description of its intended educational function, not as the official title.[33] Nevertheless, it is revealing that the phrase became common just as atrocity photographs were becoming more visible. It was clearly through *images* of the dead that the Jasenovac Memorial Area sought to open the 'eyes of the living' to the horrors of ethnic violence.

Although the 1986 exhibition was produced under the auspices of the Jasenovac Memorial Museum, its staff were not involved in its curation, beyond formally approving the final design in March 1986.[34] This was not in itself unusual given that, as we have seen in the previous chapter, the 1968 permanent exhibition was also the work of experts from outside Jasenovac. However, on this occasion, there was no collaboration with the Museum of the Revolution in Zagreb or similar institutions. The exhibition was designed – and, by all accounts, initiated – by two individuals, Antun Miletić and Dragoje Lukić.[35]

Antun Miletić's involvement in the exhibition reflected his growing reputation as the country's foremost expert on Jasenovac. In the late 1970s, as the chief archivist at the Military Historical Institute in Belgrade, Miletić was invited to write an overview of the history of the Jasenovac camp for a Sarajevo-based team working on a new, more representative memorial at Donja Gradina (the part of the Jasenovac memorial which is on Bosnian territory and where the mass graves are located).[36] The invitation led Miletić, who until then had little interest in Jasenovac, to do something that had never been attempted before: scour the archives of the Military Historical Institute for documents specifically related to the camp. In 1979, the Jasenovac Memorial Area also expressed interest in the institute's archive, so Miletić continued this work.[37] By the mid-1980s he had amassed around 400 documents, which were published in 1986 in two large volumes totalling over a thousand pages, with a third volume appearing the following year. The publication of Miletić's books was a joint venture of the Jasenovac Memorial Area and Narodna knjiga, a commercial publisher from Belgrade.[38]

Miletić's work was widely welcomed as an important and long overdue step towards more systematic historical research on Jasenovac, especially as the sheer size of the books laid bare the feebleness of the most commonly cited excuse for the paucity of historical literature on the camp, namely, that the lack of original documents made research virtually impossible.[39] On the other hand, what made Miletić's work mildly controversial was that it violated (but also exposed the shortcomings of) a long-standing principle of Yugoslav historiography, namely, that research into the history of each of Yugoslavia's six constituent republics was the prerogative of institutions from that republic.[40] Even though this decentralized and fragmented historical culture made very little sense when it came to the study of places like Jasenovac, the very fact that Miletić, who was based in Belgrade and was considered something of a maverick, conducted research outside the relevant structures, and without collaboration with institutions from Croatia, was deemed problematic.[41]

While Miletić was the expert on the topic of the touring exhibition, his co-author, Dragoje Lukić, was the main curator. As Ana Požar would later put it 'Lukić is the museologist, Miletić the connoisseur of history'.[42] At the time, Lukić was a recognized expert on the plight of the children of Kozara and an experienced curator of exhibitions on this topic.[43] Besides the museum in Bosanska Gradiška (which was mentioned in the previous chapter), he worked on the permanent exhibition at the official Kozara memorial in Mrakovica in Bosnia and on the acclaimed 1982 touring exhibition 'The Kozara Epic'. The latter probably provided inspiration for the similar project on Jasenovac.

Lukić was also an avid collector of photographs on the topic of the Second World War and the history of the Kozara region.[44] At the time of death in 2008, Lukić's personal collection – which he bequeathed to the Museum of Genocide Victims in Belgrade – numbered no less than 24,739 photographs, including hundreds on the topic of Ustasha genocide.[45] Although Lukić's personal collection is likely to have been substantially smaller in the 1980s, it was still larger than that of many state institutions, including the Jasenovac Memorial Museum.[46] As for the source of the photographs, most were obtained in the course of Lukić's curatorial work and his indefatigable, decades-long research on the fate of the Kozara children in archives and museums across Yugoslavia. Also, during his career Lukić had privileged access to valuable photographic collections, some of which were not accessible to other researchers. For instance, he worked for a while in the historical archives of the federal Ministry of the Interior. Given that many of the photographs collected by the State Commission for the Investigation of the Crimes of the Occupiers and their

Accomplices, or indeed those that had been in possession of the security services after the war, ended up with the Ministry of the Interior, it is highly likely that Lukić had access to these before they were declassified and donated to public museums and archives. Later, he worked also at the Museum of the Revolution in Belgrade, which had an extensive archive of photographs relevant to the Second World War and good connections with similar institutions across the country, not least the Military Museum in Belgrade.[47]

The authors' collaboration on the touring exhibition was in some ways an extension of Miletić's archival work on Jasenovac. Around the time of the publication of Miletić's book, the retired general Jefto Šašić, member of the Jasenovac Memorial Area's governing council, reflected on the paucity of photographic evidence relating to Jasenovac and noted that, after the war, the State Commission collected as many as '6,880 photographs' of fascist atrocities. Assuming that, like documents, the photographs existed and just needed to be found, he called for images relevant to Jasenovac to be assembled, 'subjected to scientific and historiographic study' and published as an 'album'.[48] Šašić saw photographs as a source of 'facts about the horrors of the Jasenovac concentration camp' that would complement the emerging documentary evidence.[49] Responding to the challenge, Miletić and Lukić searched the photographic collections of institutions in Belgrade, Zagreb and Sarajevo.[50] The touring exhibition, images featured in Miletić's edited volumes of documents and a small album of photographs published in May 1986 were the outcome of this effort.[51]

The touring exhibition opened in Jasenovac on 19 April 1986, as part of the annual commemoration of the anniversary of the breakout from the camp. The exhibition was displayed in the hall of the local primary school, which was regularly used as a venue for commemorative activities, lectures and workshops. Ten days later, the exhibition moved to Zagreb, from where it embarked on a three-year-long journey across Yugoslavia.

Figure 6.1 shows the layout of the touring exhibition. Densely arranged photographs, of which there were 220, were exhibited on wall displays, while 84 facsimiles of documents were presented in tabletop display cases.[52] The exhibition was divided into ten thematic sections, which took visitors through the history of the Ustasha genocide and the horrors of the Jasenovac camp.

Figure 6.1 Touring exhibition 'Concentration camp Jasenovac 1941-1945', 1986 (reproduced from 'Pukovniku ima ko da piše', *Front*, 30 May 1986, 28–9; courtesy of Ministry of Defence, Republic of Serbia).

This was the first exhibition on Jasenovac since the 1940s, which overwhelmed the audience with graphic portrayals of violence. More than half of all photographs represented Ustasha brutality, most of them concentrated in three sections of the exhibition: on the 'legalization of the crimes' (which covered the persecution of Serbs, Jews and Roma more generally), on the killings in Jasenovac and on the suffering of children in the Independent State of Croatia. The display utilized the same visual rhetoric as exhibitions of atrocity photographs organized after the war. Individually, gruesome images testified to Ustasha brutality, whereas cumulatively, they signified the scale and the scope of the genocide.

And yet, just like in Zafranović's documentary, most atrocity photographs used to illustrate the horrors of Jasenovac had little to do with the camp. It seems that it was enough for a photograph to show a mass grave for it to be designated a scene from Donja Gradina or to show an act of killing or a mutilated body to be attributed to Jasenovac. Also, photographs showing the same event (for instance, the series of photographs depicting the decapitation of captured Partisans in Slovenia or the aftermath of the execution in Sisak in May 1945) were distributed across different parts of the exhibition as if they depicted more than one crime. This suggests either that the authors did not engage with the material sufficiently carefully to notice the connection between the photographs or, more likely, that they consciously separated the exhibits in order to illustrate different aspects of Ustasha violence, create effective juxtapositions and enhance the impact of the display.[53]

The atrocity-focused nature of the exhibition was also revealed in the captions. Many of them directed the attention of the audience to the horror of the violence, often invoking the clichés of atrocity reporting and propaganda: sexual mutilation, extraction of the heart, macabre methods of torture and so on. On the other hand, some of the photographs were accompanied by unusually detailed and precise information about their subject matter. There were references to specific locations and events or even the identity of the victims or perpetrators.

Although the media at the time praised the authors of the exhibition for their 'painstaking research and verification of every fact' about the exhibits, most of the detailed captions and designations were unsubstantiated and in many cases demonstrably erroneous.[54] For instance, one of the exhibits was a photograph of the head and torso of a fresh corpse of a man laid on the ground, with a visible wound to the neck, probably inflicted with a knife (Figure 6.2). This photograph had featured in both *The Gospel of Evil* and *Blood and Ashes of Jasenovac* as a generic illustration of the proclivity among the Ustasha for throat cutting. In the 1986 exhibition, the photograph was given a much more precise caption. It was said to show 'the stabbed body of Petar Teslić, an industrialist from Sisak [...] killed in 1941'.[55] Petar Teslić was the father of Miloš Teslić, whose fate was discussed in Chapter 2 in relation to the atrocity photograph that circulated in occupied Serbia in 1941. Although the man in Figure 6.2 bears physical resemblance to Petar Teslić, it cannot be him for two reasons: first, Petar Teslić died of natural causes on 30 January 1936; and second, the photograph is one of the many showing victims executed by the Ustasha in Sisak in May 1945.[56] Therefore, except for the location, all other 'facts' about the photograph were incorrect.

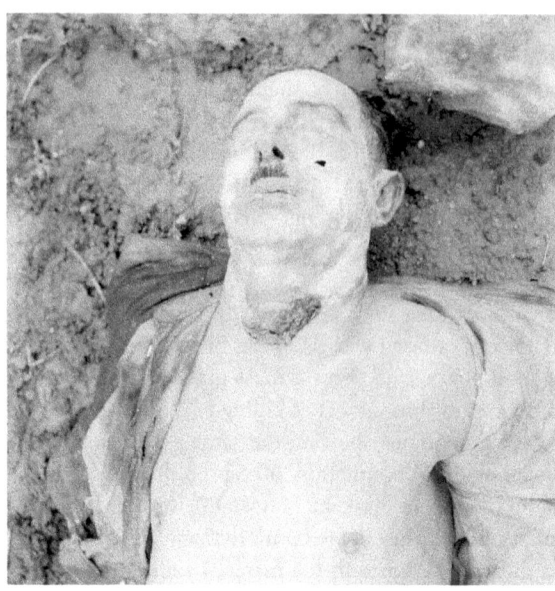

Figure 6.2 Photograph purporting to show the body of Petar Teslić (HR-HDA-1422, Z-267).

Another example is the photograph in Figure 6.3, which shows a group of six Ustasha soldiers armed with a knife, a revolver and a wooden club, subduing a victim while holding a large, two man crosscut timber saw across his neck. This trophy photograph, suggestive of the barbarity and sadism of the Ustasha, had been in circulation since the end of the Second World War, although it was only in the late 1980s that it became ubiquitous in the media, in exhibitions and documentaries.

Before 1986, the photograph was usually said to show the decapitation of a 'Yugoslav patriot', 'captured Partisan' or 'peasant'.[57] In the touring exhibition, it was described as follows: 'Ustasha cut off the head of Branko Jungić, a young man from the village of Grbavci at the foot of the Kozara mountain, with a saw in 1942. The saw is kept in the museum in Banja Luka.'[58] This was the first reference to the identity of the victim, and there is no doubt that it was Dragoje Lukić – an expert on Kozara – who made the link between the photograph and Jungić's murder. Now Lukić was correct that a man by the name of Branko Jungić lived in Grbavci and that he was tortured and murdered by the Ustasha in 1942, with a saw. It is also true that the murder weapon has been preserved in the museum in Banja Luka, after its owners (a family from Grbavci from whom the Ustasha took the saw for the purpose of killing Jungić) handed it to the authorities in 1945.[59] But this does not mean that the photograph of Ustasha soldiers posing with a saw necessarily shows *this* crime, especially as the saw in the photograph is different to that supposedly used to murder Jungić. In 2015, I was given access to the saw stored in the depot of what is today the Museum of Republika Srpska in Banja Luka and was able to establish clear differences in the tooth patterns and the shape of the blade and the handles.[60] The connection

Figure 6.3 Photograph said to show 'Ustasha cutting off the head of Branko Jungić' (Museum of Yugoslavia, III-7723).

between the photograph and the crime was, just like in many other cases, based on apparent similarity and conjecture.

Inaccuracies in the designation of these and many other photographs should not automatically be attributed to bad intentions or the desire to deceive the public. Writing about the Holocaust, Richard Raskin noted that obliterating the victims' identities was an inherent part of the Nazi project, so photographs of nameless victims sometimes reinforce, even if inadvertently, their status as 'anonymous and interchangeable units'. The process of naming a victim restores their personal identity and acts as a reminder that 'everyone in the photograph had a unique personal history', irreducible to the moment when the picture was taken.[61] Dragoje Lukić, who was a child survivor of the Kozara tragedy, spent much of his career painstakingly searching for names, photographs and life stories of the murdered children of Kozara, of his friends who 'did not survive to rejoice with me at the victory [of the Partisans]'.[62] His clumsy and error-prone endeavour to rescue victims from anonymity – including those featured in Figures 6.2 and 6.3 – was at least partly driven by the noble motive described by Raskin.

But the abundance of detailed captions in the touring exhibition had another, arguably more important dimension. When photographs are used as generic illustrations for abstract themes and motifs (such as 'Ustasha depravity'), they are 'disconnected from the concrete situation shown in the picture', and as a result, they lose their referentiality.[63] Naming the victim or victims, or stating the location or date of the crime, reinstates that referentiality and enhances the truth-value of an image. We have already seen in the case of the photographs which the Yugoslav government submitted to the Nuremberg Tribunal that being able to 'authenticate' or 'identify' a photograph, link it to a crime and even name 'the persons in the photograph' was what turned an image into a piece of evidence.[64] The frequent reference, in the 1980s, to photographs as 'documents' or 'facts', and the insistence that they constitute important source of proof and 'visual confirmation' of Ustasha crimes, fuelled the demand for more specific descriptions.[65] The reference to the murder weapon in the caption accompanying Figure 6.3 is especially noteworthy in this regard. The saw preserved in the museum is invoked as both material evidence of the depicted crime and proof of the photograph's authenticity.

The dominance of atrocity photographs in the touring exhibition reflected Lukić's well-established curatorial style, which relied on the emotional and persuasive power of photography. It was also a manifestation of the growing appreciation of violent images as 'persuasive and invaluable testimony' that 'makes one stop and think'.[66] However, the content, message and reception of the exhibition – including the greater acceptance of its graphic content– were strongly influenced by a specific event that coincided with its creation. In the spring of 1986, a trial was held in Zagreb of the former minister of the interior of the Independent State of Croatia, Andrija Artuković. This event, more than any other in the 1980s propelled the topic of Ustasha genocide to the fore of public consciousness in Yugoslavia.

Photographs as 'proof of guilt': The trial of Andrija Artuković

In February 1986, after a legal battle that lasted (on and off) for thirty-five years, the US authorities finally ceded to Yugoslavia's request to extradite the indicted war criminal Andrija Artuković.[67] Artuković had been one of the highest-ranking officials in the Independent State of Croatia, often thought of as second only to the Ustasha leader, Ante Pavelić. As the puppet state's minister of the interior, he was directly responsible for signing into law the decrees against Serbs, Jews and Roma, for sanctioning mass executions of captured communists and hostages and for the operation of Ustasha-run concentration camps and prisons. In May 1945, just before the fall of the Independent State of Croatia, Artuković fled Yugoslavia and eventually settled in the United States.

Around the time of the extradition, many saw the impending trial as 'Yugoslavia's Nuremberg', the 'trial of the century', a unique and maybe last opportunity to prosecute one of 'the intellectual masterminds and instigators of crimes of genocide, who issued the orders'.[68] It was hoped that Artuković would act as a proxy for 'the complete Ustasha movement and its leader Ante Pavelić' who had eluded justice.[69]

Publicity surrounding Artuković's extradition and trial resulted in Ustasha atrocities becoming much more visible in the Yugoslav press. Between the moment the new extradition request was submitted to the US State Department in August 1984 and the end of the trial in May 1986, almost every daily and weekly newspaper in the country published at least one lengthy series of articles on the accused's wartime record.[70] Accompanying illustrations included official photographs from Artuković's time as minister, which were used to illustrate his status within the Ustasha hierarchy, but also to provide a contrast to the figure of a frail eighty-six-year-old being stretchered off the plane in Zagreb or dozing behind bullet-proof glass in the dock. Atrocity photographs were also common. They included many of the images discussed in previous chapters, including those of Ustasha standing above mass graves or posing with a severed head, photographs of the aftermath of the execution in Sisak and so on.[71] These images would not have been unfamiliar to the Yugoslav public, but – except for the period immediately after the war – they had never been as noticeable, or as common, as in the lead up to the Artuković trial.

Soon after the extradition was approved, it became apparent that serious legal obstacles stood in the way of using Artuković to put the whole bloody legacy of the Ustasha movement on trial. In line with the doctrine of specialty in international law, Artuković could only be prosecuted for specific offences for which extradition was granted.[72] These included four counts of individual and mass murder for which the US court was satisfied there was enough evidence of Artuković's direct involvement. Crimes against humanity or genocide, or crimes committed in Jasenovac, did not feature in the official indictment at all. Caught in a bind, the court decided not to allow legal formalities to stand in the way of the 'trial of the century'. Riding roughshod over international law and the Yugoslav constitution, the prosecution team took the view, and the judges agreed, that specific 'crimes with which [the accused] has been charged were not isolated incidents', but 'the logical consequence of his overall criminal activity'.[73] The trial, and the media coverage of it, ended up focusing on Artuković's culpability for the totality of the 'horrors of Danteesque hell' of the Independent State of Croatia, including 'countless crimes against civilians and prisoners of war perpetrated by means that defy human reason'.[74]

Among the evidence presented in court were two documentary films on Jasenovac discussed in previous chapters, Gavrin and Hlavaty's *Jasenovac* from 1945 and Kastratović's *The Gospel of Evil* from 1973. Together with harrowing survivor testimonies they added an air of spectacle to the trial. The day after they were shown in the trial chamber, *Vjesnik* reported that Artuković showed no reaction to the films, but that once the lights were turned back on in the courtroom, 'the impression they left on the judges and the public gallery was evident'.[75] Just before the closing arguments, the court also reviewed still photographs of Ustasha atrocities supplied by the Jasenovac Memorial Area and the Museum of the Revolution in Zagreb.[76]

Even before the trial began, Artuković's defence objected to the inclusion of the visual material on the grounds that it was irrelevant to the counts of the indictment and that it breached the well-established rules of evidence. Beyond stating the names of the institutions which provided the photographs, the prosecution offered no proof of provenance, authenticity or relevance.[77] Similarly, there was no information about who filmed the footage included in the documentaries, whether it was subsequently edited or altered in any way, and if so, when, by whom and in what way. The objection was not only overruled, but, in the final judgement, the court firmly asserted the *evidentiary* value of the photographs and films. 'Through the scrutiny of photographs during the trial', the judges concluded, 'facts to which witnesses testified were confirmed, as were facts established by reading the contents of documents about mass executions, torture in the camps, mass religious conversion of the population and the confiscation of the property of interned persons.... These photographs were, according to historians, scientifically verified, and the court accepts them as authentic material evidence.'[78] What kind of 'verification', if any, the photographs underwent was not specified, but the evidentiary threshold was clearly quite low: on the final day of the trial, the court accepted in evidence even some photographs published in the press.[79] The judges also affirmed that 'by watching extracts from the films ... the court established beyond doubt the existence of camps where mass torture and murder of the population was perpetrated' and that the footage 'corroborated the testimonies of witnesses who attested to these facts in a convincing and vivid way'.[80]

On 15 May 1986, after a court case lasting barely a month, Artuković was found guilty and sentenced to death.[81] At the time, the process was hailed as a 'triumph for justice and fairness', although there was some resentment, especially in Serbia, over the failure of the authorities to formally try Artuković for genocide.[82] Either way, the trial was a pivotal event in the evolution of the public memory of Ustasha violence. First, frequent references to genocidal motives and actions of the Ustasha leadership signalled a gradual (and sometimes hesitant) shift away from the traditional narrative according to which communists, or Yugoslav patriots, were the primary target, towards a greater recognition of the suffering of Serbs, Jews and Roma as victims of racially motivated persecution.[83] Second, because the trial was about the actions of a leading Ustasha official, and the whole of the 'dark ideology of racial and chauvinist hatred' that underpinned the Independent State of Croatia, there was a clear focus on Ustasha exceptionalism.[84] There was much less evidence of the tendency, so prominent in previous decades, to externalize the crimes of the Ustasha and pin them on German Nazis. On the contrary, Ustasha were presented as having had both agency and 'forethought' in the planning and execution of horrific crimes. Similarly, despite attempts by some Yugoslav newspapers to maintain the mandated symmetry in guilt between Serbs and Croats by publishing articles on Serbian collaborators during the trial, the unique depravity of the Ustasha was unquestionably the flavour of the month.[85] Third, the trial led not just to greater visibility of atrocity photographs but also to them being recognized as an important form of *evidence*. In anticipation of the extradition and the trial, the Belgrade daily *Politika* embarked on a campaign, comparable to that which the State Commission initiated in 1944, whereby it invited the public to help identify and authenticate photographs of Ustasha atrocities that might help convict Artuković.[86] The media generally appeared to take it for granted that atrocity photographs 'irrefutably testify and accuse', and what is more, speak

Figure 6.4 Atrocity photographs as 'proofs' of Andrija Artuković's crimes (from *Vjesnik*, 15 May 1986, 2).

for themselves and 'don't require much explanation'.[87] Just a few hours after the death sentence was pronounced, *Vjesnik*'s five-page special edition echoed the views of the judges, when it included several atrocity photographs – records of the 'cannibalistic triumphs' of the Ustasha – among the main 'proofs of the crime' (Figure 6.4).[88]

There is no evidence that the Jasenovac Memorial Area planned for the touring exhibition on Jasenovac to coincide with the events at the Zagreb District Court. Nevertheless, the exhibition's content reflected and helped to reinforce the three motifs outlined above and, as such, it captured well the spirit of the times. The authorities certainly welcomed the exhibition as 'a form of indictment' against Artuković, and were keen to promote it as part of the broader publicity drive surrounding the trial.[89] The Zagreb leg of the tour, which coincided with the last two weeks of the court proceedings, was officially sponsored by the Coordination Committee for the Cultivation of Revolutionary Traditions and the Committee for Information for the Republic of Croatia, both important organs of official state propaganda.[90]

There is, however, another noteworthy dimension to the thematization of Ustasha genocide at the time of the Artuković trial. The rise of nationalism in the early 1980s, and the way that nationalists used historical topics to undermine the legitimacy of the country's socialist order, exposed the weaknesses of Yugoslavia's dogmatic approach to the country's past. In the years after Tito's death, many started to appreciate that the refusal to allow an open and informed discussion about the ethnic dimension of the violence in the Independent State of Croatia had created what Wolfgang Hoepken would later call the 'vacuum of memory', a series of blind spots or 'niches for "subversive" memories' that nationalists on both sides were able to exploit.[91] Thus, the tendency among Croatian revisionists to downplay the horrors of Ustasha atrocities, to claim that Jasenovac was a 'labour camp' or that Croats had suffered more than other nations during the war, was increasingly blamed on the failure to sufficiently educate the public about the horrors of Ustasha genocide. Shortly after the conclusion of the Artuković trial – which was itself a didactic exercise – Pero Pletikosa, the former editor-in-chief of the Zagreb daily *Vjesnik*, called for a more candid reckoning with the past in Croatia. He argued that the death sentence for Artuković was a watershed moment, after which Croats could finally 'look all other nations' – including Serbs – 'in the eye'. The Croatian nation no longer had anything to be ashamed of, except 'the handful of criminals who acted in its name'. Also, he argued that time had come to tell the truth. Portraying the Ustasha as mere 'servants' of the Germans should no longer be used to shelter younger generations from the reality that 'among us, among members of our nationality, there were those who joined the other side, whose hands were covered in blood'.[92] Nor should the public be protected from the full horror of Ustasha violence. Defending the aesthetic of the film *Occupation in 26 Scenes*, Pletikosa pointed out that mass killing that is stylized, toned down or merely hinted at, is less likely to be believed and is, therefore, more likely to be repeated. To prevent the tragic past from making an unwelcome return – and in order to fully appreciate the achievements of the Partisan struggle and the values of 'brotherhood and unity' – it was necessary to openly acknowledge, remember and *see*, in all its goriness, the dark, traumatic side of Yugoslavia's history. *Mladost*, the magazine of the official organization of Yugoslavia's socialist youth also called for the usual political considerations to be disregarded, and for truth about Jasenovac to be told, and *seen*, for the sake of the country's future.[93]

A similar point (albeit underpinned by a different rationale and sentiment) was made by the authors of the touring exhibition. In the preface to the third volume of Miletić's edited collection of documents on Jasenovac, published in 1987, Dragoje Lukić lamented the fact that 'for decades we lived under the illusion that we would recover from evil faster and easier if we didn't talk about it. If we left the wound alone. But that is not so. The painful past lives longest. Jasenovac is a painful wound, one that, for as long as this country exists, must be allowed to hurt.'[94] The touring exhibition, with its abundance of atrocity images and focus on the barbarity of the Ustasha and the genocidal nature of their project, was an attempt to open up Yugoslavia's 'wound'. It was an invitation to the public to start to 'talk' frankly about the past and turn the history and trauma of the Ustasha genocide into the basis for a new, common Yugoslav historical identity. The hall of the primary school in Jasenovac, where the exhibition started its tour in April 1986, was the ideal place to make a case for the more forthright approach to the memory of Ustasha genocide. The sheer number of exhibits on display, offering an unflinching look at the horror of the violence, made the more 'conventional' permanent display in the nearby Jasenovac Memorial Museum seem inadequate and antiquated, or, worse, as if it was trying to hide something.

'Penetrating the essence of the drama of Jasenovac': The revised display in the Jasenovac Memorial Museum (1988)

A year after the opening of the touring exhibition, work began on the new permanent display at the museum in Jasenovac. The idea of updating the museum's offering was first mooted in 1982, when contact was once again established with the curator of the first exhibition, Ksenija Dešković.[95] However, five years later, undoubtedly as a result of the fruitful collaboration on the touring exhibition, the museum asked Dragoje Lukić to lead the project, with Miletić as an advisor. Their work was overseen by a committee which, apart from representatives of museum staff, included Ivo Maroević, an art historian and museologist from Zagreb, the architect Petar Vovk (who designed the building of the Jasenovac Memorial Museum) and the historian Ivan Jelić.

Preliminary discussions about the new exhibition began in March 1987, when the authors were given a month to prepare the material and two months to draft the conceptual plan. The short time-frame offers an important clue that the exhibition was created from 'existing material' collected for the purpose of the 1986 touring exhibition.[96] The basic structure of the new display, which would prove its most distinctive and controversial feature, was agreed at the initial meeting. The exhibition would be dominated by photographs presented along the side walls of the hall on two levels: at the top would be a frieze of large panels containing 'the most striking and impressive' images and below it the 'thematic-chronological display' with a larger number of smaller photographs, facsimiles of documents and descriptive legends. The exhibition would also feature display cases containing additional documents and three-dimensional objects.[97]

In the preliminary conceptual plan, Lukić explained the rationale behind the proposed layout. He argued that the 'current, modest display' at the museum no longer met the needs of the public, because it did not 'allow sufficient intensity of experience'. It also did not convey 'the authenticity [and] scale of the Jasenovac tragedy, the most horrific mass grave in the Balkans'.[98] Because the museum space was relatively small, the scale and importance of Jasenovac – what Lukić and Miletić would later refer to as the 'essence of the drama of Jasenovac' – needed to be conveyed through the creative use of different 'modalities' and by harnessing the power of 'visual communication'.[99] What is more, the dominant large-format panels lining the walls would transform the museum into a 'shrine' which 'reflects the intense atmosphere, and which [visitors] will enter with piety to evoke the memory of the victims of this camp, the symbol of suffering in these lands of the kind that history has never seen'.[100]

Members of the committee tasked with overseeing the creation of the new exhibition endorsed Lukić's proposal. Ivo Maroević, for instance, praised the idea of oversized photographs as a means of 'creating an impression' and conveying the 'massive scale, the space, the deportations'. Petar Vovk suggested that 'the most horrific photographs, also those of the best quality' should be chosen for the frieze, to enhance the 'sacral' dimension of the museum.[101] On the other hand, there was widespread acknowledgement that the exhibition must never be just about creating an 'impression'. Given that schoolchildren on organized excursions were the most frequent visitors to the museum, the display should not lose sight of its educational mission. Because 'the youth is still not sufficiently informed' about the past, the story of Jasenovac needed to be told through an 'exhibition of a relatively-classic type', with a coherent narrative and 'clear, and concise legends'.[102]

Images in Figure 6.5 offer a glimpse into the layout of the new exhibition which opened in April 1988. Figure 6.5a was probably taken in the mid-1990s, when the Jasenovac Memorial Area resumed its activity following the conclusion of the war in Croatia. It shows the remaining large panels that formed the frieze.[103] Visible are eight of the ten photographs displayed on the right-hand wall, most of which illustrate the theme of torture and killing at the camp. The opposite wall featured similar panels with photographs mainly of deportations. Of the photographs that can be seen clearly enough to be identified, only one – showing a man bending over and holding his ankles – is from Jasenovac: it was taken during the investigation in 1945 by the Country Commission for the Investigation of the Crimes of the Occupiers and their Accomplices, and shows a survivor demonstrating the use of iron shackles. Others include several images from Sisak, another from the exhumations at the camp in Lepoglava in 1945, and so on.

Figure 6.5b shows one of the free-standing displays. The inclusion of a human skull alongside the mallet reflects the shift towards graphic portrayal of violence. Visible in the background are the tabletop display cases positioned against the walls, which contained the facsimiles of documents. Above them are photographs that formed part of the 'thematic-chronological display'. This was the central feature of the exhibition, presented at eye-level. It comprised 161 exhibits, of which 123 were photographs and 38 were documents. These were divided into eight 'thematic parts', containing between

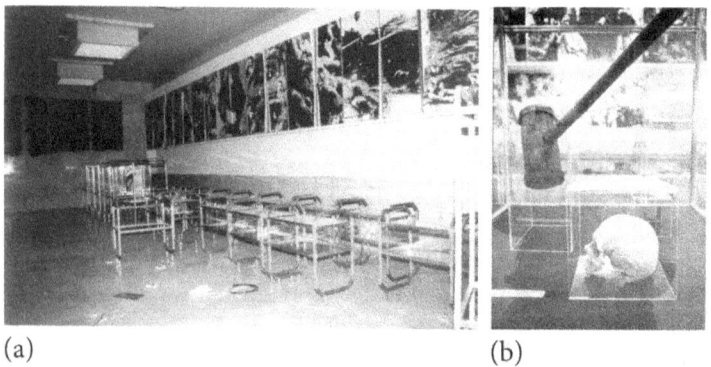

Figure 6.5 Revised permanent exhibition at the Jasenovac Memorial Museum which opened in 1988: (a) large wall panels which dominated the exhibition hall and (b) free-standing display case (courtesy of the Jasenovac Memorial Museum).

six and sixty-two exhibits each. Using descriptive legends and captions, this part of the exhibition took the visitors on a journey from the creation of the Independent State of Croatia, through the story of Jasenovac, to the 'liberation' of the camp and the investigation of the Country Commission for Croatia.[104] Graphic images of murder, mutilation, sexual violence, decomposing bodies and so on dominated the display and accounted for around a third of the photographs. This was less than in the 1986 touring exhibition, but more than would today be deemed appropriate for a museum aimed primarily at schoolchildren. Yet in the records of the various discussions about the content of the exhibition, there is no suggestion that atrocity photographs were considered anything other than a legitimate way of representing the past. The Jasenovac Memorial Area adopted a similar visual strategy in the temporary display 'Documents of the crimes' at the site of the Stara Gradiška camp, which opened around the time of the Artuković trial.[105] In addition to atrocity photographs, the exhibition in Stara Gradiška included eerie waxworks of emaciated children from Kozara.[106]

While the new permanent display at the Jasenovac Memorial Museum *looked* very different to the one from 1968, it still paid heed to some of the basic principles of Yugoslav memory culture. The legend accompanying the section on the establishment of Jasenovac identified the camp as 'the symbol of the most enormous suffering of people from these lands', that is Yugoslavs, and the place where Ustasha murdered 'hundreds of thousands of Serbs, Jews, Roma, Croats, Muslims, Slovenians and Montenegrins, and members of other of our nations and minorities'.[107] Similarly, the separate section on the suffering of children in Ustasha camps in Sisak and Jastrebarsko did not identify the victims as *Serbian* children (although they invariably were), but instead used a geographical designation – 'children from Kozara' – which was the established practice in the context of socialist Yugoslavia's 'de-ethnicized' approach to victimhood.[108] There was also the unavoidable section on resistance in the camp and the role of the Communist Party in organizing acts of sabotage and 'preserving the dignity' of the inmates. Just like in the 1968 display, the only individualizing elements – private pre-war photographs of victims accompanied by biographical details – were of communist activists. They were the only victims whose life and heroism, rather than death, were being commemorated.

On the other hand, the dominance, in the exhibition, of visual images of dead or suffering bodies signalled a dramatic shift towards the memorialization, if not sacralization, of mass *civilian* death. Genocide was no longer in the shadow of Partisan heroism; it was an object of memory in its own right. The mixture of old and new motifs was conspicuous in the basic parameters of the exhibition which Štefa Špiljak, chair of the committee that oversaw the activity of the Jasenovac Memorial Museum, set out in December 1987: 'The genocide of Serbs, Jews and Roma should be foregrounded, and the role of the Communist Party of Yugoslavia emphasised; it should list all the nations and minorities who perished in Jasenovac, and mention the [resistance] activities of the workers' movement in Zagreb.'[109]

It is noteworthy, however, that despite the emphasis on the suffering of all Yugoslavs and the genocide against 'Serbs, Jews and Roma', the interpretative legend accompanying the section on discriminatory laws enacted by the Pavelić regime singled out the persecution of Serbs. The statement that 'besides Jews and Roma', who were subjected to Nuremberg-style laws, 'the whole Serbian population of the Independent State of Croatia was outlawed' was followed by a detailed description of measures taken specifically against Serbs, including various massacres in the summer of 1941. Such open acknowledgement of the specificity and scale of Serbian victimhood – which, while unusual for socialist Yugoslavia, was neither unwarranted nor unreasonable given the history of the Independent State of Croatia – did not go unnoticed by the reviewers of the conceptual plan. A copy of an early draft preserved in the archives of the Jasenovac Memorial Area contains scribbles in the margin next to the text of the legend which ask 'Why only Serbs? Include the persecution of communists'. It is revealing that the author of this comment did not suggest adding comparable details about the persecution of Jews and Roma; the inclusion of political enemies among victims was still the default way of 'neutralizing' the unwelcome focus on Serbian victimhood. The same reviewer called for the removal from the relevant legend of any reference to specific figures regarding the number of children who perished in the Independent State of Croatia and in different camps, including in Jasenovac. This was undoubtedly because by 1987, the Jasenovac Memorial Area had started to avoid, whenever possible, getting embroiled in the controversy surrounding the number of victims. Even with the overall estimate of casualty figures, the exhibition referred to 'hundreds of thousands' of victims, rather than the previously sacrosanct figure of 700,000 dead.

The various departures from the conventional treatment of Jasenovac and Ustasha violence more generally were symptomatic of the challenges that the fragmentation of memory in Yugoslavia in the 1980s created for those charged with curating the past. By acknowledging Serbian suffering but not referring to 700,000 victims, by mentioning Partisan resistance but not foregrounding the targeting of communists, the Jasenovac Memorial Museum was trying to remain relevant in a society that, for the first time in forty years, was uncertain about its past, and where everyone – the old communist establishment, Serbian and Croatian nationalists, and everybody in between – seemed to have a different view on what Jasenovac was and what was memory-worthy about it.

Atrocity images: From an antidote to nationalism to an instrument of nationalist mobilization

As we have seen in this chapter, the transformation of the visual memory of Ustasha violence in the 1980s was the outcome first and foremost of developments *within* the Yugoslav culture of memory. For much of the decade graphic portrayals of violence were used mainly to buttress socialist Yugoslavia's ideological foundations and promote – admittedly with diminishing effectiveness – the principle of 'brotherhood and unity' among Yugoslav nations. This is an important point because in existing literature on Yugoslavia's twilight years, but also in popular narratives of the country's demise, the growing visibility of atrocity photographs and the resurgence in interest in Ustasha genocide are often viewed as a direct consequence of rising Serbian nationalism. This interpretation is especially widespread in Croatia, where the content of the touring exhibition and the 1988 permanent display are routinely attributed to the incursion of the Serbian nationalist perspective into official representations of Jasenovac. This development is sometimes traced to a single event – the visit to the Jasenovac Memorial Museum in October 1985 by a delegation of the Committee for Genocide of the Serbian Academy of Arts and Sciences.

According to this version of events (which found its way even into scholarly writing) during the two-day visit, representatives of the Committee for Genocide met with staff at the Jasenovac Memorial Area and expressed dissatisfaction with the existing museum exhibition.[110] This, it is claimed, was enough to initiate the creation of new content – the touring exhibition and the 1988 revised museum display – that would be better aligned with the ideological and aesthetic predilections of the all-powerful, and atrocity-obsessed, Serbian academicians.

While it is true that this visit took place, claims about its impact on the museum's activities are widely exaggerated. Two pieces of evidence can be cited to demonstrate this. First, relations between the Jasenovac Memorial Area and the Committee for Genocide of the Serbian Academy of Arts and Sciences were strained before, during and after the controversial visit in 1985. Jefto Šašić, who, as member of the Jasenovac Memorial Area's governing council attended several events organized by the SANU prior to the 1985 visit, later reported that he had to intervene to 'refute some of their claims' and defend the record of the Memorial Area.[111] In early October 1985, the council was so concerned about the notice of the visit from SANU that it felt compelled to inform 'the highest authorities' in Croatia and Bosnia-Herzegovina.[112] The mutual suspicion between the Jasenovac Memorial Area and the Committee for Genocide, which persisted long after the visit, makes it difficult to see how the delegation from Belgrade could have had the suggested instantaneous and decisive effect.[113] Second, this version of events neglects the fact that the 1986 touring exhibition was co-sponsored by the federal branch of the Union of Fighters of the People's Liberation War, probably the unlikeliest ally of the Serbian Academy of Arts and Sciences at the time.[114] Or that Štefa Špiljak, chair of the committee that signed off the 1988 museum display, was neither sympathetic to Serbian nationalism nor someone who would have been easily intimidated.[115] She was part of the 'old guard', married to Mika Špiljak, the former secretary of the Central Committee of the League of Communists of Croatia. Štefa Špiljak was also the chair of the publishing board of *Danas*, a newsmagazine published in Zagreb which Serbian nationalists at the time saw as unsympathetic to their cause.[116]

The reason why the simplistic, parable-like story about the sinister influence of Serbian academicians has gained such traction in Croatia is that it ties the atrocity-focused representational strategy to the Serbian nationalist project, and delegitimizes it outright as a politically suspect, anti-Croat 'foreign' imposition. For the same reason, in Croatia today, the 1986 touring exhibition on Jasenovac occupies a disproportionately central place within the teleological narrative of the war of the 1990s. For instance, during the protracted legal case before the International Court of Justice in the early 2000s – which involved Serbia and Croatia unsuccessfully suing each other for genocide perpetrated during the 1991–5 war – the Croatian side claimed that the 1986 exhibition was instrumental in whipping up nationalist sentiments among Serbs, and was deliberately designed to incite acts of genocide against Croatian civilians. 'The presentation and the exhibited material, including photographs, had a clear goal', the Croatian legal team argued, 'to connect the crimes from World War II to the allegedly "separatist" tendencies in the Socialist Republic of Croatia'. What is more, the fact that in some towns the exhibition was shown on premises owned by the military was interpreted as evidence that it was 'shown to soldiers', with the deliberate intention of stirring hatred for Croats.[117]

This interpretation of the touring exhibition, just like the account of the visit to Jasenovac from the delegation of the SANU, feeds directly into the selective and self-serving interpretation of the war of the 1990s which is today prevalent in Croatia. The assumption that preparation for the 'genocide' against Croats began as early as in 1986 helps 'backdate' the start of the conflict; it presents the events of the 1990s as premeditated and carefully planned 'Serbian aggression', rather than a civil war with complex causes, whose course was determined as much by actions of the Croatian leadership as by those of the regime in Belgrade.[118]

As this chapter has shown, the rise in the visibility of atrocity photographs in the 1980s was underpinned by a much more complex dynamic, one that had more to do with memory politics *within* Croatia than the actions of Serbian nationalists. And yet, this is not to say that there was *no* link between the proliferation of images of Ustasha atrocities and the rise of Serbian nationalism. The thematization of Ustasha genocide in public memory in the 1980s undoubtedly resonated with the emerging concerns of Serbian nationalist intellectuals, as did the increasing awareness of the shortcomings of the 'official' approach to the history of ethnic violence in Yugoslavia. Also, it could be argued that institutions in Croatia – including the Jasenovac Memorial Area – were so firmly fixated on combating *Croatian* nationalism and revisionism, that they did not pay enough attention to how the newly found focus on Ustasha exceptionalism was being interpreted in Belgrade, where the motif of 'genocidal' Croats was gaining popularity. But the direction of causality between the broader developments in the visual memory of Jasenovac and the political events in Serbia was much more complex than is often assumed.

This is especially so given that the genocide in the Independent State of Croatia, and related images, did not become the central theme in Serbian public discourse until 1988. It was only in the summer that year that Serbia witnessed a veritable 'media orgy' relating to the genocide, with 'explosive language, vast generalisations and … photographs from the war showing dead and mutilated bodies' being used to place the history of Serbian suffering at the forefront of the public's mind.[119] This development was the direct consequence of the rise to power of Slobodan Milošević. Unlike his predecessors, Milošević was willing to harness the power of rising nationalism to gain and maintain power. His aspiration to enhance Serbia's status within the Yugoslav federation was based on two related themes that by then had already been articulated by Serbian nationalist intellectuals. First, that the 1974 Yugoslav constitution put Serbia, and Serbs, in a subordinate economic and political position compared to other republics and constituent nations, and second, that Serbian communities in other parts of Yugoslavia (especially in Croatia and Kosovo) were victims of systematic discrimination and assimilation. The memory of Ustasha genocide was used to turn both themes into a source of popular anger and resentment.[120] The horrors of Ustasha violence were offered as the historical background to the contemporary threat to Serbs in Croatia, quietly ushering in the theme of 'renewed genocide'. At the same time, the claim that the history of Serbian suffering in the Independent State of Croatia had been systematically and deliberately suppressed by Yugoslav and especially Croatian communists – all in the name of forced 'ethnic appeasement' and to keep Serbia down – served to delegitimize the Yugoslav idea and present Milošević's Serbia as the bastion of Serbdom that will correct historical injustices and restore dignity to the nation.[121]

Atrocity photographs featured in the press or voluminous hardback books on Ustasha genocide published in Serbia in the late 1980s quickly became powerful visual markers for the above themes.[122] They served as icons of Serbian suffering and incontrovertible proof of the perfidy and cruelty of Croats. Also, although most of the images had been in the public domain for years (many were published around the time of the Artuković trial) they were now presented to the Serbian public as something new, as powerful, and hitherto suppressed evidence of the scale and horror of the genocide.

Therefore, Serbian nationalist agitators among historians, politicians, church leaders and journalists cannot be credited with creating the atrocity-focused visual culture of Jasenovac memory, or of imposing it on institutions in Croatia. They merely appropriated and repackaged images that had already become more visible as a result of developments examined in this chapter; they subverted their meaning and used them to plant in the minds of Serbs a sense of existential threat and the idea that coexistence between Serbs and Croats is neither possible nor desirable. The fact that, within just a few years, the *same* images of Ustasha crimes were used to convey very different, in some sense diametrically opposed political messages provides a useful reminder that the meaning of atrocity photographs is always fluid and contingent upon the ideological and affective context of their presentation and consumption. As we shall see in Chapter 7, the state-sponsored instrumentalization of the history of Serbian suffering intensified in the spring of 1991. With the onset of the war in Croatia, photographs once intended to warn Yugoslavia's youth about the perils of nationalism became an important feature of Serbian regime's sabre-rattling rhetoric, and an instrument of old-fashioned wartime atrocity propaganda.

7

Mobilizing images

Visual memory of the Ustasha genocide during and after the Yugoslav conflict of the 1990s

In April 1990, the Croatian Democratic Union (better known by the Croatian acronym HDZ) swept to power in the first multiparty elections in Croatia. The leader of the party, which ran on an openly nationalist, pro-independence and anti-communist ticket, was Franjo Tuđman, a historian and former army general who in the 1970s became an ardent nationalist and self-proclaimed protector of 'Croatian nation and culture'.[1] Throughout the 1980s, Tuđman was the main exponent of the idea that communist authorities in 'Serb-dominated' Yugoslavia had manufactured the 'Jasenovac myth' to 'emphasise the collective and permanent culpability of the Croatian nation' and make Croats feel collectively responsible for the crimes of the Ustasha.[2] Although Tuđman had always insisted that his dissident work was based on an objective analysis of historical sources and that he was motivated only by the need to 'clarify the historical record', his foray into politics exposed the darker side of his convictions.[3] In February 1990, Tuđman told the HDZ party conference that 'the Independent State of Croatia was not just a pure "quisling" creation and a "fascist crime", but also an expression of historical aspirations of the Croatian people to have their own state'.[4] Shortly after, he remarked that he was fortunate that his wife was 'neither a Serb, nor a Jew'.[5] During the election campaign, Tuđman flirted openly with pro-Ustasha organizations in the Croatian diaspora, vying for their political and financial support, even allowing their members to join HDZ.[6] Clearly, the lasting preoccupation with the 'Jasenovac distortion' and the obsession with the project of an independent Croatian nation state led Tuđman to adopt an uncritical, sometimes openly apologist stance towards the Independent State of Croatia, its history, ideology and symbols.[7]

HDZ's electoral success in 1990 is often interpreted as a reaction to events in Serbia. This is true to the extent that Tuđman's political project captured the voting public's anxiety about Slobodan Milošević's bellicose rhetoric, and frustration at the Croatian communist establishment's inability to defend the republic's interests amid the crisis that was engulfing the Yugoslav federation. But it is equally true that Milošević and Tuđman fed off each other, setting in motion disastrous self-fulfilling prophecies that ended in a lengthy and bloody civil war. Tuđman's words, actions and popularity drove the anti-Croat hysteria which the Milošević regime fomented in Serbia. His 1989 book *Horrors of War*, which reinforced his nationalist credentials and effectively launched his political career, infuriated the Serbs by downplaying the crimes of the Ustasha. Tuđman claimed that as few as 30,000–40,000 victims – 'Gypsies, Jews and Serbs, and even Croatians' – were killed in the 'labour camp' in Jasenovac and insinuated that Jewish kapos were largely responsible for the killing of Serbs.[8] He also trivialized the crime of genocide. He called genocide a 'timeless universality', something of which the Nazis and the Allies, communists and the fascists, the Ustasha and the Chetniks were equally guilty.[9] He extolled the virtues of ethnic cleansing, stating that 'radical changes' through 'deportations' and 'spontaneous migration' can lead to 'ethnic homogenization of certain nations' and 'a greater harmony between the ethnic composition of the population and the state borders of certain countries'.[10] Such inflammatory and menacing statements, coupled with the wave of threats and intimidation of Serbs that HDZ's victory unleashed in 1990, did little to counter the claim of Serbian propagandists that a new Independent State of Croatia was in the making and that Serbs across the border were in danger.[11]

In the spring of 1991, armed skirmishes broke out in eastern Croatia between local Serbs unwilling to accept the authority of the emerging Croatian state, and the Croatian police and paramilitary units sent in to restore order. After Croatia's unilateral declaration of independence in June that year, fighting intensified and spread to other parts of Croatia populated by Serbs. The intervention by the Yugoslav People's Army, initially as an ineffective mediator and, after July 1991, a highly effective armed wing of the regime in Belgrade, turned the low-intensity armed rebellion into a full-scale military conflict.[12] The following year, fighting engulfed neighbouring Bosnia-Herzegovina, and the whole region was plunged into a state of war that lasted until 1995.

Atrocity photographs and the 'renewed genocide' in Croatia

The escalation of the conflict in Croatia in 1991 prompted the Serbian regime to launch a propaganda offensive, the aim of which was to delegitimize the project of Croatian secession and mobilize the country for war. The primary focus of the propaganda was the atrocities against Serbs perpetrated by the fledgling Croatian state. Continuing the trend which began in the late 1980s, contemporary events were presented through the prism of the Ustasha genocide. The motif of a 'renewed genocide' quickly became the shorthand for explaining, and justifying, the war in Croatia.

This propaganda effort was led by the regime-controlled media, government bodies and a network of ostensibly independent institutions and individuals. The authorities published pamphlets, issued myriad 'communiqués' and 'memoranda', sponsored film and television documentaries and organized photographic exhibitions testifying to the iniquity of Tuđman's regime in Croatia.[13] Institutions such as the Military Museum in Belgrade and the Museum of Vojvodina in Novi Sad gathered evidence of contemporary atrocities, including photographs.[14] These were donated by, or procured from, Serbian photojournalists on assignment in Croatia, or were provided by pathologists who investigated the crimes, usually on behalf of the army.[15] Guns, ammunition and cold weapons supposedly used in the perpetration of the atrocities were also collected and displayed in public exhibitions. In March 1992, an under-resourced and largely ineffective Yugoslav State Commission for War Crimes and Crimes of Genocide was established with the purpose of gathering and publicizing further evidence of atrocities.[16] This feeble attempt at replicating the institutional framework from fifty years earlier, and the adoption of similar practices of investigation and dissemination, was part of the overall propaganda message. The parallels between the 1940s and the 1990s were signified not just in the alleged comparability of the crimes, but also in the supposed need for equivalent responses to them.

A particularly notable figure in the overall propaganda effort was Milan Bulajić, an international lawyer and diplomat who in 1986 attended the Artuković trial as the official 'observer' on behalf of the Serbian Academy of Arts and Sciences. After the trial, Bulajić became the leading proponent of the thesis that the failure to prosecute Artuković for genocide exposed the scale of the 'conspiracy of silence' surrounding Ustasha crimes against Serbs.[17] Hundreds of media appearances on this issue in the late 1980s transformed Bulajić into a celebrity and the go-to expert for all matters related to genocide, past or present. In 1991, Bulajić took over the leadership of the SANU's Committee for Genocide. A year later he became the secretary of the Yugoslav State Commission for War Crimes and Crimes of Genocide. He was also the founder and director of the state-sponsored Museum of Genocide Victims, which was tasked with documenting and memorializing the suffering of Serbs in the Independent State of Croatia.[18] Throughout the 1990s, Bulajić used his public profile and myriad functions to promote the theme of 'renewed genocide', often with the explicit purpose of legitimizing the Serbian expansionist project in Croatia and Bosnia and denying the reality of Serbian crimes, including the genocide in Srebrenica, the killing of Croatian prisoners of war and civilians during the siege of Vukovar and the shelling of civilian targets in Sarajevo.

The propagation of the idea of 'renewed genocide' relied heavily on the use of atrocity photographs. The historical analogy was captured in several different ways. Some publications and exhibitions included just photographs of victims of the ongoing war, with captions enunciating a link with the past. A notable example is the exhibition 'The Extermination of Serbs '91' put up by the Museum of Vojvodina in Novi Sad in October 1991.[19] The second strategy involved showing only photographs of Ustasha atrocities and leaving it to the supporting text to proclaim that a 'new genocide is afoot' and that 'resistance of Serbs in Croatia' was 'logical and necessary' because Tuđman's regime was 'applying the same methods against Serbs' as those shown in the archival photographs.[20] This was the strategy adopted in various illustrated pamphlets on the Independent State of Croatia, which the Serbian Ministry of Information published in the second half of 1991. The visually most striking of the ministry's publications was the eighty-page album of photographs of Ustasha crimes entitled *Never Again: Ustasha Genocide in the Independent State of Croatia (NDH) from 1941-1945*.[21]

The third visual strategy involved the juxtaposition of contemporary and historical images. A notable example is the touring exhibition 'Crimes of the State of Croatia

128 Picturing Genocide in the Independent State of Croatia

Figure 7.1 'History is repeating itself' extract from the catalogue of the 1992 exhibition 'Crimes of the State of Croatia '91' (from *Crimes of the State of Croatia '91*, Belgrade: Vojni muzej, 1992, 3-4, reproduced with publisher's permission).

'91' organized by the Military Museum in Belgrade.[22] Figure 7.1 shows a two-page spread from the exhibition catalogue.[23] The idea that 'history is being repeated', which is introduced in the heading, is signified in the symmetry of the pages; contemporary atrocities are presented as mirroring those of the past.[24] The visually similar photographs of rows of dead and decomposing bodies – one from Lepoglava in 1945, the other from Gospić in 1991, and of Tuđman and Pavelić attending a military parade fifty years apart – denote the 'continuity in Ustasha ideology'.[25]

A similar representational strategy was adopted in the large photographic exhibition 'Genocide against Serbs 1941-1945, 1991-1992' which opened in the Museum of Applied Arts in Belgrade in August 1992.[26] An explicit message of the exhibition, which featured 189 photographs from the period of the Independent State of Croatia and 116 of Serbian victims of the ongoing war, was that the 'nightmare' of the Second World War was returning and that 'the subterranean and poisonous waters of history are rising to the surface again'.[27] Just like in the Military Museum's exhibition, this was conveyed by using similar images to represent the two historical periods. The section on the Independent State of Croatia began with portraits of Pope Pius XII and Ante Pavelić. The one on the 'genocide' in 1991-2 featured analogous photographs of Pope John Paul II and Franjo Tuđman. Images of Pavelić being sworn in, speaking in parliament, addressing a crowd gathered in the street, attending a military parade and so on, were matched with photographs of Tuđman doing the same.[28] Parallels were expressed also through the choice of atrocity photographs.

Visual evidence of present-day suffering of Serbs comprised graphic, close-up shots of dead bodies of victims, including children. Most were of fatalities that had suffered head injuries (some showed brain matter visibly protruding from shattered skulls) or other horrific wounds that might be interpreted as evidence of mutilation. There were also photographs of dead bodies found floating in the river or washed up on riverbanks, and scenes featuring multiple victims in open spaces. This material deliberately replicated the familiar themes of representation and rhetoric of atrocity found in iconic images of Ustasha genocide, thus signalling that history was repeating itself. Also, while most contemporary photographs were presented in glorious technicolour – which made them particularly lifelike and shocking – some were deliberately displayed in the same sepia tone as photographs of Ustasha genocide. This had the effect of collapsing the distinction between crimes past and present. Visitors to the exhibition would have had to read the captions to be certain which genocide they were looking at.

Victim-centred propaganda and international public diplomacy

Strategies used to convey the motif of 'renewed genocide' in exhibitions and pamphlets featured also in the country's mainstream press and electronic media, including news reports and documentaries shown on an almost daily basis on Serbian state television. Their purpose was to incite nationalist fervour, demonize the enemy and galvanize the population for war. However, atrocity-focused propaganda was directed also at the global audience. As early as in the summer of 1991, the authorities in Serbia recognized that informing the whole world about past and present suffering of Serbs was the 'most important task'.[29] The international dimension of the propaganda effort is unsurprising given that, as we have seen in Chapter 1, there is a long-standing tradition of belligerent states using tales of enemy atrocities to legitimize their political and military objectives. In the early 1990s, this aspect of wartime international diplomacy acquired additional significance. At the time, many in the West saw the crisis in the Balkans as an important test for the post-Cold War global order. The war revived debates about international moral commitments, and the responsibility of governments and international institutions to intervene to prevent large-scale violations of human rights.[30] This inevitably encouraged both Serbs and Croats to engage in what David Bruce MacDonald called 'victim-centred propaganda'.[31] What is more, the Western press and political discourse were full of references to the past. Historical analogies – especially with the Second World War and the Holocaust – were used to make sense of the Yugoslav crisis and to validate, and contest, different responses to it.[32] The escalating war was also regularly accounted for in terms of the 'fundamental alterity' of the Balkans, a region supposedly unable to escape the endless cycle of ethnic violence.[33] Both sides in the conflict incorporated these themes in their propaganda, and cast the history of the region as a tale of enduring suffering and victimization of their own nation at the hands of the other.

In Serbia, photographs of Ustasha crimes were deemed essential to this effort.[34] It was even suggested at the time that graphic photographs of the unprecedented 'sadistic brutalization of victims' by the Ustasha should be prioritized when preparing material for international consumption. This is because the humanitarian sentiment of Western audiences was believed to have been dulled by frequent exposure to media violence.[35] One of the earliest international propaganda projects, initiated in the summer of 1991, involved the commissioning of a two-hour television documentary on Ustasha atrocities. The plan was for the Serbian state to pay for this film to be shown on 'the main television channels around the world'.[36] This and other equally ambitious initiatives (most of which were unrealized) were underpinned by the naïve assumption that Serbia's increasing international isolation was caused by bad publicity and deceitful enemy propaganda, and that as soon as 'hundreds of millions of citizens of the world' *see* evidence of the Ustasha genocide, humanity will become more sympathetic to the Serbian cause.[37]

Importance attributed to international propaganda was reflected also in the fact that state-funded publications and exhibitions targeted audiences overseas. Pamphlets issued by the Serbian Ministry of Information were printed in the English language and distributed internationally. Catalogues of the various exhibitions contained English translations of all the explanatory texts and captions, which suggests that they were intended for the eyes of foreign journalists, representatives of international NGOs and the diplomatic corps. In fact, the intention had been from the outset to take some of these exhibitions on a grand tour of Western capitals. These plans were foiled by the introduction of international economic sanctions against Serbia in May 1992. The exhibition curated by the Museum of Vojvodina was briefly shown in Paris before the sanctions came into effect, while a selection of photographs from the exhibition 'Genocide against Serbs 1941-1945, 1991-1992' made it to London in the spring of 1993, as part of an embargo-busting publicity stunt by the fringe British magazine *Living Marxism*.[38] The effect of these exhibitions on the Western public opinion was, however, negligible.

The most ambitious project of international agitation in the early 1990s was the plan to showcase the history of Serbian suffering at the centre of global decision-making, the headquarters of the United Nations in New York. In December 1991, during a scholarly visit to the city, Milan Bulajić came across the touring photographic exhibition 'Auschwitz: A Crime Against Humanity', which was displayed in the hall of the UN Headquarters in downtown Manhattan.[39] The exhibition was an attempt by post-communist Poland to promote to the world a new 'depoliticized' memory of Auschwitz, and to begin to repair the damage to its international reputation caused by decades of instrumentalization of the camp's history by the country's communist regime. In this successful exercise in public diplomacy, Bulajić saw an important 'precedent'. He promptly arranged meetings with contacts at the UN and the United States Holocaust Memorial Museum (which co-organized the Polish exhibition), with the view of organizing a similar event on Jasenovac.

An international exhibition on Jasenovac was deemed particularly relevant at the time, given the uncertain fate of the Jasenovac memorial. On 8 October 1991, the army of the Republic of Serb Krajina – the self-proclaimed independent Serb entity in Croatia – took over the village of Jasenovac and discovered that premises of the Jasenovac Memorial Area had been vandalized and looted. Windows were shattered, and papers, reels of film and furniture scattered about.[40] The likely culprits were members of a Croatian paramilitary unit that had been stationed there since the summer. Although it is often claimed in Croatia that it was the Serbs who caused the damage, this is unlikely. Jasenovac and the Jasenovac memorial were a thorn in the side of Croatian, not Serbian nationalists. Tuđman himself admitted in 1996 that he had to issue an order to prevent Croatian troops from destroying the Stone Flower, which many Croatian nationalists (including Tuđman) considered a symbol of anti-Croat Yugoslav ideology.[41] In February 1992, in anticipation of further attacks by Croatian forces, the former curator of the Jasenovac Museum, Simo Brdar, transferred the museum's entire inventory (which had been packed and prepared for evacuation to Zagreb in the summer of 1991) across the border to the Serb-held area of Bosnia. He kept it at his home in Kozarska Dubica before handing it over to Bosnian Serb authorities in Banja Luka.[42] This appropriation of Croatia's cultural heritage attracted international condemnation, although it is today widely recognized, even in Croatia, that the evacuation probably saved the collection from further damage or destruction.[43]

Like other similar initiatives, plans for the exhibition at the UN were brought to a premature end by Serbia's international isolation. In September 1992, the General Assembly of the UN passed a resolution effectively ousting the 'rump' Federal Republic of Yugoslavia (which comprised Serbia and Montenegro) from the organization. Nevertheless, work on the exhibition continued, and in April 1994, it opened in central Belgrade under the title 'Jasenovac – The system of Ustasha death camps'. The state-funded exhibition, which was co-organized by the Museum of Genocide Victims and the Museum of Vojvodina, was later shown also in Novi Sad and Kragujevac.[44] In May 1995 the exhibition was supposed to be shown in Jasenovac, but just a week before the planned opening date, the Croatian Army launched a military offensive against the Serb enclave in western Slavonia, during which it recaptured Jasenovac from the Serbs.[45]

Taking the Jasenovac exhibition overseas and conveying to the world 'the essence of the suffering of the Serbian people' remained Bulajić's main objective.[46] In 1994, he negotiated with potential partner institutions in the United States and Israel – the USHMM in Washington DC, the Simon Wiesenthal Centre in Los Angeles, Yad Vashem in Jerusalem and others – but without success. The fact that these were all institutions committed to Holocaust memorialization was not a coincidence. Bulajić genuinely believed in the comparability of the tragic experiences of Serbs and Jews during the Second World War, but, controversially, he also saw 'Jewish institutions' around the world as powerful, influential and potentially useful for the propagation of his nationalist agenda. He sought, as he put it, to 'demonstrate the suffering of the Serbian people via the Jews'.[47] At one point, the USHMM briefly considered hosting the exhibition on Jasenovac and even sent a delegation to Serbia to review it. In the end, it pulled out of the project.[48] The response from the Wiesenthal Centre and Yad Vashem was the same. Overseas institutions understood well that the exhibition was more about promoting the motif of 'renewed genocide' and legitimizing the Serbian nationalist project than about remembering the past or honouring the victims. What is more, the quality of the exhibition, whose content was driven exclusively by the propagandistic imperative, was poor. It would not have escaped the attention of the delegation from the USHMM that the photograph illustrating 'death from starvation and forced labour' in Jasenovac was in fact an iconic image from Dachau.⁴⁹ Or that among the exhibits were two versions of the *same* photograph of the pile of dead bodies on the banks of the Sava in Sisak (Figure 3.6a), accompanied by different captions.⁵⁰ Most damagingly, at least one of the images was obviously manipulated. The image in question is the 'trophy' photograph discussed in Chapter 4 which shows German soldiers posing next to a victim hanging from a tree (Figure 4.1). This iconic photograph, which had been used for decades to illustrate the brutality of the Nazi occupation of Yugoslavia, was presented in the 1994 exhibition as an illustration of the macabre Ustasha rhyming slogan '*Srbe na vrbe*', that is '[hang] Serbs on willows'. The picture was cropped to exclude the figure of the soldier standing to the side (undoubtedly because he is obviously wearing a German uniform), while the image of the soldier leaning against the tree was doctored. The distinctive light-coloured Wehrmacht eagle on the tunic pocket was blackened out.⁵¹ It is clear, just from looking at the reproduction of the image in the catalogue that the intervention was made in a very amateurish way, probably with nothing more than a black marker pen or rudimentary photo-editing software.

The failure to bring the story of Serbian suffering to the global audience did not undermine the Serbian regime's overall propaganda effort. On the contrary, the outside world's apparent refusal to partake in the commemoration of Serbian suffering was mobilized at home to fuel popular resentment towards the West, on which the Serbian regime thrived. Atrocity photographs thus became symbols not just of the suffering of Serbs but also of the world's indifference to it.

The Jasenovac exhibition did eventually make it abroad. In June and July 1995, it was briefly displayed in Vienna. The Serbian media at the time made much of the grand setting for the exhibition – the luxurious Hofburg imperial palace in the city – although they conveniently omitted to mention that the event was organized and funded by local Serbian community organizations and had little visibility or influence beyond that community.⁵² In the autumn of 1997, the exhibition finally made it to New York, albeit to a much less prestigious venue than originally planned. It was displayed at the Kingsborough Community College in Brooklyn, as part of a privately funded international conference on Jasenovac.⁵³ It is, however, revealing that the event's organizers took the trouble to hire a room at the United Nations headquarters for the final press conference. They even sought and obtained permission to record a television interview with some of the conference delegates in the iconic Security Council Chamber. This 'impressive finale' to the conference, as Bulajić called it, was a desperate attempt to create the illusion, for the benefit of the Serbian public, that the exhibition finally made a mark on international politics and fulfilled its original aim of showcasing to the world the history of Serbian suffering.⁵⁴

Jasenovac memory in Serbia in the shadow of the 1990s

The various photographic exhibitions on Ustasha genocide shown in Serbia in the 1990s closely resembled each other. More importantly, the visual material was very similar to that which had featured in the 1986 touring exhibition on Jasenovac or the 1988 permanent display in the Jasenovac Memorial Museum. Even the way in which atrocity photographs were organized into thematic sections mirrored the basic structure and aesthetic of the earlier exhibitions.[55]

These similarities have led some Croatian authors to speculate that the exhibitions in the 1990s were *identical* to those from the 1980s, and even that exhibits taken from Jasenovac by Simo Brdar ended up in Belgrade, where they were placed in the service of Serbian propaganda.[56] There is, however, no evidence to support this claim. Despite clear resemblances, there was not a perfect correspondence in terms of structure, content, or, importantly, ideological message between the Jasenovac exhibitions in the 1980s and Serbian wartime propaganda. For one thing, the captions in the 1990s were much more inflammatory. They denounced the Croatian nation rather than Croatian nationalism, and they incited ethnic hatred instead of warning against its dangers. Also, several new photographs were added, mainly for shock value. Among them was the photograph of the decapitated boy discussed in Chapter 4 (Figure 4.4). Having been used after the Second World War as evidence of the barbarity of German (or in one case Hungarian) fascists, in 1991 it was presented as proof that 'the foundations of the Ustasha state were laid on the slaughter of children'.[57] Other images were also re-versioned, or reinterpreted, not least the doctored photograph of the German soldier posing with the hanged victim.

A more plausible explanation for the similarities, but also differences, between the exhibitions and publications in the 1990s and those from the 1980s is that they were based on the same source: Dragoje Lukić's photographic collection. Lukić, who, as we have seen, curated the two main Jasenovac exhibitions in the 1980s, was credited with involvement in most of the projects in the early 1990s. However, in the case of the latter, he was not the principal curator, and there is no evidence that he had a say in the selection, ordering or captioning of the material.[58] It is more likely that the authors of the atrocity propaganda relied on Lukić's material (they may even have had access to the blueprints of his earlier exhibitions), but then adapted and manipulated both the images and the captions in line with their political and propaganda objectives.

The regularity with which the same graphic images of Ustasha violence were displayed, and, importantly, displayed *together* throughout the 1990s has had a profound and enduring impact on the memory of the Ustasha genocide in Serbia. First, the visual lexicon of Ustasha atrocities consolidated around a hundred or so snapshots of horror, which, in terms of frequency of reproduction, recognizability and perceived importance, have come to constitute the 'core' of the visual memory of the genocide. These photographs still feature regularly in the press, in books, in television news reports, on the internet and so on. What is more, their visibility has come to be regarded as the sine qua non of any authentic and truthful representation of the genocide in the Independent State of Croatia.

A second and arguably more important, and troubling, legacy of the 1990s is that images of Ustasha violence still carry connotations that reflect the ideological and political context of the war. Atrocity photographs are today seldom publicized, or consumed, simply as emotionally moving evidence of the nation's tragic past. They invariably serve also as visual markers for political motifs: the iniquity and perfidy of Croats, 'renewed genocide', the world's indifference towards Serbian suffering and so on.

A particularly illustrative example of this is the exhibition 'Jasenovac – The Right to Remembrance' which the Permanent Mission of the Republic of Serbia to the United Nations organized at the institution's headquarters in New York in January 2018. Work on this exhibition began in October 2016, following a conference on Jasenovac organized by the Serbian parliament. The Serbian Ministry of Foreign Affairs originally planned to show the exhibition at the United Nations in January 2017 but could not make the necessary arrangements in time. A version of the exhibition was displayed instead in a private gallery in New Jersey and later also in the Serbian embassy in Washington DC. In January 2018, the exhibition opened at the Delegates' Entrance of the UN building, one of the exhibit areas that is made available to member states for such displays. It is important to note, however, that the event was not co-sponsored or sanctioned by the UN's Department of Global Communications, and a disclaimer to that effect was placed at the entrance to the exhibition.

At first sight, the 'multi-media, Serbian-Jewish exhibition' on Jasenovac, prepared by an international group of scholars led by the Israeli historian Gideon Greif, looked different to that which Milan Bulajić wanted to present at the same venue in the 1990s.[59] Among the exhibits, besides atrocity photographs, were numerous works of art, including large-format sculptures, art installations, recordings of musical performances and so on.[60] Also, visitors had the opportunity to hear testimonies of survivors and 'trace the fate of several families that were imprisoned in Jasenovac'.[61] This welcome attempt to personalize the suffering had been conspicuously absent from previous exhibitions. And yet, behind the event's more contemporary feel, and commitment to 'universal values of humanity', were some less progressive or conciliatory ideological themes.[62] The choice of venue itself offered a strong hint that the exhibition was, in fact, attending to some unfinished political business from the 1990s.

In his speech at the opening ceremony, the Serbian Minister of Foreign Affairs, Ivica Dačić, explained that the main aim of the exhibition was to 'inform the international public of a little-known chapter of the Second World War'.[63] Reporting on the event, the Serbian media referred to the killings in Jasenovac as the 'hidden Holocaust'.[64] Even the title of the exhibition – 'The Right to Remembrance' – implied that Serbs were asserting a right previously denied to them. Thus, the exhibition and the choice of location were underpinned by the same assumption about the world's lack of concern for Serbian suffering that guided Bulajić's international efforts in the 1990s. Also, the fact that the 'right to remembrance' was asserted on the occasion of the International Holocaust Remembrance Day, through a 'Serbian-Jewish exhibition', suggests that the rhetoric of comparative martyrdom and the belief in the benefit of 'promoting the suffering of Serbs via the Jews' are both still present in Serbia.

Among the key 'truths' and 'facts' about Jasenovac that the organizers wanted the world to acknowledge was its unique horror. Exhibits included 'evidentiary artefacts' (i.e. replicas of primitive murder weapons used by the Ustasha), photographs, and film documentaries which were projected on a large screen. Among the mainly abstract artworks were twenty-one drawings by the artist Dragan Jelovac, with naturalistic depictions of gruesome methods of execution. These were illustrations of the vivid and exaggerated stories frequently found in accounts of Ustasha crimes: mutilations, smashed skulls and slashed necks, children being impaled on bayonets, foetuses being extracted from their mothers' womb and so on. One of the drawings was the artist's impression of the photograph showing the decapitation of a Partisan fighter in Slovenia (see Figure 5.7b). Another was an illustration of a basket full of gouged eyes, which, according to an apocryphal story dating back to the Second World War, were removed from Serbian victims by an Ustasha unit and sent to Pavelić as a gift.[65] Alongside photographic and video material, these drawings framed Jasenovac as the most 'notorious' camp in history, whose horrors exceeded those of Nazi camps. This motif was reinforced through quotes from German officials in the Independent State of Croatia in which they expressed revulsion at Ustasha barbarism. The fact that an exhibition staged at the UN during the Holocaust Memorial Week presented Nazi Germany as a civilizing influence in the Balkans obviously did not strike the organizers as insensitive.

The second objective of the exhibition was to 'warn the world of the dangerous attempts [in Croatia] to revive the ideology and political practice that brought horror and atrocities' to Jasenovac.[66] This was an implicit reference to 'renewed genocide'. On several occasions in his speech Dačić alluded to the enduring presence of extremism in Croatian political culture and called for 'vigilance' to avoid 'having the tragic destiny from the past repeated to us'.[67] Other contributors to the exhibition also spoke of the rampant neo-fascism in Croatia as a threat to peace in the region.[68] Therefore, just like in the 1990s, the object of memory was not just the history of suffering of Serbs, Jews and Roma, but also the unique and *enduring* heinousness of Croats, and the continuity in their 'genocidal intent'.[69] Finally, organizers sought to draw the world's attention to the marginalization of the Ustasha genocide in Croatian public memory, with the phrase 'combatting denial' featuring prominently in the exhibition.

The Serbian government spared no expense to bring the story of atrocities in Jasenovac to the United Nations. The state media even boasted that this was the largest and most lavish exhibition ever staged at the institution's headquarters.[70] But what is revealing about all this effort is that, despite the proclaimed importance of Jasenovac to Serbs, there is no representative national museum or memorial to victims of Ustasha genocide in Serbia itself. The Museum of Genocide Victims, which was established in 1992 for this purpose, still operates mainly as a research institution, without permanent exhibition space. This suggests that today, just like in the 1990s, official memorialization of the horrors of Jasenovac is inherently outward facing. It is motivated less by the intrinsic need to remember, honour and mourn the victims than by the belief that the horrors of Jasenovac are a tool of international diplomacy that can, and should, be mobilized to advance what the historian Vasilije Krestić referred to as the country's 'foreign policy interests'.[71]

But what foreign policy interest could the story of Ustasha atrocities have served in 2018? With the exhibition at the UN, the Serbian government undoubtedly sought to score political points in the ongoing diplomatic squabbles with Croatia. They wanted to embarrass Croatia on the international stage and damage its reputation. But there was another, much more important point to the exhibition. In New York, Serbia was managing *its own* international reputation as the 'only country charged with genocide twice', first by Bosnia and then Croatia, 'before the International Court of Justice in the

Hague'.⁷² The horrors of Ustasha atrocities, displayed in a 'well-balanced, politically thoughtful' exhibition, were supposed to show to the world what *real* genocide in the Balkans looks like, and in doing so position Serbs as victims, rather than as alleged perpetrators of genocide.⁷³

This was not the first time since the 1990s that visual imagery of Ustasha atrocities was mobilized for this purpose. At a press conference held in 2009, the then president of Serbia, Boris Tadić, and his counterpart from Republika Srpska, Milorad Dodik, announced that their governments would co-sponsor a feature film on Jasenovac and would pitch the idea to Steven Spielberg. Bringing to life the 'cruel methods of killing' and showing them to the world was singled out as the key aim of the 'Serbian *Schindler's List*'.⁷⁴ But particularly noteworthy was the timing of the announcement. It came just a week before the European Parliament was scheduled to pass a resolution that instituted the annual commemoration of the 1995 Srebrenica genocide throughout the European Union. During the press conference, Dodik openly admitted that, amid the world's enduring preoccupation with the fate of 'several thousand Muslims' killed in Srebrenica, the film would show who the real victims were.⁷⁵ The same objective underpinned other similar initiatives put forward in subsequent years. These invariably involved the creation of films or exhibitions, and, just like the event at the UN, they were about getting the world to *see* the truth about the fate of Serbs in the Independent State of Croatia.⁷⁶ What this suggests is that in both Serbia and Republika Srpska, the practices of displaying and looking at graphic images of suffering in the Independent State of Croatia remain rooted in the political context of the 1990s, and intrinsically tied up with the process of managing, if not covering up, the difficult heritage from that decade.

Croatian victim-centred propaganda during the 'Homeland war'

An important driver of Serbian atrocity propaganda in the early 1990s was the perception that Croatia had a much more effective public relations machinery.⁷⁷ Even Milan Bulajić's initial plan to take the story of Serbian suffering to the United Nations was motivated in part by the perception that Croatia was gaining advantage in the propaganda war. 'In front of the United Nations building' Bulajić lamented at the time, Croats 'are displaying photographs in full colour of dismembered bodies of victims, supposedly killed by the "Chetniks"'.⁷⁸

Croatian wartime atrocity propaganda was very similar to that disseminated in Serbia. In September 1991, the Zagreb daily *Večernji list* published a 160-page album of black-and-white photographs entitled *War Crimes Against Croatia*.⁷⁹ The tone of the introductory text, printed in both Croatian and English, suggests that the publication was intended for the international audience. It explained to readers unversed in Balkan history and politics that Croatia was the victim of unprovoked aggression by the 'last European Bolsheviks' and exponents of the 'century-old Serbian expansionist policy'. These peculiar ideological bedfellows were said to be aided in their anti-Croat efforts by 'terrorists recruited from among Serbs in Croatia'.⁸⁰ The aim of the alleged aggression was said to be genocidal: it involved nothing less than the 'eradication of the biological and spiritual roots' of Croats.[81] In line with the well-established iconography of atrocity propaganda, the threat to national and cultural identity was signified through the image of a destroyed religious temple. On the front cover of *War Crimes Against Croatia* was a photograph of the remains of a shelled spire of a Catholic church.

Besides photographs of destroyed homes and churches, deserted streets, heroic Croatian soldiers, defiant civilians and refugees fleeing the war zone, the album featured a section on atrocities. Its title – 'Stigmata of crime' – framed the photographs of mutilated corpses as a form of religious witness to the Christ-like, collective suffering of the Croatian nation. The choice of atrocity images (most of which were taken during forensic medical examinations) and the wording of the captions focused on the wickedness of the perpetrators. Horrific injuries visible in the photographs were said to have been inflicted with cold weapons, axes and blades. There was even the allegation that the Yugoslav People's Army was using illegal 'dum-dum' bullets, a perennial theme of atrocity propaganda since the First World War.[82]

Just like in Serbian propaganda, the supposed barbaric methods of killing signified the enemy's depravity and 'irrational hatred'. 'Chetnik massacres' were said to have been perpetrated by a particularly dangerous and uncivilized category of criminal, the 'Barbaricus Balkanicus'.[83] The improvised Latin name, of the kind typically reserved for animals or prehistoric humans, presented Serbs as inherently primitive and violent. The dehumanizing stereotype was not a far cry from that propagated in Ustasha publications fifty years earlier.[84]

In the atrocity propaganda, but also in the country's mainstream media and political discourse, the present-day existential threat to the Croatian nation was seldom presented as historically isolated. The album of photographs described the Serbian aggression as an attempt to fulfil the 'age-old Greater Serbian dream'.[85] What was happening to Croatia was, therefore, merely a link in the longer chain of Serbian genocidal oppression. The opening paragraph of a recently published 700-page exegesis of this thesis – the book *Ideology and Propaganda of Greater Serbian Genocide against Croats* by Stjepan Lozo – provides a useful summary of the Croatian take on the motif of 'renewed genocide':

> Greater-Serbian genocide against Croats began as early as 1941, and it was carried out by both Chetniks and Partisans. The genocide was a well planned and executed strategic military and political project. Simultaneously with the onset of the genocide, through vocal propaganda Croats were vilified as perpetrators of a genocide against Serbs, which they never committed. At the end of the Second World War, in 1945, mass crimes against Croats were perpetrated by an industry of death, unique on the world's stage. After that, Croats came under communist dictatorship, but also a Serbian hegemony of sorts.[86]

Lozo's reference to the unprecedented, post-war 'industry of death' is an allusion to the core motif of the Croatian national martyrology, the 'Bleiburg massacre'. Over the years, this term has become a shorthand for the execution, in multiple locations, of around 50,000 Croatian collaborators who fled Yugoslavia in May 1945 (often accompanied by their families) but were then forcibly repatriated after surrendering to the Allies and returned into the hands of Yugoslav authorities.[87] In the late 1980s, Bleiburg became the symbol of Croatian suffering, a 'countermyth' used in Croatian nationalist discourse to 'offset' the atrocities perpetrated by the Ustasha at Jasenovac, and present Croats as the main victims of the Second World War.[88]

Throughout the conflict in the 1990s, revisionist writers in Croatia published tendentious and selective quasi-historical analyses of Serbian nationalism, the aim of which was to prove that 'history is, regrettably, repeating itself'.[89] Visual analogies used to capture the parallels between genocides past and present were virtually identical to those featured in Serbian propaganda. Just as the latter frequently juxtaposed images of Pavelić and Pius XII, and Tuđman and John Paul II to illustrate the continuity in the Catholic Church's support for the persecution of Serbs, so in publications printed in Zagreb, the role of the Serbian Orthodox Church in the pursuit of the 'Greater-Serbian imperialist politics' was illustrated with a photograph from 1945 of the Chetnik warlord Momčilo Đujić in the company of the Serbian Orthodox bishop Nikolaj Velimirović, presented alongside a contemporary photograph of the Serbian bishop Lukijan Vladulov blessing the nationalist politician and would-be Chetnik warlord Vojislav Šeselj.[90] Also, a Second World War-era trophy photograph showing a group of Chetniks posing with a victim featured in several publications in the 1990s as an illustration of the continuity of Serbian genocide (Figure 7.2). It was often accompanied by the same caption: 'Chetnik throat cutters themselves documented their horrific crimes for posterity. Are they creating similar records of their mass atrocities in the current war against Croatia and Bosnia-Herzegovina?'[91]

The reverence of Croatian suffering and the demonization of Serbs helped cast a veil of silence over the memory of Ustasha genocide in Croatian society. This, of course, had a profound impact on the memorialization of Jasenovac. In April 1996, eight months after the end of the war, President Franjo Tuđman openly told journalists that the 'Croatian nation could not accept' the Jasenovac memorial 'in its present shape' and that a new approach to the site's history was required.[92] The new approach involved transforming Jasenovac into a symbol of Croatian patriotism and suffering. Tuđman envisaged two parallel memorials at the site, one to all those who perished in Jasenovac because they 'opposed Nazi-fascist ideology' and another honouring the 'victims of Communism who were killed in Jasenovac as well as those whose remains have been found in other mass grave sites'.[93] The suggestion that Jasenovac was a place of communist as well as fascist oppression was based on an unsubstantiated claim dating back to the 1970s that a communist-run camp existed in Jasenovac between 1945 and 1948. Tuđman even linked the suffering of Croats at this (non-existent) facility to Bleiburg, when he argued that, after the war, Jasenovac was 'a camp for those who returned from Bleiburg'.[94] With the two memorials in place, Jasenovac would effectively become a site of national unity and reconciliation, a place where Croats would come together to honour the sacrifices of (Croatian) antifascists but also of Ustasha and Domobrani fighters, all of whom, it was claimed, fought and laid their lives for Croatia 'in their own way'.[95] Crucially, in this pantheon of Croatian suffering, Tuđman envisaged a third, no less controversial memorial, to 'victims of the recently concluded war for the liberation of Croatia from Serbian aggression'.[96] Tying the 'Homeland War' to Jasenovac in this way was a tendentious and cynical attempt to undermine the Serbs' claim to victimhood:

institutions around the world and make Jasenovac an intrinsic part of 'European cultural heritage'.[105] Also, they wanted the exhibition to offer a radically *new* way of looking at Jasenovac: an early conceptual plan mentioned the slogan 'Truth – but in a different way' as an informal moto of the exhibition.[106]

What was the 'truth' that the museum was hoping to showcase, and what was it 'different' from? The exhibition's main aim certainly wasn't to admonish the revisionism and denialism of the Tuđman era, or to confront the enduring nationalist myths in Croatia. These were barely mentioned as relevant concerns in the museum's conceptual plan and rationale. Rather, the exhibition was envisaged first and foremost as a corrective to, and repudiation of, the atrocity-focused representational strategy which defined the museum's work in the 1980s.

The importance attributed to differentiating the new exhibition from its previous incarnations was apparent in the fact that the exhibition hall was given a radical makeover. Adopting the approach pioneered by the USHMM, and to create what Edward T. Linenthal called the 'mood of memory', the once well-lit open space of the museum's exhibition hall was converted into a claustrophobic maze with blackened uneven and slanting walls, and no central lighting.[107] This new design, with its dark and oppressive atmosphere, is meant to provoke in visitors a sense of unease, disorientation and rupture. The sense of disorientation is enhanced further by the absence of a logical route through the exhibition. The display does not follow a clear chronological narrative, which, as we have seen in previous chapters, had always been an essential feature of the Jasenovac Memorial Museum's 'methodical-didactic' approach to representing the past. Instead, visitors are encouraged to wonder through meandering hallways and move back and forth between different stages of the victims' lives: their 'existence before the deportation, their life in the camp and the place of execution'. This is meant to convey the 'fragile boundary between life and death'.[108]

Eschewing narrative in favour of visceral experience was not just an aesthetic or artistic choice. It was a convenient way of avoiding confrontation with the issue of what Jasenovac actually was and why it is worth remembering. The exhibited 'artefacts, photographs, documents and other museum material' are meant to speak for themselves, with deliberately scant descriptive captions conveying only 'specific content or idea, but without the authors of the display interpreting and imposing specific ideological and emotive frameworks of meaning'.[109] In other words, the display offers impressions and sensations, but little in the way of much needed historical interpretation, contextualization or critique.

The discontinuity with previous museum displays was signified most directly in the decision to exclude atrocity photographs. The museum's director Nataša Jovičić was adamant from the start that photographs of slaughter, of rotting bodies or of mass graves would not feature in the main display at all. Instead, a selection would be made available through a computerized database accessible to visitors in the museum's visitor centre. One reason for this decision, which was seldom explicitly stated, but never concealed or denied, was that the manner in which Serbian nationalists instrumentalized atrocity photographs to 'generate and inspire' war crimes against Croats during the war of the 1990s rendered them unusable as vessels of memory.[110] Another reason was that atrocity images were deemed an outdated and ethically compromised means of representing victims, whose presence in the display would amount to 'renewed violence' against the dead.[111] In particular, their use was seen as incompatible with the preferred 'Western model of representing the Holocaust' which focuses on 'the victim as an individual'.[112] To enable visitors to 'feel and comprehend the horrors of Ustasha crimes' and empathize with the victims, the museum would highlight that 'the crime was committed against tens of thousands of *individuals* with a name and surname', not the 'anonymous mass' of victims portrayed in atrocity photographs.[113]

What does the 'victim as an individual' look like?

In the Jasenovac exhibition, the personalization of suffering implicit in the idea of the 'victim as an individual' is manifested in four ways. First, suspended from steel structures built into the ceiling above the entire museum space are large glass panels containing names of over 80,000 victims. Names of the dead are displayed also on a screen in a continuous loop. Second, emulating the aesthetic of the 'Tower of Faces' at the USHMM and the 'Hall of Names' at Yad Vashem – where victims' faces, names and personal stories are used to overcome the 'fascination with the technique of destruction' – the Jasenovac exhibition features sixty-eight private photographs of individual victims and survivors taken before arrest and deportation or, in a small number of cases, after the war.[114] These are accompanied with basic information about each person's place of birth, profession and ethnicity.[115] Third, camp experience is conveyed through the voices and faces of survivors, whose audiovisual testimonies feature prominently in the exhibition. Finally, most of the artefacts among the exhibits are *personal* possessions of the inmates: blankets, watches, clothes, keys, ashtrays and so on.

An important outcome of these individualizing elements, which foreground 'individual human destinies' and whose aim is the 'affirmation of life', is that they, somewhat conveniently, detract from the genocidal aspects of the Ustasha project. The focus on the 'victim as an individual' obscures the differences between Serbs, Croats, Jews or Roma in terms of why, by whom and in what numbers they were brought to Jasenovac and killed. Thus, although the horror of Ustasha crimes is not denied – Jasenovac is said to have been 'above all a death camp' in which killing was carried out 'in the most primitive way: throat cutting, beatings, starvation and hard labour' – the word 'genocide' is hardly mentioned.[116] One caption even lists *all* victims, including Croatian antifascists, as victims of 'crimes of genocide'. Similarly, there is no reference anywhere in the exhibition to the broader reign of terror against Serbs, or to the reasons *why* they were targeted. On the contrary, most mentions of the persecution of Serbs are worded in a way that suggests that other 'undesirable elements', including Croatian antifascists, were targeted in a similar way and, therefore, that there was nothing distinctive about their fate.

An additional problem is that the approach to victims 'as individuals' is not consistently applied. For instance, the only category of victims which is dealt with separately in the exhibition is the Roma. The rationale for singling out their fate was that 'none of the discriminated against racial or national communities were persecuted as systematically and consistently as the Roma'.[117] This is a reference to the fact that the mortality rate among the Roma in Jasenovac was close to a 100 per cent. Also, the separate section was a way of compensating for the fact that no photographs of Roma from before the war could be found for the display of portraits of individual victims, and the fact that Roma voices were absent from the survivor testimonies featured in the exhibition.

The section on Roma comprises a handful of exhibits: a brief descriptive legend, a copy of an Ustasha document and four photographs. The latter are Ustasha propaganda images taken in late summer of 1942 in Uštica, part of the Jasenovac camp where the Roma were interned. Two of the photographs are of identically dressed children (e.g. Figure 7.3), who, in one case, are identified solely by their affiliation to a specific subgroup of the Roma people. The description states: 'Uštica, the Gypsy camp, September 1942, a little Roma girl from Bajaši [Boyash] tribe'.[118] The reference to the 'tribe' directly contradicts the museum's commitment to representing victims as individuals. What is more, nowhere is it stated that these are Ustasha propaganda photographs or that the information about the girls' 'tribal' affiliation was probably collected as relevant *by the photographer* who sought to capture the racialized 'romance of the exotic'.[119] Thus, by inviting visitors to visualize the Roma in Jasenovac through the colonial, 'ethnographic eye' of the propaganda photographer, the exhibition normalizes the perpetrators' othering gaze, and does little to subvert or overcome the 'Gypsy fetish' that still pervades visual representations of the Roma.[120]

A similar problem is to be found in the portrayal of Serbs from western Bosnia, of whom tens of thousands were rounded up and sent to Jasenovac during the Kozara offensive in the summer of 1942. One of the screens in the exhibition shows, on a continuous loop and without any accompanying contextual information, nine photographs of columns of captured men and women – 'Serbian Orthodox population from Kozara' – being escorted to concentration camps by armed Ustasha, Domobrani

Figure 7.3 Photograph of Roma in Jasenovac featured in the new permanent display at the Jasenovac Memorial Museum (courtesy of the Jasenovac Memorial Museum).

Figure 7.4 Deportation to Ustasha camps of Serb population from Kozara (courtesy of the Jasenovac Memorial Museum).

or German soldiers (e.g. Figure 7.4). There is little in these photographs – the only ones in the exhibition that represent the suffering of Serbian civilians – that 'personalizes' the victims. On the contrary, they are reduced to the kind of 'anonymous mass' that the authors were committed to *not* showing. More importantly, as we have seen in Chapter 2, photographs of such orderly columns of prisoners were created by the Ustasha as visual evidence of the triumph over the Serbs, and were used in propaganda literature to reinforce racial stereotypes about the Serbian population and deny reports of mass slaughter. As in the case of the Roma inmates, by saying nothing about the provenance of the photographs or their role in the dehumanization and humiliation of victims, the exhibition allows perpetrators to visually define the object of memory.[121] Not to mention that such uncritical use of perpetrator-generated photographs directly contradicts the museum's proclaimed commitment to not showing the victims 'from the perspective of the executioner'.[122]

The argument here is not that these images should have been excluded from the exhibition, but that they should have been framed, presented and contextualized differently. More importantly, their use calls into question the rationale behind the complete absence of photographs of atrocities. Why is photographic depiction of *humiliated* men and women, with their fear and desperation laid bare before the banal gaze of the public, any less a manifestation of 'renewed violence' against them, than photographs showing executions or their aftermath?

More importantly, the content of the Jasenovac Memorial Museum's new display was informed by the assumption that a 'victim-focused' approach characteristic of the contemporary, 'Western model of memory' precludes the use of atrocity photographs. And yet, this is not the case. While contemporary Holocaust museums, including those which inspired the new display in Jasenovac, do generally take a measured approach to shocking or graphic portrayals of violence, few if any show none. Instead, institutions seek to strike a balance between, on the one hand, the demands of 'commemorative civility' and the mandate to remember the past in ethically appropriate ways and, on the other hand, the 'educational imperative' that calls for an accurate historical representation of past horrors.[123] There is no evidence that the creators of the Jasenovac exhibition even tried to negotiate between the two competing demands. Besides, the restrained use of atrocity photographs in contemporary Holocaust museums is not informed solely by abstract principles regarding public decency or the ethics of spectatorship. It reflects the wishes of Holocaust survivors and descendants of victims, who have fought long and hard to reclaim the story of the Holocaust from the once dominant images of anonymous 'corpses and skeletal prisoners'.[124] The authors of the Jasenovac exhibition imported these concerns – which reflect a specific trajectory of Holocaust representation, primarily in the United States – and superimposed them, unthinkingly, on the Croatian cultural and political context. A genuine adoption of the 'Western model of memory' would have involved greater engagement with representatives of Serbian, Jewish and Roma communities, and proper consultation on how best to represent their suffering.

There are doubts about whether the authors of the Jasenovac museum exhibition took adequate notice of the views of the descendants of victims. In 2004, the draft conceptual plan for the exhibition was sent out to reviewers, among them several historians and representatives of Serbian and Jewish communities in Croatia. One of the reviewers was Đuro Zatezalo, a historian who at the time was working on several book projects on the Ustasha genocide.[125] He was also the representative of the Serbian community in Croatia on the governing council of the Jasenovac Memorial Area.[126] Zatezalo submitted extensive feedback on the conceptual plan, in which he praised the authors' efforts, but argued that the exhibition needed to be supplemented with additional 'photographs, documents and extracts from testimonies'. Foreseeing criticisms that would later be directed at the exhibition, he pointed to the 'uneven treatment' of different ethnic groups, and the fact that the scale and scope of the genocide against Serbs was not adequately represented.[127] He also called for the inclusion of atrocity photographs and other evidence of Ustasha brutality. Five pages of 'reviewer's suggestions' contained many references to specific photographs which Zatezalo felt should be included. While not all of these suggestions were reasonable – most, in fact, reflected the misattributions and misinterpretations explored in previous chapters – Zatezalo was making an important, and valid, broader point. To avoid 'creating doubt' in the minds of visitors regarding the nature of the camp, the museum had to show Jasenovac 'the way it was'. This was necessary in order 'to avoid, once again, reopening the wounds of those who lost their loved ones in the Jasenovac camp'.[128]

The authors of the exhibition disregarded Zatezalo's concerns. Unwavering commitment to not showing atrocity photographs prevented them from engaging with what it means to show Jasenovac 'the way it was', or from considering why, after a decade of denials and trivialization of the Ustasha genocide in Tuđman's Croatia, this was such an important matter to so many survivors and descendants of victims. Instead, once all the reviews were in, Nataša Jovičić commissioned the right-wing historian Mario Jareb to wade through the different and often conflicting comments from reviewers and advise on the way forward. In his report, Jareb concluded that the authors of the exhibition were not obliged to take on board any of the 'purely advisory' recommendations. He also declared that the conceptual plan was 'well thought-through' and that the focus on the 'victim as an individual' was the correct approach to take.¹²⁹ Importantly, Jareb singled out Zatezalo's comments for special criticism and questioned his competence and scholarly credentials. This censure was, in some respects, less about Zatezalo personally than about excoriating the atrocity-focused perspective on Jasenovac and legitimizing its omission from the exhibition. In his comments on the final draft of the exhibition, which he completed on 6 February 2006 – the same day that Jareb submitted his report – Đuro Zatezalo could only observe, with a mixture of resignation and regret, that none of his recommendations had been taken up.¹³⁰ His plea that, even at this late hour, things could still be resolved with a 'phone call between the authors and the reviewers' went unheeded.

Something old, something new: The echoes of the 1960s and 1970s in the new Jasenovac exhibition

The dilemma that the authors of the new display in the Jasenovac museum faced in the early 2000s was not new. As we have seen in Chapter 5, the memorialization of Jasenovac in socialist Yugoslavia was also informed by the need to remember the camp's tragic history in a way that downplayed the genocidal nature of the crimes and overlooked Ustasha exceptionalism. It should, therefore, come as no surprise that the 2006 exhibition revived some of the representational strategies dating back to that that era. In other words, to distance itself from the maligned, atrocity-focused iconography of the 1980s, the new display embraced some visual elements from the late 1960s and 1970s, and embellished them with motifs of the Croatian take on the 'Western model of memory'.

For instance, despite the long-standing contempt for Bogdanović's Stone Flower among Croatian nationalists, in the 2000s Croatia rediscovered an affinity for the monument. Recall that when it was constructed in the 1960s, the main appeal of the monument's abstract form and life-affirming message was that it *did not* evoke 'images of horror and disgust'.¹³¹ As such it allowed the politically sensitive aspects of the history of Jasenovac to be marginalized. After 2000, praises lavished on the monument's artistic merit, complex symbolism and 'profound humanist message' were a way of once again aestheticizing and de-historicizing Jasenovac, and diverting attention from what happened there.¹³² Importantly, the Stone Flower no longer stood for the common fate of Yugoslav nations, but for more generic values to which post-Tuđman Croatia was keen to demonstrate allegiance: non-violence, tolerance, democracy, human rights and so on.¹³³ More controversially, the insistence that the Jasenovac memorial teaches about 'all forms of violence and genocide', and condemns not just Ustasha ideology but 'every totalitarian ideology and ideologization', opened the space for linking Jasenovac to communist crimes or those perpetrated by Serbs in the 1990s.¹³⁴

Also, in the museum display, horrors of Jasenovac are represented obliquely, through photographs of places. Included are images of landscapes: the 'Poplar of Horror' in Donja Gradina, a large tree under which torture and executions took place (Figure 7.5a) and the 'Grove of Sighs', the location from where inmates were transported by barge across the river to the execution grounds (Figure 7.5b). As we have seen in Chapter 5, images of landscapes that hint at the violence without showing it have been used extensively during the socialist period.[135] This representational strategy first featured in Nikola Nikolić's 1948 book on Jasenovac and was later adopted in the 1968 display in the museum.[136] The new exhibition also includes images taken by Partisan photographers in Stara Gradiška in April 1945, shortly after they entered the abandoned camp. None of these are of mutilated bodies of the camp's last inmates. Instead of showing the horrors of the killings, there is a photograph of a bloodied staircase which alludes to the violence (Figure 7.6a) and another of inmates' possessions scattered around one of the cells (Figure 7.6b). The latter, focusing on physical remnants, draws on the iconic

Figure 7.5 Landscapes as a proxy for atrocities: (a) 'Poplar of Horror' in Donja Gradina and (b) 'Grove of Sighs' in Jasenovac (courtesy of the Jasenovac Memorial Museum).

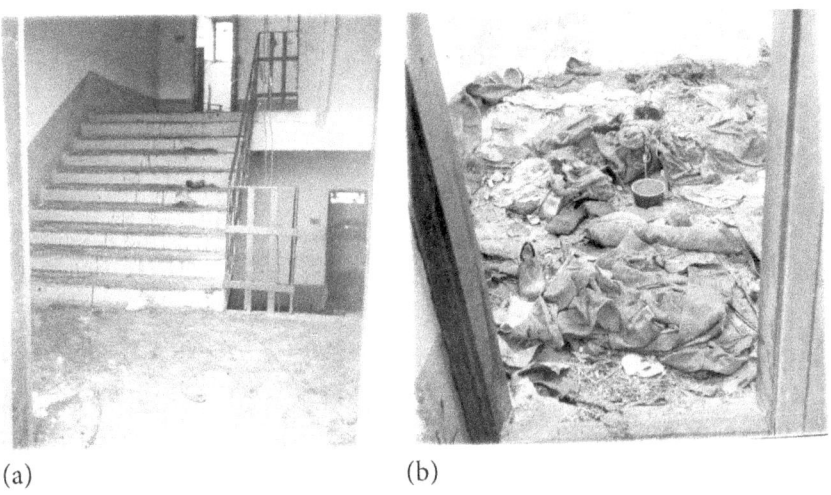

Figure 7.6 Scenes from Stara Gradiška, April 1945: (a) bloodied staircase in the main building and (b) a pile of inmates' possessions (courtesy of the Jasenovac Memorial Museum).

mode of representation deployed in contemporary Holocaust museums, where piles of objects, or photographs of them, are used to personalize suffering and signify the 'brokenness of lives'.[137]

Finally, just like in socialist Yugoslavia, the exhibition externalizes the responsibility for Ustasha crimes to foreign occupiers, especially Nazi Germany. The display features seven photographs of occupying troops marching through Croatian cities, or of Ustasha in the company of German or Italian officials. The fact that Ustasha leaders are visible *only* in the company of foreign officials presents the Independent State of Croatia as a Nazi satellite and therefore as an entity of diminished agency and accountability. Particularly prominent is the photograph of Ante Pavelić being greeted by Hitler on the steps of the Berghof, the German leader's residence in Berchtesgaden, in June 1941 (Figure 7.7). According to the exhibition's conceptual plan, this photograph was placed on the central axis of the display in order to emphasize 'the dependence of the Independent State of Croatia on the Third Reich'.[138] The legend accompanying the photograph explains that during the visit, Hitler gave 'full support for Pavelić's genocidal policy towards the Serb population'. The composition of the image, which shows Hitler in a dominant position, looking down towards (and on) the Ustasha leader, is suggestive of where the power and responsibility lie. It is noteworthy also that the legend describes 'Dr. Ante Pavelić' simply as the 'leader of the Ustasha movement' and the 'head of the Independent State of Croatia' who 'emigrated to Spain' after the war. There is no reference to Pavelić's culpability for hundreds of thousands of deaths or to the inherently criminal nature

Figure 7.7 Hitler giving his 'full support' to the genocide against Serbs, Jasenovac Memorial Museum (author's personal collection).

of the state which he led. This is an important departure from how the Ustasha were represented in socialist Yugoslavia. Clearly, in their effort to remain 'objective' and avoid imposing on visitors 'specific ideological ... frameworks of meaning', the authors opted for a description of the Ustasha leader which is 'neutral' to the point of deference.[139]

The presence of photographs of foreign, mainly German officials and soldiers is important because there are no comparable images of the Ustasha. In fact, perpetrators are conspicuously absent from the Jasenovac exhibition. They feature in no more than a dozen images, usually loitering in the background, cast in the role of prison guards rather than killers. This aspect of the display, ostensibly motivated by the desire to focus on victims rather than perpetrators, helps to 'avoid dealing with the fact that Jasenovac was one of the rare cases in which it was not the Nazis, but their local collaborators, who ran the death camp all by themselves'.[140] What is more, the complete absence of images of Ustasha 'at work' is incompatible with the 'Western model of memory' which the museum seeks to emulate. Holocaust museums, including the USHMM, have always clearly identified, and showed 'the human face of evil', in order to avoid mass murder being construed as a 'metaphysical', 'superhuman force'.[141] More importantly, when it comes to crimes of collaborators, showing perpetrators and assigning responsibility is especially important. It is a way of bringing into the conversation other sensitive topics, such as everyday collaboration, the conduct of bystanders and the 'moral choices made by ordinary people who were not victims'.[142] These topics are conspicuously absent from the Jasenovac exhibition, but also from the wider, sanitized historical memory in contemporary Croatia, within which Serbian victims of genocide remain largely invisible.

Jasenovac memory and the fog of war

As we have seen in this chapter, in the early 1990s, Serbia and Croatia found themselves compelled to forge new, post-Yugoslav and post-communist, historical identities. Because this process took place in time of war and nationalist euphoria (which resulted in both sides relying on stretched historical analogies and nationalist mythologies), narratives of the events of the 1940s and 1990s became intertwined in the public imagination. In Serbia, through the stubborn motif of 'renewed genocide', the persecution of Serbs in the Independent State of Croatia became the prism for interpreting the war of the 1990s. What is more, the atrocity-focused memory of the Ustasha genocide became a tool for sidelining, minimizing and justifying crimes perpetrated by Serbian forces during the conflict of the 1990s. In Croatia, on the other hand, the 'Homeland War' provided a lens for re-interpreting the events of the 1940s. The trauma of the 'Serbian aggression' and the way it was interpreted in Tuđman's Croatia produced an enduring taboo around the idea of Serbian victimhood and engendered intolerance to any interpretation of the past that disrupted the comforting narrative according to which Serbs are 'perpetrators' and Croats 'victims'. This has prevented any serious and critical reckoning with the legacy of the genocide in the Independent State of Croatia and created an enduring, deafening silence around Serbian suffering. The very different, even diametrically opposed attitudes towards atrocity photographs in evidence in the two countries today are the outcome, and reflection, of these developments.

Notably, the divergent cultures of visual memory in Serbia and Croatia are closely linked and mutually dependent. Ever since the late 1980s, the selective and strategic memorialization of the history of Ustasha genocide has been informed, on both sides, by the desire to admonish and counterbalance the other's perspective.[143] The importance attributed to, and the uncritical use of, atrocity images in Serbia is even today fuelled by their invisibility in Croatian public memory. Meanwhile, the more prominent the images are in Serbia, and the more they are linked to the motif of 'renewed genocide', the stronger is the impulse in Croatia to reject them as alien and anti-Croat. This endless cycle of mutual reinforcement of self-serving nationalist agendas – which are, in both countries, closer to the mainstream than is healthy for any modern democracy – has proven extremely hard to break. As such, the state of visual memory of the Ustasha genocide provides a powerful reminder of the extent to which the traumas, and ideological and political agendas of the 1990s, continue to shape the politics of memory in post-Yugoslav societies. Clearly, a critically informed, historically grounded memory of the Ustasha genocide, and a more sensible and measured approach to atrocity images, have yet to emerge from fog of the recent war.

8

Conclusion

Atrocity photographs beyond idolatry and oblivion

This book offered the first detailed examination of the role which atrocity photographs have played in shaping the public memory of the genocide in the Independent State of Croatia. Focusing mainly on the example of the Jasenovac concentration camp – a potent symbol of both Ustasha depravity and the contested nature of the memory of the Second World War in the former Yugoslavia – it explored the origins and history of atrocity images and scrutinized the dynamic behind their collection, distribution and exhibition. It analysed their changing importance, visibility and connotations over the past eighty years, and considered how they were used, at different times and in different social and political contexts – in the Independent State of Croatia, Nazi-occupied Serbia, socialist Yugoslavia and two of its successor states, Serbia and Croatia – to remember the past, but invariably also make sense of the present.

The role of photographs as vehicles for imagining and remembering human suffering is well documented. Wars in particular are often represented through symbolic and dramatic images that capture – but also produce and perpetuate – what is deemed to be the essence of a conflict.[1] Notably, because wars are inherently divisive and emotionally charged events, so are the images used to represent them. As this book demonstrated, atrocity photographs are always contested and inherently political. Over the years, depictions of Ustasha barbarity have seldom been shown or looked at for their aesthetic or illustrative properties, or as a source of dispassionate insight into the past. They were stances in an argument, deployed, usually alongside words, to get things done.[2]

One of the objectives of the book has been to complicate the history of the images of Ustasha atrocities and debunk many of the over-simplifications and misunderstandings that continue to inform their dissemination and consumption. As we have seen, in Croatia, atrocity images are today often dismissed as a deeply compromised instrument of anti-Croat manipulation and propaganda. Indeed, the present book exposed numerous instances of deliberate, propagandistic misuse, not least during the conflict of the 1990s. But it also demonstrated that over the years, photographs were often used in good faith, as part of genuine and legitimate, although often inept and ill-conceived efforts to render visible the horrors of Ustasha violence, or counter resurgent Croatian nationalism and revisionism. In other words, atrocity images are not intrinsically corrupt; there are reasons other than malicious 'atrocity propaganda' for showing and looking at them. At the same time, the book demonstrated how delicate the boundary sometimes is between the legitimate use of atrocity photographs on the one hand and indefensible propagandistic abuse on the other. In doing so it pointed to the importance of moderation, and careful and informed curation of photographic material.

Having considered the past and the present of the visual culture of atrocity in the former Yugoslavia, we will now turn to its future. How might one go about fashioning a new, critically informed way of looking at the past, one that would allow violent images which at present polarize the region to be wrested from controversy, and incorporated into public memory in a more constructive and conciliatory way? Two fundamental questions that underpin ongoing debates about the use of violent images provide a convenient starting point: What are these images for, and how, if at all, should the public engage with them as they seek insight into and a connection with the past?

Atrocity images: To look or not to look?

Within literature on the visual record of the Holocaust, myriad reasons have been put forward for why it may be time to call a halt on what Janina Struk called 'the repetitive and frequently reckless use of [atrocity] photographs'.[3] The most commonly cited reasons concern the ethics of spectatorship. Several writers have argued that the dissemination and consumption of violent images – many of which depict torment and death and were taken with the specific purpose of degrading and humiliating victims – amounts to vicarious participation and collusion in the act of cruelty.[4] Susan Sontag termed this the 'indecency of ... co-spectatorship'.[5] It has even been suggested that the 'soiled lineage' of most atrocity images – the fact that they were taken by the killers and invariably without the victims' consent – renders them inadmissible and unusable.[6] As we have seen in the previous chapter, a version of this argument was cited by the authors of the 2006 permanent exhibition at the Jasenovac Memorial Museum as the main reason for the complete exclusion of atrocity images from the display.

A second reason, which also concerns ethics, is that, once images of atrocities are placed in the public domain, it becomes impossible to regulate the response of the audience and mitigate against undesirable reactions. Repeated exposure may, for instance, lead to the effect of shocking images wearing off, resulting in passive indifference towards human suffering. Alternatively, images might provoke revulsion towards the powerless victim or admiration for the perpetrators' superiority and dominance. Some spectators might even develop an unsavoury fascination with images of horror and go on to seek them out as a source of prurient pleasure.[7] The prospect of pleasure or satisfaction being derived from looking at atrocity images is particularly important. Observed pain of others is always a potential source of pleasure: the pleasure of one's own virtue manifested in the experience of horror or sympathy, or relief provoked by the realization that one has been spared from the observed suffering. Susan Sontag alluded to a further dimension of the pleasure of spectatorship when she wrote that moral satisfaction can be derived both from the act of flinching before images of unbearable suffering and from the knowledge that one can look at the images *without* flinching.[8] This pleasure is believed by some to be unethical, because it compounds the injury to the victims. Victims of historical injustices are beyond help, so images serve no purpose other than to provide the viewer with 'the pleasure of affective intensity without the cost of ethical responsibility'.[9]

While ethical arguments against the use of atrocity images are well-articulated and persuasive, they are not without weaknesses. First, ethical objections overlook the possibility that the meaning of an atrocity image can be subverted. As Roger Simon put it in relation to photographs of lynching in the United States, it is sometimes possible to render 'what were once viewed as tokens of racial dominance and superiority into dreadful yet instructive scenes documenting instances of historical injustice and shameful barbarity'.[10] Suzie Linfield makes a similar point when she argues that once photographs of victims' vulnerability and defeat are curated into 'evidence of the crimes committed', they become 'self-portraits of Nazi degradation' and a depiction of 'the photographer as much as the subject'.[11] In other words, the audience does not necessarily have to adopt the gaze of the photographer; it can choose to look *through the photograph* and turn its sights on the wrongdoing of the killers.

Second, the objections do not take sufficient account of ethical remembering as a situated social practice, whose parameters and meaning are determined by the local political context. As we have seen in Chapter 7, in some cases, such as in the 2006 display at the Jasenovac Memorial Museum, ethical considerations can be mobilized to facilitate forgetting, to exclude from public memory not just the contentious images but also the nature of the murderous project that produced them and which they evidence. What is more, there are clearly occasions when pictures of atrocities can be legitimately placed in the service of ethical conduct. It is not uncommon, for instance, for 'shocking', 'heart-breaking' or 'harrowing' images from present-day conflicts to be publicized in order to convey a sense of urgency and inspire some form of meaningful social action.[12] The same faith in the power of atrocity photographs to compel belief, elicit emotions, inspire solidarity and move the audience on an instinctive, 'visceral' level mandates their use as 'ethical reference points' to guide our approach to the past.[13] This is especially the case in societies where the threat of revisionism and denialism hangs over the memory of past suffering.[14] It is, therefore, perhaps unsurprising that the new wave of right-wing historical revisionism which swept Croatia in recent years led some in that country to question the appropriateness of the 'aestheticized' approach to the past epitomized by the Jasenovac Memorial Museum.[15] The historian Ivo Goldstein, one of the original reviewers of the exhibition, who in 2006 cautiously welcomed its novel approach, noted recently that in a country facing a 'revisionist offensive', where Jasenovac remains a political issue and an object of constant manipulation, an exhibition that shows the victims but not the crime, and which does not expose fully the reality of the horrors of Jasenovac, has become difficult to justify.[16]

On the other hand, indiscriminate and uncritical use of atrocity photographs is just as inexcusable. This is not just for ethical reasons but also because atrocity photographs sustain a highly simplistic view of the past. As Max Begholtz observes, the problem with any historical memory that is reliant on 'graphic descriptions of violence, the presentation of large, yet precise body counts and disturbing survivor testimonies' is that it substitutes description for explanation.[17] It leaves the audience 'shocked by the horror of violence' without guiding them to 'ask questions about the causes, dynamics and effects of violence'.[18] As we have seen, this kind of atrocity-focused memory is often mediated through, and sustained by, photographs. Because of their credentials of objectivity, atrocity images create the illusion that the 'reality' of a past event has been truthfully and unproblematically captured and remembered. As such, they prevent engagement with other sources of knowledge that might illuminate the past's inherent complexity or reveal aspects of it that elude visual representation.[19] This is what Susan Sontag had in mind when she said that 'the problem is not that people remember through photographs, but that they remember only the photographs'.[20] Moreover, because atrocity images provoke a limited range of emotions, mainly horror and outrage, they impede a more dynamic, reflexive relationship with the past. In Claude Lanzmann's words, violent images are 'images without imagination'; they 'petrify thought and kill any power of evocation'.[21]

All these different arguments and concerns provide a helpful reminder of the complex issues and challenges that engagement with atrocity photographs poses for both consumers of images and professionals involved in their curation. They also help put in perspective some of the often taken-for-granted assumptions that underpin the divided visual memories in the former Yugoslavia: that atrocity images inevitably retraumatize victims or, conversely, that they provide a superior, objective and clear-cut insight into the horrors of the past. On balance however, the arguments seem to suggest that the question that we need to ask is not *whether* we should ever show or look at images of atrocities – there are clearly instances when this is both legitimate and desirable – but *how* we can do so in a socially and ethically responsible way.

As we have seen throughout this book, probably the greatest problem with images of Ustasha violence is the abundance of incorrect and often misleading captions and attributions. For this reason, the first step towards a more responsible, and constructive, engagement with atrocity images must involve an attempt to 'clean up' the somewhat chaotic visual record and establish the provenance of, and correct attribution for, at least some of the photographs. Preceding chapters contain numerous examples that suggest that doing so is both possible and useful. It is also *necessary*, because, as Susan Crane points out, historians, and indeed scholars of other disciplines, have an ethical as well as professional duty to 'find out more' about images of human suffering, before they start treating them as '"representative" of humanity or of history'.[22] On the other hand, anyone undertaking this project of identification and verification should be mindful that many of the misattributions and mislabelling that their endeavour seeks to correct were themselves the outcome of the desire, by different people over the years, to restore the referentiality and authenticity of anonymous photographs by tying them to specific places or events.

The effort to trace the origins of photographs will inevitably be hampered by the fact that the visual record of Ustasha genocide is inherently messy and imperfect. The ways in which photographs were collected and curated over the years means that most photographs will probably never be correctly or reliably identified. However, this does not render them worthless, especially in instances where it is possible to ascertain, from the photographs themselves or from relevant records, that they show an Ustasha crime. Trophy photographs are particularly useful in this respect. Despite their many flaws (including the fact that we often do not know where they were taken or by whom), they make it impossible to deny, as Roland Barthes put it, 'that *the thing has been there*'.[23] They possess a unique kind of authenticity that means that, providing they are appropriately contextualized and all the limitations are priced in, they can help capture some broader truth about past horrors and injustices.

There is however a further step towards a more responsible and productive engagement with atrocity photographs. It involves broadening Susan Crane's injunction to 'find out more' to include the quest for information not just about the images themselves but also about the history of their uses as vessels of memory. This entails applying the critical lens of the kind I used in this book to map the trajectory of the dissemination and consumption of a specific image or images, and scrutinize their changing visibility and meaning over time. This knowledge, which would become part of a photograph's record – its historical, or biographical 'meta-data' – could be used to mediate the audience's relationship with the image and with the past that it purports to represent. It would also help reclaim the photographs from those who over the years sought to instrumentalize them. This would be beneficial because it would help move the discussion on from the simplistic question about whether an atrocity image tells us everything or nothing about the past. It would, instead, invite those engaging with images to participate in a more reflexive kind of spectatorship, which involves thinking about how others have looked at an image before, what photographs can and cannot show, and how they become invested with meaning.

Perhaps the biggest advantage of this approach is that it would help reset our relationship with images of the traumatic past and relieve them of the burden of responsibility to convey historical truths. As the philosopher J. M. Bernstein put it, when engaging with controversial or imperfect images, the question we need to ask is not 'how has this image failed' but rather 'how have we failed this image'.[24] Critical interrogation of atrocity photographs must entail an equally critical and rigorous interrogation of ourselves and the history of our often imperfect ways of looking.

Notes

Chapter 1

1 *Trial of the Major War Criminals before the International Military Tribunal: Nuremberg 14 November 1945–1 October 1946*, Vol. II (Nuremberg: International Military Tribunal, 1947), 99–100.
2 Ibid.
3 Ibid., 130, 99.
4 Ibid., 433; also, Lawrence Douglas, 'Film as witness: Screening Nazi concentration camps before the Nuremberg Tribunal', *The Yale Law Journal* 105, no. 2 (1995): 452.
5 Cited in Jeremy Hicks, *First Films of the Holocaust: Soviet Cinema and the Genocide of the Jews, 1938-1946* (Pittsburg, PA: University of Pittsburg Press, 2012), 207.
6 Rebecca West, *A Train of Powder* (New York: Viking Press, 1955), 3.
7 Daniel H. Magilow and Lisa Silverman, *Holocaust Representations in History: An Introduction* (London: Bloomsbury Academic, 2015), 26.
8 Susan Sontag, *Regarding the Pain of Others* (London: Penguin Books, 2003), 21.
9 *Trial of the Major War Criminals*, Vol. II, 431.
10 Barbie Zelizer, *Remembering to Forget: Holocaust Memory through the Camera's Eye* (Chicago: University of Chicago Press, 1998), 13. See also Carolyn J. Dean, *The Moral Witness: Trials and Testimony after Genocide* (Ithaca, NY: Cornell University Press, 2019), Chapter 4.
11 See Janina Struk, *Photographing the Holocaust: Interpretations of the Evidence* (London: I.B. Tauris, 2004).
12 John J. Michalczyk, *Filming the End of the Holocaust: Allied Documentaries, Nuremberg and the Liberation of the Concentration Camps* (London: Bloomsbury, 2014), 18.
13 Zelizer, *Remembering to Forget*; Barbie Zelizer, *Visual Culture and the Holocaust* (London: Athlone Press, 2000); Struk, *Photographing the Holocaust*; Sontag, *Regarding the Pain of Others*; Susie Linfield, *The Cruel Radiance: Photography and Political Violence* (Chicago: University of Chicago Press, 2010); David Shneer, *Through Soviet Jewish Eyes: Photography, War, and the Holocaust* (New Jersey: Rutgers University Press, 2010); Marianne Hirsch, 'Surviving images: Holocaust photographs and the work of postmemory', *The Yale Journal of Criticism*, 14, no. 1 (2001): 5–37; Ulrich Baer, *Spectral Evidence* (Cambridge, MA: MIT Press, 2005); Georges Didi-Huberman, *Images in Spite of All: Four Photographs from Auschwitz*, trans. Shane B. Lillis (Chicago: University of Chicago Press, 2007); Hildegard Frübis, Clara Oberle and Agnieszka Pufelska, *Fotografien aus den Lagern des NS-Regimes. Beweissicherung und ästhetische Praxis* (Vienna: Böhlau Verlag, 2019); Christian Delage, *La Vérité par l'image: De Nuremberg au procès Milosevic* (Paris: Éditions Denoël, 2006) etc.
14 See, for instance, Nina Tumarkin, *The Living and the Dead: The Rise and Fall of the Cult of World War II in Russia* (New York: Basic Books, 1994); Lucy S. Dawidowics, *The Holocaust and the Historians* (Cambridge, MA: Harvard University Press, 1981).
15 E.g. Michael Shafir, *Between Denial and 'Comparative Trivialization': Holocaust Negationism in Post-Communist East Central Europe* (Jerusalem: SICSA, 2002);

Michal Kopeček, *Past in the Making: Historical Revisionism in Central Europe after 1989* (Budapest: CEU Press, 2008); John-Paul Himka and Joanna Beata Michlic, eds. *Bringing the Dark Past to Light: The Reception of the Holocaust in Postcommunist Europe* (Lincoln, NE: University of Nebraska Press, 2013).

16 Zelizer, *Remembering to Forget*; David Campbell, 'Atrocity, memory, photography: Imaging the concentration camps of Bosnia – the case of ITN versus *Living Marxism*, Part 1', *Journal of Human Rights* 1, no. 1 (2002): 1–33; Jamie Frederic Metzl, *Western Responses to Human Rights Abuses in Cambodia, 1975–80* (Basingstoke: Palgrave Macmillan, 1996); Angi Buettner, *Holocaust Images and Picturing Catastrophe: The Cultural Politics of Seeing* (London: Routledge, 2011).

17 E.g. Jovan Mirković, *Zločini nad Srbima u Nezavisnoj Državi Hrvatskoj – Fotomonografija* (Belgrade: Svet Knjige, 2014); *Jasenovac: Suština užasa*, directed by Milan Stevanović (Belgrade: Filmske Novosti, 2008); Permanent exhibition 'Jasenovac: Sistem ustaških logora smrti' at the Museum of Republika Srpska, Banja Luka, Bosnia – Herzegovina.

18 'Zbirka fotografija i foto artefakata', website of the Military Museum, Belgrade, available at http://www.muzej.mod.gov.rs/sr/muzejska-delatnost/zbirke/zbirka-fotodokumentacije (accessed 3 December 2018).

19 Nataša Jovičić, 'Jasenovac Memorial Museum's permanent exhibition – the victim as an individual', *Review of Croatian History* 2, no.1 (2006): 295–9.

20 E.g. Amir Obhođaš et al., *Ustaška vojnica*, Vols 1 and 2 (Zagreb: Despot, 2013).

21 E.g. the Facebook page 'Ustaše su najveća sramota Hrvata' ('Ustasha are the biggest disgrace to Croats') (https://www.facebook.com/ustasesramota/).

22 Vladimir Dedijer and Antun Miletić, *Protiv zaborava i tabua (Jasenovac 1941-1991)* (Sarajevo: Pregres, 1991).

23 Franjo Tudjman, *Horrors of War: Historical Reality and Philosophy* (New York: M. Evans and Company, 1996), 15, 245.

24 E.g. Tomislav Vuković, *Drugačija povijest (o Srbu, Jasenovcu, Glini…)* (Zagreb: Glas Koncila, 2012); Josip Pečarić, *Srpski mit o Jasenovcu: Skrivanje istine o beogradskim konc-logorima* (Zagreb: Dom & Svijet, 1998).

25 The figures are based on the records of the Jasenovac Memorial Area, whose database currently contains the names of 83,145 victims (see http://www.jusp-jasenovac.hr/Default.aspx?sid=6711). There is, however, widespread recognition among scholars in the region that these figures are incomplete and that the total number of victims is likely to be closer to 100,000. For the history of Jasenovac, see Ivo Goldstein, *Jasenovac* (Zagreb: Fraktura, 2018).

26 Demographic analyses carried out in the 1980s and the 1990s suggest that Yugoslavia's direct losses incurred during the Second World War were around one million, rather than 1.7 million. See Bogoljub Kočović, *Sahrana jednog mita: žrtve Drugog svetskog rata u Jugoslaviji* (Belgrade: Otkrovenje, 2005); Vladimir Žerjavić, *Opsesije i megalomanije oko Jasenovca i Bleiburga: Gubici stanovništva Jugoslavije u drugom svjetskom ratu* (Zagreb: Globus, 1992).

27 See Ivo Goldstein, *Holokaust u Zagrebu* (Zagreb: Novi Liber, 2001); Pål Kolstø, 'The Serbian-Croatian controversy over Jasenovac', in *Serbia and the Serbs in World War Two*, ed. Sabrina P. Ramet and Ole Listhaug (Basingstoke: Palgrave Macmillan, 2011), 225–46; Jozo Tomasevich, *War and Revolution in Yugoslavia, 1941-1945: Occupation and Collaboration* (Stanford: Stanford University Press, 2001).

28 Nataša Mataušić, *Koncentracioni logor Jasenovac: Fotomonografija* (Zagreb: Spomen Područje Jasenovac, 2008).

29 Ibid., 18.
30 See Struk, *Photographing the Holocaust*, Zelizer, *Remembering to Forget*.
31 Pečarić, *Srpski mit o Jasenovcu*; Vuković, *Drugačija povijest*.
32 For the background on the Ustasha and their rise to power, see Fikreta Jelić-Butić, *Ustaše i NDH* (Zagreb: Liber, 1977); Tomasevich, *War and Revolution in Yugoslavia*; Tomislav Dulić, *Utopias of Nation: Local Mass Killing in Bosnia and Herzegovina, 1941-1942* (Uppsala, Sweden: Uppsala University Library, 2005).
33 Tomasevich, *War and Revolution in Yugoslavia*, 233.
34 The Ustasha regarded Muslims in Bosnia as an integral part of the Croatian national body, based on the false assumption that Muslims were ethnically Croatian. See Tomislav Dulić, 'Mass killing in the Independent State of Croatia, 1941-1945: A case for comparative research', *Journal of Genocide Research* 8, no. 3 (2006): 255–81.
35 Cited in Slavko Goldstein, *1941, The Year That Keeps Returning* (New York: New York Review of Books, 2013), 106.
36 Tomasevich, *War and Revolution in Yugoslavia*, 738; Kočović, *Sahrana jednog mita*, 51, 56.
37 For detailed discussion of the wartime losses and the challenges of calculating them, see Žerjavić, *Opsesije i megalomanije oko Jasenovca i Bleiburga*; Tomasevich, *War and Revolution in Yugoslavia*, Chapter 17; Kočović, *Sahrana jednog mita*.
38 See, Dulić, *Utopias of Nation*, 313–14. Remaining Serbian losses are accounted for mainly by Partisans killed in combat or 'collateral deaths'. For a higher estimate of Serbian victims of genocide, see Dragan Cvetković, 'Koncentracijski logor Jasenovac i njegova uloga u uništavanju naroda NDH – izračun mogućeg broja žrtava na temelju djelomično revidiranog popisa iz 1964. godine', in *Jasenovac manipulacije, kontroverze i povijesni revizionizam*, ed. Andriana Benčić, Stipe Odak and Danijela Lucić (Jasenovac: JUSP Jasenovac, 2018), 171–220.
39 Marko Attila Hoare, *Genocide and Resistance in Hitler's Bosnia: Partisans and the Chetniks 1941-1943* (Oxford: Oxford University Press, 2007), 19.
40 Dulić, 'Mass killing in the Independent State of Croatia', 264; Alexander Korb, 'Understanding Ustaša violence', *Journal of Genocide Research* 12, no. 1–2 (2010): 1–18.
41 Tomasevich, *War and Revolution in Yugoslavia*, 440.
42 Most Jewish victims perished in the Jadovno camp which operated in 1941 and in Jasenovac in 1941 and 1942. The remaining Jews, mainly from Zagreb, were deported to Auschwitz in August 1942 and in 1943. See Goldstein, *Holokaust u Zagrebu*.
43 Narcisa Lengel-Krizman, *Genocid nad Romima: Jasenovac 1942* (Jasenovac: JUSP Jasenovac, 2003).
44 Dulić, *Utopias of Nation*, 316.
45 Almost 70 per cent of Serbian victims perished in the first eighteen months of the war. The reduction in the scale of the killing after 1942 came about following an intervention from Nazi Germany, which was concerned that the indiscriminate murder of Serbs played into the hands of the Partisan resistance. This resulted in a change in personnel at the head of the Ustasha security apparatus and a policy shift in favour of assimilation. However, small-scale atrocities persisted until the end of the war. See Tomasevich, *War and Revolution in Yugoslavia*, 440.
46 See Jelić-Butić, *Ustaše i NDH*, 170.
47 See Max Bergholtz, *Violence as a Generative Force: Identity, Nationalism, and Memory in a Balkan Community* (Ithaca: Cornell University Press, 2016).

48 Dulić, *Utopias of Nation*, 357.
49 For an examination of the symbolic aspects of the Ustasha killing methods, see John Allcock, *Explaining Yugoslavia* (London: Hurst & Company, 2000), Chapter 13; Radu Harald Dinu, 'Honor, shame and warrior values: The anthropology of Ustasha violence', in *Utopia of Terror: Life and Death in Wartime Croatia*, ed. Rory Yeomans (Rochester: University of Rochester Press, 2015), 119–41; Goldstein, *Jasenovac*, Chapter VI.
50 Gideon Greif in 'Izraelski profesor: Jasenovac je bio gori od Aušvica', *Blic*, 26 July 2017; Jaša Almuli in Slobodan Kljakić, 'Jasenovac gori od Aušvica', *Politika*, 7 February 2010.
51 See Dulić, 'Mass killing in the Independent State of Croatia'; Aleksander Korb, *Intertwined Genocides: Mass Violence in Western Yugoslavia during the Second World War* (Oxford: Oxford University Press, 2020).
52 See Korb, 'Understanding Ustaša violence', 10–11, also Jovan Byford, 'When I say "the Holocaust", I mean "Jasenovac": Remembrance of the Holocaust in contemporary Serbia', *East European Jewish Affairs* 37, no. 1 (2007): 51–74. For more on the appropriation of the Holocaust in Eastern Europe, see Jelena Subotić, *Yellow Star, Red Star: Holocaust Remembrance after Communism* (Ithaca, NY: Cornell University Press, 2019).
53 Hoare, *Genocide and Resistance in Hitler's Bosnia*, 20.
54 See Vladimir Dedijer and Antun Miletić, *Genocid nad Muslimanima 1941–1945* (Sarajevo: Svetlost, 1990).
55 See Dulić, *Utopias of Nation*, 317; Cvetković, 'Koncentracijski logor Jasenovac', 180.
56 Allcock, *Explaining Yugoslavia*, 381–2.
57 Ibid., 382–3.
58 For a recent analysis of Ustasha cruelty, see Goldstein, *Jasenovac*, Chapter VI.
59 Allcock, *Explaining Yugoslavia*, 395.
60 Ibid., 398.
61 Frances Larson, *Severed: A History of Heads Lost and Heads Found* (London: Granta, 2015), 75.
62 Allcock, *Explaining Yugoslavia*, 402.
63 Marc Bloch, 'Reflections of a historian on the false news of the war (1921)', trans. James P. Holoka, *Michigan War Studies Review*, 1 July 2013, available at http://www.miwsr.com/2013-051.aspx (accessed 15 December 2018).
64 Davide Rodogno, *Against Massacre: Humanitarian Interventions in the Ottoman Empire, 1815-1914* (Princeton: Princeton University Press, 2011), 32.
65 David G. Bromley, Anson D. Shupe and J. C. Ventimiglia, 'Atrocity tales, the Unification Church and the social construction of evil', *Journal of Communication* 29, no. 3 (1979): 43.
66 Rodogno, *Against Massacre*.
67 Ibid., see also, Y. Doğan Çetinkaya, 'Atrocity propaganda and the nationalization of the masses in the Ottoman Empire during the Balkan Wars (1912–13)', *International Journal of Middle East Studies* 46 (2014): 759–78.
68 David Welch, 'Atrocity propaganda', in *Propaganda and Mass Persuasion: A Historical Encyclopedia, 1500 to the Present*, ed. Nicholas J. Cull, David Culbert and David Welch (Santa Barbara, CA: ABC-CLIO, 2003), 24.
69 Michel Foucault, *Discipline and Punish* (New York: Pantheon Books, 1977), 8. In atrocity literature, the term 'medieval' has always served as a shorthand for barbarism and cruelty. This trend continues to the present day. See Chris Jones, 'Is Islamic State Medieval?' available at https://researchtheheadlines.org/2014/09/18/is-islamic-state-medieval/ (accessed 5 December 2018).

70 For the analysis of the pornography of pain in the context of humanitarian campaigns, see Karen Halttunen, 'Humanitarianism and the pornography of pain in Anglo-American culture', *The American Historical Review* 100, no. 2 (1995): 303–34.
71 A particularly notable early example is photographs of victims of atrocities perpetrated in the Belgian Congo in the early 1900s. See Kevin Grant, 'The limits of exposure: Atrocity photographs in the Congo reform campaign', in *Humanitarian Photography: A History*, ed. Heide Fehrenbach and Davide Rodogno (Cambridge: Cambridge University Press, 2015), 64–88.
72 See, for instance, Edwin Munsell Bliss, *Turkey and the Armenian Atrocities: A Reign of Terror* (Philadelphia: Hubbard Publishing, 1896); Tollemache Sinclair, *A Defence of Russia and the Christians of Turkey* (London: Chapman and Hall, 1877).
73 Cited in Howard G. Brown, *Mass Violence and the Self* (Ithaca: Cornell University Press, 2018), 177.
74 Welch, 'Atrocity propaganda', 24; Brown, *Mass Violence and the Self.*
75 'Rat za slobodu i civilizaciju', *Ilustrovana ratna kronika*, 31 October 1912, 1.
76 The earlier incarnation of *Ilustrovana ratna kronika* was established by Stevan Popović, a well-known Serbian politician, author and publicist. He was assisted by two political exiles from Serbia, Pera Todorović and Pera Velimirović, and by the famous children's poet Jovan Jovanović-Zmaj, whose task was to inject some humour into the chronicle of the war. *Ilustrovana ratna kronika* mainly contained portraits of Russian officers, and illustrations of landscapes and battles. Illustrations of atrocities were comparatively rare but contained the same motifs as those found in Figure 1.2. See, for instance, *Ilustrovana ratna kronika*, no. 4, November 1877, 234, also no. 5, December 1877, 266. For more on the 1877–8 edition of the publication, see Milić J. Milićević, 'Ilustrovana ratna kronika – časopis i tvorci', in *Ilustrovana ratna kronika 1877-1878,* Reprint, ed. Milić J. Milićević (Belgrade: Srpski genealoški centar, 2011), vii–xv.
77 Similar material was published in the illustrated supplement of *Le Petit Parisien*. For instance, the front cover of the issue published on 27 October 1912 was very similar, in terms of the main symbolic themes, to Figure 1.2. At the time, it was common practice for illustrated magazines published in Serbian to procure visual material from the foreign press, or even from rival publications at home. See Milićević, 'Ilustrovana ratna kronika – časopis i tvorci', xiii.
78 Identical motifs featured in Turkish propaganda at the time, except with minarets instead of church towers. Y. Doğan Çetinkaya, 'Illustrated atrocity: The stigmatisation of non-Muslims through images in the Ottoman Empire during the Balkan Wars', *Journal of Modern European History* 12, no. 4 (2014): 460–78.
79 See John Horne and Alan Kramer, *German Atrocities 1914: A History of Denial* (New Haven: Yale University Press, 2001). On the absence of evidence of atrocities, see Susan D. Moeller, *Shooting War: Photography and the American Experience of Combat* (New York: Basic Books, 1989), 108.
80 E.g. Dragomir Patchoff and Danail V. Katzeff, *The Roumanian Atrocities* (Sofia: Royal Court Printing Press, 1919); *Album des Crimes Bulgares* (Paris: publisher unknown, 1919).
81 Voyslav M. Yovanovitch, 'Preface', in *Report upon the Atrocities Committed by the Austro-Hungarian Army during the First Invasion of Serbia*, ed. Rodolphe A. Reiss (London: Simpkin, Marshall, Hamilton, Kent & Co, 1917), v. For more on Reiss's involvement in Serbia, see Zdenko Levental, *Švajcarac na Kajmakčalanu* (Belgrade: Prosveta, 1984).

82 Rodolphe A. Reiss, *La Photographie Judiciaire* (Paris: Mendel, 1903).
83 Cited in Luce Lebart, 'Rodolphe A. Reiss: Traces, narks, prints: Revealing details invisible to the naked eye', in *Images of Conviction: The Construction of Visual Evidence*, ed. Diane Dufour (Paris: Le Bal, 2015), 39.
84 Rodolphe A. Reiss, *Report upon the Atrocities Committed by the Austro-Hungarian Army during the First Invasion of Serbia* (London: Simpkin, Marshall, Hamilton, Kent & Co, 1917), 29; also Reiss, *How Austria-Hungary Waged War in Serbia: Personal Investigations of a Neutral* (Paris: Librarie Armand Colin, 1916).
85 Reiss, *Report upon the Atrocities*, 97.
86 Rodolphe A. Reiss, *Infringements of the Rules and Laws of War Committed by the Austro-Bulgaro-Germans: Letters of a Criminologist on the Serbian Macedonian Front* (London: George Allen & Unwinn, 1919), 73.
87 Ibid., 77–8.
88 Ibid., 80. The First World War trophy images, mainly from Austrian sources, are considered in more detail in Anton Holzer, *Das Lächeln der Henker. Der unbekannte Krieg gegen die Zivilbevölkerung 1914-1918* (Dormstadt: Primus Verlag, 2008).
89 Sabine T. Kriebel and Andrés Mario Zervigón, *Photography and Doubt* (London: Routledge, 2017).
90 Sontag, *Regarding the Pain of Others*, 9; Judith Keilbach, 'Photographs, symbolic images, and the Holocaust: On the (im)possibility of depicting historical truth', *History and Theory* 47, no. 2 (2009): 60.
91 Zelizer, *Remembering to Forget*, 239.
92 Jennifer L. Mnookin, 'The image of truth: Photographic evidence and the power of analogy', in *Images of Conviction: The Construction of Visual Evidence*, ed. Diane Dufour (Paris: Le Bal, 2015), 14.
93 Zelizer, *Remembering to Forget*, 12.

Chapter 2

1 Struk, *Photographing the Holocaust*, 34–46.
2 Janina Struk, *Private Pictures: Soldiers' Inside View of War* (London: I.B. Tauris, 2011), Chapter 4; Struk, *Photographing the Holocaust*, Chapter 2.
3 *Soviet Documents on Nazi Atrocities* (London: Hutchinson, 1942); *We Shall Not Forgive! The Horrors of the German Invasion in Documents and Photographs* (Moscow: Foreign Languages Pub. House, 1942); *New Soviet Documents on Nazi Atrocities* (London: Hutchinson, 1943).
4 Struk, *Photographing the Holocaust*, 49.
5 *The Polish Atrocities against the German Minority in Poland* (Berlin: Volk und Reich Verlag, 1940), 5.
6 'Truth about Katyn', published as supplement to the *Soviet War News Weekly*, 1944, precise date of publication unknown, 4.
7 For the history of the Extraordinary Commission, see Marina Sorokina, 'Peoples and procedures: Towards a history of the investigation of Nazi crimes in the USSR', *Kritika: Explorations in Russian and Euroasian History* 4 (2005): 797–831; and Kirik Feferman, 'Soviet investigation of Nazi crimes in the USSR: Documenting the Holocaust', *Journal of Genocide Research* 5, no. 4 (2003): 587–602.

8 David Engel, *Facing the Holocaust: the Polish Government-in-Exile and the Jews, 1943-1945* (Chapel Hill, University of North Carolina Press, 2012), 71.
9 Slobodan Nešović, 'Saveznička štampa o genocidu and Srbima, Jevrejima i Ciganima u Drugom svetskom ratu', in *Genocid nad Srbima u Drugom svetskom ratu*, ed. Radovan Samardžić (Belgrade, Muzej žrtava genocida, 1995), 438–48.
10 *Martyrdom of the Serbs* (Chicago: Palandech Press, 1943).
11 For the effect of atrocity reports on the Yugoslav government in exile and the diaspora in the United States, see Lorraine M. Lees, *Yugoslav-Americans and National Security during World War II* (Chicago: University of Illinois Press, 2007) and Ljubo Boban, *Hrvatska u arhivima izbjegličke vlade, 1941–1943* (Zagreb: Globus, 1985).
12 'Poslije osam i pol stoljeća uskrsla je nova Hrvatska', *Hrvatski Narod*, 14 April 1941: 1.
13 Tomasevich, *War and Revolution in Yugoslavia*, 396.
14 'Izveštaj o streljanju Srba u selu Gudovcu u toku okupacije' (1945), HDA, Fond 306, Box 691, 2–3.
15 Goldstein, *1941*, 111.
16 'Izveštaj o streljanju Srba u selu Gudovcu', 2.
17 'Javnom tužilaštvu okruga Bjelovar 27. X. 1955', HDA, Fond 306, Box 691, 1.
18 See Jelić-Butić, *Ustaše i NDH*, 173.
19 Testimony of Marta Popović, 15 July 1942, cited in Atanasije Jevtić, *Od Kosova do Jadovna* (Trebinje: Manastir Tvrdoš, 2007), 480–6.
20 Jonathan E. Gumz, 'Wehrmacht perceptions of mass violence in Croatia, 1941–1942', *The Historical Journal* 44, no. 4 (2001): 1019.
21 *Zbornik dokumenata*, Part XII, Vol. 2, 390.
22 Gumz, 'Wehrmacht perceptions of mass violence in Croatia', 1035–6.
23 Goldstein, *1941*, 112. Unlike some of his colleagues, Kasche was supportive of Ustasha aims and methods, and was a reliable advocate of the regime for the duration of the war. See Ben Shepard, *Terror in the Balkans* (Cambridge, MA: Harvard University Press, 2012), 95.
24 Gumz, 'Wehrmacht perceptions of mass violence in Croatia', 1038.
25 See *Zločini na jugoslovenskim prostorima u Prvom i Drugom svetskom ratu: Zbornik dokumenata, Knjiga 1* (Belgrade: Vojnoistorijski institut, 1993), 720.
26 AV, Fond 562, Folder 3.1.1.2, docs 442 and 443.
27 See Mila Mihajlović, *Jugoslavija, April 1941–September 1943* (Belgrade: Udruženje srpskih izdavača, 2012).
28 These camps were part of the so-called Gospić complex of concentration camps which operated between May and August 1941. Besides Serbs, among the estimated 25,000 victims were around 2,500 Jews. See Goldstein, *Holokaust u Zagrebu*, 301.
29 Đuro Zatezalo, *Jadovno, kompleks ustaških logora*, vol. 2 (Belgrade: Muzej žrtava genocida, 2007), 745–77. Zatezalo's book contains translations of original Italian reports on Ustasha atrocities. See also Alexander Korb, 'The disposal of corpses in an ethnicized civil war', in *Human Remains and Mass Violence: Methodological Approaches*, ed. Jean-Marc Dreyfus and Élisabeth Anstett (Manchester: University of Manchester Press, 2014), 106–28.
30 Cited in Davide Rodogno, *Fascism's European Empire: Italian Occupation during the Second World War* (Cambridge: Cambridge University Press, 2006), 185.
31 Ibid., 150, 176.
32 See Francis O. Wilcox, 'The use of atrocities in war', *The American Political Science Review* 36, no. 6 (1940): 1169–75.
33 Dulić, *Utopias of Nation*, 168–72.

34 Milan Slani, 'Susak u prvim danima ustanka', in *Ustanak naroda Jugoslavije 1941*, vol. 5 (Belgrade: Vojno Delo, 1964), 576.
35 *Zločini na jugoslovenskim prostorima*, 781–2; *Zbornik dokumenata*, Part V, Vol. 1, 406–12.
36 John Berger, *About Looking* (London: Vintage, 1991), 56.
37 See examples in AV, Fond 562, Folder 3.1.1.2.
38 Radmila Radić, *Država i verske zajednice, 1945-1970*, vol. 1 (Belgrade: INIS, 2002), 58.
39 See Tomislav Dulić, 'Mapping out the "Wasteland": Testimonies from the Serbian Commissariat for Refugees in the service of Tudjman's revisionism', *Holocaust and Genocide Studies* 23, no. 2 (2009): 263–84.
40 Stanislav Krakov, *Prepuna čaša čemera: General Milan Nedić, knjiga druga* (Munich: Iskra, 1968), 184.
41 Radić, *Država i verske zajednice*, 58.
42 The commission collected 4,504 testimonies and received copies of further 3,032 from the Commissariat for Refugees with which it cooperated closely. See Atanasije Jevtić, ed. *Srpska crkva u Drugom svetskom ratu: iz arhiva Sv. Arhijerejskog Sinoda Srpske Pravoslavne Crkve* (Belgrade: Publisher unknown, 1992), 100–1.
43 Borivoje Karapandžić, *Građanski rat u Srbiji, 1941-1945* (Belgrade: Nova Iskra, 1993), 40; also, Velibor Džomić, ed. *Mitropolit Skopski Josif: Memoari* (Cetinje: Svetigora, 2006), 170.
44 Karapandžić, *Građanski rat u Srbiji*, 41.
45 See Veselin Đuretić, *Vlada na bespuću* (Belgrade: Narodna knjiga, 1982), 159–88.
46 See for example AV, Fond 562, Folder 3.1.1.2., docs 69 and 73.
47 See AV, Fond 562, Folder 3.1.1.2.
48 *Zločini na jugoslovenskim prostorima*, 139–42.
49 Ibid., 142.
50 Karapandžić, *Građanski rat u Srbiji*, 40.
51 Stanislav Krakov, *Na oštrici noža: Milan Nedić, knjiga prva* (Munich: Iskra, 1963), 143. Krakov was a controversial writer, journalist and filmmaker, who in the late 1930s supported the fascist movement Zbor, led by the pro-Nazi politician Dimitrije Ljotić. During the occupation, Krakov edited *Novo Vreme* and *Obnova*, the main mouthpieces of the collaborationist government led by his uncle Milan Nedić. See Olivera Milosavljević, *Potisnuta istina: Kolaboracija u Srbiji 1941-1944* (Belgrade: Helsinški odbor za ljudska prava u Srbiji, 2006).
52 For examples see AV, Fond 562, Folder 3.1.1.2.
53 'The memorandum of the Serbian Orthodox Church', in *Martyrdom of the Serbs* (Chicago: Palandech Press, 1943), 204.
54 Milosavljević, *Potisnuta istina*, 54–5.
55 See Jovan Byford, 'The collaborationist administration and the treatment of the Jews in Nazi-occupied Serbia', in *Serbia and the Serbs in World War Two*, ed. Sabrina Ramet and Ola Listhaug (Basingstoke: Palgrave Macmillan, 2011), 109–27.
56 Ratko Parežanin, *Drugi Svetski Rat i Dimitrije V. Ljotić* (Munich: Iskra, 1971), 339.
57 Cited in Aleksandar Vojinović, *NDH u Beogradu* (Zagreb: Naklada Pavičić, 1995), 130.
58 Ibid., 228.
59 See Boban, *Hrvatska u arhivima izbjegličke vlade*, 284–8. For evidence that the letter was a forgery see same volume, 288–92.
60 Vojinović, *NDH u Beogradu*, 142, 157. Nikšić claimed that the distribution of atrocity propaganda was officially prohibited, but that authorities did little to limit its availability.

61 E.g. Karapandžić, *Građanski rat u Srbiji*, 80–1; Krakov, *Na oštrici noža*, 139; Krakov, *Prepuna čaša čemera*, 198; Đoko Slijepčević, *Jugoslavija* (Munich: Iskra, 1978), 303. There is no evidence that Berlin ever planned such a measure, although it is possible that German officials in Belgrade used the threat as a ploy to induce obedience among collaborators.
62 For more on the Teslić business empire founded by Miloš Telić's father, Petar, see Mira Kolar-Dimitrijević, 'Društveno-ekonomski razvoj Siska 1919-1941.godine', *Radovi – Zavod za hrvatsku povjest* 27 (1994): 271–88.
63 Jelić-Butić, *Ustaše i NDH*, 159.
64 *Martyrdom of the Serbs*, 148.
65 Radovan Pilipović, 'Tragedija jedne srpske porodice iz Siska 1941', *Dveri srpske* 47–50 (2011): 61.
66 In October 1941, the wife of Miloš Teslić, Jelena, told the Serbian Commissariat for Refugees that she had it on good authority that her husband was killed by the Ustasha after enduring 'horrific torture' at the hands of the 'Croatian parasites'. However, it is unclear whether the source of this information was someone in Sisak or whether she learned the details of her husband's fate upon arrival in Serbia. For Jelena Teslić's statement, see Pilipović, 'Tragedija jedne srpske porodice iz Siska 1941', 61.
67 Aleksandar Ajzenberg, 'Sekire, maljevi, kame', *Jevrejski pregled* XXIII, no. 4 (2014): 17.
68 Gavrilo Dožić, *Memoari Patrijarha srpskog Gavrila* (Belgrade: Sfairos, 1990), 330.
69 *Martyrdom of the Serbs*, 149.
70 Ibid., 141.
71 Ibid., 236.
72 Over the years several other photographs have been used to illustrate the tragic fate of the Teslić family. Some were even said to depict Miloš's slain son (who, in fact, survived the war), or his father Petar, who died in 1936. See *Martyrdom of the Serbs*, 155; Mirković, *Zločini nad Srbima u Nezavisnoj Državi Hrvatskoj*, 129; Lazo M. Kostich, *Holocaust in the Independent State of Croatia* (Chicago, IL: Liberty, 1981), 275.
73 E.g. *Državna komisija za utvrđivanje zločina okupatora i njihovih pomagača, Saopštenja br. 66-93* (Belgrade: Državna komisija, 1946), 772; Ljubomir Durković-Jakšić, *Platon Jovanović, Episkop Banjalučki* (Kragujevac: Kalenić, 1986), front matter; Mladenko Kumović, *Jasenovac, sistem ustaških logora smrti* (Belgrade: Muzej žrtava genocida, 1997), 33.
74 E.g. testimony of Vitomir Vukić, ABiH, Records of the Country Commission for the Investigation of Crimes of the Occupiers and their Accomplices, Reports, Box I, Doc. 15, 1.
75 *Novi sveštenomučenici i mučenici Pravoslavne crkve prosijavši u pravoslavnom srpskom narodu* (Cetinje: Svetigora, 2000), 54.
76 ABiH, Records of the Country Commission for the Investigation of Crimes of the Occupiers and their Accomplices, Reports, Box I, Doc. 28, Inv. Br. 47366, 20. The fact that the victim had to be identified by his distinctive clothing suggests that the body was badly decomposed.
77 After the war, the photograph was regularly published as showing Bishop Platon's body even though the church leadership was fully aware of the state in which corpse was found. Mačkić's account of the bishop's death was formally endorsed in the Synod's report on the activities of the Serbian Orthodox Church between 1941 and 1946. See Jevtić, *Srpska crkva u Drugom svetskom ratu*, 94–6.

78 Krakov, *Na oštrici noža*, 142.
79 AV, Fond 562, Folder 3.1.1.2., docs 553–68. Figure 4.2 is doc. 560. In 1949, Boško Kostić, a man close to the collaborationist government in Serbia, published his memoirs in France, in which he included five images of the Gudovac massacre, including Figure 2.4; see Boško Kostić, *Za istoriju naših dana* (Lille: Jean Lausier, 1949), 27.
80 *Martyrdom of the Serbs*, 29, 141, 66. In the publication aimed at the American audience, a photograph from Gudovac that the editors must have known shows German officers investigating an Ustasha atrocity (Figure 2.1) was labelled in a way that implied that Germans took part in the execution.
81 *Martyrdom of the Serbs*, 161.
82 Vojinović, *NDH u Beogradu*, 130.
83 Matija Kovačić (ed.), *Odmetnička zvjerstva i pustošenja u Nezavisnoj Državi Hrvatskoj u prvim mjesecima života hrvatske narodne države* (Zagreb: Naklada Hrvatskog izdavalačkog bibliografskog zavoda, 1942).
84 Ibid., 5.
85 Ibid.
86 Franjo Rubina, *Kozara: Grob partizana* (Zagreb: Nakladna knjižara Velebit, 1942); Rubina, *Krvave tajne planine Kozare* (Zagreb: Naklada odgojnog dela ustaške vojnice, 1942).
87 Božidar Novak, *Hrvatsko novinarstvo u 20. stoljeću* (Zagreb: Golden Marketing – Tehnička Knjiga, 2005), 285.
88 Rory Yeomans, *Visions of Annihilation: The Ustasha Regime and the Cultural Politics of Fascism* (Pittsburgh, PA: University of Pittsburgh Press, 2013), 140, 315. See also, Rory Yeomans, '"For us, beloved commander, you will never die!" Mourning Jure Francetić, Ustasha death squad leader', in *In the Shadow of Hitler: Personalities of the Right in Central and Eastern Europe*, ed. Rebecca Haynes and Martyn Rady (London: I.B. Tauris), 193–4.
89 Both books were printed by the same company, 'Ustasha' from Zagreb.
90 *Odmetnička zvjerstva*, 22.
91 Ibid., 20.
92 This is typical of atrocity propaganda. See Horne and Cramer, *German Atrocities 1914*, 118.
93 Kovačić, *Odmetnička zvjerstva*, photoplates, ix.
94 Ibid., photoplates, iv, v and xxi.
95 Ibid., photoplates, iii, xxi and xxv.
96 Lukas Meissel, 'Perpetrator photography: The pictures of the *Erkennungsdienst* at Mauthausen Concentration Camp', in *Fotografien aus den Lagern des NS-Regimes. Beweissicherung und ästhetische* Praxis, ed. Hildegard Frübis, Clara Oberle and Agnieszka Pufelska (Vienna: Böhlau Verlag, 2019), 32.
97 *Kozara, groblje partizana*, 77.
98 See Yeomans, *Visions of Annihilation*, 154–7.
99 *Kozara, groblje partizana*, 60.
100 Ibid., 83, 85.
101 Thousands of mostly Serbian children were saved from these facilities by Diana Budisavljević, a humanitarian of Austrian descent, see Nataša Mataušić, 'Diana Budisavljević: The silent truth', in *Revolutionary Totalitarianism, Pragmatic Socialism, Transition: Tito's Yugoslavia, Stories Untold*, ed. Gorana Ognjenović and Jasna Jozelić (Basingstoke: Palgrave Macmillan, 2016), 49–97.

102 *Sjeverozapadna Hrvatska u narodnooslobodilačkoj borbi i socijalističkoj revoluciji*, vol. 2 (Zagreb: Institut za historiju radničkog pokreta Hrvatske, 1984), 324 and 310; see also Dušan Korać, *Kordun i Banija u narodnooslobodilačkoj borbi i socijalističkoj revoluciji* (Zagreb: Školska Knjiga, 1986), 260, and *Zbornik dokumenata*, Part V, Vol. 1, 301–3.
103 A number of these images have been published in Obhođaš et al., *Ustaška vojnica 1*.
104 Walter Manoschek, *Holokaust u Srbiji: Vojna okupaciona politika i uništavanje Jevreja, 1941–1942* (Belgrade: Službeni list SRJ, 2007), 89.
105 See Shepherd, *Terror in the Balkans*, 122, also Manoschek, *Holokaust u Srbiji*, 88–9.
106 Hirsch, 'Surviving images: Holocaust photographs and the work of postmemory', 25–6.
107 See Mataušić, *Jasenovac - Fotomonografija*, 29. It is unclear whether Stöger was in charge of the filming or whether this was undertaken by a different crew. The similarity in content suggests that the photographs and the film footage were created around the same time.
108 Struk, *Photographing the Holocaust*, 19–20.
109 Hermann Proebst, 'Jasenovac nije ni lječilište ni mučilište', *Spremnost*, 3 March 1942, cited in Antun Miletić, *Koncentracioni logor Jasenovac*, vol. 1 (Belgrade: Narodna knjiga, 1986), 174–7. As many as 70 per cent of the total number of victims of Jasenovac perished in 1942, most of them in the summer months, see Cvetković, 'Koncentracijski logor Jasenovac', 206.
110 Article in the Ustasha publication *Hrvatski narod*, 9 September 1942, cited in Miletić, *Koncentracioni logor Jasenovac*, vol. 1, 444.
111 E.g. 'Junački se treba osvetiti', *Vjesnik* 14 (July 1942): 21–2. See also Predrag Matvejević, 'Naša književnost pobune i otpora', in *Kultura i umjetnost u NOB-u i socijalističkoj revoluciji u Hrvatskoj*, ed. Ivan Jelić, Dunja Rihtman-Auguštin and Vice Zaninović (Zagreb: August Cesarec, 1975), 83–92. Also, Dunja Rihtman-Auguštin, 'Folklor kao komunikacija u NOB-u', same volume, 151–65.
112 The quote is from a Partisan oath used by units in Bosnia. Cited in Hoare, *Genocide and Resistance in Hitler's Bosnia*, 38.
113 *Zbornik dokumenata*, Part V, Vol. 3, 144.
114 *Zbornik dokumenata*, Part V, Vol. 30, 183–9.
115 Žorž Skrigin, *Rat i pozornica* (Belgrade: Turistička stampa, 1968), 19.
116 *Zbornik dokumenata*, Part II, Vol. 13, 226–35, also Part II, Vol. 11, 46–8.
117 For more on Partisan photography, see Davor Konjikušić, *Crveno Svjetlo: Jugoslavenska partizanska fotografija i društveni pokret, 1941–1945* (Zagreb/Belgrade: Kolektor/Roza Luxemburg Stiftung, 2017).
118 Ibid., Part II, Vol. 6, 248–58.
119 'U čast Pavelićevog rođendana zaklano 1.000 djece', *Borba*, 21 November 1942. The article was preceded by a piece on Chetnik crimes which explicitly condemned revenge killings of Croats by Serbs, 'Zločini četnika u dolini Rame…', *Borba*, 21 November 1942.
120 *Zbornik dokumenata*, Part II, Vol. 6, 249, also 257–8.
121 Vyacheslav Molotov, 'The responsibility of Hitlerite invaders and their accomplices for crimes perpetrated in occupied Europe (October 14, 1942)', in *Soviet Government Statements on Nazi Atrocities* (London: Hutchinson & Co., 1945), 51–5. The full text of the note was published in *Borba*, alongside the translation of an editorial from the

Soviet newspaper *Pravda*, 'Izjava sovjetske vlade o odgovornosti hitlerovskih osvajača i njihovih pomagača za zločine koje su izvršili u okupiranim državama Evrope' and 'Zločinačku Hitlerovu kliku na odgovornost', *Borba*, 22 October 1942, 1.
122 *Zbornik dokumenata*, Part II, Vol. 6, 249–58.

Chapter 3

1 Antifašističko veće narodnog oslobođenja Jugoslavije (AVNOJ) was founded in November 1942 at the first assembly held in Bihać. It was replaced by a temporary parliament in 1945.
2 'Odluka o vrhovnom zakonodavnom i izvršnom narodnom predstavničkom telu Jugoslavije i Nacionalnom komitetu oslobođenja Jugoslavije', in *Jugoslavija 1918- 1988. Tematska zbirka dokumenata. Drugo izmenjeno i dopunjeno izdanje*, ed. Branko Petranović and Momčilo Zečević (Belgrade: Rad, 1988), 655–6.
3 'Declaration on atrocities', in *United Nations Documents 1941–1945* (Oxford: Oxford University Press, 1946), 15–16.
4 Aleksandar Levi, 'Krivična dela protiv čovečnosti i međunarodnog prava iz aspekta jugoslovenskog zakonodavstva', *Jevrejski almanah* (Belgrade: Savez jevrejskih opština Jugoslavije, 1963–1964), 103–28.
5 The reference to six subsidiaries as 'zemaljske komisije', that is 'country' or 'land commissions' was a way of emphasizing the status of nascent Yugoslav republics as geopolitical, rather than national or ethnic entities. The term 'zemaljska' has proven notoriously difficult to translate into English. Even translators working for the State Commission could not agree on the terminology, and ended up using two different translations interchangeably, namely 'State Commission' followed by the name of the republic (e.g. State Commission for Croatia) or 'national commission' (e.g. National Commission for Serbia). Throughout the book, I will be using the term 'Country Commission', which better captures the term's political connotations.
6 Albert Vajs, 'Rad Komisije za utvrđivanje zločina okupatora i njihovih pomagača', *Anali Pravnog fakulteta* 9, no. 1 (1961): 392.
7 The Soviet Extraordinary Commission was established in November 1942.
8 'Državna komisija za utvrđivanje zločina okupatora i njihovih pomagača: Izveštaj Dr Nedeljkovića o radu D. komisije za period 1943–1948', AJ, Fond 110, box, doc. 132, 17 (henceforth 'Izveštaj Dr Nedeljkovića').
9 'Izveštaj Dr Nedeljkovića', 4.
10 Ibid., 43. Three quarters of this number (49,245) were 'domestic traitors'.
11 AJ, Fond 110, box 1, doc. 2.
12 E.g. 'Okružnom organu Zemkom-a za okrug Kozara', 5 March 1945, ARS, Records of the regional office of the [Bosnian] Country Commission for the Investigation of the Crimes of the Occupiers, Kozara, Box 1.
13 'Prikupljajte fotografije', undated, ABiH, Records of the Country Commission for the Investigation of Crimes of the Occupiers and their Accomplices, Reports, Box I, doc. 126.
14 In the final months of the war, undercover Partisan operatives were tasked with photographing leading Ustasha officials and other collaborators for the purpose of subsequent identification; see Nikola Brezović Prebeg, 'Teritorijalna obavještajna služba i Odjeljenje zaštite naroda (OZN) Zagrebačke oblasti u NOR-u, od jeseni 1943.

do proljeća 1945. godine s osvrtom na grad Zagreb (fragmenti)', in *Sjeverozapadna Hrvatska u NOB-u*, 816.
15 'Izveštaj Dr Nedeljkovića', 29–30.
16 Ibid., 25.
17 Ibid. Upon receipt, the photographs were assigned an official 'inventory number' (which was standard practice for all forms of evidence), re-photographed and assigned a separate 'negative number'.
18 'Organ zemaljske komisije za utvrđivanje zločina okupatora i njihovih pomagača za okrug Kozare, Izvještaj za mjesec decembar 1944.', ARS, Records of the regional office of the [Bosnian] Country Commission for the Investigation of the Crimes of the Occupiers, Kozara, Box 1.
19 'Okružnom organu Zemkom-a za okrug Kozara', 5 March 1945, ARS, Records of the regional office of the [Bosnian] Country Commission for the Investigation of the Crimes of the Occupiers, Kozara, Box 1.
20 'Izveštaj Dr Nedeljkovića', 21, 30.
21 'Yugoslav War Crimes Commission: Report to the International Military Tribunal, Nuremberg', AJ, Fond 110, box 809, docs 415–502.
22 Cited in Martina Grahek-Ravančić, *Narod će im suditi: Zemaljska komisija za utvrđivanje zločina okupatora i njihovih pomagača za Zagreb, 1944–1948* (Zagreb: Hrvatski institut za povjest, 2013), 113.
23 'Izveštaj Dr Nedeljkovića', 30.
24 'Prikupljajte fotografije', see also AJ, Fond 110, Box 1, doc. 10; Article 5 of the State Commission's statute, *Zbornik dokumenata*, Part 2, Vol. 6, 252.
25 AJ, Fond 110, box 31, doc. 32. The photographs submitted to Nuremberg will be examined in more detail in Chapter 4.
26 'Uverenje', 23 January 1946, National Archives and Records Administration, Washington DC, RG 238, entry (NM66) 3 Box 22, USSR – 442.
27 ABiH, Records of the Country Commission for the Investigation of Crimes of the Occupiers and their Accomplices, Reports, Box I, doc. 173.
28 AJ, Fond 110, box 1, doc. 791.
29 'Anketa državne komisije za utvrdjivanje zločina okupatora i njihovih pomagača', *Borba*, 30 November 1944, 5.
30 'Anketa državne komisije', *Borba*, 16 January 1945, 6.
31 *Zbornik dokumenata*, Part 2, Vol. 6, 255.
32 Robert Wolfe, *Captured German and Related Records: A National Archives Conference* (Dayton, OH: University of Ohio Press, 1974), 95; see also Donald Bloxham, *Genocide on Trial: War Crimes Trials and the Formation of Holocaust History and Memory* (Oxford: Oxford University Press, 2001), 62.
33 See Jovan Byford, '"Shortly afterwards, we heard the sound of the gas van": Survivor testimony and the writing of history in socialist Yugoslavia', *History and Memory* 22, no. 1 (2010): 5–47.
34 For instance, a photograph of the execution of Lepa Radić hanged in Bosanska Krupa in February 1943 was said to show the execution of 'captured Partisan Darinka Živković-Stanić, a teacher'. Another showing the mutilated body of a partisan fighter had appeared earlier in a communiqué on Italian crimes.
35 ZAVNOH, *Zbornik dokumenata, 1944* (Zagreb: Institut za historiju radničkog pokreta Hrvatske, 1975), 353.
36 Srđan Milošević, *Istorija pred sudom: interpretacija prošlosti i pravni aspekti u rehabilitaciji kneza Pavla Karađorđevića* (Belgrade: Fabrika knjiga, 2013), 71–81.

37 Tomislav Dulić, 'Forging brotherhood and unity: War propaganda and transitional justice in Yugoslavia, 1941–1948', in *Utopia of Terror: Life and Death in Wartime Croatia*, ed. Rory Yeomans (Rochester, NY: University of Rochester Press, 2015), 241–59.
38 *Zbornik dokumenata*, Part 2, Vol. 12, 487.
39 This points to another similarity between the Yugoslav State Commission and its Soviet counterpart. The Soviet Extraordinary State Commission was also independent of Soviet courts, prosecutor's office or the secret police, in part because Stalin wanted the commission to be seen as impartial outside the Soviet Union. This is also why individuals with academic credentials, rather than technical knowledge or skills, were placed at its helm. See Sorokina, 'Peoples and procedures'.
40 'Izveštaj Dr Nedeljkovića', 82.
41 Ibid., 47.
42 Ibid., 82.
43 'Izveštaj Dr Nedeljkovića', 83–4. The exhibition was shown for fifteen days in Sarajevo and Cetinje, sixteen days in Ljubljana and twenty-four days in Zagreb.
44 Ibid. The State Commission also provided material for photographic exhibitions put up by propaganda sections of different army units and local authorities.
45 Cited in Slavko Komarica and Slavko Odić, *Zašto Jasenovac nije oslobodjen?* (Belgrade: Institut za savremenu istoriju, 2005), 70.
46 'U čast Pavelićevog rođendana zaklano 1,000 djece'.
47 Nikola Pavlić, ed., *Jasenovački logor: izkazi zatočenika koji su pobjegli iz logora* (Propagandni odsjek Narodno-oslobodilačkog vijeća Jugoslavije, 1942).
48 The liberation of Majdanek and the horrors encountered there were reported extensively in the Soviet press in August 1944. 'Report of the Polish-Soviet Extraordinary Commission for the Investigation of Crimes Committed by the German fascist invaders in the extermination camp at Majdanek in the town of Lublin' was first published in *Soviet War News* 965 (19 September 1944), and was later picked up by the *London Illustrated News* and other newspapers. See Zelizer, *Remembering to Forget*, 57–61.
49 *Zbornik dokumenata*, Part V, Vol. 34, 548.
50 A smaller investigation was carried out in a section of the camp a week earlier, by the local branch of the commission from Novska. The commission's investigators returned to Jasenovac again in June 1945. See Đorđe Mihovilović, *Jasenovac 1945–1947: Fotomonografija* (Jasenovac: JUSP Jasenovac, 2016). The first photographs of the destroyed village of Jasenovac were taken by a photojournalist working for the Yugoslav news agency Tanjug, who was embedded with the Partisan unit that liberated the area in early May 1945.
51 Examples of photographs taken during the Country Commission's investigations at Jasenovac are reproduced in Mihovilović, *Jasenovac 1945–1947*.
52 Ibid., 284. One of the photographs from Stara Gradiška was published in the Belgrade daily *Borba* shortly after they were taken, in a report on the Stara Gradiška camp. However, they do not seem have featured in the press published in Zagreb which opens the possibility that they were sent directly to Belgrade. 'Strašna zverstva ustaša u logoru Stara Gradiška', *Borba*, 6 May 1945, 2.
53 See Mataušić, *Koncentracioni Logor Jasenovac – Fotomonografija*, 70. There is also a series of five images which show a group of men arriving at Jasenovac and being stripped of their belongings. However, it is unclear when these were discovered; ibid., 125–8.
54 Zemaljska komisija Hrvatske za utvrđivanje zločina okupatora i njihovih pomagača, *Zločini u Logoru Jasenovac* (Zagreb: Zemaljska komisija Hrvatske, 1946), 19.
55 Ibid., 19–27.

56 Ibid., 23. Some of these implements were later put on display at the Jasenovac Memorial Museum.
57 Ibid., 73.
58 There is also a third image from Sisak in the report on Jasenovac. A photograph of a body with a heavy object tied to their arms accompanies the claim that Ustasha attached weights to the bodies of victims before dumping them in the river, to prevent them from floating. Zemaljska komisija Hrvatske, *Zločini u Logoru Jasenovac*, 73.
59 'Ustaški koljači poubijali su u Sisku noć prije svog povlačenja oko 400 građana i seljaka', *Vjesnik,* 19 May 1945, 3; 'Dan pre oslobođenja Siska, Ustaše su pobile 400 zatvorenika iz logora u staklani Teslić', *Borba,* 28 May 1945, 3.
60 See Zdravko Dizdar, et al., *Partizanska i komunistička represija i zločini u Hrvatskoj, 1944.-1946. Dokumenti* (Slavonski brod: Hrvatski institut za povijest, 2005), 108–11. The report on the execution published in *Borba* reconciled the two figures by stating that the number of those killed was 400, but that only 150 bodies were recovered from the river; see 'Dan pre oslobođenja Siska'.
61 The collection can be found in the Croatian State Archives, HR-HDA-1422, Z-161-325.
62 Images HR-HDA-1422 Z-219 and Z-234 for Figure 3.5(a) and Z-220 and Z-246 for Figure 3.5(b).
63 The identity of the photographer who documented this event has been impossible to establish. It has been suggested by several authors that it was Hugo Fischer-Ribarić, a well-known Partisan photographer, although this claim is based on hearsay, rather than reliable evidence. For example, Mataušić, *Koncentracioni Logor Jasenovac – Fotomonografija*, 21; and Rhea Ivanuš, *Hugo Fischer (Ribarić), Ratne fotografije* (Zagreb: Galerija 'Milan i Ivo Steiner', 1998), 21.
64 'Film o Jasenovcu', *Borba,* 11 August 1945, 5.
65 Alongside the images from Sisak were some taken during exhumations in Lepoglava, but also photographs published in Ustasha propaganda literature purporting to show Partisan executions of Croatian civilians.
66 *Jasenovac*, directed by Gustav Gavrin and Kosta Hlavaty (Zagreb: Filmsko poduzeće FDJ, 1945).
67 See the review of the film published in *Narodni List*, 'Dvije zančajne filmske premijere: "Jasenovac" i "Preporod Staljingrada"', *Narodni List*, 18 September 1945, 5.
68 For examples see Mataušić, *Koncentracioni Logor Jasenovac – Fotomonografija*, 19–25.
69 Egon Berger, *44 meseca u Jasenovcu* (Zagreb: Grafički zavod Hrvatske, 1966), 65.
70 Zelizer, *Remembering to Forget*, 99–100. This well-established visual trope is to be found in illustrations of atrocities as far back as the Paris Commune and the 'Bloody Week' of 1871, see Brown, *Mass Violence and the Self.*
71 'Koncentracioni logori: Stara Gradiška', *Vjesnik,* 19 May 1945, 5.
72 'Koncentracioni logori: Nožem i maljem', *Vjesnik,* 20 May 1945, 5.
73 'Strahote logora u Lepoglavi', *Narodni List*, 31 May 1945, 3.
74 Jennifer L. Mnookin, 'The image of truth: Photographic evidence and the power of analogy', *Yale Journal of Law & the Humanities* 10, no. 1 (1998): 6.
75 'Kao grobar video sam mnoge strahovite ustaške zločine', *Vjesnik,* 31 May 1945, 4; 'Dokumenat ustaškog terora', *Narodni List*, 6 June 1945, 3.
76 'Kako su ustaški razbojnici opljačkali', *Narodni List*, 31 May 1945, 3.
77 'Ustaški koljači…', 5. The glass factory where the prisoners were held once belonged to Miloš Teslić, the Sisak entrepreneur whose death was examined in Chapter 2.
78 Dizdar et al., *Partizanska i komunistička represija i zločini u Hrvatskoj*, 109.

79 Ibid., 110.
80 AJ, Fond 110, RZ-II-281.
81 See Zelizer, *Remembering to Forget*, Chapter 4.
82 Ibid., 9.
83 Sontag, *Regarding the Pain of Others*, 9.

Chapter 4

1 This was one reason why the Yugoslav government wanted the closing statement of the Prosecution at Nuremberg to recognize Yugoslavs as victims of genocide alongside 'Jews, Poles and Gypsies'. See AJ Fond 110, Box 809, doc. 193.
2 'Prikupljajte fotografije!'
3 AJ, Fond 110, Box 1, docs 74 and 128.
4 Ivan Meštrović, *Uspomene na političke ljude i događaje* (Buenos Aires: Knjižnica Hrvatske Revije, 1961), 397–8.
5 *Saopštenje o zločinima Austrije i austrijanaca protiv Jugoslavije i njenih naroda* (Belgrade: Državna komisija, 1947), 88.
6 Ibid., 5.
7 ZAVNOH, *Zbornik Dokumenata, 1944*, 505.
8 *Notes Relating to the Italian Occupation of Yugoslavia* (date and publisher unknown), 94. This pamphlet was published by the Italian Ministry of Foreign Affairs and the Ministry of War in response to the indictment of senior Italian officers by the Yugoslav government. See Filippo Focardi and Lutz Klinkhammer, 'The question of Fascist Italy's war crimes: The construction of a self-acquitting myth (1943–1948)', *Journal of Modern Italian Studies* 9, no. 3 (2004): 330–48; also Filippo Focardi, 'Italy as occupier in the Balkans: Remembrance and war crimes after 1945', in *Experience and Memory: The Second World War in Europe*, ed. Jorg Echternkamp and Stefan Martens (London: Berghahn Books, 2010), 135–46.
9 ZAVNOH, *Zbornik Dokumenata, 1944*, 506.
10 *Report on Italian Crimes against Yugoslavia and Its Peoples* (Belgrade: Državna komisija, 1946).
11 *Državna komisija za utvrđivanje zločina okupatora i njihovih pomagača, Saopštenja br. 66-93*, 768.
12 Ibid., also *Report on Italian Crimes*, 176, 180.
13 'Za zajedničke zločine – istu pravednu kaznu', *Borba*, 1 April 1946, 4.
14 AJ, Fond 110, Box 809, doc. 10.
15 *Izveštaj jugoslovenske Državne komisije za utvrđivanje zločina okupatora i njihovih pomagača Međunarodnom vojnom sudu u Nürnbergu* (Belgrade: Državna komisija, 1947), 58.
16 'U izlaganju sovjetske optužbe jugoslovenskom optužnom materijalu poklonjena je naročita pažnja', *Borba*, 17 February 1946, 6.
17 See Bloxham, *Genocide on Trial*. Also, Lawrence Douglas, *The Memory of Judgment: Making Law and History in the Trials of the Holocaust* (New Heaven, CT: Yale University Press, 2001).
18 Bloxham, *Genocide on Trial*, 60–1.
19 Articles 19 and 21 of the Nuremberg Charter, see *Trial of the Major War Criminals*, vol. I, 15.

20 'Izveštaj Dr Nedeljkovića', 44, also AJ, Fond 110, Box 809, doc 8.
21 AJ, Fond 110, Box 809, docs 5 and 8. A total of 160 documents were submitted to the tribunal, of which 63 were presented in evidence during the trial; *Izveštaj jugoslovenske Državne komisije*, 2.
22 The film was made with the assistance of Lee Abbott, member of the US delegation at Nuremberg, who is credited in the Commission's documents for the quality of the film and its effectiveness at Nuremberg. The film was produced by Merlin Productions Ltd, a private company based in London (see AJ, Fond 110, Box 809, docs 12 and 53).
23 AJ, Fond 110, Box 31, doc. 32; *Trial of The Major War Criminals,* vol. VIII, 293. For an analysis of the Soviet documentaries which were shown around the same time, see Hicks, *First Films of the Holocaust: Soviet Cinema and the Genocide of the Jews, 1938-1946.*
24 Douglas, 'Film as witness', 452.
25 'Sutra se otvara izložba koju priređuje Državna komisija za utvrđivanje zločina okupatora i njihovih pomagača', *Politika*, 15 March 1946, 5.
26 AJ 110, Box 809, doc. 36, also 168.
27 AJ 110, Box 809, doc. 19.
28 AJ 110, Box 809, doc. 36.
29 The list of items and the captions have been preserved in the archives of the State Commission, AJ, Fond 110, Box 809, docs 336-57, and Box 31, docs 33-49. The photographs themselves were included in the Serbo-Croatian translation of the Yugoslav government's report published in 1947; *Izveštaj jugoslovenske Državne komisije*, 60-112. Some of the documents relating to the photographs suggest that there were eighty-nine rather than ninety photographs but that is because, for some reason, two photographs were listed under the same number, as 84a and 84b.
30 *Izveštaj jugoslovenske Državne komisije*, 62.
31 Ibid., 93.
32 'Sutra se otvara izložba', 5. See also 'Mogu li ovakvi zločinci uživati pravo utočišta u Trstu?', *Borba*, 10 March 1946, 4.
33 'Hitlerovski antisemitizam ispoljava se u surovom uništavanju nevinih ljudi', *Borba*, 2 March 1946, 5.
34 Among them was the photograph in Figure 4.1.
35 See Laurence Douglas, 'The shrunken head of Buchenwald: Icons of atrocity at Nuremberg', *Representations* 63 (1998): 42.
36 *Trial of the Major War Criminals*, vol. II, 102, 126.
37 'Yugoslav War Crimes Commission: Report to the International Military Tribunal, Nuremberg', AJ, Fond 110, box 809, docs 415 502, also doc. 105.
38 AJ, Fond 110, Box 809, docs 10-11.
39 For a discussion of attempts by the psychiatric profession in Yugoslavia to explain the psychology of collaborators, see Ana Antić, *Therapeutic Fascism: Experiencing the violence of the Nazi New Order in Yugoslavia* (Oxford: Oxford University Press, 2017), 229-33.
40 Dr. Dušan Nedeljković, 'Novost fašističkog i petokolonaškog zločina u istoriji zločinstva', date unknown, AJ 110, box 28, docs 1024-1028. I was unable to determine when the essay was written and if it was ever published. The fact that it was filed among State Commission's documents suggests that it was written while Nedeljković was at the helm of the commission and that it was deemed relevant to its work.
41 Cited in Timothy R. Vogt, *Denazification in Soviet-Occupied Germany* (Cambridge, MA: Harvard University Press, 2000), 18.

42 Nedeljković, 'Novost fašističkog i petokolonaškog zločina', 1.
43 Ibid., 2.
44 Ibid.
45 Ibid., 3.
46 *Izveštaj jugoslovenske Državne komisije*, 58.
47 'Hitlerovski antisemitizam ispoljava se u surovom uništavanju nevinih ljudi', 5.
48 See Vladimir Dedijer, *Novi prilozi za biografiju Josipa Broza Tita* (Rijeka: Liburnija, 1981), Chapter 18; also Ivo Goldstein, *Tito* (Zagreb: Profil, 2015), 362–83.
49 E.g. 'Narodima Hrvatske!', 9 September 1944, AJ, Fond 110, Box 1, docs 419–21. In Croatia, local officials were advised to tone down the rhetoric of revenge in majority-Croatian areas where the population feared 'collective retribution'; see ZAVNOH, *Zbornik Dokumenata, 1944,* 505.
50 'Narod sam kažnjava ratne zločince i pomaže narodnim vlastima u otkrivanju ustaških krvnika', *Vjesnik*, 3 June 1945, 3.
51 Milovan Đilas, 'Plemenita mržnja', *Borba,* 9 October 1942, 1.
52 Ibid.
53 Milovan Djilas, *Wartime* (New York: Harcourt Brace Jovanovich, 1977), 202. For more on Ehrenburg's work see Joshua Rubenstein, *Tangled Loyalties: The Life and Times of Ilya Ehrenburg* (Tuscaloosa, AL: University of Alabama Press, 1999).
54 *Zbornik dokumenata*, Part II, Vol. 6, 249.
55 'Okružnom organu Zemkom-a za Okrug Kozara', ARS, Records of the regional office of the [Bosnian] Country Commission for the Investigation of the Crimes of the Occupiers, Kozara, Box 1.
56 'Narodima Bosne i Hrecegovine', ABiH, Records of the Country Commission for the Investigation of Crimes of the Occupiers and their Accomplices, Reports, Box I, doc. 269; 'Apel Zemaljske komisije za utvrđivanje zločina okupatora i njihovih pomagača', *Vjesnik*, 30 May 1945, 1.
57 'Smrt nemačkim okupatorima: Osvetimo krv i patnje naše braće iz slovenačkog primorja', *Borba*, 29 November 1944, 4.
58 Ibid. The photographs were later included in the submission to Nuremberg and were described by the Yugoslav media as particularly 'striking' illustrations of fascist criminality. 'Hitlerovski antisemitizam ispoljava se u surovom uništavanju nevinih ljudi', 5.
59 'Jedna slika iz albuma nemačkog vojnika', *Borba*, 15 March 1945, 2.
60 *Državna komisija za utvrđivanje zločina okupatora i njihovih pomagača, Saopštenja br. 7-33* (Belgrade, 1945), 236.
61 'Jedna slika iz albuma nemačkog vojnika'.
62 Ibid. The reference to 'severed arms' suggests that the author of the article interpreted the fact that the boy's left arm is bent at the elbow, and is therefore not visible, as a sign that the limbs too had been severed. Also, the dark stain on the boy's back appears to have been mistaken for a bullet wound.
63 Ibid.
64 The fascination with Ehrenburg at the time was reflected in the fact that he was invited to visit the Yugoslav capital. See Goldstein, *Tito*, 373.
65 The Sarajevo daily *Oslobođenje* also published several articles on the character of the 'German beasts', including one by Ilya Ehrenburg. 'Nijemci zveri', *Oslobođenje*, 31 August 1944, 7, Ilya Ehrenburg, 'Nijemac', *Oslobođenje*, 4 November 1944, 4.
66 'Dvije značajne filmske premijere', 5.

67 ABiH, Records of the Country Commission for the Investigation of Crimes of the Occupiers and their Accomplices, Reports, Box I, docs 173–6.
68 AJ Fond 110, Box 32, docs 37–9.
69 Cited in Dizdar et al., *Partizanska i komunistička represija i zločini*, 113.
70 See Grahek-Ravančić, *Narod će im suditi*, 132–3. Articles published in *Vjesnik* in May and June 1945 often stressed that retribution was a precondition for a brighter future, 'Kažnjavanje fašističkih zločinaca jedan je od preduslova za našu svijetliju budućnost', *Vjesnik*, 13 April 1945, 1.
71 AJ, Fond 110, Box 32, doc. 38. The exhibition later toured seventeen Croatian cities.
72 'Izložba o zvjerstvima okupatora', *Ilustrirani Vjesnik*, 15 September 1945, 12; 'Izložba slika o okupatorskim zvjerstvima u salonu Ulrich', *Vjesnik*, 31 August 1945, 5.
73 AJ Fond 110, Box 32, doc. 38.
74 'Jedna slika iz albuma nemačkog vojnika'. There was also the ubiquitous reference to duplicitous Western governments, whose reluctance to extradite indicted Nazi officials amounted to 'sheltering German criminals'.
75 E.g. 'Izvještaj o izložbi fotografija ratnih zločina Zemaljske komisije za utvrđivanje zločina okupatora i njihovih pomagača za B.H', ABiH, Records of the Country Commission for the Investigation of Crimes of the Occupiers and their Accomplices, Reports, Box I, docs 173–6.
76 'Hrvatska javnost i štampa zalažu se za najstrožije kažnjavanje ustaša i koljača', *Politika*, 3 June 1945, 3.
77 'Narod će im suditi', *Naprijed*, 10 April 1946, 4.
78 AJ Fond 110, Box 809, doc. 550.
79 Ibid, listed as Exhibit 532. The image also featured in the State Commission's communiqué on 'Chetnik-Ustasha cooperation', see *Saopštenja br. 66-93*, 663.
80 See 'Za zajedničke zločine – istu pravednu kaznu', also 'Ante Pavelić i Draža Mihailović zajedno su vršili zločine nad našim narodima, zajedno moraju odgovarati pred narodnim sudom', *Borba*, 17 April 1946, 3.
81 'Apel Zemaljske komisije za utvrđivanje zločina okupatora i njihovih pomagača', *Vjesnik*, 30 May 1945, 1. A similar appeal from 9 September 1944 also only mentioned Ustasha crimes, AJ, Fond 110, Box 1, doc. 420.
82 Cruelty as a 'specialty' of the Ustasha was noted also in the Country Commission's 1946 report on Jasenovac; see Zemaljska komisija Hrvatske, *Zločini u Logoru Jasenovac*, 79.
83 AJ, Fond 110, Box 32, doc. 38.

Chapter 5

1 AJ, Fond 110, Box 32, doc. 161.
2 Ibid., docs 162–4.
3 AJ, Fond 110, Box 809, doc. 35.
4 Vajs, 'Rad komisije', 392.
5 James E. Young, *The Texture of Memory: Holocaust Memorials and Meaning* (New Haven, CT: Yale University Press, 1994), 63.
6 See Karel C. Berkhoff, *Motherland in Danger: Soviet Propaganda in World War II* (Cambridge, MA: Harvard University Press, 2012).

7 Jill Irvine, *The Croat Question: Partisan Politics in the Formation of the Yugoslav Socialist State* (San Francisco, CA: Westview Press, 1993), 237.
8 Carol Lilly, *Power and Persuasion: Ideology and Rhetoric in Communist Yugoslavia 1944-1953* (Boulder, CO: Westview Press, 2001), 115.
9 Heike Karge, 'Mediated remembrance: Local practices of remembering the Second World War in Tito's Yugoslavia', *European Review of History: Revue europeenne d'histoire* 16, no.1 (2007): 52.
10 See Jovan Byford, *Staro sajmište: Mesto sećanja, zaborava i sporenja* (Belgrade: Beogradski centar za ljudska prava, 2011), Chapter 5.
11 See Heike Karge, 'Sajmište, Jasenovac, and the social frames of remembering and forgetting', *Filozofija i društvo* 23, no. 4 (2012): 106-18.
12 See Byford, *Staro sajmište*, 87-8.
13 Letter from the local Communist Party organization in Jasenovac to the headquarters of the Union of Fighters of the People's Liberation War, 15 May 1952. Cited in Heike Karge, *Sećanje u kamenu – okamenjeno sećanje* (Belgrade: XX vek, 2014), 197.
14 Ibid.
15 Ibid., 215.
16 Cited in ibid., 128.
17 Bogdan Bogdanović, *Ukleti neimar* (Split: Feral Tribune, 2001), 155.
18 Karge, *Sećanje u kamenu*, 128.
19 Karge, 'Mediated remembrance', 57.
20 Bogdanović, *Ukleti neimar*, 156.
21 Karge, *Okamenjeno sećanje*, 206.
22 Cited in *Jasenovac* (Sisak: Jedinstvo, 1966), 1.
23 Bogdanović, *Ukleti neimar*, 149.
24 Cited in Radovan Trivunčić, *Spomen područje Jasenovac* (Zagreb: Turistkomerc, 1976), 75.
25 Ibid. In 1966, the mass graves in Donja Gradina, across the river from the main site of the Jasenovac camp, were officially designated as 'graves of the participants in the Struggle for National Liberation and victims of fascist terror', see Milan Bulajić, *Ustaški zločini genocida*, vol. 4 (Belgrade: Rad, 1988), 1170.
26 'Jasenovac camp', United States Holocaust Memorial Museum, Steven Spielberg Film and Video Archive, RG-60.3878.
27 Josip Broz – Tito, *Sabrana djela*, vol. VII (Belgrade: Bigz, 1982), 134. For a similar account of Jasenovac and the prioritization of Partisan fighters and communists, see Nedo Zec, 'Umesto predgovora', in *Da se ne zaboravi*, ed. Zdravko Čolić, Aziz Hadžihasanović and Milan Mučibabić (Sarajevo: Veselin Masleša, 1961), 5.
28 Emil Kerenji, 'Jewish citizens of socialist Yugoslavia: Politics of Jewish identity in a socialist state, 1944-1974', unpublished PhD thesis, University of Michigan, 2008, 120; see also Tea Sinbaek, *Usable History? Representations of Yugoslavia's Difficult Past from 1945 to 2002* (Aarhus: Aarhus University Press, 2012).
29 'Idejna koncepcija stalne izložbe u Jasenovcu', *JUSP Jasenovac*, 1965, 1. Ksenija Dešković made the same claim in a subsequent interview to the magazine *Poruke*, see 'Upoznajmo stvaraoce umjetničkih elemenata i cjelina u prostoru spomen-područja Jasenovac', *Poruke*, 2 November 1974, 6.
30 'Idejna koncepcija stalne izložbe u Jasenovcu', 1.
31 Ibid., 10.
32 Egon Berger, *44 mjeseca u Jasenovcu* (Zagreb: Grafički zavod Hrvatske, 1966); Mirko Peršen, *Ustaški logori* (Zagreb: Stvarnost, 1966).

33 Mataušić, *Fotomonografija*, 53.
34 The collection of original artefacts began in 1957, shortly after the creation of the Jasenovac Memorial Area was formally announced. Further calls for donations were issued by the Museum of the Revolution in the early 1960s. See Jefto Šašić, 'Pregled istraživanja genocida u Jasenovcu', *Naše teme* 30, no. 9 (1986): 1293.
35 The unaccounted-for images are mainly generic ones, whose descriptions could not be matched precisely to any specific source.
36 Nikola Nikolić, *Jasenovački logor* (Zagreb: Nakladni zavod, 1948).
37 For more on the Photographic Documentation Agency, see Hrvoje Gržina, 'Agencija za fotodokumentaciju – pozitivizam stvaratelja u postskrbničkome vremenu', *5. kongres hrvatskih arhivista*: *Arhivi u Hrvatskoj – (Retro)perspektiva* (Zagreb: Hrvatsko arhivističko društvo, 2017), 321–36.
38 According to the Museum of the Revolution's inventory books, several of the acquisitions and donations relevant to Jasenovac were received in the *autumn* of 1968, and therefore after the Jasenovac exhibition opened. However, the records of the Jasenovac Memorial Museum's photo archive suggest that some of this material was available earlier and was included in the exhibition. It is therefore possible that the Museum of the Revolution received the material early in 1968, but formally entered it in the inventory books after the work on the exhibition was completed.
39 Nikolić, *Jasenovački logor*, 5–7. For more on the official memory of the Second World War in Yugoslavia, see Sinbaek, *Usable History?*.
40 Gojko Nikoliš, *Korijen, stablo, pavetina* (Zagreb: Sveučilišna naklada Liber, 1981), 557.
41 Nikolić, *Jasenovački logor*, 8.
42 According to Vladimir Dedijer, Nikolić submitted a proposal for a memorial at Jasenovac to the leadership of AVNOJ as early as in 1944, while the camp was still in existence. See Vladimir Dedijer, *Vatikan i Jasenovac* (Belgrad: Rad, 1987), 667.
43 Nikolić, *Jasenovački logor*, 363.
44 Wolfgang Hoepken, 'War, memory and education in a fragmented society: The case of Yugoslavia', *East European Politics and Society* 13, no. 1 (1999): 203.
45 Trivunčić, *Spomen područje Jasenovac*, 75.
46 'Pronadene grobnice', *Poruke*, 15 September 1973, 3; 'Otkrivena još jedna masovna grobnica', *Poruke*, 10 October 1981, 3; 'Još jedna grobnica na gradinskoj strani', *Poruke*, 15 June 1984, 7; 'Istraživanja: Nove grobnice', *Poruke*, 15 April 1986, 2.
47 'Skraćeni zapisnik sa sjednice Savjeta S-P Jasenovac, 3.10.1985', JUSPJ, 1985, 3.
48 Berger, *44 mjeseca u Jasenovcu*. Included were some of the photographs from the Sisak execution explored in Chapter 3.
49 Ibid., 64.
50 Similar references to the extraction of the teeth can be found in captions accompanying two photographs of the exhumation of bodies at the Lepoglava camp in 1945, which the Croatian Secretariat of the Interior released to the Museum of the Revolution in Belgrade in the 1960s (MIJ III 7126 and 7127).
51 Berger, *44 mjeseca u Jasenovcu*.
52 Nikola Nikolić, *Jasenovački logor smrti* (Sarajevo: NIŠP Oslobođenje, 1975).
53 Ibid. For more on the origin of these photographs, see https://www.jewishvirtual library.org/photographs-captured-by-gilbert-di-loreto. The photographs featured in the collection of the State Commission for the Investigation of the Crimes of the Occupiers and their Accomplices, and were published in 1946 in a communiqué on Nazi concentration camps in Germany, see *Državna komisija, Saopštenja br 66-93*, 651.

54 Duško Lončar, *Deset godina Spomen-područja Jasenovac* (Jasenovac: JUSP Jasenovac, 1977), 26.
55 Photo archive of the Historical Museum of Bosnia-Herzegovina, FNOB 2589. What was then the regional archive in Banja Luka (now Archives of Republika Srpska) also had the same image in its collection, with the accompanying description suggesting that it is from Jasenovac, see ARS, Photo Collection, Inv. No. 7565.
56 Dušan Azanjac, Ivo Frol and Đorđe Nikolić, *Otpor u žicama: Sećanja zatočenika Knjiga prva* (Belgrade: Vojnoizdavački zavod, 1969), 64. The caption accompanying the photograph in this volume alluded to sexual violence when it described the young woman visible in the image as a victim of Ustasha 'orgy'. In the same volume, the other image from Dachau featured in Nikolić's book was published as having been taken at Auschwitz (204).
57 Dragoje Lukić, *Rat i djeca Kozare* (Belgrade: Narodna knjiga, 1978); *Kozarsko detinjstvo* (Belgrade: Narodna knjiga, 1973).
58 HR-HDA-1442, Z-526 and Z-527.
59 The photograph of the Chetnik execution was also sometimes published as representing Ustasha violence, but not as often. See for instance 'Svjedočanstvo užasa', *Vjesnik*, 30 June 1985, 6, or the 1983 documentary *Blood and Ashes of Jasenovac*, discussed in the next chapter.
60 Lončar, *Deset godina Spomen-područja Jasenovac*, 42. The screenplay for *The Gospel of Evil* was written by Stevo Bulajić, who also worked on *Battle of Neretva*.
61 See Byford, *Staro sajmište*, 121–8.
62 Just like in Žižić's film, most of the photographs were of victims of the Sisak execution in May 1945. According to the credits, they too were obtained from the archives of the Photographic Documentation Agency in Zagreb.
63 'Prikazuje se dokumentarni film "Evanđelje zla"', *Poruke*, 2 November 1972, 8.
64 Ibid.
65 Lončar, *Deset godina Spomen-područja Jasenovac*, 42, 'Prikazuje se dokumentarni film "Evanđelje zla"', 8.
66 For more on the Croatian Spring see Jill Irvine, 'The Croatian Spring and the dissolution of Yugoslavia', in *State Collapse in South-Eastern Europe: New Perspectives on Yugoslavia's Disintegration*, ed. Lenard J. Cohen and Jasna Dragović-Soso (Lafayette, IN: Purdue University Press, 2007), 149–78; Tvrtko Jakovina, ed. *Hrvatsko proljeće 40 godina poslije* (Zagreb: Centar za demokratiju i pravo Mika Tripalo, 2012); and Dennison Rusinow, *Yugoslavia: Oblique Insights and Observations* (Pittsburgh: University of Pittsburgh Press, 2008).
67 Bruno Bušić, 'Žrtve rata', *Hrvatski književni list* 2, no. 15 (1969): 2–3.
68 Vjekoslav Kaleb, 'Govorim o toleranciji', *Hrvatski tjednik* 1, no. 31 (1971): 15.
69 Novak, *Hrvatsko novinarstvo u 20. stoljeću*, 623, 680.
70 The statement was published in the daily *Vjesnik*. See Dedijer and Miletić, *Protiv zaborava i tabua*, 337.
71 'Primjedbe na program rada S-P Jasenovac za 1971. Godinu', JUSPJ, institutional archive, 1971.
72 Ibid.
73 Lončar, *Deset godina Spomen-područja Jasenovac*, 25, 39; Ana Požar, 'Dvadeset godina rada Spomen-područja Jasenovac', *Poruke*, 4 July 1988, 2.
74 Lončar, *Deset godina Spomen-područja Jasenovac*, 30; Spomen područje Jasenovac, *Izvještaj (Analiza i smjernice razvoja)* (Jasenovac: SPJ, 1980), 29.
75 Lončar, *Deset godina Spomen-područja Jasenovac*, 25.

76 Đuka Kaurić, cited in Trivunčić, *Spomen područje Jasenovac*, 76.

Chapter 6

1. Cited in Goldstein, *Tito*, 796.
2. Jasna Dragović-Soso, *Saviours of the Nation? Serbia's Intellectual Opposition and the Revival of Nationalism* (Montreal: McGill-Queens University Press, 2003), Chapter 2.
3. On the gradual introduction of the theme of genocide in Yugoslav historiography, see Sinbaek, *Usable History?*, Chapter 6.
4. See Slobodan Kljakić, 'Kratka istorija Odbora SANU za sakupljanje građe o genocidu nad srpskim narodom i drugim narodima Jugoslavije u XX veku', in *Catena Mundi II*, ed. Predrag Dragić-Kijuk (Kraljevo: Ibarske novosti, 1992), 498–512.
5. Vjekoslav Perica, *Balkan Idols: Religion and Nationalism in Yugoslav States* (Oxford: Oxford University Press, 2002), 150.
6. Holy Synod of the Serbian Orthodox Church, *Večan pomen. Jasenovac: mjesto natopljeno krvlju nevinih* (Belgrade: SPC, 1990). See also Byford, 'When I say "Holocaust"'.
7. 'Bili smo razbijeni pre izlaska na front', *Intervju*, 5 August 1983, 4–9.
8. E.g. 'Govor nadbiskupa Kuharića na komemorativnoj misi za kardinala Stepinca', *AKSA – Aktualnosti kršćanske sadašnjosti: informativni bilten* 6 (1981): 1–7. Ivan Supek, *Crown Witness against Hebrang* (Chicago, IL: Markanton Press, 1983), 169.
9. 'Desno od svake stvarnosti', *Vjesnik*, 13 January 1985; Novak, *Hrvatsko novinarstvo u 20. stoljeću*, 907, 922.
10. Cited in 'Negovanje revolucionarnih tradicija u funkciji ostvarivanja aktuelnih programskih ciljeva socijalističkog saveza', Archives of the Jewish Historical Museum, Belgrade, K.KSO-20, 410/88, see also 'Susret i savetovanje', *Četvrti jul*, 10 July 1984, 3.
11. 'Odlučno protiv falsificiranja istine o broju poginulih u Jasenovcu', *Poruke*, 22 April 1981, 1.
12. Jefto Šašić, 'Predgovor', in *Koncentracioni logor Jasenovac, 1941-1945*, ed. Antun Miletić, vol. 1 (Belgrade: Narodna Knjiga, 1986), 14.
13. Požar, 'Dvadeset godina rada Spomen-područja Jasenovac', 2.
14. 'Odlučno protiv falsificiranja istine', 1.
15. See Ana Požar, 'Jasenovac traži više istraživanja', in *Okrugli Stol, 21 April 1984*, ed. Radovan Trivunčić (Jasenovac: JUSP Jasenovac, 1984), 13.
16. Ibid.
17. 'S-P Jasenovac, Tekući plan za 1982. godinu', JUSPJ, 1982, 4.
18. 'Pokretna izložba "Koncentracioni logor Jasenovac"', *Poruke*, XVI, 4 July 1988, 10.
19. Ibid.
20. For more on the film and Zafranović's work more generally, see Daniel J. Goulding, *Liberated Cinema: The Yugoslav Experience* (Bloomington, IN: University of Indiana Press, 2003); and Dina Iordanova, *Cinema in Flames: Balkan Film, Culture and the Media* (London: BFI, 2001).
21. In '"Okupacija u 26 slika": Krik protiv zla Jasenovca', *Večernje Novosti*, 15 December 2018, available at http://www.novosti.rs/vesti/kultura.71.html:766130-OKUPACIJA-U-26-SLIKA-Krik-protiv-zla-Jasenovca (accessed 1 February 2019).
22. 'Arhitektura zla na filmskoj vrpci', *Danas*, 6 May 1986, 27.
23. 'Dokumentarni film o logoru Jasenovac', *Poruke*, 22 April 1981, 6.

24 The only major difference is that the film accords greater prominence to the suffering of the children of Kozara, a theme that entered public consciousness only in the 1970s.
25 The editors of the two-volume edition of survivor testimonies published in 1969 under the title *Resistance among the Wires* rejected testimonies that mentioned cannibalism in Jasenovac. They also noted that 'despite the warnings' none of the submissions 'mentioned the Germans, but only Ustasha' as the perpetrators. See 'Rezultati prve ocene rukopisa', AJ, Fond 297, Box 114.
26 See 'Dosije *Mladosti*. Tato, Jezus i Marija! - konc-logor Jasenovac', *Mladost*, 8–21 December 1986, 27; 'Delo i nedjelo', *Danas*, 20 January 1987, 44–5.
27 See for example 'Veliko interesovanje za film "Krv i pepeo Jasenovca"', 8; 'Iza žice bio je užas', *Večernji list*, 7 May 1986, 7. The educational potential of the film in the age of resurgent nationalism was acknowledged also in Anđelko Barbić, 'Protiv manipulacija', *Naše teme* 30, no. 9 (1986): 1297.
28 Zafranović in the television documentary *NDH – muk, ponor, strah* [Independent State of Croatia – Silence, Abyss, Fear] Directed by Stevan Kostić (Belgrade, Serbian Radio Television, 2016), Part 2.
29 'Mrtvi živima otvaraju oči', *Poruke*, 15 June 1984, 1.
30 'Pokretna izložba "Koncentracioni logor Jasenovac"', 10.
31 Mataušić, *Jasenovac: Fotomonografija*, 23; Nataša Jovičić, 'Jasenovac Memorial Museum's permanent exibition – The victim as an individual', *Review of Croatian History* 2, no. 1 (2006): 295–9.
32 E.g. 'S-P Jasenovac, Tekući plan za 1982. godinu', 3.
33 'Mrtvi živima otvaraju oči', 1.
34 'Kratak izvjetaj o radu odbora', JUSPJ, 1986, 3.
35 Jovan Kesar, a journalist based in Belgrade was also involved in the early stages of the work on this exhibition, but Miletić and Lukić are usually credited as the authors.
36 The institute was the main archive and research institution of the Yugoslav National Army, and the central repository for archival material pertaining to the Second World War in Yugoslavia.
37 'Spomen područje Jasenovac: Izvršenje programa za 1979. godinu. Prilog 7', JUSPJ, 1979.
38 Despite Miletić's affiliation to the Military Historical Institute, the institute never endorsed Miletić's work on Jasenovac or sought to associate itself with it. The edited collections of documents were very much Miletić's personal project.
39 E.g. Žejko Krušelj, 'Pakao u ravnici', *Danas*, 6 May 1986, 29; 'Nove knjige', *Poruke*, 15 April 1986, 1. For the reception of Miletić's book among Yugoslav historians, see Singaek, *Usable History?*, 165–6.
40 See Sinbaek, *Usable History?*, 94.
41 E.g. Ivan Jelić, 'Vrijedan poticaj daljnjim sitraživanjima', *Naše teme* 30, no. 9 (1986): 1309–11.
42 'Zapisnik sa sastanka za izradu nove muzejske postavke 12.11.1987', JUSPJ, 1987, 3.
43 For more on Lukić's life and work, see Jovan Mirković, *Dragoje Lukić – Roditelj pokošenog naraštaja* (Belgrade: Muzej žrtava genocida, 2008).
44 See Jasmina Tutunović-Trifunov, 'Zbirka dokumentarnih fotografija Dragoja Lukića (Muzej žrtava genocida)', in *Proceedings of the Fourth International Conference with International Participation on Suffering if Serbs, Jews and Roma in the Former Yugoslavia* (Belgrade, 2017), 207–14.
45 Mirković, *Zločini and Srbima*, 6.

46 In the late 1980s, Lukić made a large donation of photographs to the Jasenovac Memorial Museum, and until the mid-2000s this remained the largest single collection of photographs in the museum's archive. See Mataušić, *Fotomonografija*, 79. A document from 1987 indicates that the donation numbered 620 photographs and that Lukić arranged a donation of around 100 additional photographs from the Museum of the Revolution in Sarajevo. See 'Skraćeni zapisnik sa sednice Odbora za muzejsku djelatnost, 9.05.1987', JUSPJ, 1987, 5.
47 Mirković, *Dragoje Lukić*, 347.
48 Šašić, 'Pregled istraživanja genocida u Jasenovcu', 1290.
49 Šašić, 'Predgovor', 13.
50 Miletić, personal communication.
51 Dragoje Lukić, *Koncentracioni logor Jasenovac: Istorijske fotografije* (Belgrade: BIGZ, 1986).
52 'Pokretna izložba "Koncetracioni logor Jasenovac"', 10.
53 In Chapter 2 we already examined a similar dynamic in the way photographs of the Gudovac massacre were used in occupied Serbia.
54 'Pukovniku ima ko da piše', *Front*, 30 May 1986, 29.
55 'Muzejsko-ekspozicioni plan izložba 'Koncentracioni logor Jasenovac', JUSPJ, 1985. Exhibit no. 3.16.
56 I am grateful to the staff at the City Museum in Sisak for the information regarding the date of Teslić's death. Two versions of this image are among the photographs of the exhumation in Sisak: HDA, Collection of the Photographic Documentation Agency, HR-HDA-1422, Z-223 and Z-267.
57 'Mogu li ovakvi zločinci uživati pravo utočišta u Trstu', *Borba*, 10 March 1946, 4; Nikola Popović, *Koreni kolaboracionizma* (Belgrade: Narodna knjiga, 1974), 224; Photo archive of the Museum of Bosnia-Herzegovina Sarajevo, FNOB 929.
58 'Muzejsko-ekspozicioni plan izložba 'Koncentracioni logor Jasenovac' Exhibit no. 6.29; also, Lukić, *Koncentracioni logor Jasenovac*, 19.
59 Bogdan Šmitran, *Hronika potkozarskog sela Grbavci* (Gradiška: Prosvjeta, 2002), 306.
60 The saw was initially entered in the museum's inventory books as artefact no.70 but was later reclassified as no. 501. The inventory books mention that the saw was used to 'decapitate Partisan fighters in Grbavci under the Kozara mountain after the Kozara offensive' but do not mention Jungić by name.
61 Richard Raskin, *A Child at Gunpoint* (Aarhus, Denmark: Aarhus University Press, 2004), 98.
62 See, Lukić, *Rat i djeca Kozare*, 5.
63 Keilbach, 'Photographs, symbolic images, and the Holocaust', 67.
64 AJ, Fond 110, Box 31, doc. 32.
65 E.g. Dedijer and Miletić, *Protiv zaborava i tabua*, 337.
66 Branislava Milošević, 'Prezentacija spomen-područja-muzeja koncentracionih logora', in *Okrugli Stol 'Jasenovac 1986'*, ed. Ana Požar (Jasenovac: JUSP Jasenovac, 1986), 246.
67 For more on this legal and diplomatic battle, see Henry Friedlander and Earlean McCarrick, 'The Extradition of Nazi Criminals: Ryan, Artukovic, and Demjanjuk', *Simon Wiesenthal Centre Annual* 4 (1987): 65–98; also Allan A. Ryan, *Quiet Neighbours: Prosecuting Nazi War Criminals in America* (New York: Harcourt Brace Jovanovich, 1984), Chapter 5.

68 Bulajić, *Ustaški zločini genocida*, vol. 1, 12; Srđa Popović, *Poslednja instanca*, vol. 3 (Belgrade: Helsinški odbor, 2003), 1241; 'Nikad nije kasno za pravdu', *Front*, 7 March 1986, 20–2.
69 Interview with historian Bogdan Krizman in 'Suđenje Artukoviću je i suđenje celokupnom ustaštvu', *Front*, 4 April 1986, 3–5; Bulajić, *Ustaški zločini genocida*, vol. 1, 11.
70 Bogdan Krizman, 'Andrija Artuković – jugoslavenski Himmler', *Danas*, 11 parts, 27 November 1984–5 February 1985; Vojinović Aleksandar, 'Poslijeratni dosije ustaškog zločinca Andrije Artukovića', *Večernji List*, 10 parts, 20 November 1984–3 December 1984; Stanivuković and Kerbler, 'Artuković – ustaški Himler', *Večernje Novosti*, 13 parts, 11 November 1984–5 December 1984; Both *Danas* and the Slovenian daily *Delo* serialized Allan Ryan's book *Quiet Neighbors* (e.g. 'Mirni Sosedje', *Delo*, 6 parts, 16 March–29 April 1985), Bogdan Krizman, 'Artuković i njegovo vrijeme', *Danas*, 4 parts, 25 February 1986–18 March 1986.
71 See Branimir Stanojević, *Ustaški ministar smrti* (Belgrade: Nova knjiga, 1985); 'Artuković – nestor nacistov v Ameriki', *Delo*, 6 April 1985; Bogdan Krizman, *Ustaški logori*, 11 March 1986, 72–5; Bogdan Krizman, 'Artuković – Krvavi zlocinac', 45 parts. 14 February 1986–15 March 1986.
72 Bulajić, *Ustaški zločini genocida*, vol. 1, 198.
73 Popović, *Poslednja instanca*, vol. 3, 1270.
74 Jovo Popović, *Suđenje Artukoviću, i što nije rečeno* (Zagreb: Stvarnost, 1986), 32; Popović, *Poslednja instanca*, vol. 3, 1248.
75 'Slike užasa', *Vjesnik*, 6 May 1986, 4.
76 Popović, *Suđenje Artukoviću*, 154. It was recorded in the transcript that Artuković was 'unable' to review the images due to his poor eyesight.
77 This point was made by Artuković's legal representatives at the appeal stage. See Popović, *Poslednja instanca*, vol. 3, 1247.
78 Ibid., 1270.
79 Popović, *Suđenje Artukoviću*, 155.
80 Popović, *Poslednja instanca*, vol. 3, 1270.
81 The sentence was never carried out. Artuković died of natural causes in a prison hospital in Zagreb in January 1988.
82 'Presuda i oko nje', *Politika*, 25 May 1986, 6.
83 Xavier Bougarel, 'Od krivičnog zakona do memoranduma: upotrebe pojma "genocid" u komunističkoj Jugoslaviji', *Političke perspective* 2 (2011): 7–24.
84 'Da se nikad ne ponovi', *Oslobodjenje*, 17 May 1986, 1.
85 Sinbaek, *Usable History?*, 170.
86 'Jednom viđena fotografija', *Politika*, 18 January 1985, 12. See also Pilipović, 'Trgedija jedne srpske porodice', 62. The photograph in question was the one allegedly showing the mutilated body of Miloš Teslić (see Figure 2.3, this volume).
87 Bogdan Krizman, 'Artuković – Krvavi zlocinac', *Večernji List*, 20 February 1986, 25.
88 'Dokazi zločina', *Vjesnik*, 15 May 1986 (special edition), 2.
89 'Pokretna izložba "Koncentracioni logor Jasenovac"', 10.
90 Ibid.
91 Hoepken, 'War, memory and education', 202.
92 Pero Pletikosa, in the foreword to Popović, *Suđenje Arukoviću*, 6–9.
93 'Dosije *Mladosti*', 25–8.
94 Dragoje Lukić, 'Umjesto predgovora', in *Koncentracioni logor Jasenovac 1941-1945*, ed. Antun Miletić, vol. 3 (Belgrade: Narodna Knjiga, 1987), 6.

95 'S-P Jasenovac, Tekući plan za 1982. godinu', JUSPJ, 1982, 4.
96 'Radna zabeleška sa sastanka Radne grupe oko izrade nove muzejske postavke, 17.3.1987', JUSPJ, 1987.
97 Ibid.
98 'Osnovne komponente sadržaja za izradu tematsko-ekspozicionog plana nove muzejske postavke', JUSPJ, 1987, 1. Also, 'Tematsko-ekspozicioni plan sa materijalizacijom stalne postavke Memorijalnog muzeja', JUSPJ, 1987, 1.
99 'Osnovne komponente sadržaja', 1.
100 Ibid.
101 'Zapisnik sa sastanka komisije za izradu nove muzejske postavke, 4.12.1987', JUSPJ, 1987, 1.
102 Ibid., 2.
103 The fate of the Jasenovac Memorial Museum during the war of the 1990s will be examined in the next chapter.
104 'Zapisnik sa sastanka komisije za izradu nove muzejske postavke, 12.11.1987', JUSPJ, 1987, 1.
105 'Iza žice bio je užas', *Večernji list*, 7 May 1986, 7. The exhibition was continuously updated in subsequent years.
106 These can be seen in Vladimir Tadej's 1988 documentary *The Tower of Death* about Stara Gradiška, the last film commissioned by the Jasenovac Memorial Area. The film will not be analysed here, as the use of atrocity photographs was similar to that in *Blood and Ashes of Jasenovac*.
107 'Tematsko-ekspozicioni plan sa materijalizacijom stalne postavke Memorijalnog muzeja', 8.
108 Ibid., 18; Hoepken, 'War, memory and education', 200.
109 See 'Sedamnaesta sednica Savjeta Spomen područja Jasenovac, 18.12.1987', JUSPJ, 1987.
110 This explanation can be found in Jovičić, 'Jasenovac Memorial Museum's permanent exibition', 295, also Andriana Benčić, 'Koncentracijski logor Jasenovac: konfliktno ratno nasljeđe i osporavani muzejski postav', *Polemos: časopis za interdisciplinarna istraživanja rata i mira* 21, no. 41 (2018): 48.
111 'Skraćeni zapisnik sa sjednice Savjeta Spomen-područja Jasenovac, 3.10.1985', JUSP, 1985, 2; Jefto Šašić, 'Izvještaj o radu SPJ 1984/1985', JUSP 1985, 6.
112 'Skraćeni zapisnik sa sjednice Savjeta Spomen-područja Jasenovac, 3.10.1985', JUSP, 1985, 2.
113 Also, at the time, the SANU had more notoriety than political clout, even in Serbia. On the relations between the SANU and the Serbian leadership at the time, see Dejan Jović, *Jugoslavija - Država koja je odumrla* (Belgrade: Reč, 2003), 347–67.
114 'Skraćeni zapisnik sa sednice Odbora za muzejsku djelatnost, 9.05.1987', JUSPJ, 1987, 6.
115 Also, as we have seen, the creation of the museum display was overseen by a committee with a multi-ethnic composition, whose members certainly did not share the views of the Serbian Academy of Arts and Sciences.
116 See Dejan Jović, 'Reassessing socialist Yugoslavia, 1945-90: The case of Croatia', in *New Perspectives on Yugoslavia: Key Issues and Controversies*, ed. Dejan Djokić and James Ker-Lindsay (London: Routledge, 2011), 136.
117 ICJ-118, Reply of the Republic of Croatia, vol. 1 (December 2010), available at http://www.icj-cij.org/files/case-related/118/18198.pdf (accessed 3 August 2018), 51.

118 This version of events also omits the fact that up until 1991, the army was firmly and dogmatically devoted to preserving Yugoslav unity and the socialist order. It came into conflict with the Croatian leadership only in 1990, when the Tuđman-led government started to form its armed forces, outside the army's command structure. The Yugoslav People's Army's ideological alignment and collusion with the Serbian regime did not begin until the spring and summer of 1991. See Jović, *Jugoslavija - Država koja je odumrla*, 472–81.
119 Dragović-Soso, *Saviours of the Nation*, 112.
120 See Zoran Marković, 'Nacija – žrtva i osveta', in *Srpska strana rata, II deo*, ed. Nebojša Popov (Belgrade: Samizdat B92, 2002), 205–29.
121 Hoepken, 'War, memory and education', 211. For examples of claims about the 'conspiracy of silence' surrounding the genocide, see Kosta Nikolić, *Prošlost bez istorije* (Belgrade: ISI, 2003), 279–374.
122 E.g. Dedijer, *Vatikan i Jasenovac*; Bulajić, *Ustaški zločini genocida*, vols 1–4.

Chapter 7

1 Tuđman, *Horrors of War*, 7.
2 Ibid., 17. See also Zlatko Čepo, 'Dva decenija Instituta za historiju radničkog pokreta Hrvatske', *Časopis za suvremenu povijest* 14, no. 1 (1982): 7–58; Mladen Pavković, *Dr Franjo Tudjman u sudskim dosjeima* (Koprivnica: Alineja, 2007), 50.
3 Tuđman, *Horrors of War*, 7.
4 Cited in Tvrtko Jakovina, 'Nezavisna Država Hrvatska u Hitlerovom osovinskom sustavu', in *Spomen područje Jasenovac*, ed. Tea Benčić Rimay (Jasenovac: Spomen Područje Jasenovac, 2006), 42.
5 Ivo Goldstein, *Dvadeset godina samostalne Hrvatske* (Zagreb: Novi Liber, 2010), 222.
6 Jović, *Jugoslavija - Država koja je odumrla*, 475.
7 See Ivo Goldstein and Goran Hutinec, 'Neki aspekti revizionizma u hrvatskoj historiografiji devedesetih godina XX stoljeća – motivi, metode i odjeci', in *Revija prošlosti na prostorima bivše Jugoslavije*, ed. Vera Katz (Sarajevo: Institut za istoriju, 2007), 187–210.
8 Tuđman, *Horrors of War*, 233. See also Dulić, 'Mapping out the "Wasteland"'. Reference to the responsibility of Jewish kapos was removed from the English translation of the book. See Viktor Ivančić, *Točka na U* (Split: Feral Tribune, 2000), 127.
9 Tuđman, *Horrors of War*, 123.
10 Ibid., 125.
11 For other examples of Croatian officials speaking favourably of the Independent State of Croatia, see Andrijana Perković Paloš, 'Je li hrvatska vlast 1990-ih bila antisemitska?' *Časopis za suvremenu povjest* 48, no. 2 (2016): 291–329.
12 See Miroslav Hadžić, 'Armijska upotreba trauma', in *Srpska strana rata: Trauma i katarza u istorijskom pamćenju*, ed. Nebojša Popov (Belgrade: Samizdat B92, 2002), 125–47.
13 For examples of memoranda issued in the early 1990s, see Radovan Samardžić, *Ratni zločini i zločini genocida* (Belgrade: SANU, 1993), 171–91.
14 See Javorka Računica, 'Prikupljanje fotografije i druge muzealije u Istorijskom muzeju Vojvodine o stradanju i žrtvama srpskog naroda 1991-1992. godine', in *Ratni*

zločini i zločini genocida 1991-1992, ed. Radovan Samardžić (Belgrade: SANU, 1993), 485–7.
15 In August 1992, Zoran Stanković, a military pathologist who conducted autopsies on bodies of Serbian victims, criticized journalists for selling rather than donating atrocity photographs to public institutions. Cited in Samardžić, *Ratni zločini i zločini genocida*, 504.
16 See 'Uvodno izlaganje dr-a Milana Bulajića', in Samardžić, *Ratni zločini i zločini genocida*, 8–9.
17 See Bulajić, *Ustaški zločini genocida*.
18 See Byford, *Staro sajmište*, Chapter 7. Also, Byford, 'When I say "Holocaust"'.
19 Milan Lučić, *Teror nad Srbima '91 – The extermination of Serbs '91* (Novi Sad: Pokrajinski sekretarijat za informacije AP Vojvodine, 1991). The exhibition was co-organized by the Secretariat of Information for the province of Vojovodina and the daily *Dnevnik* published in Novi Sad.
20 Rastislav Petrović, *The Extermination of Serbs on the Territory of the Independent State of Croatia* (Belgrade: Ministry of Information of the Republic of Serbia, 1991), 9; Slobodan Kljakić, *A Conspiracy of Silence* (Belgrade: Ministry of Information of the Republic of Serbia, 1991), 45.
21 *Never Again: Ustashi Genocide in the Independent State of Croatia (NDH) from 1941-1945* (Belgrade: Ministry of Information of the Republic of Serbia, 1991). The publication was reprinted in 1995.
22 The exhibition was shown in Belgrade, Podgorica, Niš and Užice in early 1992. See Dragan Jerković, 'Predmeti i dokumenti kao dokaz o izvršenim ratnim zločinima i zločinima genocida', in *Ratni zločini i zločini genocida 1991-1992*, ed. Radovan Samardžić (Belgrade: SANU, 1993), 497.
23 Stanoje Jovanović and Dragan Jerković, *Zločin hrvatske države '91 = Crimes of the State of Croatia '91* (Belgrade: Vojni muzej, 1992).
24 The back page of the catalogue featured a photograph of a child killed in Croatia in 1991 alongside the image of an emaciated child from one of the Ustasha-run concentration camps.
25 Jerković, 'Predmeti i dokumenti', 493; Jovanović and Jerković, *Zločin hrvatske države '91*, 2.
26 Bojana Isaković, *Genocid and Srbima 1941-1945, 1991/92: Žrtve* (Belgrade: Muzej primenjene umetnosti, 1992).
27 Ibid., 5. Further sixty-five photographs were of destroyed churches and cultural heritage. These were included in a second volume of the exhibition catalogue. Bojana Isaković, *Genocid and Srbima 1941-1945, 1991/92: Spomenici* (Belgrade: Muzej primenjene umetnosti, 1992).
28 The same strategy was used in the partly state-funded 1993 documentary *God and Croats*, directed by Krsto Škanata.
29 Serbian politician Batrić Jovanović during a debate on the atrocities against Serbs in Croatia, Belgrade, August 1992. Cited in Samardžić, *Ratni zločini i zločini genocida*, 33.
30 See Elazar Barkan, *The Guilt of Nations: Restitution and Negotiating Historical Injustices* (New York: WW Norton & Company, 2000).
31 David Bruce MacDonald, *Balkan Holocausts? Serbian and Croatian Victim-centred Propaganda and the War in Yugoslavia* (Manchester: Manchester University Press, 2002).
32 Zelizer, *Remembering to Forget*, Chapter 7.

33 Allcock, *Explaining Yugoslavia*, 395.
34 See Milan Bulajić's introduction to *Never Again*, 4.
35 Samardžić, *Ratni zločini i zločini genocida*, 59.
36 See Batrić Jovanović in Samardžić, *Ratni zločini i zločini genocida*, 33.
37 Ibid.
38 Računica, 'Prikupljanje fotografije i druge muzealije', 486. The March 1993 issue of *Living Marxism* featured a selection of photograph from the London exhibition. These were considered too 'gruesome and unacceptable' to be displayed on the shelves in UK newsagents, so the issue was sold under the counter. See 'The pictures they don't want you to see', *Living Marxism* 53 (March 1993): 19–30.
39 The touring exhibition was displayed at the UN once before, in 1985. See Kazimierz Smoleń and Teresa Świebocka, *Auschwitz: A Crime against Mankind* (Oświęcim: Auschwitz State Museum, 1985).
40 See 'Letter dated 92/02/10 from the Permanent Representative of Yugoslavia to the United Nations Office at Geneva addressed to the Under-Secretary-General for Human Rights', UN Archives, E/CN.4/1992/7. For images of the damage see Milan Bulajić, *Jasenovac: Ustaški logor smrti, srpski mit?* (Belgrade: Stručna knjiga, 1999), 302–4.
41 Interview with Franjo Tuđman, Croatan state broadcaster HTV, 22 April 1996, cited in Foreign Broadcast Information Service (FBIS), FBIS-EEU-96-084, 41. Monument to victims of Ustasha violence at other locations including Jadovno, Slana on the island of Pag and others had been destroyed by Croatian forces during the war; see Subotić, *Yellow Star, Red Star* (Ithaca: Cornell University Press, 2019).
42 Mataušić, *Jasenovac, 1941-1945*, 157.
43 The material was returned to Croatia in November 2001, with the USHMM acting as an intermediary.
44 The exhibition later toured Novi Sad and Kragujevac. See Bulajić's memo to the Holy Synod of the Serbian Orthodox Church, 21 June 1995, cited in Bulajić, *Jasenovac: Ustaški logor smrti*, 645–6.
45 Ibid. 646.
46 Ibid.
47 Milan Bulajić, *Deset godina Muzeja žrtava genocida* (Belgrade: Stručna knjiga, 2003), 465.
48 Milan Bulajić, *Uloga Vatikana u nacističkoj Hrvatskoj* (Belgrade: Pešić i sinovi, 2007), 312.
49 Mladenko Kumović, *Jasenovac: Sistem ustaških logora smrti* (Belgrade: Muzej žrtava genocida/Novi Sad: Muzej Vojvodine, 1994), 53.
50 Ibid., 63. In the catalogue the two photographs were printed on the same page, virtually side by side.
51 Ibid., 69.
52 Bulajić, *Deset godina Muzeja žrtava genocida*, 156; 'U bečkom dvoru Hofburg izložba o Jasenovcu i film o Vukovaru', *Politika ekspres*, 10 July 1995, 10.
53 See Barry M. Lituchy, *Jasenovac and the Holocaust in Yugoslavia* (New York: Jasenovac Research Institute, 2006).
54 See Bulajić, *Deset godina Muzeja žrtava genocida*, 221.
55 Documentary films on the Independent State of Croatia produced in Serbia in the 1990s also adopted the same visual style, and often used the same footage and images, as the atrocity-focused films from the 1980s, most notably Zafranović's *Blood and Ashes of Jasenovac*.

56 Mataušić, *Jasenovac: 1941-1945*, 158; Andriana Benčić, 'Koncentracijski logor Jasenovac: konfliktno ratno nasljeđe i osporavani muzejski postav', *Polemos* 21, no. 1 (2018): 37–63.
57 *Never Again*, 63.
58 A recent bibliography of Lukić's work does not mention involvement in the 1992 exhibition at the Museum of Applied Arts or the 1994 exhibition on Jasenovac, even though his contribution was acknowledged in both. Mirković, *Dragoje Lukić – Roditelj pokošenog naraštaja*, 336–7.
59 *Pravo na nezaborav*, TV programme, RTS (Serbia), 12 May 2018.
60 'Jasenovac – The Right to Remembrance', website of the Serbian Orthodox Church, available online: http://www.spc.rs/eng/jasenovac_right_remembrance (accessed 2 May 2019).
61 'United Nations Department of Public Information 2018 Holocaust Remembrance Calendar of Events', available online: https://www.un.org/en/holocaustremembrance/2018/calendar2018.shtml (accessed 2 May 2019).
62 Ibid.
63 'Minister Dačić opens exhibition "Jasenovac – The Right to Remembrance" at the United Nations', website of the Ministry of Foreign Affairs of the Republic of Serbia, available online: http://www.mfa.gov.rs/en/about-the-ministry/minister/ministry-speeches/17384-minister-dacic-opens-exhibition-jasenovac-the-right-to-remembrance-at-the-united-nations (accessed 2 May 2019).
64 *Pravo na nezaborav*.
65 E.g. Petrović, *The Extermination of Serbs*, 43. The myth about the basket of eyes first featured in an anecdote described in the 1944 book *Kaputt* by the Italian journalist Curzio Malaparte. See Korb, 'Understanding Ustaša violence', 4.
66 'Minister Dačić opens Exhibition "Jasenovac – The Right to Remembrance"'.
67 Ibid.
68 *Pravo na nezaborav*.
69 The historian Vasilije Krestić in '27 January 2017, International Holocaust Day and exhibition "Jasenovac - The Right to Rememberance"', website of the Ministry of Foreign Affairs of the Republic of Serbia. Available online: http://www.mfa.gov.rs/en/statements-archive/statements2017/16132-27-january-2017-international-holocaust-day-and-exhibition-jasenovac-the-right-to-rememberance (accessed 2 May 2019). Krestić was the first to formulate the theory about the 'continuity' in Croatian 'genocidal intent' against Serbs in a controversial article published in 1986. Vasilije Krestić, 'O genezi genocida and Srbima u NDH', *Književne novine*, 15 September 1986, 1, 4–5.
70 'Izložba "Jasenovac - pravo na nezaborav" u UN', http://www.rts.rs/page/rts/sr/Dijaspora/story/1518/vesti/3015367/izlozba-jascnovac--pravo-na-nezaborav-u-un.html (accessed 5 June 2019).
71 '27 January 2017, International Holocaust Day and exhibition "Jasenovac - The right to rememberance"'.
72 Ibid.
73 Ibid.
74 The lead role was going to be offered to Robert De Niro. 'Srbi angažiraju De Nira i Spielberga za film o Jasenovcu', *Jutanji list*, 2 January 2009, https://www.jutarnji.hr/arhiva/srbi-angaziraju-de-nira-i-spielberga-za-film-o-jasenovcu/3997140/ (accessed 5 June 2019).
75 Ibid.
76 See 'Dodik: Stradanje Srba u NDH proglasiti genocidom', *Dnevni avaz*, 10 April 2016, https://avaz.ba/vijesti/229841/dodik-stradanje-srba-u-ndh-proglasiti-genocidom

(accessed 1 June 2019); 'Srbija i Srpska podižu spomenik žrtvama Jasenovca', *Politika*, 22 December 2018, http://www.politika.rs/articles/details/418729 (accessed 1 June 2019).

77 Milan Koljanin, 'Propaganda u oružanom sukobu u Jugoslaviji 1991-1992. godine', in *Ratni zločini i zločini genocida*, ed. Radovan Samardžić (Belgrade: SANU, 1993), 474.
78 Bulajić in *Genocid and Srbima u Drugom svetskom ratu*, 30.
79 Ivo Lajtman, *War Crimes against Croatia/ Ratni zločini protiv Hrvatske* (Zagreb: Večernji list, 1991).
80 Ibid., 3.
81 Ibid.
82 Ibid., 123.
83 Ibid., 124.
84 Another old stereotype featured in the book was that Croatia, located on the 'historical border between East and West', represents the bulwark of European civilization; ibid., 3.
85 Ibid.
86 Stjepan Lozo, *Ideologija i propaganda velikosrpskog genocida na Hrvatima* (Split: Podstrana, 2019), 15.
87 See Slavko Goldstein and Ivo Goldstein, *Jasenovac i Bleiburg nisu isto* (Zagreb: Novi Liber, 2011).
88 Hoepken, 'War, memory and education', 214–5.
89 Ljubica Štefan, *Srpska pravoslavna crkva i fašizam* (Zagreb: Globus, 1996), 11. See also Tomilav Vuković and Edo Bojović, *Pregled srpskog antisemitizma* (Zagreb: Altair, 1992); Anto Knežević, *Analysis of Serbian Propaganda* (Zagreb: Domovina TT, 1992); Pečarić, *Srpski mit o Jasenovcu: Skrivanje istine o beogradskim konc-logorima*; Philip Cohen, *Serbia's Secret War: Propaganda and the Deceit in History* (College Station, TX: A&M University Press, 1996).
90 Štefan, *Srpska crkva i fašizam*, 196, 198.
91 Ibid., 201; Pečarić, *Srpski mit o Jasenovcu*, 143.
92 Tuđman's interview to Croatian media, 22 April 1996, in FBIS-EEU-96-084, 30 April 1996, 40.
93 See Letter from the Office of the President of the Republic of Croatia to Miles Lerman, Chairman of the United States Holocaust Memorial Council, 6 May 1996, USHMM institutional archive, 04/2007.84, Collections, Box 1.
94 Tuđman's interview to Croatian media, 22 April 1996, in FBIS-EEU-96-084, 30 April 1996, 40.
95 As Tuđman himself acknowledged, inspiration for this approach came from the way in which the Spanish Civil War was commemorated in Franco's Spain.
96 Letter from the Office of the President of the Republic of Croatia to Miles Lerman.
97 See Ljiljana Radonić, 'Croatia: Exhibiting memory and history at the "Shores of Europe"', *Culture Unbound* 3 (2011): 355–67.
98 E.g. Miles Lerman, Chair of the US Holocaust Memorial Council, letter to President Franjo Tuđman, 18 March 1996, USHMM institutional archive, 04/2007.84, Collections, Box 1; 'A plan that's bad to the bone', *The Wall Street Journal*, 3 April 1996, A14.
99 'Izvješće of radu za 1998. godinu', JUSPJ, 1998, 1–4; 'Stalni postav Memorijalnog muzeja Spomen-područja Jasenovac: Muzeološka koncepcija', November 2004, JUSPJ, 2004, 3.

100 Izvješće of radu za 1998. godinu', JUSPJ, 1998, 1–4; 'Stalni postav Memorijalnog muzeja Spomen-područja Jasenovac: Muzeološka koncepcija', November 2004, JUSPJ, 2004, 3.
101 See Mataušić, *Jasenovac 1941-1945*, 163–74. According to the museum's records, 6,531 objects were retrieved, while the rest of the up to 14,000 objects are still considered missing. See Ivo Pejaković, 'Jasenovac Memorial Site and "difficult heritage"', *Temoigner – entre histoire et memoire* 115 (December 2012): 52.
102 Mark Biondich, 'Representations of the Holocaust and historical debates in Croatia since 1989', in *Bringing the Dark Past to Light: Reception of the Holocaust in Postcommunist Europe*, ed. John-Paul Himka and Joanna Beata Michlic (Lincoln, NE: University of Nebraska Press, 2013), 142.
103 Claus Leggewie and Anne Lang, *Der Kampf um die europäische Erinnerung. Ein Schlachtfeld wird besichtigtct* (München: C.H. Beck, 2011), 15, cited in Ljiljana Radonić, 'Slovak and Croatian invocation of Europe: The Museum of the Slovak National uprising and the Jasenovac Memorial Museum', *Nationalities Papers: The Journal of Nationalism and Ethnicity* 42, no. 3 (2014): 490.
104 Radonić, 'Slovak and Croatian invocation of Europe', 490.
105 'Stalni postav Memorijalnog muzeja Spomen područja Jasenovac', November 2004, JUSPJ, 2004, 14. Božo Biškupić, Croatian Minister of Culture, cited in Benčić-Rimay, *Jasenovac*, 5.
106 'Stalni postav Memorijalnog muzeja Spomen područja Jasenovac', November 2004, 14.
107 Edward T. Linenthal, *Preserving Memory: The Struggle to Create America's Holocaust Museum* (New York: Columbia University Press, 2001), 170. For a more detailed analysis of the architecture of the Jasenovac Museum, see Ana Kršinić Lozica, 'Između memorije i zaborava: Jasenovac kao dvostruko posredovana trauma', *Radovi Instituta za povijest umjetnosti* 35 (2011): 297–308.
108 'Stalni postav Memorijalnog muzeja Spomen područja Jasenovac: Muzeološka koncepcija. Jasenovac', April 2005. JUSPJ, 2005, 16.
109 Jovičić, 'Jasenovac Memorial Museum's permanent exhibition', 298.
110 Ibid.
111 Ibid., 296.
112 Benčić, 'Koncentracijski logor Jasenovac', 49.
113 'Stalni postav Memorijalnog muzeja Spomen područja Jasenovac', April 2005, 13.
114 Linenthal, *Preserving memory*, 171.
115 The reference to ethnicity was added after complaints from several reviewers. It is also noteworthy that Croats are over-represented in the portraits of individual victims, which was highlighted as problematic, but was not addressed. See Ivo Goldstein, 'Očitovanje', 13 March 2006, JUSPJ, 2006, 2.
116 Some of the murder weapons – a mallet, a hammer and a dagger – feature among the exhibits, although they were included only after a public outcry over the absence of any representation of the brutality of the killings. A table providing the breakdown of victims by ethnicity was also added later, for the same reason.
117 'Stalni postav Memorijalnog muzeja Spomen područja Jasenovac', April 2005, 17.
118 Ivo Goldstein, 'Očitovanje', 13 March 2006, JUSPJ, 2006, 2.
119 Stuart Hall, 'Cultural Identity and Diaspora', in *Identity: Community, Culture, Difference*, ed. Jonathan Rutherford (London: Lawrence & Wishart 1990), 233.
120 See Paloma Gay y Blasco, 'Picturing "Gypsies": Interdisciplinary Approaches to Roma Representation', *Third Text* 22, no. 3 (2008): 297–303; Annabel Tremlett, 'Visualising

everyday ethnicity: Moving beyond stereotypes of Roma minorities', *Identities* 24, no. 6 (2017): 720–40.
121 The same applies to the use in the exhibition of Edmund Stöger's propaganda photographs. Several of them are on display in the section devoted to conditions in the camp, without any reference to their provenance. Only the legend displayed next to a screen showing the film footage taken around the same time mentions that these are 'extracts from an Ustasha propaganda film'.
122 'Stalni postav Memorijalnog muzeja Spomen područja Jasenovac', November 2004, 13.
123 See Linenthal, *Preserving Memory*, 192.
124 James E. Young, *Writing and Rewriting the Holocaust: Narrative and the Consequences of Interpretation* (Bloomington: Indiana University Press, 1988), 163; see also Byford, 'Remembering Jasenovac'.
125 Đuro Zatezalo, *Radio sam svoj seljački i kovački posao: svjedočanstva genocida* (Zagreb: Srpsko kulturno društvo Prosvjeta, 2005); Zatezalo, *Jadovno, kompleks ustaških logora*.
126 See Mataušić, *Jasenovac 1941-1945*, 167. At the time, Zatezalo was also the vice president of Croatia's State Council for National Minorities.
127 Đuro Zatezalo, 'Recenzija scenarija novog stalnog postava Memorijalnog muzeja Jasenovac', 27 October 2004, JUSPJ, 2004, 3. For criticism of the display, including the absence of photographs, see for instance Solomon Jazbec, *Magnissimus Crimen* (Zagreb: Margelov Institut, 2008), 229, 274; Julija Koš, 'Concentration camp Jasenovac today: History rewritten. Tuđman's idea ultimately realized', paper presented at the Fourth International Conference on Jasenovac, Banja Luka, 30–31 May 2007. For more scholarly critiques of the exhibition see the already cited works by Ljiljana Radonić, also Kršinić Lozica, 'Između memorije i zaborava', and Vjeran Pavlaković, 'Sukobljena jasenovačka kultura sjećanja: postkomunistički memorijalni muzej u Jasenovcu u doba povjesnog revizionizma', in *Jasenovac - manipulacije, kontroverze i povijesni revizionizam*, ed. Andriana Benčić, Stipe Odak and Danijela Lucić (Jasenovac: JUSP Jasenovac, 2018) , 111–42.
128 Zatezalo, 'Recenzija scenarija novog stalnog postava', 1, 3.
129 Mario Jareb, 'Objašnjenje položaja recenzenta i dodatno stručno mišljenje o scenariju stalnog postava Memorijalnog muzeja Jasenovac – povjesni dio', 6 February 2006, JUSPJ, 2006, 1–11.
130 Đuro Zatezalo, 'Predmet: Recenzentima muzeološke koncepcije', 6 February 2006, JUSPJ, 2006, 1–2.
131 *Jasenovac*, 1.
132 Nataša Jovičić, 'Žrtva je pojedinac', in *Spomen područje Jasenovac*, ed. Tea Benčić Rimay (Jasenovac: Spomen Područje Jasenovac, 2006), 9. See also, Nataša Jovičić and Tea Benčić Rimay, *Geneza cvijeta Bogdana Bogdanovića* (Jasenovac: Spomen područje Jasenovac, 2009).
133 See Ljiljana Radonić, 'Univerzalizacija holokausta na primjeru hrvatske politike prošlosti i spomen-područja Jasenovac', *Suvremene teme* 3, no. 1 (2010): 53–61.
134 Jovičić, 'Žrtva je pojedinac', 9; 'Stalni postav Memorijalnog muzeja Spomen područja Jasenovac', April 2005, 13. For examples of unfitting comparisons made by some Croatian politicians between, on the one hand, the fate of Jews under Nazism and, on the other hand, the suffering of Croats either at Bleiburg in 1945 or during Serbian 'fascist aggression' in the 1990s, see Jelena Subotić, *Yellow Star, Red Star*.

135 The same strategy is present in museums in other parts of post-communist Eastern Europe. See Ljiljana Radonić, 'Visualising perpetrators and victims in post-communist memorial museums', *Yad Vashem Studies* 44, no. 2 (2016): 181.
136 Some of the images of landscapes included in the 2006 exhibition originate from Nikolić's photographic collection.
137 Young, *The Texture of Memory*, 132.
138 'Stalni postav Memorijalnog muzeja Spomen područja Jasenovac', November 2004, 14.
139 The caption remained despite the comment by one of the reviewers, the historian Ivo Goldstein, that it should be stated clearly that Pavelić was 'the initiator and sponsor of terror, chiefly responsible for the horrors of Jasenovac', see Goldstein, 'Očitovanje', 4. The caption was also commented on by Mario Jareb in his assessment of the exhibition, although his objections were quite different. The thing that troubled him was that the authors failed to mention that Pavelić spent time in Argentina before moving to Spain and that he had survived an assassination attempt by the Yugoslav secret service. Jareb, 'Objašnjenje položaja recenzenta', 6.
140 Radonić, 'Visualising perpetrators and victims', 184.
141 Linenthal, *Preserving Memory*, 210, 201.
142 Ibid.
143 See Hoepken, 'War, memory and education', for a similar argument specifically about the 1990s.

Chapter 8

1 See Zelizer, 'When war is reduced to a photograph'.
2 See Ariella Azoulay, *The Civil Contract of Photography* (New York: Zone Books, 2008); Laura Levin, 'The performative force of photography', *Photography and Culture* 2, no. 3 (2009): 327–36; Susan Ash, 'The Barnardo's babies: Performativity, shame and the photograph', *Continuum: Journal of Media & Cultural Studies* 19, no. 4 (2005): 507–21.
3 Struk, *Photographing the Holocaust*, 215.
4 Ibid.; Andrea Liss, *Trespassing through Shadows: Memory, Photography and the Holocaust* (Minneapolis: University of Minnesota Press, 1998); Susan A. Crane, 'Choosing not to look: Representation, repatriation, and Holocaust atrocity photography', *History and Theory* 47, no. 3 (2008): 309–30; Sharrona Pearl, 'Believing is not seeing: Teaching atrocity without images', *Afterimage* 40, no. 6 (2013): 16–20.
5 Sontag, *Regarding the Pain of Others*, 54.
6 See Crane, 'Choosing not to look', 309–30. Suzie Linfield, who used the term 'soiled heritage' offers a cogent argument against the 'rejectionist' school of thought; Linfiled, *The Cruel Radiance*, 73.
7 Linfiled, *The Cruel Radiance*, 75–76.
8 Sontag, *Regarding the Pain of Others*, 37.
9 J. M. Bernstein, 'Preface', in *Ethics and Images of Pain*, ed. Asbjørn Grønstad and Henrik Gustafsson (London: Routledge, 2012), xii.
10 Roger I. Simon, *A Pedagogy of Witnessing: Curatorial Practice and the Pursuit of Social Justice* (New York: SUNY Press, 2014), 8.
11 Linfield, *The Cruel Radiance*, 71.

12 Jovan Byford, 'The emotional and political power of images of suffering: Discursive psychology and the study of visual rhetoric', in *Peace and Conflict: Discursive Psychology Perspectives*, ed. Stephen Gibson (London: Springer, 2019), 285–302.
13 Halla Beloff, *Camera Culture* (Oxford: Blackwell, 1985), 121. See also Zelizer, *Visual Culture and the Holocaust*.
14 See Bernd Hüppauf, 'Emptying the gaze: Framing violence through the viewfinder', *New German Critique* 72, no. 3 (1997): 3–44.
15 Since 2012, numerous books published in Croatia have sought to revive old myths about Jasenovac being a labour camp or about the existence of a post-war communist camp at the site. Particularly prominent in disseminating these ideas has been the revisionist Association for the Research on the Triple Camp Jasenovac. Exponents of right-wing revisionist ideas have received a worrying amount of media coverage as well as support from mainstream institutions. For example, Vladimir Horvat, Igor Vukić, Stipo Pilić and Blanka Matković, *Jasenovački logori – istraživanja* (Zagreb: Društvo za istraživanje trostrukog logora Jasenovac, 2015); Igor Vukić, *Radni logor Jasenovac* (Zagreb: Naklada Pavičić, 2018); Vuković, *Drugačija povijest*; Lozo, *Ideologija i propaganda*, and so on.
16 Goldstein, *Jasenovac*, 786.
17 Bergholtz, *Violence as a Generative Force*, 7.
18 Ibid.
19 Linfield, *The Cruel Radiance*, 90.
20 Sontag, *Regarding the Pain of Others*, 79.
21 Claude Lanzmann, 'Le monument contre l'archive?' *Cahiers de médiologie* 11 (2001): 241.
22 Crane, 'Choosing not to look: Representation, repatriation, and Holocaust atrocity photography', 324, 311.
23 Roland Barthes, *Camera Lucida* (London: Vintage Classics, 1980), 76.
24 Bernstein, 'Preface', xiv.

Bibliography

Archives

Arhiv Bosne i Hercegovine (ABiH) – Archives of Bosnia - Herzegovina, Sarajevo
Arhiv Jugoslavije (AJ) – Archives of Yugoslavia, Belgrade, Serbia
Arhiv Republike Srpske (ARS) – Archives of Republika Srpska, Banja Luka, Bosnia-Herzegovina
Arhiv Vojvodine (AV) – Archives of Vojvodine, Novi Sad, Serbia
Hrvatski državni arhiv (HAD) – Croatian State Archives, Zagreb, Croatia
Hrvatski povjesni muzej (HPM) – Croatian History Museum, Zagreb, Croatia
Javna ustanova Spomen područje Jasenovac (JUSPJ) – Public Institution Jasenovac Memorial Area, Jasenovac, Croatia
Muzej istorije Jugoslavije (MIJ) – Museum of Yugoslavia, Belgrade, Serbia

Films

Blood and Ashes of Jasenovac [Krv i pepeo Jasenovca]. Directed by Lordan Zafranović. Jasenovac: JUSP Jasenovac, 1983.
Gospel of Evil [Evanđelje zla]. Directed by Gojko Kastratović. Jasenovac/Zagreb: JUSP Jasenovac/Jadran Film, 1973.
Jasenovac. Directed by Bogdan Žižić. Zagreb: Zagreb Film, 1966.
Jasenovac. Directed by Gustav Gavrin and Kosta Hlavaty. Zagreb: Filmsko poduzeće FDJ, 1945.
Jasenovac: The Essence of Horror [Jasenovac: Suština užasa]. Directed by Milan Stevanović. Belgrade: Filmske Novosti, 2008.
Occupation in 26 Scenes [Okupacija u 26 slika]. Directed by Lordan Zafranović. Zagreb: Jadran Film, 1978.
The Tower of Death [Kula smrti]. Directed by Vladimir Tadej. Jasenovac/Zagreb: JUSP Jasenovac/ Luna Film, 1988.

Books and articles

Ajzenberg, Aleksandar. 'Sekire, maljevi, kame'. *Jevrejski pregled* 23, no. 4 (2014): 17.
Album des Crimes Bulgares. Paris: publisher unknown, 1919.
Antić, Ana. *Therapeutic Fascism: Experiencing the Violence of the Nazi New Order in Yugoslavia*. Oxford: Oxford University Press, 2017.
Ash, Susan. 'The Barnardo's babies: Performativity, shame and the photograph'. *Continuum: Journal of Media & Cultural Studies* 19, no. 4 (2005): 507–21.

Azanjac, Dušan, Frol, Ivo and Nikolić, Dordje. *Otpor u žicama: Sećanja zatočenika*. Belgrade: Vojnoizdavački zavod, 1969.
Azoulay, Ariella. *The Civil Contract of Photography*. New York: Zone Books, 2008.
Baer, Urlich. *Spectral Evidence*. Cambridge, MA: MIT Press, 2005.
Barkan, Elazar. *The Guilt of Nations: Restitution and Negotiating Historical Injustices*. New York: WW Norton & Company, 2000.
Bathes, Roland. *Camera Lucida*. London: Vintage Classics, 2000.
Beloff, Halla. *Camera Culture*. Oxford: Blackwell, 1985.
Benčić, Andriana. 'Koncentracijski logor Jasenovac: konfliktno ratno nasljeđe i osporavani muzejski postav'. *Polemos* 21, no. 1 (2018): 37–63.
Berger, Egon. *44 mjeseca u Jasenovcu*. Jasenovac: JUSP Jasenovac, 1978.
Berger, Egon. *44 mjeseca u Jasenovcu*. Zagreb: Grafički zavod Hrvatske, 1966.
Berger, John. *About Looking*. London: Vintage, 1991.
Berkhoff, Karel C. *Motherland in Danger: Soviet Propaganda in World War II*. Cambridge, MA: Harvard University Press, 2012.
Bernstein, J. M. 'Preface'. In *Ethics and Images of Pain*, edited by Asbjørn Grønstad and Henrik Gustafsson, xi–xiv. London: Routledge, 2012.
Biondich, Mark. 'Representations of the Holocaust and historical debates in Croatia since 1989'. In *Bringing the Dark Past to Light: Reception of the Holocaust in Postcommunist Europe*, edited by John-Paul Himka and Joanna Beata Michlic, 131–65. Lincoln, NE: University of Nebraska Press, 2013.
Bliss, Edwin Munsell, *Turkey and the Armenian Atrocities: A Reign of Terror*. Philadelphia: Hubbard Publishing, 1896.
Bloch, Marc. 'Reflections of a Historian on the false news of the war (1921)'. Translation by James P. Holoka. *Michigan War Studies Review*, 1 July 2013, available at http://www.miwsr.com/2013-051.aspx.
Bloxham, Donald. *Genocide on Trial: War Crimes Trials and the Formation of Holocaust History and Memory*. Oxford: Oxford University Press, 2001.
Boban, Ljubo. *Hrvatska u arhivima izbjegličke vlade, 1941–1943*. Zagreb: Globus, 1985.
Bogdanović, Bogdan. *Ukleti neimar*. Split: Feral Tribune, 2001.
Bougarel, Xavier. 'Od krivičnog zakona do memoranduma: upotrebe pojma "genocid" u komunističkoj Jugoslaviji', *Političke perspektive* 2 (2011): 7–24.
Bromley, David G., Shupe, Anson D. and Ventimiglia, J. C. 'Atrocity tales, the Unification Church and the social construction of evil'. *Journal of Communication* 29, no. 3 (1979): 42–53.
Brown, Howard G. *Mass Violence and the Self*. Ithaca: Cornell University Press, 2018.
Broz -Tito, Josip. *Sabrana djela*, vol. VII. Belgrade: BIGZ, 1982.
Buettner, Angi. *Holocaust Images and Picturing Catastrophe: The Cultural Politics of Seeing* London: Routledge, 2011.
Bulajić, Milan. *Deset godina Muzeja žrtava genocida*. Belgrade: Stručna knjiga, 2003.
Bulajić, Milan. *Jasenovac: Ustaški logor smrti, srpski mit?* Belgrade: Stručna knjiga, 1999.
Bulajić, Milan. *Uloga Vatikana u nacističkoj Hrvatskoj*. Belgrade: Pešić i sinovi, 2007.
Bulajić, Milan. *Ustaški zločini genocida*, vols 1–4. Belgrade: Rad, 1988–1989.
Byford, Jovan. 'Remembering Jasenovac: Survivor testimonies and the cultural dimension of bearing witness'. *Holocaust and Genocide Studies* 28, no. 1 (2014): 58–84.
Byford, Jovan. '"Shortly afterwards, we heard the sound of the gas van": Survivor testimony and the writing of history in socialist Yugoslavia'. *History and Memory* 22, no. 1 (2010): 5–47.

Byford, Jovan, *Staro Sajmište: Mesto sećanja, zaborava i sporenja*. Belgrade: Beogradski centar za ljudska prava, 2011.

Byford, Jovan. 'The collaborationist administration and the treatment of the Jews in Nazi-occupied Serbia'. In *Serbia and the Serbs in World War Two*, edited by Sabrina P. Ramet and Ola Listhaug, 109–27. Basingstoke: Palgrave Macmillan, 2011.

Byford, Jovan. 'When I say "the Holocaust", I mean "Jasenovac": Remembrance of the Holocaust in contemporary Serbia'. *East European Jewish Affairs* 37, no. 1 (2007): 51–74.

Campbell, David. 'Atrocity, memory, photography: Imaging the concentration camps of Bosnia – the case of ITN versus *Living Marxism*, Part 1'. *Journal of Human Rights* 1, no. 1 (2002): 1–33.

Čepo, Zlatko. 'Dva decenija Instituta za historiju radničkog pokreta Hrvatske'. *Časopis za suvremenu povijest* 14, no. 1 (1982): 7–58.

Çetinkaya, Y. Doğan. 'Atrocity propaganda and the nationalization of the masses in the Ottoman Empire during the balkan wars (1912–13)'. *International Journal of Middle East Studies*, 46 (2014): 759–78.

Çetinkaya, Y. Doğan. 'Illustrated atrocity: The stigmatisation of non-Muslims through images in the Ottoman Empire during the Balkan Wars'. *Journal of Modern European History* 12, no. 4 (2014): 460–78.

Cohen, Philip. *Serbia's Secret War: Propaganda and the Deceit in History*. College Station, TX: A&M University Press, 1996.

Crane, Susan A. 'Choosing not to look: Representation, repatriation, and Holocaust atrocity photography'. *History and Theory* 47, no. 3 (2008): 309–30.

Cvetković, Dragan. 'Koncentracijski logor Jasenovac'. In *Jasenovac – manipulacije, kontroverze i povijesni revizionizam*, edited by Andriana Benčić, Stipe Odak and Danijela Lucić, 171–220. Jasenovac: JUSP Jasenovac, 2018.

Dawidowics, Lucy S. *The Holocaust and the Historians*. Cambridge, MA: Harvard University Press, 1981.

Dean, Carolyn J. *The Moral Witness: Trials and Testimony after Genocide*. Ithaca NY: Cornell University Press, 2019.

Dedijer, Vladimir. *Novi prilozi za biografiju Josipa Broza Tita*. Rijeka: Liburnija, 1981.

Dedijer, Vladimir. *Vatikan i Jasenovac*. Belgrade: Rad, 1987.

Dedijer, Vladimir and Miletić, Antun. *Genocid nad Muslimanima 1941-1945*. Sarajevo: Svetlost, 1990.

Dedijer, Vladimir and Miletić, Antun. *Protiv zaborava i tabua (Jasenovac 1941–1991)*. Sarajevo: Pregres, 1991.

Delage, Christian. *La Vérité par l'image: De Nuremberg au procès Milosevic*. Paris: Éditions Denoël, 2006.

Didi-Huberman, Georges. *Images in Spite of All: Four Photographs from Auschwitz*, trans. Shane B. Lillis. Chicago: University of Chicago Press, 2007.

Dinu, Radu Harald. 'Honor, shame and warrior values: The anthropology of Ustasha violence'. In *Utopia of Terror: Life and Death in Wartime Croatia*, edited by Rory Yeomans, 119–41. Rochester: University of Rochester Press, 2015.

Dizdar, Zdravko, Geiger, Vladimir, Pojić, Milan and Rupić, Mate. *Partizanska i komunistička represija i zločini u Hrvatskoj, 1944.–1946. Dokumenti*. Slavonski brod: Hrvatski institut za povijest, 2005.

Djilas, Milovan. *Wartime*. New York: Harcourt Brace Jovanovich, 1977.

Douglas, Lawrence. 'Film as witness: Screening Nazi Concentration Camps before the Nuremberg Tribunal'. *The Yale Law Journal* 105, no. 2 (1995): 449–81.

Douglas, Lawrence. *The Memory of Judgment: Making Law and History in the Trials of the Holocaust*. New Heaven, CT: Yale University Press, 2001.
Douglas, Lawrence. 'The shrunken head of Buchenwald: Icons of atrocity at Nuremberg', *Representations* 63 (1998): 39–64.
Dožić, Gavrilo. *Memoari Patrijarha srpskog Gavrila*. Belgrade: Sfairos, 1990.
Dragović-Soso, Jasna. *Saviours of the Nation: Serbia's Intellectual Opposition and the Revival of Nationalism*. Montreal: McGill-Queens University Press, 2003.
Državna komisija za utvrđivanje zločina okupatora i njihovih pomagača, Saopštenja br 7–33. Belgrade: Državna komisija, 1945.
Državna komisija za utvrđivanje zločina okupatora i njihovih pomagača, Saopštenja br 66–93. Belgrade: Državna komisija, 1946.
Dulić, Tomislav. 'Forging brotherhood and unity: War propaganda and transitional justice in Yugoslavia, 1941–1948'. In *Utopia of Terror: Life and Death in Wartime Croatia*, edited by Rory Yeomans, 241–59. Rochester, NY: University of Rochester Press, 2015.
Dulić, Tomislav. 'Mapping out the "Wasteland": Testimonies from the Serbian Commissariat for refugees in the Service of Tudjman's revisionism'. *Holocaust and Genocide Studies* 23, no. 2 (2009): 263–84.
Dulić, Tomislav. 'Mass killing in the Independent State of Croatia, 1941–1945: A case for comparative research', *Journal of Genocide Research* 8, no. 3 (2006): 255–81.
Dulić, Tomislav. *Utopias of Nation: Local Mass Killing in Bosnia and Herzegovina, 1941-1942*. Uppsala, Sweden: Uppsala University Library, 2005.
Đuretić, Veselin. *Vlada na bespuću*. Belgrade: Narodna knjiga, 1982.
Durković-Jakšić, Ljubomir. *Platon Jovanović, Episkop Banjalučki*. Kragujevac: Kalenić, 1986.
Džomić, Velibor. *Mitropolit Skopski Josif: Memoari*. Cetinje: Svetigora, 2006.
Engel, David. *Facing the Holocaust: The Polish Government-in-Exile and the Jews, 1943–1945*. Chapel Hill, University of North Carolina Press, 2012.
Feferman, Kirik. 'Soviet investigation of Nazi crimes in the USSR: Documenting the Holocaust'. *Journal of Genocide Research* 5, no. 4 (2003): 587–602.
Focardi, Filippo. 'Italy as occupier in the Balkans: Remembrance and war crimes after 1945'. In *Experience and Memory: The Second World War in Europe*, edited by Jorg Echternkamp and Stefan Martens, 135–46. London: Berghahn Books, 2010.
Focardi, Filippo and Klinkhammer, Lutz. 'The question of Fascist Italy's war crimes: The construction of a self-acquitting myth (1943–1948)', *Journal of Modern Italian Studies* 9, no. 3 (2004): 330–48.
Foucault, Michel. *Discipline and Punish*. New York: Pantheon Books, 1977.
Friedlander Henry and McCarrick, Earlean. 'The extradition of Nazi criminals: Ryan, Artukovic, and Demjanjuk', *Simon Wiesenthal Centre Annual* 4 (1987): 65–98.
Frübis, Hildegard, Oberle, Clara and Pufelska, Agnieszka. *Fotografien aus den Lagern des NS-Regimes. Beweissicherung und ästhetische Praxis*. Vienna: Böhlau Verlag, 2019.
Gay y Blasco, Paloma. 'Picturing "Gypsies": Interdisciplinary approaches to Roma representation'. *Third Text* 22, no. 3 (2008): 297–303.
Germans: Letters of a Criminologist on the Serbian Macedonian Front. London: George Allen & Unwinn, 1919.
Goldstein, Ivo. *Dvadeset godina samostalne Hrvatske*. Zagreb: Novi Liber, 2010.
Goldstein, Ivo. *Holokaust u Zagrebu*. Zagreb: Novi Liber, 2001.
Goldstein, Ivo. *Jasenovac*. Zagreb: Fraktura, 2018.
Goldstein, Ivo, *Tito*. Zagreb: Profil, 2015.

Goldstein, Ivo and Hutinec, Goran. 'Neki aspekti revizionizma u hrvatskoj historiografiji devedesetih godina XX stoljeća – motivi, metode i odjeci'. In *Revija prošlosti na prostorima bivše Jugoslavije*, edited by Vera Katz, 187–210. Sarajevo: Institut za istoriju, 2007.

Goldstein, Slavko. *1941, The Year That Keeps Returning*. New York: New York Review of Books, 2013.

Goldstein, Slavko and Goldstein, Ivo. *Jasenovac i Bleiburg nisu isto*. Zagreb, Novi Liber, 2011.

Goulding, Daniel J. *Liberated Cinema: The Yugoslav Experience*. Bloomington, IN: University of Indiana Press, 2003.

Grahek-Ravančić, Martina. *Narod će im suditi: Zemaljska komisija za utvrđivanje zločina okupatora i njihovih pomagača za Zagreb, 1944–1948*. Zagreb: Hrvatski institut za povjest, 2013.

Grant, Kevin. 'The limits of exposure: Atrocity photographs in the Congo reform campaign'. In *Humanitarian Photography: A History*, edited by Heide Fehrenbach and Davide Rodogno, 64–88. Cambridge: Cambridge University Press, 2015.

Grønstad, Asbjørn and Gustafsson, Henrik. *Ethics and Images of Pain*. London: Routledge, 2012.

Gržina, Hrvoje. 'Agencija za fotodokumentaciju – pozitivizam stvaratelja u postskrbničkome vremenu', *5. kongres hrvatskih arhivista: Arhivi u Hrvatskoj – (Retro) perspektiva*, 321–36. Zagreb: Hrvatsko arhivističko društvo, 2017.

Gumz, Jonathan E. 'Wehrmacht perceptions of mass violence in Croatia, 1941–1942', *The Historical Journal* 44, no. 4 (2001): 1015–38.

Hadžić, Miroslav. 'Armijska upotreba trauma'. In *Srpska strana rata: Trauma i katarza u istorijskom pamćenju*, edited by Nebojša Popov, 125–47. Belgrade, Samizdat B92, 2002.

Hall, Stuart. 'Cultural identity and diaspora'. In *Identity: Community, Culture, Difference*, edited by Jonathan Rutherford, 222–37. London: Lawrence & Wishart, 1990.

Hall, Stuart. 'The Determination of news photographs', in *The Manufacture of News: Social Problems, Deviance, and the Mass Media*, edited by Stanley Cohen and Jock Young, 226–47. London: Sage, 1981.

Halttunen, Karen. 'Humanitarianism and the pornography of pain in Anglo-American culture'. *The American Historical Review* 100, no. 2 (1995): 303–34.

Hicks, Jeremy. *First Films of the Holocaust: Soviet Cinema and the Genocide of the Jews, 1938–1946*. Pittsburg, PA: University of Pittsburg Press, 2012.

Himka, John-Paul and Michlic, Joanna Beata. *Bringing the Dark Past to Light: The Reception of the Holocaust in Postcommunist Europe*. Lincoln, NE: University of Nebraska Press, 2013.

Hirsch, Marianne. 'Surviving images: Holocaust photographs and the work of postmemory', *The Yale Journal of Criticism*, 14, no. 1 (2001): 5–37.

Hoare, Marko Attila. *Genocide and Resistance in Hitler's Bosnia: Partisans and the Chetniks 1941–1943*. Oxford: Oxford University Press, 2007.

Hoepken, Wolfgang. 'War, memory and education in a fragmented society: The case of Yugoslavia', *East European Politics and Society* 13, no. 1 (1999): 207–18.

Holy Synod of the Serbian Orthodox Church, *Večan pomen Jasenovac: mjesto natopljeno krvlju nevinih*. Belgrade: SPC, 1990.

Holzer, Anton. *Das Lächeln der Henker. Der unbekannte Krieg gegen die Zivilbevölkerung 1914–1918*. Dormstadt: Primus Verlag, 2008.

Horne, John and Kramer, Alan. *German Atrocities 1914: A History of Denial*. New Haven: Yale University Press, 2001.

Horvat, Vladimir, Vukić, Igor, Pilić, Stipo and Matković, Blanka. *Jasenovački logori – istraživanja*. Zagreb: Društvo za istraživanje trostrukog logora Jasenovac, 2015.
Hüppauf, Bernd. 'Emptying the gaze: Framing violence through the viewfinder'. *New German Critique* 72, no. 3 (1997): 3–44.
Iordanova, Dina. *Cinema in Flames: Balkan Film, Culture and the Media*. London: BFI, 2001.
Irvine, Jill. *The Croat Question: Partisan Politics in the Formation of the Yugoslav Socialist State*. San Francisco, CA: Westview Press, 1993.
Irvine, Jill. 'The Croatian Spring and the dissolution of Yugoslavia'. In *State Collapse in South-Eastern Europe: New Perspectives on Yugoslavia's Disintegration*, edited by Lenard J. Cohen and Jasna Dragović-Soso, 149–78. Lafayette, IN: Purdue University Press, 2007.
Isaković, Bojana. *Genocid and Srbima 1941-1945, 1991/92: Spomenici*. Belgrade, Muzej primenjene umetnosti, 1992.
Isaković, Bojana. *Genocid and Srbima 1941-1945, 1991/92: Žrtve*. Belgrade, Muzej primenjene umetnosti, 1992.
Ivančić, Viktor. *Točka na U*. Split: Feral Tribune, 2000.
Ivanuš, Rhea. *Hugo Fischer (Ribarić), Ratne fotografije*. Zagreb: Galerija 'Milan i Ivo Steiner', 1998.
Izveštaj jugoslovenske Državne komisije za utvrđivanje zločina okupatora i njihovih pomagača Međunarodnom vojnom sudu u Nürnbergu. Belgrade: Državna komisija, 1947.
Jakovina, Tvrtko. *Hrvatsko proljeće 40 godina poslije*. Zagreb, Centar za demokratiju i pravo Mika Tripalo, 2012.
Jakovina, Tvrtko. 'Nezavisna Država Hrvatska u Hitlerovom osovinskom sustavu'. In *Spomen područje Jasenovac*, ed. Tea Benčić Rimay, 17–43. Jasenovac: Spomen područje Jasenovac, 2006.
Jasenovac. Sisak: Jedinstvo, 1966.
Jelić, Ivan. 'Vrijedan poticaj daljnjim sitraživanjima', *Naše teme* 30, no. 9 (1986): 1309–11.
Jelić-Butić, Fikreta. *Ustaše i NDH*. Zagreb: Liber, 1977.
Jerković, Dragan. 'Predmeti i dokumenti kao dokaz o izvrsenim ratnim zlocinima i zločinima genocida'. In *Ratni zločini i zločini genocida 1991-1992*, edited by Radovan Samardžić, 493–89. Belgrade: SANU, 1993.
Jerković, Nebojša (ed.). *Never Again: Ustashi Genocide in the Independent State of Croatia (NDH) from 1941-1945*. Belgrade: Ministry of Information of the Republic of Serbia, 1991.
Jevtić, Atanasije. *Od Kosova do Jadovna*. Trebinje: Manastir Tvrdoš, 2007.
Jevtić, Atanasije. *Srpska crkva u Drugom svetskom ratu: iz arhiva Sv. Arhijerejskog Sinoda Srpske Pravoslavne Crkve*. Belgrade: Publisher unknown, 1992.
Jovanović, Stanoje and Jerković, Dragan. *Zločin hrvatske države '91 = Crimes of the State of Croatia '91*. Belgrade: Vojni muzej, 1992.
Jović, Dejan. *Jugoslavija - Država koja je odumrla*. Belgrade: Reč, 2003.
Jović, Dejan. 'Reassessing socialist Yugoslavia, 1945–90: The case of Croatia'. In *New Perspectives on Yugoslavia: Key Issues and Controversies*, edited by Dejan Djokić and James Ker-Lindsay, 117–42. London: Routledge, 2011.
Jovičić, Nataša. 'Jasenovac Memorial Museum's permanent exhibition – the victim as an Individual'. *Review of Croatian History* 2, no. 1 (2006): 295–99.
Jovičić, Nataša. 'Žrtva je pojedinac'. In *Spomen područje Jasenovac*, ed. Tea Benčić Rimay, 9–10. Jasenovac: Spomen Područje Jasenovac, 2006.
Karapandžić, Borivoje. *Građanski rat u Srbiji, 1941–1945*. Belgrade: Nova Iskra, 1993.

Karge, Heike. 'Mediated remembrance: Local practices of remembering the Second World War in Tito's Yugoslavia', *European Review of History: Revue europeenne d'histoire* 16, no. 1 (2007): 49–62.

Karge, Heike. 'Sajmište, Jasenovac, and the social frames of remembering and forgetting', *Filozofija i društvo* 23, no. 4 (2012): 106–18.

Karge, Heike. *Sećanje u kamenu – okamenjeno sećanje*. Belgrade: XX vek, 2014.

Keilbach, Judith. 'Photographs, symbolic images, and the Holocaust: On the (im)possibility of depicting historical truth'. *History and Theory* 47, no. 2 (2009): 54–76.

Kerenji, Emil. 'Jewish citizens of socialist Yugoslavia: Politics of Jewish identity in a socialist state, 1944–1974', unpublished PhD thesis, University of Michigan, 2008.

Kljakić, Slobodan. *A Conspiracy of Silence*. Belgrade: Ministry of Information of the Republic of Serbia, 1991.

Kljakić, Slobodan, 'Kratka istorija Odbora SANU za sakupljanje gradje o genocidu nad srpskim narodom i drugim narodima Jugoslavije u XX veku'. In *Catena Mundi II*, edited by Predrag Dragić-Kijuk, 498–515. Kraljevo: Ibarske novosti, 1992.

Knežević, Anto. *Analysis of Serbian Propaganda*. Zagreb, Domovina TT, 1992.

Kočović, Bogoljub. *Sahrana jednog mita: Žrtve Drugog svetskog rata u Jugoslaviji*. Belgrade: Otkrovenje, 2005.

Kolar-Dimitrijević, Mira. 'Društveno-ekonomski razvoj Siska 1919–1941. godine'. *Radovi – Zavod za hrvatsku povjest* 27 (1994): 271–88.

Koljanin, Milan. 'Propaganda u oružanom sukobu u Jugoslaviji 1991-1992. godine'. In *Ratni zločini i zločini genocida, 1991–1992*, edited by Radovan Samardžić, 473–6. Belgrade: SANU, 1993.

Kolstø, Pål. 'The Serbian-Croatian controversy over Jasenovac'. In *Serbia and the Serbs in World War Two*, edited by Sabrina P. Ramet and Ole Listhaug, 225–46. Basingstoke: Palgrave Macmillan, 2011.

Komarica, Slavko and Odić, Slavko. *Zašto Jasenovac nije oslobođen?* Belgrade: Institut za savremenu istoriju, 2005.

Konjikušić, Davor. *Crveno svjetlo: Jugoslavenska partizanska fotografija i društveni pokret, 1941–1945*. Zagreb/Belgrade: Kolektor/Roza Luxemburg Stiftung, 2017.

Kopeček, Michal. *Past in the Making: Historical Revisionism in Central Europe after 1989*. Budapest, CEU Press, 2008.

Korać, Dušan. *Kordun i Banija u narodnooslobodilačkoj borbi i socijalističkoj revoluciji*. Zagreb: Školska Knjiga, 1986.

Korb, Alexander, *Intertwined Genocides: Mass Violence in Western Yugoslavia during the Second World War*. Oxford: Oxford University Press, 2020.

Korb, Alexander. 'The disposal of corpses in an ethnicized civil war'. In *Human Remains and Mass Violence: Methodological Approaches*, edited by Jean-Marc Dreyfus and Élisabeth Anstett, 106–28. Manchester: University of Manchester Press, 2014.

Korb, Alexander. 'Understanding Ustaša violence'. *Journal of Genocide Research* 12, no. 1–2 (2010): 1–18.

Kostić, Boško. *Za istoriju naših dana*. Lille: Jean Lausier, 1949.

Kostich, Lazo M. *Holocaust in the Independent State of Croatia*. Chicago: Lazo M Kostich Fund, 1981.

Kovačić, Matija. *Odmetnička zvjerstva i pustošenja u Nezavisnoj Državi Hrvatskoj u prvim mjesecima života hrvatske narodne države*. Zagreb, Naklada Hrvatskog izdavalačkog bibliografskog zavoda, 1942.

Krakov, Stanislav. *Na oštrici noža: Milan Nedić, knjiga prva*. Munich: Iskra, 1963.

Krakov, Stanislav. *Prepuna čaša čemera: General Milan Nedić, knjiga druga*. Munich: Iskra, 1968.
Kriebel, Sabine T. and Zervigón, Andrés Mario. *Photography and Doubt*. London: Routledge, 2017.
Kršinić Lozica, Ana. 'Između memorije i zaborava: Jasenovac kao dvostruko posredovana trauma'. *Radovi Instituta za povijest umjetnosti* 35 (2011): 297–308.
Kumović, Mladenko. *Jasenovac: Sistem ustaških logora smrti*. Belgrade: Muzej žrtava genocida/Novi Sad: Muzej Vojvodine, 1994.
Kumović, Mladenko. *Jasenovac, sistem ustaških logora smrti*. Belgrade: Muzej žrtava genocida, 1997.
Lajtman, Ivo. *War Crimes against Croatia/ Ratni zločini protiv Hrvatske*. Zagreb: Večernji list, 1991.
Lanzmann, Claude. 'Le monument contre l'archive?'. *Cahiers de médiologie* 11 (2001): 271–9.
Larson, Frances. *Severed: A History of Heads Lost and Heads Found*. London: Granta, 2015.
Lebart, Luce. 'Rodolphe A. Reiss: Traces, marks, prints: Revealing details invisible to the naked eye'. In *Images of Conviction: The Construction of Visual Evidence*, edited by Diane Dufour, 37–9. Paris: Le Bal, 2015.
Lees, Lorraine M. *Yugoslav-Americans and National Security during World War II*. Chicago: University of Illinois Press, 2007.
Lengel-Krizman, Narcisa. *Genocid and Romima: Jasenovac 1942*. Jasenovac: JUSP Jasenovac, 2003.
Levental, Zdenko. *Švajcarac na Kajmakčalanu*. Belgrade: Prosveta, 1984.
Levi, Aleksandar. 'Krivična dela protiv čovečnosti i međunarodnog prava iz aspekta jugoslovenskog zakonodavstva', *Jevrejski almanah* 10–11, (1963–4): 103–28.
Levin, Laura. 'The performative force of photography'. *Photography and Culture* 2, no. 3 (2009): 327–36.
Lilly, Carol. *Power and Persuasion: Ideology and Rhetoric in Communist Yugoslavia 1944–1953*. Boulder, CO: Westview Press, 2001.
Linenthal, Edward T. *Preserving Memory: The Struggle to Create America's Holocaust Museum*. New York: Columbia University Press, 2001.
Liss, Andrea. *Trespassing through Shadows: Memory, Photography and the Holocaust*. Minneapolis: University of Minnesota Press, 1998.
Lituchy, Barry M. *Jasenovac and the Holocaust in Yugoslavia*. New York: Jasenovac Research Institute, 2006.
Lončar, Duško. *Deset godina Spomen-područja Jasenovac*. Jasenovac: JUSP Jasenovac, 1977.
Lozo, Stjepan. *Ideologija i propaganda velikosrpskog genocida nad Hrvatima*. Split: Podstrana, 2019.
Lučić, Milan. *Teror and Srbima '91 – The extermination of Serbs '91*. Novi Sad: Pokrajinski sekretarijat za informacije AP Vojvodine, 1991.
Lukić, Dragoje. *Koncentracioni logor Jasenovac: Istorijske fotografije*. Belgrade: BIGZ, 1986.
Lukić, Dragoje, *Kozarsko detinjstvo*. Belgrade: Narodna knjiga, 1973.
Lukić, Dragoje. *Rat i djeca Kozare*. Belgrade, Narodna knjiga, 1978.
Lukić, Dragoje. 'Umjesto predgovora'. In *Koncentracioni logor Jasenovac 1941–1945*. vol. 3, edited by Antun Miletić, 5–6. Belgrade: Narodna Knjiga, 1987.
MacDonald, David Bruce. *Balkan Holocausts? Serbian and Croatian Victim-centred Propaganda and the War in Yugoslavia*. Manchester: Manchester University Press, 2002.

Magilow, Daniel H. and Silverman, Lisa. *Holocaust Representations in History: An Introduction*. London: Bloomsbury Academic, 2015.

Manoschek, Walter. *Holokaust u Srbiji: Vojna okupaciona politika i uništavanje Jevreja, 1941-1942*. Belgrade: Službeni list SRJ, 2007.

Marković Zoran M. 'Nacija – žrtva i osveta'. In *Srpska strana rata, II deo*, edited by Nebojša Popov, 205–29. Belgrade: Samizdat B92, 2002.

Martyrdom of the Serbs: Persecutions of the Serbian Ortodox Church and Massacre of the Serbian People, Documents and Reports of the Trustworthy United Nations and of Eyewitnesses. Chicago: Palandech Press, 1943.

Mataušić, Nataša. 'Diana Budisavljević: The silent truth'. In *Revolutionary Totalitarianism, Pragmatic Socialism, Transition: Tito's Yugoslavia, Stories Untold*, edited by Gorana Ognjenović and Jasna Jozelić, 49–97. Basingstoke: Palgrave Macmillan, 2016.

Mataušić, Nataša. *Koncentracioni logor Jasenovac: Fotomonografija*. Zagreb: Spomen Područje Jasenovac, 2008.

Matvejević, Predrag. 'Naša književnost pobune i otpora'. In *Kultura i umjetnost u NOB-u i socijalističkoj revoluciji u Hrvatskoj*, edited by Ivan Jelić, Dunja Rihtman-Auguštin and Vice Zaninović, 83–92. Zagreb: August Cesarec, 1975.

Meissel, Lukas. 'Perpetrator photography. The pictures of the Erkennungsdienst at Mauthausen Concentration Camp'. In *Fotografien aus den Lagern des NS-Regimes. Beweissicherung und ästhetische Praxis*, edited by Hildegard Frübis, Clara Oberle and Agnieszka Pufelska, 25–47. Vienna: Böhlau Verlag, 2019.

Meštrović, Ivan. *Uspomene na političke ljude i događaje*. Buenos Aires: Knjižnica Hrvatske Revije, 1961.

Metzl, Jamie Frederic. *Western Responses to Human Rights Abuses in Cambodia, 1975–80*. Basingstoke: Palgrave Macmillan, 1996.

Michalczyk, John J. *Filming the End of the Holocaust: Allied Documentaries, Nuremberg and the Liberation of the Concentration Camps*. London: Bloomsbury, 2014.

Mihajlović, Mila. *Jugoslavija, April 1941-Septembar 1943*. Belgrade: Udruženje srpskih izdavača, 2012.

Mihovilović, Đorđe. *Jasenovac 1945 – 1947: Fotomonografija*. Jasenovac: JUSP Jasenovac, 2016.

Miletić, Antun, *Koncentracioni logor Jasenovac*, vols 1–3. Belgrade: Narodna knjiga, 1986–1987.

Miletić, Antun. 'Predstoji i treći tom', *Naše teme: časopis za društvena pitanja* 30, no. 9 (1986): 3015–6.

Milićević, Milić J. 'Ilustrovana ratna kronika – časopis i tvorci'. In *Ilustrovana ratna kronika 1877-1878*, Reprint, edited by Milić J. Milićević, vii–xv. Belgrade: Srpski genealoški centar, 2011.

Milosavljević, Olivera. *Potisnuta istina: Kolaboracija u Srbiji 1941-1944*. Belgrade: Helsinški odbor za ljudska prava u Srbiji, 2006.

Milošević, Branislava, 'Prezentacija spomen-područja-muzeja koncentracionih logora'. In *Okrugli Stol 'Jasenovac 1986'*, edited by Ana Požar, 241–5. Jasenovac: JUSP Jasenovac, 1986.

Milošević, Srđan. *Istorija pred sudom: interpretacija prošlosti i pravni aspekti u rehabilitaciji kneza Pavla Karađorđevića*. Belgrade: Fabrika knjiga, 2013.

Mirković, Jovan. *Dragoje Lukić – Roditelj pokošenog naraštaja*. Belgrade: Muzej žrtava genocida, 2008.

Mirković, Jovan. *Zločini nad Srbima u Nezavisnoj Državi Hrvatskoj – Fotomonografija*. Belgrade: Svet Knjige, 2014.
Mnookin, Jennifer L. 'The image of truth: Photographic evidence and the power of analogy', *Yale Journal of Law & the Humanities* 10, no. 1, Article 1 (1998): 1–74.
Mnookin, Jennifer, L. 'The image of truth: Photographic evidence and the power of analogy'. In *Images of Conviction: The Construction of Visual Evidence*, edited by Diane Dufour, 9–15. Paris: Le Bal, 2015.
Moeller, Susan D. *Shooting War: Photography and the American Experience of Combat*. New York: Basic Books, 1989.
Nešović, Slobodan. 'Saveznička štampa o genocidu and Srbima, Jevrejima i Ciganima u Drugom svetskom ratu'. In *Genocid nad Srbima u Drugom svetskom ratu*, edited by Radovan Samardžić, 438–48. Belgrade, Muzej žrtava genocida, 1995.
New Soviet Documents on Nazi Atrocities. London: Hutchinson, 1943.
Nikolić, Kosta. *Prošlost bez istorije: Polemike u jugoslovenskoj istoriografiji, 1961–1991*. Belgrade: ISI, 2003.
Nikolić, Nikola. *Jasenovački logor*. Zagreb: Nakladni zavod, 1948.
Nikolić, Nikola. *Jasenovački logor smrti*. Sarajevo: NIŠP Oslobođenje, 1975.
Nikoliš, Gojko. *Korijen, stablo, pavetina*. Zagreb: Sveučilišna naklada Liber, 1981.
Nikčević, Radomir (ed.). *Novi sveštenomučenici i mučenici Pravoslavne crkve prosijavši u pravoslavnom srpskom narodu*. Cetinje: Svetigora, 2000.
Novak, Božidar. *Hrvatsko novinarstvo u 20. stoljeću*. Zagreb: Golden Marketing – Tehnička Knjiga, 2005.
Obhođaš, Amir, Werhas, Mario, Dimitrijević, Bojan and Zvonimir Despot. *Ustaška vojnica*, vols 1 and 2. Zagreb: Despot, 2013.
Parežanin, Ratko. *Drugi Svetski Rat i Dimitrije V. Ljotić*. Munich: Iskra, 1971.
Patchoff, Dragomir and Katzeff, Danail V. *The Roumanian Atrocities*. Sofia: Royal Court Printing Press, 1919.
Pavković, Mladen, *Dr Franjo Tudjman u sudskim dosjeima*. Koprivnica: Alineja, 2007.
Pavlaković, Vjeran, 'Sukobljena jasenovačka kultura sjećanja: postkomunistički memorijalni muzej u Jasenovcu u doba povjesnog revizionizma'. In *Jasenovac – manipulacije, kontroverze i povijesni revizionizam*, edited by Andriana Benčić, Stipe Odak and Danijela Lucić, 111–42. Jasenovac: JUSP Jasenovac, 2018.
Pavlić, Nikola. *Jasenovački logor: izkazi zatočenika koji su pobjegli iz logora*. Propagandni odsjek Narodno-oslobodilačkog vijeća Jugoslavije, 1942.
Pearl, Sharrona. 'Believing is not seeing: Teaching atrocity without images'. *Afterimage* 40, no. 6 (2013): 16–20.
Pečarić, Josip. *Srpski mit o Jasenovcu: Skrivanje istine o beogradskim konc-logorima*. Zagreb: Dom & Svijet, 1998.
Pejaković, Ivo. 'Jasenovac Memorial Site and "difficult heritage"'. *Temoigner – entre histoire et memoire* 115 (December 2012): 48–58.
Perica, Vjekoslav. *Balkan Idols: Religion and Nationalism in Yugoslav States*. Oxford: Oxford University Press, 2002.
Perković Paloš, Andrijana. 'Je li hrvatska vlast 1990-ih bila antisemitska?' *Časopis za suvremenu povjest* 48, no. 2 (2016): 291–329.
Peršen, Mirko. *Ustaški logori*. Zagreb: Stvarnost, 1966.
Petranović Branko and Momčilo, Zečević, *Jugoslavija 1918–1988. Tematska zbirka dokumenata. Drugo izmenjeno i dopunjeno izdanje*. Belgrade: Rad, 1988.
Petrović, Rastislav. *The Extermination of Serbs on the Territory of the Independent State of Croatia*. Belgrade: Ministry of Information of the Republic of Serbia, 1991.

Pilipović, Radovan. 'Tragedija jedne srpske porodice iz Siska 1941'. *Dveri srpske*, 47–50 (2011): 60–2.
Popović, Jovo. *Suđenje Artukoviću, i što nije rečeno*. Zagreb: Stvarnost, 1986.
Popović, Nikola, *Koreni kolaboracionizma*. Belgrade: Narodna knjiga, 1974.
Popović, Srđa. *Poslednja instanca, Vol 3*. Belgrade: Helsinški odbor, 2003.
Požar, Ana. 'Jasenovac traži više istraživanja'. In *Okrugli Stol, 21 April 1984*, edited by Radovan Trivunčić, 12–17. Jasenovac: JUSP Jasenovac, 1984.
Prosser, Jay. 'Introduction'. In *Picturing Atrocity: Photography in Crisis*, edited by Geoffrey Batchen, Mick Gidley, Nancy K. Miller and Jay Prosser, 7–13. London: Reaction Books, 2011.
Računica, Javorka. 'Prikupljanje fotografije i druge muzealije u Istorijskom muzeju Vojvodine o stradanju i žrtvama Srpskog naroda 1991–1992. godine'. In *Ratni zločini i zločini genocida 1991–1992*, edited by Radovan Samardžić, 485–7. Belgrade: SANU, 1993.
Radić, Radmila. *Država i verske zajednice, 1945–1970*. Belgrade: INIS, 2002.
Radonić, Ljiljana. 'Croatia: Exhibiting memory and history at the "Shores of Europe"'. *Culture Unbound* 3 (2011): 355–67.
Radonić, Ljiljana. 'Slovak and Croatian invocation of Europe: The Museum of the Slovak National Uprising and the Jasenovac Memorial Museum'. *Nationalities Papers: The Journal of Nationalism and Ethnicity* 42, no. 3 (2014): 489–507.
Radonić, Ljiljana. 'Univerzalizacija holokausta na primjeru hrvatske politike prošlosti i spomen-područja Jasenovac'. *Suvremene teme* 3, no. 1 (2010): 53–61.
Radonić, Ljiljana. 'Visualising perpetrators and victims in post-communist memorial museums'. *Yad Vashem Studies* 44, no. 2 (2016): 173–201.
Raskin, Richard. *A Child at Gunpoint*. Aarhus: Aarhus University Press, 2004.
Reiss, Rodolphe A. *How Austria-Hungary Waged War in Serbia: Personal Investigations of a Neutral*. Paris: Librarie Armand Colin, 1916.
Reiss, Rodolphe A. *Infringements of the Rules and Laws of War Committed by The Austro-Bulgaro-Germans: Letters of a Criminologist on the Serbian Macedonian Front*. London: George Allen & Unwinn, 1919.
Reiss, Rodolphe A. *La Photographie Judiciaire*. Paris: Mendel, 1903.
Reiss, Rodolphe A. *Report upon the Atrocities Committed by the Austro-Hungarian Army during the First Invasion of Serbia*. London: Simpkin, Marshall, Hamilton, Kent & Co, 1917.
Report on Italian Crimes against Yugoslavia and Its Peoples. Belgrade: Državna komisija, 1946.
Rihtman-Auguštin, Dunja. 'Folklor kao komunikacija u NOB-u'. In *Kultura i umjetnost u NOB-u i socijalističkoj revoluciji u Hrvatskoj*, edited by Ivan Jelić, Dunja Rihtman-Auguštin and Vice Zaninović, 151–65. Zagreb: August Cesarec, 1975.
Rodogno, Davide. *Against Massacre: Humanitarian Interventions in the Ottoman Empire, 1815–1914*. Princeton: Princeton University Press, 2011.
Rodogno, Davide. *Fascism's European Empire: Italian Occupation during the Second World War*. Cambridge: Cambridge University Press, 2006.
Rubenstein, Joshua, *Tangled Loyalties: The Life and Times of Ilya Ehrenburg*. Tuscaloosa, AL: University of Alabama Press, 1999.
Rubina, Franjo. *Kozara: Grob partizana*. Zagreb: Nakladna knjižara Velebit, 1942.
Rubina, Franjo. *Krvave tajne planine Kozare*. Zagreb: Naklada odgojnog dela ustaške vojnice, 1942.
Rusinow, Dennison. *Yugoslavia: Oblique Insights and Observations*. Pittsburgh: University of Pittsburgh Press, 2008.

Ryan, Allan A. *Quiet Neighbours: Prosecuting Nazi War Criminals in America*. New York: Harcourt Brace Jovanovich, 1984.
Samardžić, Radovan. *Ratni zločini i zločini genocida 1991-1992*. Belgrade: SANU, 1993.
Saopštenje o zločinima Austrije i austrijanaca protiv Jugoslavije i njenih naroda. Belgrade: Državna komisija, 1947.
Šašić, Jefto. 'Predgovor'. In *Koncentracioni logor Jasenovac, 1941-1945, Vol. 1*, edited by Antun Miletić, 1–14. Belgrade: Narodna Knjiga, 1986.
Šašić, Jefto. 'Pregled istraživanja genocida u Jasenovcu', *Naše teme: časopis za društvena pitanja* 30, no. 9 (1986): 1288–96.
Shafir, Michael. *Between Denial and 'Comparative Trivialization': Holocaust Negationism in Post-Communist East Central Europe*. Jerusalem: SICSA, 2002.
Shepard, Ben. *Terror in the Balkans*. Cambridge, MA: Harvard University Press, 2012.
Shneer, David. *Through Soviet Jewish Eyes: Photography, War, and the Holocaust*. New Jersey: Rutgers University Press, 2010.
Simon, Roger I. *A Pedagogy of Witnessing: Curatorial Practice and the Pursuit of Social Justice*. New York: SUNY Press, 2014.
Sinbaek, Tea. *Usable History? Representations of Yugoslavia's Difficult Past from 1945 to 2002*. Aarhus: Aarhus University Press, 2012.
Sinclair, Tollemache. *A Defence of Russia and the Christians of Turkey*. London: Chapman and Hall, 1877.
Sirotković, Hodimir. *ZAVNOH, Zbornik Dokumenata, 1944*. Zagreb: Institut za historiju radničkog pokreta Hrvatske, 1975.
Sjeverozapadna Hrvatska u narodnooslobodilačkoj borbi i socijalističkoj revoluciji, vols 1–10. Zagreb: Institut za historiju radničkog pokreta Hrvatske, 1981–1989.
Skrigin, Žorž. *Rat i pozornica*. Belgrade: Turistička stampa, 1968.
Slani, Milan. 'Susak u prvim danima ustanka'. In *Ustanak naroda Jugoslavije 1941, Vol.5*, edited by Milinko Burović, 575–80. Belgrade: Vojno Delo, 1964.
Slijepčević, Đoko. *Jugoslavija*. Munich: Iskra, 1978.
Šmitran, Bogdan. *Hronika potkozarskog sela Grbavci*, Gradiška: Prosvjeta, 2002.
Smoleń, Kazimierz and Świebocka, Teresa. *Auschwitz: A Crime against Mankind*. Oświęcim: Auschwitz State Museum, 1985.
Sontag, Susan. *On Photography*. London: Penguin, 1979.
Sontag, Susan. *Regarding the Pain of Others*. London: Penguin Books, 2003.
Sorokina, Marina. 'Peoples and procedures: Towards a history of the investigation of Nazi crimes in the USSR'. *Kritika: Explorations in Russian and Euroasian History* 4 (2005): 797–831.
Soviet Documents on Nazi Atrocities. London: Hutchinson, 1942.
Stanojević, Branimir. *Ustaški ministar smrti*. Belgrade: Nova knjiga, 1985.
Štefan, Ljubica. *Srpska pravoslavna crkva i fašizam*. Zagreb: Globus, 1996.
Struk, Janina. *Photographing the Holocaust: Interpretations of the Evidence*. London: I.B. Tauris, 2004.
Struk, Janina. *Private Pictures: Soldiers' Inside View of War*. London: I.B. Tauris, 2011.
Subotić, Jelena. *Yellow Star, Red Star: Holocaust Remembrance after Communism*. Ithaca, NY: Cornell University Press, 2019.
Supek, Ivan. *Crown Witness against Hebrang*. Chicago, IL: Markanton Press, 1983.
The Polish Atrocities against the German Minority in Poland. Berlin: Volk und Reich Verlag, 1940.
Tomasevich, Jozo. *War and Revolution in Yugoslavia, 1941–1945: Occupation and Collaboration*. Stanford: Stanford University Press, 2001.

Tremlett, Annabel. 'Visualising everyday ethnicity: Moving beyond stereotypes of Roma minorities'. *Identities* 24, no. 6 (2017): 720–40.
Trial of the Major War Criminals before the International Military Tribunal: Nuremberg 14 November 1945–1 October 1946, vol. II. Nuremberg: International Military Tribunal, 1947.
Trivunčić, Radovan. *Spomen područje Jasenovac*. Zagreb: Turistkomerc, 1976.
Tuđman, Franjo, *Horrors of War: Historical Reality and Philosophy*. New York: M. Evans and Company, 1996.
Tumarkin, Nina. *The Living and the Dead: The Rise and Fall of the Cult of World War II in Russia*. New York: Basic Books, 1994.
Tutunović-Trifunov, Jasmina. 'Zbirka dokumentarnih fotografija Dragoja Lukića (Muzej žrtava genocida),' in *Proceedings of the Fourth International Conference with International Participation on Suffering of Serbs, Jews and Roma in the Former Yugoslavia*, 207–14. Belgrade, 2017.
United Nations Documents 1941–1945. London: Royal Institute of International Affairs, 1946.
Vajs, Albert. 'Rad Komisije za utvrđivanje zločina okupatora i njihovih pomagača', *Anali Pravnog fakulteta* 9, no. 4 (1961): 387–400.
Vogt, Timothy R. *Denazification in Soviet-Occupied Germany*. Cambridge, MA: Harvard University Press, 2000.
Vojinović, Aleksandar. *NDH u Beogradu*. Zagreb: Naklada Pavičić, 1995.
Vučak, Ivica. 'Dr Nikola Nikolić – od Jasenovca do Golog otoka', *Liječničke novine* 14, no. 142 (2015): 66–73.
Vukčević, Slavko. *Zločini na jugoslovenskim prostorima u Prvom i Drugom svetskom ratu: Zbornik dokumenata, Knjiga 1*. Belgrade, Vojnoistorijski institut, 1993.
Vukić, Igor. *Radni logor Jasenovac*. Zagreb: Naklada Pavičić, 2018.
Vuković, Tomislav. *Drugačija povijest (o Srbu, Jasenovcu, Glini…)*. Zagreb: Glas Koncila, 2012.
Vuković, Tomilav and Bojović, Edo. *Pregled srpskog antisemitizma*. Zagreb: Altair, 1992.
We Shall Not Forgive! The Horrors of the German Invasion in Documents and Photographs. Moscow: Foreign Languages Pub. House, 1942.
Welch, David. 'Atrocity Propaganda'. In *Propaganda and Mass Persuasion: A Historical Encyclopedia, 1500 to the Present*, edited by Nicholas J. Cull, David Culbert and David Welch, 23–6. Santa Barbara, CA: ABC-CLIO, 2003.
West, Rebecca. *A Train of Powder*. New York: Viking Press, 1955.
Wilcox, Francis O. 'The use of atrocities in war'. *The American Political Science Review* 36, no. 6 (1940): 1169–75.
Wolfe, Robert. *Captured German and Related Records: A National Archives Conference*. Dayton, OH: University of Ohio Press, 1974.
Yeomans, Rory. '"For us, beloved commander, you will never die!" Mourning Jure Francetić, Ustasha death squad leader'. In *In the Shadow of Hitler: Personalities of the Right in Central and Eastern Europe*, edited by Rebecca Haynes and Martyn Rady, 188–205. London: I.B. Tauris, 2011.
Yeomans, Rory. *Visions of Annihilation: The Ustasha Regime and the Cultural Politics of Fascism*. Pittsburgh, PA: University of Pittsburgh Press, 2013.
Young, James E. *The Texture of Memory: Holocaust Memorials and Meaning*. New Haven, CT: Yale University Press, 1994.
Young, James E. *Writing and Rewriting the Holocaust: Narrative and the Consequences of Interpretation*. Bloomington: Indiana University Press, 1988.

Zatezalo, Đuro. *Jadovno, kompleks ustaških logora*, vols 1 and 2. Belgrade: Muzej žrtava genocida, 2007.

Zatezalo, Đuro. *Radio sam svoj seljački i kovački posao: svjedočanstva genocida*. Zagreb: Srpsko kulturno društvo Prosvjeta, 2005.

Zbornik dokumenata i podataka o narodnooslobodilačkom ratu jugoslovenskih naroda. Belgrade: Vojnoistorijski institut Jugoslovenske narodne armije, 1954–, Parts 2, 4, 5, 12.

Zec, Nedo. 'Umesto predgovora'. In *Da se ne zaboravi*, edited by Zdravko Čolić, Aziz Hadžihasanović and Milan Mučibabić, 5. Sarajevo: Veselin Masleša, 1961.

Zelizer, Barbie. *Remembering to Forget: Holocaust Memory through the Camera's Eye*. Chicago: University of Chicago Press, 1998.

Zelizer, Barbie. *Visual Culture and the Holocaust*. London: Athlone Press, 2000.

Zelizer, Barbie, 'When war is reduced to a photograph'. In *Reporting War: Journalism in Wartime*, edited by Stuart Allan and Barbie Zelizer, 115–35. London: Routledge, 2004.

Žerjavić Vladimir. *Opsesije i megalomanije oko Jasenovca i Bleiburga. Gubici stanovništva Jugoslavije u drugom svjetskom ratu*. Zagreb: Globus, 1992.

Zločini u Logoru Jasenovac. Zagreb: Zemaljska komisija za utvrđivanje zločina okupatora i njihovih pomagača Hrvatske, 1946.

Index

Abbott, Lee 173 n.22
Aćimović, Milan 30, 33
Ajzenberg, Aleksandar 32, 36
Amerikanski Srbobran (periodical) 24
Antifascist Council of National Liberation of Yugoslavia (AVNOJ) 45, 46, 168 n.1
Artuković, Andrija 112, 182 nn.76–7, 81
  trial of 112–17
atrocities
  Chetnik 11, 13, 27, 37, 43, 64, 78, 97, 136
  Italian 64–6
  Nazi 1–4, 8, 9, 23–4, 26–7, 35, 46, 61, 64, 66, 148
  Partisan 8, 37, 40, 41
  Ustasha 12–14, 24, 27–9, 33, 76, 113, 116, 122, 127, 133
atrocity, meaning and significance of 14–15
atrocity drawings 15–16
atrocity photographs
  evidentiary and illustrative function of 3, 20, 61–2, 71
  and international diplomacy 64–6, 130–2, 135–6, 137
  as legal proof 48–51, 113–14
  misattribution of 7–8, 22, 53, 95, 109–11, 131–2, 145, 154
  in occupied Serbia, politics of 29–36
  politics of 12–18
  and propaganda 8, 13, 23, 28, 33, 38–42, 44, 52, 62, 64–5, 76–8, 109, 123, 126–7, 129, 133, 136–8, 151
  purpose of 19–20
  and revenge 71–7
  as source of sadistic gratification 68–71
  as weapon against nationalism in Yugoslavia 80, 98–100, 120–3

Auschwitz 54, 130
Austria 64, 69
Austro-Hungary 16–17

Bader, Paul 27
Banjica (concentration camp) 47
Battle of Neretva (film) 98
Belgian Congo 161 n.71
Belgrade 21, 29–33, 48, 68, 72, 76, 81, 108, 121, 122, 128, 133, 165 n.61, 170 n.52, 177 n.50, 185 n.29
Berger, Egon 59, 90, 93
Bishop Platon. *See* Jovanović, Platon
Bleiburg massacre 137–8
Blood and Ashes of Jasenovac (documentary) 87, 104–6, 109, 180 n.24, 183 n.106, 186 n.55
Bogdanović, Bogdan 85–6
Borba (newspaper) 44, 50, 52, 53, 57, 60, 72
Bosanska Gradiška 95, 107
Bosanska Krajina 95
Bosnia-Herzegovina 5, 9, 47, 49, 75, 95, 103, 121, 126, 127, 135, 138
Bosnian Muslims 4, 11, 43, 119, 136, 159 n.34
Brdar, Simo 131, 133
brotherhood and unity 5, 78, 81–4, 96–100, 102, 104, 116, 120
Budisavljević, Diana 166 n.101
Bulajić, Milan 127, 130–2, 134, 136, 176 n.25, 186 n.40
Bulajić, Veljko 98

cannibalism 70–2, 79, 105, 115, 180 n.25
Cetinje 52
chauvinism 80, 102, 105, 114
Chetniks
  atrocities 11, 13, 27, 37, 43, 64, 78, 97, 136
  collaboration with Italians 65–6

collaboration with Ustasha 78–9
similarities with Ustasha 71, 76,
  78–80, 97–8, 126
Chile 98
collaboration/collaborators 4–5, 30–1,
  43, 47, 48, 91, 137, 149, 165 n.61,
  168 n.14, 173 n.39
 in Serbia 29–32, 91
 visual representation of 64–6, 69,
  78–9, 95, 148
Commissariat for Refugees 29, 164
  nn.39, 42, 165 n.66
Country Commission for the Investigation
  of the Crimes of the Occupiers and
  their Accomplices
 for Bosnia 47, 72, 76
 for Croatia 47, 53–5, 60, 79, 90, 119
 for Slovenia 47
 for Vojvodina 46, 47
Committee for Information for the
  Republic of Croatia 115
Committee for the Collection of Material
  on the Genocide against the
  Serbian People and Other Nations
  on the Territory of Yugoslavia in
  the First and the Second World War
  (SANU) 101, 121
Croatia 42, 116, 121–3, 125–6, 131,
  136–9, 146, 149, 174 n.49, 192 n.15
Croatian Democratic Union (HDZ) 125
Croatian Spring 99, 102, 178 n.66
Croats
 as 'genocidal' 122
 as victims 36–8, 99, 137–8, 149
Czechoslovakia 66

Dachau 2, 42, 54, 82, 94–5, 132, 178 n.56
Dačić, Ivica 134, 135
Danas (periodical) 121
Danckelmann, Heinrich 29
decapitation 12–13, 72–4, 97, 98, 104,
  105, 133, 135, 181 n.60
decomposed bodies 35, 54, 56, 58, 97,
  119, 128, 165 n.76
Dedijer, Vladimir 177 n.42
depravity 32, 62, 63, 67, 98, 105, 112,
  114, 137, 151
 of perpetrators 18, 19, 36, 70, 77
Dešković, Ksenija 87, 117, 176 n.29

Đilas, Milovan 72, 174 n.53
Dodik, Milorad 136
Donja Gradina 105, 106, 109, 146, 147,
  176 n.25
Dožić, Gavrilo 33
Drezga, Branko 57, 61
Đujić, Momčilo 138
Džamonja, Dušan 87

Ehrenburg, Ilya 72, 75, 174 nn.53, 64–5

fascism 53, 70–2, 75–80, 98, 100,
  103, 105
 victims of 83–5, 90, 114, 119
Filipović-Majstorović, Miroslav 91
Fischer-Ribarić, Hugo 171 n.63
Fotić, Konstantin 24

Gavrin, Gustav 57, 96, 113
genocide. *See also* Independent State of
  Croatia; 'renewed genocide'; Serbs
 Artuković trial and 127
 of Bosnian Muslims 11–12
 controversies over definition of 10
 in Srebrenica 127, 136
 Tuđman on 126
 Yugoslav wars of the 1990s and
  121–2, 136
God and Croats (documentary) 185 n.28
Goldstein, Ivo 153, 191 n.139
Gošnjak, Ivan 85
Gospel of Evil, The (documentary) 98,
  99, 109, 113
Greif, Gideon 134
Grgić, Ivan 81
Grisogono, Prvislav 31
Gudovac 25–7, 30, 35, 166 n.79
Gutić, Viktor 34

heroism 16, 21, 44, 71, 78, 85, 91, 95, 119
Historical Archives of Belgrade 81
Hitler, Adolf 31, 70, 72, 78, 98, 148
Hlavaty, Kosta 57, 96, 113
Holocaust 3, 10, 111, 144–5, 160 n.52
Homeland War 149
 victim-centred propaganda
  during 136–9
Hrvatski književni list (periodical) 99
Hrvatski narod (periodical) 25, 42

Illustrierter Beobachter (periodical) 42
Ilustrovana ratna kronika
    (periodical) 15–16, 161 n.76
Independent State of Croatia
    genocide in 8–12, 25–6, 116, 125, 128
    history of 8–12
    revisionist interpretations of 5, 6, 99, 102, 122, 141, 151, 153
Italian atrocities. *See* atrocities
Italy 27–9, 64, 69

Jackson, Robert H. 1, 2, 69
Jadovno (concentration camp) 159 n.42
Jajinci 47
Jareb, Mario 145–6, 191 n.139
Jasenovac (documentary, 1945) 57, 58, 75–6, 79, 105, 113
Jasenovac (documentary, 1966), 96–8, 104
Jasenovac (concentration camp) 47, 83
    authenticity of photographs of 7–8, 42, 109
    breakout from 89, 108
    documentary about on 57
    exhibitions about (*see* Jasenovac Memorial Museum; photographic exhibitions)
    mass executions in 54, 57, 59, 89, 105
    memorialization challenges, in post-war Yugoslavia 84–6
    as metonymy for genocide in Independent State of Croatia 7, 95
    polemics over number of victims 7–8, 85, 89, 99, 102, 105, 120, 126
    post war investigations at 53–4
    remains of 55
    torture and killings at 56–7
    visualizing the scale of killing at 58–61, 109–10, 145
Jasenovac Memorial Area 86, 87, 92–4, 98, 99, 102–7, 113, 118–22, 131, 139, 158 n.25, 177 n.34
Jasenovac Memorial Museum 87–91, 121, 133, 139, 140, 177 n.38, 181 n.46
    first permanent display (1968) 87–91
    new display (2006) 140–9
    second permanent display (1988) 117–20
Jastrebarsko (concentration camp) 119

Jelić, Ivan 117
Jelovac, Dragan 134
Jericault, Theodore 74
Jerković, Dragan 185 n.22
Jevtić, Atanasije 164 n.42, 165 n.77
Jews, persecution of 9–11
Jovanović, Ljubo 34–5
Jovanović, Platon 34–5, 165 n.77
Jovanović-Zmaj, Jovan 161 n.76
Jovičić, Nataša 140, 141, 145, 183 n.110, 190 n.134
Jungić, Branko 110

Kaleb, Vjekoslav 99
Kasche, Siegfried 27, 163 n.23
Kastratović, Gojko 98, 99, 104, 113
Katyn 24
Kaurić, Đuka 92
Kesar, Jovan 180 n.35
Kovač, Leonida 140
Kovačić, Ivan Goran 86
Kozara offensive 40, 119, 180 n.24
Krakov, Stanislav 30, 36, 164 n.51
Krasnaya Zvezda (newspaper) 72
Krestić, Vasilije 135, 187 n.69
Kvaternik, Eugen Dido 25

landscapes, as proxy for atrocities 92, 146–7
Lanzmann, Claude 154
Le Petit Parisien (periodical) 161 n.77
Lepoglava (concentration camp) 47, 60, 171 n.65, 177 n.50
L'illustration (periodical) 16
Lisak, Erih 49
Living Marxism (periodical) 130, 186 n.38
Ljubljana 52
Lončar, Duško 104
Lozo, Stjepan 137
Lukić, Dragoje 96, 106–8, 110, 111, 116, 117, 133, 180 nn.35, 43, 181 n.46, 187 n.58

Mačkić, Dušan 34, 35
Majdanek 53, 170 n.48
Malaparte, Curzio 187 n.65
Maroević, Ivo 117–18
Mataušić, Nataša 8, 140
Meštrović, Ivan 64

Miletić, Antun   106–8, 117, 180 nn.35, 38
Military Museum (Belgrade)   6, 126
Milošević, Slobodan   122, 125
Mladost (periodical)   116
Moscow Declaration on Atrocities
    (1943)   46, 63
Museum of Applied Arts (Belgrade)   128
Museum of Genocide Victims
    (Belgrade)   135
Museum of Republika Srpska
    (Banja Luka)   110
Museum of the Revolution   81, 87, 90–1,
    177 nn.34, 38
    in Belgrade   81, 108
    in Sarajevo   95
    in Zagreb   87, 90–1, 106, 113
Museum of Vojvodina (Novi Sad)   126,
    127, 130
mutilation   6, 13, 15–17, 24, 30–8, 40–1,
    65, 71, 74, 78, 105, 109, 119, 122,
    129, 137, 182 n.86

Naprijed (newspaper)   78
Narodni List (newspaper)   52, 58, 60
nationalism   5–7, 9, 78, 82, 103, 125
    Croatian   42, 43, 80, 99, 102, 122, 131,
        138, 146
    Serbian   11, 21, 43, 102, 120–3, 131,
        138, 140, 141
Nedeljković, Dušan   49, 52, 67, 70, 71,
    77, 81, 173 n.40
Nedić, Milan   29, 164 n.51
New Martyrs of Jasenovac   102
Nikolić, Nikola   90, 91–2, 94, 95, 147,
    177 n.42, 191 n.136
Nikšić, Ante   31, 36, 164 n.60
Nordhausen (concentration camp)   59
Nova Hrvatska (newspaper)   37
Novi Sad   15, 35, 126, 127
Nuremberg Military Tribunal   1, 49–51,
    66–71, 112
    involvement of Yugoslavia in   49, 51,
        66–71
    photographs and film footage at   2–3,
        67–8

Occupation in 26 Scenes (film)   103–4,
    116, 179 n.20
Oslobođenje (newspaper)   52, 174 n.65

Partisan movement   4, 27, 43–4, 82–3,
    89, 92
Pavelić, Ante   9, 25, 36, 112, 113, 119,
    128, 148, 191 n.139
Paver-Njirić, Helena   140
Peršen, Mirko   90
Photographic Documentation Agency
    (Zagreb)   83, 90, 97, 177 n.37
photographic exhibitions   2, 20, 23,
    64, 82
    'Concentration Camp Jasenovac,
        1941–1945' (1986–9)   106–12
    'Crimes of the State of Croatia '91'
        (1992)   127–8
    'Extermination of Serbs '91'
        (1991)   127
    'Genocide against Serbs   1941–1945,
        1991–1992' (1992)   128, 130
    'Jasenovac–The Right to
        Remembrance' (2018)   134–6
    'Jasenovac–The system of Ustasha
        death camps' (1994)   131–2
    'Kozara Epic' (1982)   107
    State Commission and   49, 52, 64,
        76–8
    Ustasha propaganda and   42
Pijade, Moša   44, 53, 72
Pletikosa, Pero   116
Pokrovsky, Yuri   2
Poland   53, 66, 130
Polish government in exile   24
Politika (newspaper)   52, 68, 114
Poruke (periodical)   93
Požar, Ana   103, 107

Radić, Lepa   169 n.34
Ranković, Aleksandar   85
Reiss, Rodolphe Archibald   16–18, 64
'renewed genocide'   123, 126–9, 137, 149
Republic of Serb Krajina   130–1
Republika Srpska   5, 136
resistance   3, 63, 89, 92, 96, 104, 119
    Partisan   27, 31, 43, 44, 83, 95, 120,
        159 n.45
revisionism   4, 101, 102, 105, 116, 122,
    138, 151, 153, 192 n.15
Roma   9–11, 142–3
Rubina, Franjo   37
Rudenko, Roman   67

Sajmište (concentration camp) 47
Sarajevo 30, 43, 47, 52, 95, 108, 127,
    181 n.46
Šašić, Jefto 108, 121, 177 n.34
Schröder, Ludwig von 29
Serbia 5, 6, 121, 130, 149. *See also* Serbs;
    suffering
  Jasenovac memory in 132-6
  Nazi-occupied 20, 33, 35, 37
Serbian Academy of Arts and Sciences
    (SANU) 101, 102, 121, 122, 127,
    183 n.113
Serbian Orthodox Church 29, 84, 102
Serbs. *See also* Serbia
  as arch-enemy of the Ustasha 9
  deportation to Ustasha camps 143-4
  genocide against 4, 9-11, 25, 27,
    29-36, 89, 120
  Serbian women, depiction of 39-40
Šešelj, Vojislav 138
sexual violence 12, 119, 178 n.56
Simon Wiesenthal Centre
    (Los Angeles) 131
Sisak 33, 62, 92, 119, 132, 171 n.58
  executions in (May 1945) 57-61,
    95, 105, 109, 113, 118
Skrigin, Žorž 43-4
Smirnov, Lev 67
Srebrenica 127, 136
Soviet Extraordinary State Commission for
    the Establishment and Investigation
    of Atrocities Committed by the
    German-Fascist Invaders and their
    Accomplices 24, 46, 162 n.7,
    170 n.39
Soviet Union 24, 53
Soviet War News Weekly (periodical) 23
spectatorship
  ethics of 152
  pleasure of 152-3
  reflexive kind of 155
Špiljak, Mika 121
Špiljak, Štefa 119, 121
Stara Gradiška (concentration camp) 47,
    54, 60, 119, 147, 148, 170 n.52
State Commission for the Investigation of
    the Crimes of the Occupiers and
    their Accomplices 20, 44, 45, 50,
    61-5, 81, 83, 107-8, 177 n.53

creation of 44, 45-6
at Nuremberg Tribunal 49-51, 66-71
political function of 51-3
structure and remit of 46-8
Stepinac, Alojzije 31
Stöger, Edmund 42, 55, 167 n.107,
    190 n.121
Stone Flower monument 85-6, 131, 146
Subotić, Kamenko 15, 16
suffering 3, 6, 16, 32, 70, 86, 152,
    192 n.12
  of children 93, 95, 109, 119,
    180 n.24
  Christ-like 34, 137
  of Croats 37-9, 99, 138, 190 n.134
  personalization of 134, 142, 148
  remote 5
  of Serbs 21, 40, 95, 101, 102, 120,
    122-3, 127, 129-32, 134-6, 140,
    144, 150
  of Yugoslavs 44, 52, 53, 68, 88, 89

Tadić, Boris 136
Tašković, Mato 54
Terzić, Velimir 102
Teslić, Miloš 31-3, 36, 109, 171 n.77,
    182 n.86
Teslić, Petar 109, 165 n.62
Tito, Josip Broz 6, 45, 63, 85, 89, 99, 100,
    176 n.27
torture 14-15, 30-40, 105, 110, 114, 118,
    147, 165 n.66
Tower of Death, The (documentary)
    183 n.106
Trivunčić, Radovan 87
trophy photographs 12, 17-18, 20, 64,
    70, 71, 75, 132. *See also* atrocity
    photographs
  examples of 13, 110, 111, 138, 139
  significance of 154
Tuđman, Franjo 6, 125-8, 131, 138, 139,
    140, 145, 184 n.118, 188 n.95
Turkish atrocities 15
Turner, Harald 29-30, 35

Union of Fighters of the People's
    Liberation War 83, 84, 102, 121
United Nations War Crimes
    Commission 46

United States Holocaust Memorial Museum (USHMM)   131, 132, 139, 142, 149
Ustasha   4–5, 8–13. *See also* genocide
  brutality   10–11, 27, 28, 55, 58, 78, 98, 109, 145
  exceptionalism   77–80, 98, 114, 122
Uštica   143

Vajs, Albert   67, 81–2
Večernji list (newspaper)   136
Velimirović, Nikolaj   138
victim-centred propaganda
  during 'Homeland War'   136–9
  and international public diplomacy   129–32
victims   78, 129. *See also* suffering
  Croatian   37–9, 99, 138
  as individuals   142–6
  Roma   9–11, 142–3
  Serbian   4, 9–11, 21, 25, 27, 29–36, 40, 89, 95, 101, 102, 120, 122–3, 127, 129–32, 134–6, 140, 144, 150

Vjesnik (newspaper)   52, 60, 79, 113, 115, 175 n.70
Vladulov, Lukijan   138
Vojvodina   46
Volksdeutche   68, 69
Vovk, Petar   117, 118

West, Rebecca   2
Wiertz, Antoine   74

Yad Vashem (Jerusalem)   131, 142
Yugoslavia. *See* individual entries
Yugoslav People's Army   126, 184 n.118
Yugoslav State Commission for War Crimes and Crimes of Genocide (1992)   127

Zafranović, Lordan   87, 103, 104, 105, 179 n.20, 186 n.55
Zagreb   29, 30, 36, 42, 43, 52, 76, 77, 79–80, 87, 90–1, 106, 113, 119, 159 n.42
Zatezalo, Đuro   145, 146, 163 n.29, 190 n.127
Žižić, Bogdan   96, 98, 104

www.ingramcontent.com/pod-product-compliance
Lightning Source LLC
Chambersburg PA
CBHW072234290426
44111CB00012B/2087